THE HOME COMPUTER COMPANION

John Pivovarnick
Clayton Walnum
Judy Salpeter

alpha
books

A Division of Macmillan Computer Publishing

201 West 103rd Street, Indianapolis, Indiana 46290 USA

International Standard Book Number: 1-56761-431-0

Library of Congress Catalog Card Number: 94-70521

96 95 94   8 7 6 5 4 3 2 1

Interpretation of the printing code: the rightmost number of the first series of numbers is the year of the book's printing; the rightmost number of the second series of numbers is the number of the book's printing. For example, a printing code of 94-1 shows that the first printing of the book occurred in 1994.

Printed in the United States of America

Publisher   *Marie Butler-Knight*
Managing Editor   *Elizabeth Keaffaber*
Product Development Manager   *Faithe Wempen*
Acquisitions Manager   *Barry Pruett*
Production Editors   *Michelle Shaw, Phil Kitchel*
Copy Editor   *Audra Gable*
Cover Designer   *Karen Ruggles*
Designer   *Barbara Webster*
Indexer   *Charlotte Clapp*
Production Team   *Gary Adair, Dan Caparo, Brad Chinn, Kim Cofer, Lisa Daugherty, Jennifer Eberhardt, Mark Enochs, Beth Rago, Bobbi Satterfield, Kris Simmons, Carol Stamile, Robert Wolf*

Special thanks to C. Herbert Feltner for ensuring the technical accuracy of this book.

Introduction

I may be going out on a limb here, but since you picked up this book, I'm guessing that you recently bought (or started to seriously think about buying) a computer for your home. I'll even go a little further out on that limb and guess that your computer (or the thought of buying one) intimidates you on some level.

Well, let's put some basic facts on the table right away:

◆ Buying and using a computer will not turn you into a geek overnight. You won't just wake up one morning to find a pair of broken horn-rimmed glasses on your face—unless that's how you went to bed the night before.

◆ A computer will not hurt you. No game of "Clue" is ever going to end with somebody saying, "It was the Macintosh Performa in the drawing room with the lead pipe."

◆ And, despite movies like *2001: A Space Odyssey* and *Colossus: The Forbin Project*, computers are not out to enslave you. They will affect your daily life only as little or as much as you let them.

If that isn't reassuring enough, let me add that it's good that you're finally considering a computer for your home. While these spunky little machines may not be bent on world domination in a "do what I tell you or else" kind of way, they are certainly dominating the world in a "wouldn't it be much simpler to get a computer to do this" kind of way.

Computers Are Everywhere

If you pay the slightest attention as you go about your business, you can't help but notice how computers have infiltrated daily life. In businesses and offices, computers are all over the place. It's gotten to the point (for me at least) that I'm more surprised to see a desk *without* a computer on it than I am to see one with a computer.

However, there are still more computers flying around than you may have ever dreamt of: bank cash machines are computers; Nintendo and Sega game players are computers; the itemized check you got from your waitress at lunch was printed by a computer—and that same computer probably told the chef what your party wanted to eat. You'll find computers in auto repair shops and even in your car. Not all of these machines are what you would traditionally think of as computers, since they only perform a limited range of functions, but they are computers nonetheless.

With all the computers you come across day in and day out, why shouldn't you have a computer for your home? There's got to be something to them, if they're becoming so indispensable in the world at large, right? Of course, right.

What *Is* a Home Computer?

In the simplest of terms, a "home computer" is pretty much the same thing as a "business computer," except that you keep it in your home and use it for some different things.

Generally speaking a computer consists of these three things:

◆ A central unit, the main box that contains the part that does the work.

◆ A monitor (a kissing cousin to a television), that lets you watch what you're doing while you work.

◆ A keyboard and probably a mouse to get your information into the computer and onto the monitor so you can tinker with it.

There are more parts of course, and there's some optional stuff that you may or may not need, but we're taking it easy. Any computer will have these parts, and (generally) you can buy the pieces all together as a set, or individually, like a component stereo system.

And therein lies the most difficult thing about buying computer equipment. If computers were like stereos, you could buy one part by Sanyo, another by Panasonic, and another by RCA, and they would all work well together. Unfortunately, with computers that isn't always the case. Some parts by one manufacturer won't work with parts by another manufacturer. In some cases two parts by the same manufacturer won't even work together.

Although there's no secret to matching up what works with what, the mere thought of it, as well as the computerese terminology, may intimidate the heck out of some people. That's why it's a good thing you've laid your hands on this book. We promise to be gentle.

What This Book Offers and How To Use It

It may not be the wisdom of the ages, but in this book you'll find everything you need to know about buying a computer (if you don't already have one), setting up and using a computer in your home, and getting the maximum enjoyment and work out of it. You'll also find life-saving information on keeping your computer running, fixing problems as they crop up, and buying and using software and other computer doohickeys as your needs and your skills increase. In short, this book will be helpful for a long time to come.

To get the most out of this book, don't try to sit down and read it from start to finish. Look at all of this information on a need-to-know basis. When you're about to embark on a new aspect of computing (whether that's a new piece of software, hardware, or some other new experience), consult the table of contents or the index, and read only the material that applies.

For example, if you're about to buy a computer, stop and read Part I, which will help you select the computer that's best for you and your family. It explains all the basic components and what your choices are, and even helps you narrow down the field to the one that's right for you.

If you've already bought your computer, and now you want to know what to do with it, you may want to read some of Part I (like Chapter 6, if your computer isn't set up yet, or Chapters 7 and 8 on maintaining it and setting up the house rules for computer use).

After your new baby is set up and humming right along, you'll probably want to read the sections of Part II that apply to your computer. You probably won't want (or need) to read the chapter devoted to DOS if you bought a Macintosh (or vice versa). You will, however, want to read the sections on protecting your data (Chapter 12) and diagnosing problems (Chapter 13—it would be 13, wouldn't it?).

Part III is devoted to helping you become a savvy software shopper. Chapters 14, 15, and 16 help you select, install, and survive almost any computer program. The rest of the section gives you quick and informative reviews of dozens of popular software programs by category. You may want to consult the appropriate chapter(s) before you make your final buying decision.

Kids and computers are an amazing combination. If you have children, or if young folks will have access to your computer, you'll probably want to check out Part IV before you let them at your machine, or before you spend money on software or accessories just for them.

As you become more comfortable with your system and the core of basic programs you use daily, you might want to pop into Part V and see some of the cool other stuff you can do with your computer. You get articles on adding multimedia hardware ("Multimedia"), setting up a home office ("Setting Up a Home Office"), getting into the world of on-line services like CompuServe ("On-Line Services"), and lots more.

All along the way you'll find useful tidbits of information, helpful hints, and cool words and phrases you can bandy about to impress your technologically impaired friends.

As you can see, there's so much information crammed in here, you'd hurt yourself if you tried to absorb it all from cover to cover. Pace yourself. Save some fun stuff for later.

Contents

Part I

Introducing the Home Computer

Considering all the media hype surrounding computers and technology, it's a perfectly normal reaction for people to want a home computer without knowing if they actually need one. That's the point of hype, after all: to make you want stuff. But, while the hype instills the desire, it doesn't always follow through and explain what you need or where to find it, much less what to do with it once you've gotten it.

Part I will fill in all the blanks surrounding your desire to own a home computer. It will start with helping you decide if you actually need one; if you need one, what kind you need; and then how to shop for that computer system. It will also give you tips on setting it up and caring for it once you get it home, and how to introduce it to the rest of your family.

In some ways, choosing a home computer is a lot like choosing a new pet. Getting an animal on the spur of the moment can cause some serious problems on the homefront—ask anyone who lives in a small apartment with a big dog. "It's cute" isn't a good reason to buy a pet or a computer. Just as you need to select a pet that will suit your lifestyle, you need to find a computer that will suit your needs and goals, and grow with you as those needs and goals change over time.

Chapter 1

Do I Really Need a Home Computer?

D on't panic if you answer "no" to that question right now. A lot of folks aren't clear on all the things a computer can do for them. And if you don't know what all a computer can do, how will you ever know if you need one? In this chapter, you'll get a peek at some of the jobs a computer may help you with, and you'll find a simple quiz to help you decide if you really need a computer.

Computer-Type Things to Do

To help you get a handle on what a computer can do for you, here's a quick look at some of the things people do with home computers. Not all of them will appeal to you. Some ideas may sound too heavy duty, others may sound ridiculous and/or frivolous. Don't worry about it. The point is for you to find things that you may like to do or try, so only pay attention to what strikes your fancy right now.

You never know—some of the things you poo-poo today may become very important to you once you have a computer of your own. Stranger things have happened.

Putting the Cart Before the Horse

Talking about things to do with your computer before you've officially decided to buy one may seem like putting the cart well before the horse. In one sense, that's true: how can you figure out what you want to do with a computer if you don't own one? In another sense, though, how can you decide what kind of computer you want to own if you don't have some idea of what you want to do with it?

Home Management

Regardless of whether you're single or married, have children, are co-habitating, or *what*, you may find yourself feeling like you're living in the middle of Grand Central Station. There are always places to go, people to see, things to do, things you forgot to do. I don't know many people who couldn't use a little more organization in their lives.

With a home computer, you can produce daily, weekly, or monthly calendars with all the things you and your family or friends need to do. You can schedule activities so you don't have to be in two places (or three) at once—like a doctor's appointment and a dentist's appointment within minutes of each other.

You can keep track of car maintenance so you'll know exactly the last time you changed the oil and about when you should do it again. Plus, you'll be able to remind yourself in advance when you need to register the kids for summer camp, put the deposit down on your much-needed vacation, or order the cake for Aunt Mildred's 105th birthday and send her photo to Willard Scott.

Education

If you've got kids of your own (or just borrow someone else's), computers can help with almost every facet of their education—from learning to tell time and tie shoes, to preparing to take the College Boards.

No kids? No problem. You can teach yourself a new language, brush up on your history and geography, and generally prepare yourself for the day Alex Trebek calls and asks you to be on "Jeopardy!"

Ride the Info-Highway

With a modem and a membership to an on-line service, you can gain access to an entire world of information, useful to you and everyone you know (computerless/modemless friends are always asking me to find some scoop for them). Be the first kid on the block with access to the Internet. Win friends. Influence people. Run up your phone bill.

Have Fun

Computer games just keep getting cooler and cooler. Stereo sound effects, video-quality animation, and all kinds of other whiz-bang novelties are available to "make your games come true."

In addition, with that modem and membership to an on-line service, you can not only be informed, you can be the life of the on-line party, meeting, greeting, and corresponding with other members of the on-line world— including the President and Vice-President of the U.S. of A.

Spend More Time at Home

Do you find yourself spending extra hours at work because you can't take your computer-related work home? Well, you could go home a lot sooner if you had your own computer at home. You'd still have to do the work, but at least you'd be present and accounted for—not missing in action.

If your employer is amenable, your family agreeable, and your job adaptable, you could conceivably work from home all or most of the time. *Telecommute* instead of commuting: the worst traffic you'd run into would be a busy signal.

Tired of being pushed around? Want to murder your boss? Don't do it. Instead, start a business in your home with the power of your new computer. When business starts taking off, you might just want to quit that day job. Remember, the best revenge is living well.

Be Philanthropic

Donate your computer and skills for a couple of hours each week or month to your favorite local non-profit organization. They always need something done: publish a flyer or newsletter; maintain a database of clients or donors; generate form letters about fund raisers. You'll not only learn more about your own computer and what it can do, you'll feel all warm and fuzzy inside.

But Wait! There's More . . .

If there wasn't more, this would be a pretty shabby, thin, and uninformative book.

I know you need a home computer—I think everybody does. But if you still aren't sure you want or need one, flip through the book. Read the chapters that strike your fancy. All of the topics above are covered, plus many more.

Need additional information on a particular subject? In the back there's an index that cross-references topics, and a resource list for finding information elsewhere.

But don't let us bully you into anything (not that we would, of course).

Night of the Living Self-Test: Are YOU Ready for a Home Computer?

This is not a timed test, so take as little or as much time as you need. There are no right or wrong answers. You might, however, want to make a copy of the blank test and let every member of your household who will contribute to the purchase of a home computer take a whack at it.

Quizzical Looks

Question	Yes	No	Maybe
1. Do you use a computer at work?	❏	❏	❏
2. Do you ever put in extra hours on that computer just for the fun of it, or to learn things you don't have time to learn during the course of your regular day?	❏	❏	❏
3. Do you have school-age children?	❏	❏	❏
4. Are you in school yourself?	❏	❏	❏
5. Do you regularly type or write letters? Reports? Short stories? Articles? Novels? Scholarly work?	❏	❏	❏
6. Do you maintain a lot of personal records (financial, medical, family history, important dates, appointments)?	❏	❏	❏

Question	Yes	No	Maybe
7. Do you have a hobby, like collecting, where you maintain an inventory of your collectibles and their history (for yourself or for insurance purposes)?	❑	❑	❑
8. Do you often waste a lot of time looking for important reference materials in your own book or magazine library?	❑	❑	❑
9. Are you active in community organizations?	❑	❑	❑
10. Do you leave a trail of Post-It notes and scraps of paper with reminders on them wherever you go?	❑	❑	❑
11. Do you have difficulty getting out of the house to meet people (because of shyness, physical impairment, etc.), but long for social contact?	❑	❑	❑
12. Do you run a small business from your home? Do you want to?	❑	❑	❑
13. Are you the kind of person who can't or won't balance a checkbook?	❑	❑	❑
14. Do you (or will you) have an investment or stock portfolio that you monitor on a regular basis?	❑	❑	❑
15. Do you work late or work weekends? Do you go into the office just to use the computer?	❑	❑	❑
16. Do you find the idea of an Information Super Highway such a great idea that you're trembling in anticipation?	❑	❑	❑

Question	Yes	No	Maybe
17. Do friends, colleagues, and/or business associates ask you for your personal e-mail address? Are you embarrassed to admit that you don't have one?	❑	❑	❑
18. When you travel for business, do you have to take an extra suitcase for reports, charts, and other paper reference materials?	❑	❑	❑
19. Do you do your own taxes?	❑	❑	❑
20. Do some of your co-workers work primarily at home, and come into the office only once or twice a week/month? Do you envy them?	❑	❑	❑

Go Figure

There's no clever scoring to this quiz. You don't get three points for each Yes answer, two for each Maybe, and so on. Instead, look down the list and see how many times you answered Yes. How many Maybe's?

If you have a majority of Yes answers, you have a need for a home computer. If you have a lot of Maybe answers, you might need one, and you probably want one. If your answers are mostly No, it's less likely that you need or want a home computer.

If more than one person in your home took the quiz, you may want to average the number of each Yes/No/Maybe responses (add up each response and divide by the number of folks taking the quiz). Go ahead and make the math as complicated as you like—the results will still be valid.

You should now have a fair idea of the reasons for and against buying a computer for your home. If the test came up against a computer, so long, it's been nice knowing you. But you might want to poke around in the later chapters and see if we can't change your mind.

If the quiz came up for the purchase of a computer, plow on. We're here to help you every step of the way.

Chapter 2

What Makes Up a Home Computer System?

T hese days, buying a computer is similar to buying component stereo
equipment. When buying a stereo, it's important to get all the pieces
you'll need to listen to all the types of music you have (good luck
finding an actual turntable, though). With computers, you need to be sure you
get all of the components you need to meet your immediate goals. Everyone
will need the basic system stuff, but (depending on your needs and desires)
you may or may not need some of the various add-ons and accessories.

This chapter is a brief introduction to the various parts (with descriptions and
suggestions) that you can use to formulate a generic list of things to get. The
next chapter will help you put that generic list into a specific context:
Macintosh, PC, PowerPC; desktop, laptop, or other.

Basic System Hardware

There are four main components you need before you can truly say you own
a computer: CPU, monitor, disk storage, and input devices. Omit any one,
and it's like buying a car without wheels: you'll have a computer, but you
won't be able to do anything with it.

The Central Processing Unit

The *Central Processing Unit* (CPU) is the part that does the actual computing;
it's the computer that makes a computer. Sometimes you'll hear folks refer to
the boxy part of a computer system as the CPU. That's misleading. The box is
the part that contains the CPU. The CPU is actually a little-bitty chip inside
the box that does the work. It's that chip that distinguishes one "box" from
another.

The differences between chips are generally discussed in terms of the chip model (386 vs. 486 for PCs, or 68030 vs. 68040 for Macs) and the chip's clock speed (how fast it works). When considering what processor chip you want in your computer, a general rule of thumb is that the latest, greatest models have higher numbers than their predecessors: a 386 is newer/more powerful than a 286, and a 68040 is newer/more powerful than a 68030.

The newer models also tend to be more expensive than the older ones. Currently, the cutting edge CPU for IBM and IBM-compatible machines is the *Pentium* (sometimes called the 586 chip). For Macs, it's the chip behind the PowerPC, the 601 chip.

This Way to the PowerPC

If you're thinking about buying a PowerPC, you might want to skip ahead to the article "The Power PC" in Part V, which discusses the advantages and disadvantages of jumping on the PowerPC bandwagon.

Different versions of the same CPU chip may vary in terms of their clock speed. When you look at advertising information (or when a salesman is blathering in your ear about a machine's virtues), you may see/hear a chip referred to as a 486/50MHz. The 486 is the kind of chip; 50MHz refers to that chip's clock speed.

MHz means *megahertz*, and it's a measure of how many instructions the chip can carry out in one second. A chip that runs at 1MHz can do a million things per second. One that runs at 50MHz can do fifty million things in that same second. A higher clock speed means that the chip can do more in the same amount of time, so the computer will work faster than a similar machine with a lower clock speed.

Monitors

The choice of monitor is nearly as important as the choice of CPU. For just about every minute you use your computer, you'll be staring at the monitor. If you get a monitor that's too small or too hard to read, you'll be complaining about eyestrain and headaches in short order.

In some ways, choosing a monitor is like choosing a TV set, only it's a little more complicated. Like a television set, monitor size is measured diagonally, from one corner of the picture tube to the other. Larger models are more expensive. 13- and 14-inch monitors seem to have become the norm. Smaller ones are hard to find; larger ones abound. If you want to do serious graphics work or desktop publishing, a larger monitor may be helpful. In addition to the size, you must also choose from monochrome, grayscale, and color monitors.

Monochrome monitors display one color (usually amber, green, or white) against a black background. Although monochrome monitors are the least expensive, they are inappropriate for many uses and are hard on the eyes.

Grayscale monitors are better for your eyes. They display shades of gray, instead of stark black-and-white. If you're only interested in data processing and desktop publishing (without the use of color), a grayscale monitor will serve you well.

If you want to play games in color, deal with color images, or work with color in any way, you need a *color monitor* (duh). Depending on your computer's video capability (see "Video Considerations" in the sidebar) you may be able to see up to millions of colors on your screen, although 256 colors will serve most users nicely.

Video Considerations

If you're buying a PC, you'll also need to buy a video adapter card—one that's appropriate for the monitor you've chosen. The majority of new PC applications that require color monitors also require a VGA (video graphics array) or SVGA (super video graphics array) adapter card. Of the two, SVGA is better. Make sure you get a name-brand SVGA card—not some cheap generic model—and make sure it has at least 512KB of memory (preferably 1 megabyte) on the video card.

If you're buying a Mac, don't sweat it. Most Macs come with built-in video support (generally enough to display from 256 to thousands of colors on a 14-inch monitor). Depending on your needs, and the monitor you choose, you probably won't need an additional video card.

Finally, when selecting a monitor, you'll be confronted with monitors of the same size that have different resolution. "Resolution" refers to how many pixels (the dots that form the screen image) there are per inch of monitor. The more pixels per inch, the finer the detail you'll be able to see. A high resolution monitor is easier on your eyes, and is better for detailed work (like retouching digital photographs). Look for a monitor that displays at least 1,024 × 768 pixels.

You may also run into the terms "interlaced" and "non-interlaced" when shopping for a monitor. An *interlaced* monitor draws images and information on the screen in two phases: the first phase draws the contents of every other line, and the second phase fills in the remaining lines. *Non-interlaced* monitors draw the entire screen in one pass, eliminating the annoying flicker that is common with interlaced monitors. Non-interlaced monitors cost more, but they're much easier on the eyes than the interlaced varieties.

Disk Storage

Most new computers come with two kinds of disk storage space: floppy disk drives and hard drives.

A *hard drive* is a high volume storage medium to which your computer has access all of the time. Your hard drive is where you'll store your operating system (more on that later) and the applications you use all the time. Most computers come with an internal hard drive, which comes inside the box that houses the CPU. You can also add external hard drives that sit on your desk and are connected to your computer via a cable.

The amount of data a hard drive holds is measured in megabytes (MB). An 80MB hard drive holds twice what a 40MB drive holds. Given the size of most new applications, you don't want a hard drive smaller than 80MB: it will fill up too fast. A hard drive larger than 80MB would be even better.

Floppy disk drives read data from, and store data to smaller storage media: floppy disks. The disk drive makes it possible for you to get programs into your computer and get data out of it. Floppy disks (and their drives) come in two sizes: 5.25 and 3.5 inches. Each of these also come in two capacities: low (double) density (abbreviated DD) and high density (HD). High density drives can write to both double and high density disks, so don't fiddle with low density drives.

You want at least one 3.5-inch high density drive. You may or may not want a high density 5.25-inch drive. 5.25 disks are slowly becoming extinct, so unless you know you need to use them (if it's the size you use at work, for instance), you may not want to bother with 5.25-inch disks and drives at all.

Input Devices

You need a keyboard to get thoughts from your head onto the digital page. As essential as one is, believe it or not, they don't always come with your CPU.

There is a wide variety of keyboard designs that will be more or less comfortable depending upon how you work. Try several out before you buy one.

A mouse is also essential if you're buying a Mac or if you plan to use Windows or *any* graphics-based applications on your PC. If you don't like mice, there are less-common alternatives, such as trackballs, that you might want to investigate instead. A trackball is basically an upside-down mouse. A roller ball sits in a stationary base, and you roll the ball with your fingers instead of moving a mouse.

Since your mouse and keyboard can affect your work, and (in some cases) your health, you might want to read the article "Computing Health and Safety" in Part V before you select either.

Add-on Accessories

There are mountains of other things you can add to your computer. Depending on how you plan to use your computer, you may want or need to add some of the following.

A Printer

A printer gets your work out of your computer and onto a printed page. Most people will want one. You can choose from three varieties: dot-matrix, inkjet, and laser.

Dot-matrix printers are inexpensive and produce acceptable quality printing for personal correspondence, school reports, personal data files. Tiny pins on the printhead strike a ribbon (like on a typewriter) to form the characters. Because the dots that make up the characters are definitely visible, even on the highest quality dot-matrix printout, if you need professional-looking output you probably will want to consider a different printer.

Inkjet printers are moderately priced, falling in between dot-matrix and laser printers. They use a fine spray of ink to draw letters and characters on the page. When duplicated, printing from an inkjet printer can be mistaken for laser printing. If you have only an occasional need for laser-quality output, an inkjet may serve you well. If you need occasional color output, color inkjets are much more affordable than color laser printers.

Laser printers produce the most consistently professional-looking results. They are also fairly expensive to buy (starting at around $600) and to maintain (toner cartridges cost from $70–$100). However, if you're starting a home business, or will be producing materials for your job or for reproduction, a laser printer may be essential.

Depending on your needs and household, it might be more cost-effective for you to buy two printers. Perhaps a cheap, dot-matrix printer for your children, drafts of work documents, or non-business work, and a laser printer for your professional, finished products. Or you might find a different combination beneficial.

Modem

A *modem* is a device that allows two computers to communicate via common telephone lines. The word is a cross between the two words *mo*dulating and *dem*odulating, which describe the process of turning computer information into sound (modulating) and then back into data (demodulating). A modem can be internal or external, and in addition to connecting you to another computer, many can also send and/or receive fax documents (although you can't run a paper document through one).

A modem and phone line attached to your computer give you access to the rest of the digital world. If you want to join an on-line service or telecommute to your job, you'll have to have one.

In addition to their location (internal/external) and fax capability, modems are distinguished by speed. Modem speed is expressed in *baud rate* or *BPS* (bits per second). Both are measurements of how much data they can move. The slowest acceptable modem speed is 2400 baud, but that is very slow by today's standards. Most on-line services will let you call in at 9600 baud— some at 14400 and higher. A faster modem means less time spent on-line, and lower phone bills. Buy as fast a modem as you can afford. High speed modems can slow down, if the need arises, but slow modems can't speed up.

CD-ROM

CD-ROM stands for Compact Disk Read-Only Memory. A CD-ROM drive reads data from a CD just like your CD player in your stereo. CDs can hold hundreds of times as much information as floppy disks.

Software manufacturers have come to realize that they can release very complicated and flashy programs on CDs and distribute them for the cost of a single compact disc. In fact, that's exactly what they're doing. There's a growing assortment of multimedia software: educational materials, voluminous reference materials, and some amazing games, most of which incorporate elaborate sound and video files that never would have fit on ordinary floppy disks.

If you have kids, are in school yourself, or if anyone in your home is a gamester, a CD-ROM might be a valuable addition to your computer. The article, "Multimedia" in Part V discusses CD-ROMs and multimedia in detail.

Sound Card and Speakers

To get the fullest enjoyment out of some games, applications, and multimedia CDs, you might want to consider adding a sound card and speakers to your PC. A sound card gives your PC the capability to produce richer sound than that produced by the average PC's tinny built-in speaker. A set of external speakers can further enhance sound or make your computer a music machine (if you have a CD-ROM drive that can play audio CDs, too).

All Macs come with the functionality of a sound card already built-in, but Mac owners may want to add speakers to pump up the volume.

Removable Media Drives

While internal hard drives are wonderful storage devices, they aren't especially helpful if you need to carry that data around with you (for instance, if you want to take a huge project home, make changes to it, then bring it back to work). Not easy with an internal drive or a ton of diskettes.

However, a variety of *removable media* drives is available. They allow you to pop out a high-capacity disk, tape, or cartridge, and carry it wherever you're going. You pop it in a compatible drive at your destination, and you can access the data again. These are also handy for backing up the valuable data on your hard drive for safe keeping. (More about backups in Chapter 12.)

Average users probably won't need a removable media drive immediately, if ever. If it will make your work life easier, ask the person in charge of the computers where you work for a recommendation for an appropriate drive before you buy one.

The Operating System

Every computer needs an operating system. It tells the computer's CPU how to do everything you and/or your applications want it to do. Macs run the Macintosh Operating System, usually shortened to just "System" followed by the version number. System 7.5 is the latest version of the Macintosh operating system. The Mac's operating system is *graphical*, meaning you work with menus and icons instead of typing commands (see Chapter 11 for details).

Most PCs run MS-DOS (Microsoft Disk Operating System), though there are other operating systems available. MS-DOS is not graphical like the Mac. (See Chapter 9 for details.) You tell the computer what you want it to do by typing specific commands at the command prompt, C:\>.

PC owners who dislike the command prompt have flocked to graphics-based DOS "shells" such as Microsoft Windows to give their DOS machines the friendlier look and feel of a graphical interface (see Chapter 10 for details).

For PC shoppers, the choice of operating system and shell program is almost as important as the choice of computer. The operating system and shell program will dictate the kind and number of applications you can run on your computer. Potential Mac owners need to consider their Mac model more than the operating system, since it's fairly standard between Mac models. The choice of Mac may limit the kinds of software you can run.

The Applications

Applications are the reason you're buying your computer in the first place. They're what help you get work done. Part III of this book explains the major software categories and their hardware requirements, and gives you reviews of some of the more popular names in each category.

Before buying your computer, find out if there is a specific software package or class of software you have to use (for your job, home business, or hobby). If there is, track down a copy in your local computer store, check its system requirements, and make sure the computer you plan to buy will run that application. You don't want to shell out major dollars for an essential application, only to be frustrated when your computer can't handle it.

Well, now you know the barest of the basics, but it's okay if you're not quite ready to buy a computer yet. The next chapter will help you narrow the field down to the computer system that's perfect for you.

Chapter 3

Before You Buy

B efore you run out to the store to buy a computer, you need to think about a few more things: What kind of computer will you buy? What size? What do you want it to do? And (among others) where should you buy it? These aren't questions anyone can answer for you (since everyone is different), but they are questions you can get some help with. Here's the help.

IBM-Compatible or Macintosh? Which Is for You?

There was a time when choosing between an IBM and a Mac was a make-or-break decision. If you bought an IBM-compatible (sometimes called PC compatible or just PC), you were limited to dull, businesslike applications. If you bought a Mac, you were limited to funky, graphical, unbusinesslike applications. Today, both platforms have their share of funky and dull applications. In fact, most major applications are available for either computer type and (on the IBM-compatible side) Windows and non-Windows versions, too.

So how do you decide? The best place to start is with the reason you're buying your computer in the first place:

◆ If you're buying a computer (primarily) to be able to take work home from your day job, what kind of computer do you use at work?

◆ If you're buying one for your school-aged kids so they can have an edge, what kind of computer are they using at school?

◆ If it's going to be used primarily by a college student, does the college have a computer requirement? If the college requires students to have a particular kind of computer (some do), you've got yourself a Hobson's choice—and that's no choice at all.

◆ If the goal is a child's education, do you want a multimedia computer (with a built-in CD-ROM drive and audio accessories)? See the article "Multimedia" in Part V for more details.

Why Not Have It All?

Buying the same kind of computer that the primary user has used before (and will use again) is the path of least resistance. You can, however, buy against that advice. If you just need to exchange data, there are software programs available that let your Mac read and format DOS-formatted disks (DOS=IBM-compatible), and your DOS machine read and format Mac disks. If you use an IBM-compatible at work, but would prefer a Mac for your home, there are software and hardware add-ins that allow your Mac to emulate an IBM-compatible if you need to run specific DOS software. Be warned, however, that emulations are often sluggish and slow compared to "the real thing."

Apple even makes a Mac that has a built-in IBM-compatible processor; so one minute it can be a Mac and the next a 386 PC. It costs a bit more, and neither the Mac side nor the IBM-compatible side runs quite as well as a single-purpose computer would, but that's the price you pay for versatility.

And what about the much-hyped PowerPCs? The result of the joint venture between Apple and IBM, they're supposed to be the future of computing. If you think you'd like a PowerPC, check out the article "The PowerPC" in Part V for the advantages and disadvantages of buying one of the new machines.

If your kids use an Apple IIe at school, and you'd like them to be able to use one at home, you don't have to buy a IIe. Apple makes an expansion card that will let your Mac pretend it's a IIe. It was designed for the LC series of Macs, but will work with many of the Performas, too. Your kids can have the computer they're familiar with, and you can have a Mac.

Maybe you want a computer for a different reason—or maybe just to have one. Then how do you decide? Consider two things. First, you can buy the kind of computer you're already familiar with. If you learned on an IBM-compatible PC (and liked it), buy a PC. If you learned on a Mac, buy a Mac. People are generally happier buying a system they already know than they would be having to learn a completely new one. However, if you don't have any computer experience (or if you know what kind of computer you want but you aren't sure about the model), you'll need another way to decide: go shopping for software first.

What Do You Want It to Do?

Even after considering the suggestions above, some of you still may not know what kind or what model of a computer you want or need. One way to be sure you buy a computer you will use is to go looking for software first. (You might want to skim through Part III for a roundup of the major software categories and reviews of popular packages.)

When you see a software package you think you might want to own and use, check out the back of the box. Every package has on the back (or side) a list of the minimum system requirements needed to use the software. Some packages require high-power computers; some will run on just about anything. Some have versions available for Macintosh, DOS, and Windows computers. (Chapter 14 will help you to interpret those system requirements, and to make intelligent software decisions.) Find the software you think will be most important to you (right away or in the near future) and make sure the computer you select will meet or exceed the software's minimum system requirements.

Does Size Count?

Actually, size can count for computers. If you want one you can travel with, it probably isn't a good idea to buy a huge desktop model. Here's a quick breakdown of your size options (the smaller models are discussed in more detail in the article "Laptops and Other Portable Computers" in Part V).

◆ As a class, portable computers are generally smaller versions of desktop machines. They aren't especially small, but they'll fit in a bag and are, well, portable.

◆ Laptops are small enough and light enough that you can work with them balanced on your knees or in your lap.

◆ A desktop machine is probably what you think of when you think "computer." It's the kind designed to sit on top of a desk and not travel very far.

◆ A tower machine is one where the CPU stands vertically like a tower instead of lying horizontally on a desk. They can sit on top of your desk beside the monitor, but many people set them on the floor *under* the desk—especially when desktop real estate is at a premium.

Do You Need a Tower Case?

You don't have to buy a computer with a tower case to stand it on the floor under your desk. You can buy a desktop machine and buy a CPU stand. The stand gives the non-tower model the support and bracing to stand on its side.

Be warned, though. Using a CPU stand can put your disk drives in a position that's hard to reach. It can also put your hard drive(s) at risk. You know how record albums (remember those) that have been stored on their edge for a long time sometimes don't lay quite flat on the turntable? Well, after you've left a disk drive in a certain position for a long time, it might be just a fraction of an inch out of alignment if you suddenly tilt it; and that small alignment error can cause disk problems with some types of hard drives.

Minimum Requirements

Based on what you've learned in Chapter 2 and in this chapter, and the input from your family, friends, co-workers, and whoever else you pumped for advice, you should be able to come up with a bare-minimum list of things you need to meet your computing goals. You can write the information in this handy form, or photocopy it, or just write the information down on a piece of paper.

I NEED:

A(n) _____ (Mac/IBM), _____ (model name/processor)_____ MHz (clock speed).

With __MB of RAM, and a ___MB hard drive.

And the latest version of the appropriate operating system (MS-DOS 6.2, System 7.5, or other).

I want one 3.5-inch high density floppy drive, and _____ (another drive if you desire). Plus a box of floppy disks.

I need a(n) ___-inch monitor (diagonal measurement), _____ (VGA, SVGA, if appropriate) and a compatible video card (if appropriate).

If not included, I want a(n) _____ (extended, or 101 key, etc.) keyboard, and a mouse/trackball (circle one).

I'd also like a(n) _____ (make and model) printer, with the appropriate cable, paper, ribbons/cartridges/toner so I can use it right away. (Of course, if you don't want a printer, skip it.)

After you use this list to shop for the computer, hang on to it; it'll come in handy for matching the hardware requirements on software packages.

The Extras

Use this list for things you'd like to get if your budget allows, or things that you have to have but that aren't considered part of a basic system.

I WANT:

___MB of additional RAM (appropriate to the computer) installed.

An internal/external CD-ROM: _____ (make and model), with appropriate sound and/or controller card, cables, and speakers.

A(n) _____(baud rate) modem, with/without fax capability.

And (fill in whatever additional hardware you might want: Scanner, hard drive, removable media drive, etc. Include make and model numbers if you know them.)

_____

_____

_____

I'd also like the following software:

_____

_____

_____

_____

Tips for Ballparking the Price

With the way computer hardware prices keep fluctuating, there's no tried and true way of saying such-and-such computer system will cost you X dollars. Well, there is, but it would be wrong before the ink dried on the page.

The easiest way to figure out (roughly) what you'll pay for a particular kind of system is to look through a current issue of a magazine devoted to that kind of computer. For example, look through the ads in *PC World* for current PC pricing, or in *MacWorld* for Mac pricing. (The article "Computer Pubs" in Part V is devoted to all manner of computer publications, by the way.)

The prices in the ads won't be quite up to date. It takes a couple months for a magazine to hit the stands. While editors struggle to keep the informational content up-to-the-minute, most advertisers will list the price that's current as of the date the ad is placed. They may be a little high, or low, depending on the current pricing trend.

Figure out the cost of your ideal system from the magazine, then add the cost of any extras you may want. Finally, add approximately another 10–20% as a hedge against inflation. If the prices drop, instead of going up, you can always spend the money on software or other goodies on your extras list.

Deciding Where to Buy

Gosh, you can buy computers practically anywhere these days: computer stores, superstores, electronics stores, Sears, office supply stores, and by mail order. Hey, even QVC and the Home Shopping Club sell computers from time to time. The question to consider is where will be best for *you*.

An established computer store that's close to home has advantages for a first time buyer. It's nearby, and you can go there if you forgot to get something or run into a problem. All they sell is computer-related items, so you can probably get technical help if you need it. Some of the chain superstores, like MicroCenter, even offer training and have professional service departments. That's a plus.

Electronics, office supply, and retail stores (like Silo, Staples, and Sears, respectively) are good choices, too. However, their sales staffs often are not as informed as the staff of a dedicated computer store, most don't have service departments, and most don't offer training. The same applies to discount stores like Sam's Club, and other Club-type stores. They aren't in the business of computers; they're in the business of selling—period. The advantages are pricing and location (if there's one nearby).

Mail order companies often offer the same advantages as computer stores: they have telephone support, so you can call with your questions; many service what they sell; and pricing is usually good. The problem inherent in ordering by phone is you can't look at what you're buying before you buy it. You can't tell how long the company has been in business, or whether their customers are generally satisfied with them. In addition, if you have a problem with a mail order product, you have to ship it away for repair or replacement. That's a drag. Even speedy service will leave you without a computer for a day or two.

For most first time buyers (unless you've had gobs of experience with computers at work or have a friend who knows the ropes with other retail outlets), I recommend the safer (if a little more expensive) computer store/superstore route—at least for the computer. You may want to try getting software and one or two extras by mail order, just to check it out. Later, when you've honed your alternate shopping skills and are a little more savvy with computers in general, feel free to try other retail outlets, traveling computer shows and sales, and mail order. The first time out, I say go for safety and stress reduction. After all, who needs the gray hair?

Chapter 4

The Shopping Safari

S hopping for a home computer isn't nearly as dangerous as going on an actual safari. No rampaging lions and pusillanimous pachyderms to worry about. You may, however, have to hack through a lot of dense verbiage, or feel a tickle at the back of your neck that suggests you're being stalked by a wily salesclerk.

This chapter is all about coping with the silicon jungle, and it's chock-a-block with hints and suggestions to help you bag a computer in its natural habitat.

Dealing with Salesclerks

When traveling abroad, it's fairly rude to expect an entire country to accommodate your ignorance of their language. When shopping for a computer, it isn't necessarily rude not to speak the language, but it could be expensive.

The great truth about computer salesclerks is that many of them work on commission—that is, their paychecks are bigger when they sell more (or more expensive) stuff. It's an incentive to sell. That's not saying commissions are good or bad, or that clerks are evil, but it's the way things are. So, if you go into a computer store to buy a computer, but you haven't got a clue about what you want, the clerk is going to start out trying to sell you something expensive and work down from there. The best defense is to do your homework before you go shopping. You should know the following things before you set out on your big adventure:

- ◆ How much you want to spend

- ◆ A rough idea of the kind of computer you want (Mac vs. IBM and/or different models (486 vs. Pentium or Quadra vs. PowerPC)

◆ The minimum other components you need in order to get started (software and peripherals)

◆ Extra items you want—the stuff that's nice, but not exactly necessary right away (perhaps a CD-ROM drive or modem)

Fortunately, Chapter 3 (and the rest of this book) should give you everything you need to get that information set in your mind, and on paper. When a clerk asks, "How may I help you?" you can say something on the order of:

"I'm trying to decide between a 486 and a low-end Quadra—something that's upgradable and expandable. I'd like to put a system together for about $1500. Can I play with some floor models?"

The clerk will then know not to waste her time pushing a Pentium, PowerPC, or other high-end machine. She'll also know your price range (though you may want to hold a few hundred dollars in reserve so you have room to negotiate: tell her you've got $1500, but be prepared to spend $1700 or $1800).

Knowing roughly what you want puts you in charge of the sale. State it up front, and then remind the clerk of it if strange and horribly expensive computers keep popping up in your conversation. Once you're in charge of the sale, you can get as much (or as little) help as you need from the clerk.

Remember My Name . . .

Since many clerks work on commission, be sure to get the name of the clerk that first helped you. If he or she leaves you alone to play with floor-model computers, another clerk may offer to assist you. Say, "Thanks, so-and-so is helping me."

Clerks on commission tend to introduce themselves by name, and say "Ask for me if you have any questions, or when you've made up your mind." Great salesclerks know when to leave a customer alone to experiment or make up his mind. Don't punish a good clerk by letting another one close the sale and earn the commission.

Words to Watch Out For

You shouldn't go to France without learning enough French to ask, "Where is the bathroom, please?" and "Which way to the Louvre?" Likewise, you shouldn't go computer shopping without learning some computerese. Computer salesclerks, computer geeks, and computer book authors tend to speak in buzzwords, assuming that the folks they're speaking to understand the buzz. Here are some buzzable words you'll probably run into (these and many more will also be found in the glossary in the back of this book).

Alphabet soup   The assortment of letters thrown into chip numbers, like a 486SX or DX, or the 68LC040. They are used to indicate variations in a family of chips. If they start throwing letters at you that you don't understand, ask for a translation.

Bus   The path through which data and other impulses travel from your computer to attached devices.

Riding the 386 Bus

386 computers come in two varieties: 386SX and 386DX. The difference is the bus width: 386SX has a 16-bit bus, while the 386DX has a 32-bit bus.

Bus architecture   The structure of the bus, referring to how much information the bus can handle at one time. 8-, 16-, and 32-bit bus architectures are most common right now. 16-bit architecture can handle twice the data of 8-bit; 32-bit architecture can handle twice that of 16-bit.

CPU   The central processing unit. This term is used to refer to the chip that runs the computer, or to the box that holds the chip, disk drive(s), and so on. The rule of thumb: the higher the chip number, the newer and more powerful it is.

Clock speed   A measure of how fast the CPU chip works, expressed in megahertz (MHz). A 33MHz computer is faster than a 20MHz computer. Note, however, that the clock speed is not the be-all and end-all deciding factor when selecting a CPU. The design of the rest of the system (like the *bus*) may cripple a processor's ability to work efficiently. Just because the chip *can* do twenty million things per second doesn't mean it *will*. If you try out a computer with a 20MHz clock speed, and it seems faster than a computer with a 33MHz clock speed, go with the 20MHz clock speed.

Who Made the Chip?

Potential PC buyers also should consider who made the CPU chip. Intel is the company that designs the industry standard DOS CPU chips, but they aren't the only company that makes and sells them.

Other companies duplicate, or make their own versions of Intel's chips. Some of these imitations are fine; others cut corners and aren't up to Intel's standards. If you want to be certain you're getting an industry standard chip, look for the "Intel Inside" label on the computer or its advertising propaganda.

Mac buyers don't have to worry about it. All of Apple's chips are made by the same company: Motorola.

Expandable   Having the potential to take on extras in order to increase the computer's functionality. You add functions via *expansion cards*, so the computer must have *expansion slots* to hold them. Your video and disk controller cards (for PCs) are expansion cards. After you've added the cards you currently need, you should have a slot or two left over for future expansion.

MPC   Multimedia Personal Computer. MPC is a set of standards for IBM-compatible computers that come equipped with a CD-ROM drive and other multimedia hardware. There are two sets of standards: MPC (or MPC1) and MPC2. MPC2 is the latest, greatest set of standards. (If you're thinking about buying a multimedia computer, you might want to check out the article "Multimedia" in Part V for important additional buying information.)

MTBF   Mean-Time Between Failures. A rough indication of how long a product should last before something goes wrong with it. To find this figure, computer manufacturers run a bunch of the same hardware constantly, until it breaks down. Then they average all those times (in hours) together, and the result is the MTBF.

Math Chip/Coprocessor   An additional chip that helps your computer whip through math-intensive applications like 3-D rendering and some graphics applications (oddly enough, most spreadsheets don't require one). You may or may not want one, but the computer you buy should have a socket to accept one, should you decide to add it later.

486s and Coprocessors

Just when you thought things couldn't get any more confusing... A page or so ago you read that 386 computers' SX and DX designations referred to the bus width. Well, in 486 computers SX and DX mean something totally different. 486DX CPUs have built-in math coprocessors; 486SX CPUs do not. That is the only difference between them.

Motherboard   The main circuit board inside the computer. It holds the CPU chip, expansion slots, and system RAM.

RAM   Random Access Memory. The amount of temporary space the computer has in which to hold an application and your data files while you're working with them. Not to be confused with storage space (like a hard drive). When you turn off the computer, everything in RAM is lost. The data on your hard drive stays put until you erase it. Computers come with a minimal amount of RAM installed and slots to add more.

No matter what kind of computer you're considering, I wouldn't get one with less than 4MB of RAM, more if you plan to use Windows (for your PC) or run graphics-intensive programs on a Mac.

Turbo   A DOS-compatible computer that runs at two clock speeds (like 12MHz and 22MHz turbo). You set the desired clock speed with a switch on the CPU.

Upgradeable   The potential of many current 486 machines and Mac Quadras to be upgraded to the higher Pentium and PowerPC computers. The upgrade may mean adding a card, a chip, or a new motherboard.

The Package Deal

Ah, the path of least resistance! Walk into a computer store, point at a system, and say "Give me that!"

Knowing that most people are somewhat phobic about computers, some stores and manufacturers put together computer bundles that give you everything you need to get up and running with a minimum of fuss. Usually you get the CPU, monitor, keyboard, mouse, and some software. Sometimes you'll get extra goodies, like a modem or CD-ROM drive.

Is buying a bundled system getting a good deal, or is it getting screwed? Well, that depends on what you set out to buy in the first place.

Say you wanted a 486SX/33MHz, with an 80MB hard drive and 8MB of RAM. You planned to add a 14-inch Super VGA monitor, a fancy keyboard, and a trackball (instead of a mouse), and Microsoft Windows and a suite of Windows applications. That's what you wanted and you were prepared to spend $1500.

What you found was a 486DX/20MHz bundle that came with a 40MB hard drive and 4MB of RAM. It came with a 14-inch SVGA monitor, a no-name keyboard and mouse, and a bundle of software, including Windows. It cost $1099.

Did you get a deal? Dollar-wise, sure. You saved $400 of your budget, but you didn't get the computer you wanted. If you wanted that computer for a reason (there were specific things you wanted to do that required specific computing power), you may have been screwed. You could spend the $400 you saved (and more) just decking out that one-size-fits-all computer in extra hardware to meet your needs.

The best advice to avoid getting burned on a bundle is this: do your homework. Decide exactly what you need as a minimum to accomplish your goals. Then look at the bundles and see if you can find one that meets or exceeds your needs. If you can, great. If you can't, piece a system together that does, while still staying within your budget.

Figuring the Cost of Living

While you listen to the salesperson extol the virtues of the various computer components (especially printers), keep your eyes peeled for hidden costs associated with the various products. For example, a laser printer that's on sale may be a bargain up front, but may not be so cheap in the long run. All laser printers need toner cartridges: is one included? How long will it last? How much does it cost? Do you keep them in stock? Can I find them elsewhere?

Some laser printers also require you to replace an imaging drum, which may or may not wear out at the same time as the toner cartridge: the same questions apply.

Some ink jet printers require special coated paper to get the best print out of them: what does it cost? Do I have to use it all the time? What about ink cartridges?

Don't just consider the price you have to pay for a peripheral now, also consider what it will cost you in care and feeding expenses over the life of the equipment. Some stores will provide an information sheet for printers that includes a PPP entry. PPP means *price per page* (sometimes cost per page), which gives you a means of comparing printer costs over the long term. One printer may be more expensive in the store, but may save you money in the long run because of extremely low maintenance costs.

The Top 10 Ways to Avoid Getting a Bad Deal

10.   Do your homework: an informed shopper is harder to bamboozle.

9.   Set a budget and stick to it. If you can't afford the minimum system you need, wait. You can either save up the money, or the price may drop. Stranger things have happened.

8.   Take a shopping list with you—and stick to it (this works in any shopping situation). Don't settle for less than you need, but don't get suckered into buying more than you need, unless it's still within your budget.

7.   If you don't understand something the salesclerk is saying, don't pretend to understand it just to avoid looking stupid. *That* is stupid. Ask lots of questions.

6.   Don't be pressured into buying something you aren't sure you need. If you feel pressured, stop the clerk, say you need to think about it, and leave. Go home and do more research if you have to, or just go sit outside and think without a pushy clerk breathing down your neck. Err in haste, repent in a leisure suit (or something like that).

5.   Take someone with you whose opinion you trust, and let him play devil's advocate. Do "reality checks" and compare notes. And ask that person to keep you from going on a spending spree.

4.   If you get tired of shopping but haven't found what you need, stop. Tired brains make mistakes. Take a break.

3.   Make sure the store has a liberal return policy in case the machine doesn't live up to your expectations—or the clerk's sales pitch.

2.   Shop in several stores before you buy. Comparison shopping is the number one way to sniff out bogus claims on "Low, low pricing!" Make sure you're comparing the same systems, or similar systems from different manufacturers. Write down everything—even the names of the clerks who helped you (see "Remember My Name" in the sidebar above).

1.   Remember who's in charge. You are. You're spending your money for your computer. Don't buy the computer of the salesclerk's dreams—buy the computer of your own dreams.

Chapter 5

Getting Ready for the New Arrival

You wouldn't bring home a puppy without an adequate supply of newspapers on hand, would you? Nor would you bring home (or adopt) a baby without getting a crib, diapers, and all that other baby stuff first.

Fortunately, computers aren't the poop factories that puppies and babies are, but you still don't want to bring one home without having a special space for it all set up and ready to go. If you can, you should have the area set up before you bring the computer home because that makes the situation less stressful and lets you concentrate on the computer, not the furniture. If you can't (say, you're buying your desk at the same time you're buying your computer), set up the area first, take a break, and then set up the computer. All that "insert tab A into slot B" jazz can wear you out.

Where Should It Go?

Your computer should go wherever you have room for the desk and other furniture. Preferably, it should be placed away from high-traffic areas (so you can work undisturbed as well as for any safety issues). If at all possible, you should set up the computer in a permanent spot so you don't have to assemble and disassemble the computer every time you want to use it (what a pain). A good computer area should also include the following:

◆ A desk or table that's sturdy enough to hold the computer system and is large enough for the machine, peripherals (like a printer), and any other materials you'll need. There should also be room for non-computer work. The desk should be comfortable to work at: not too high, not too low, but just right.

◆ Electrical outlet(s). You need at least one outlet. If you've only got one outlet handy, you need to get one of those multiple outlet surge protectors to turn that one outlet into several.

◆ A phone or phone jack nearby, so you can talk on the phone while you work or hook up a modem when the need arises.

◆ A comfy chair.

◆ A source of light (so you can see what you're doing).

You can go plain or fancy: use a solid wood (*not* a hollow core) door over a couple of saw horses, special computer furniture, or even a Queen Anne desk and Louis XIV chair. You can be as cheap or extravagant as you like. Expense and good looks aren't the issue. Flimsiness is the issue. *Flimsy is bad.*

Whatever you use for a desk, make sure it's stable (doesn't wobble) and strong (an average-sized adult should be able to sit *on* the desk without it groaning or cracking). You don't want your new digital baby landing in your lap—or (the horror) hitting the floor.

"Computer furniture" has the advantage of being designed to accommodate all the fiddly bits of a computer system: a drawer for the keyboard, a shelf to hold the monitor at eye-level, space for a mouse and mouse pad, sometimes even a drawer or stand to hold a printer and supplies. They also have the advantage of being ergonomically designed (more about ergonomics in a minute). Of course, the disadvantage is that most folks buying their first computer don't already own computer furniture. You have to buy it. Go figure.

If you're buying your computer to set up a home business or to telecommute to work, you may have additional needs. Check out the articles "SOHO, SOHO, It's Off to Work We Go" and "Telecommuting" in Part V for more information.

Ergonomics

Ergonomics is the science of designing things that are easier (and healthier) to work with. Chairs that support your lower back, and mouse pads with wrist rests built-in to reduce the risk of carpal tunnel syndrome are examples of ergonomic design. Believe it or not, there may be as many potential dangers in sitting at a desk and working with a computer for long hours as there are in more obviously dangerous jobs. Check out the article "Computing Health and Safety" in Part V, if you don't believe me.

Regardless of whether you're cobbling together a work area from things you already have around the house or you're outfitting one from scratch, you should be aware that your furniture and computer equipment's design can have an impact on how long (and how well) you'll be able to work. You should consider acquiring a few more things soon after you buy your computer (if not right off the bat):

◆ A desk or desk accessory that lets you adjust the height and position of your monitor to avoid neck and eye strain.

◆ A real desk chair with arm rests and back support that is fully adjustable. It will help prevent lower back pain.

◆ A mouse pad with a wrist rest to help prevent carpal tunnel syndrome.

◆ A keyboard wrist rest to help avoid the repetitive stress injuries associated with heavy-duty typing. (Learning *how* to type will also help, since it teaches you the proper way to hold your hands, wrists, and the rest of your body while typing.)

◆ An antiglare/antiradiation filter for your monitor to cut down on eyestrain and any threat from electromagnetic radiation.

Again, the article "Computing Health and Safety" covers these things in more detail. You should read it. Really.

Surging Right Along

While you think about protecting yourself from the hazards of computing, you should also think about protecting your computer from the hazards of electrical surges. Even though the lights in your home may look like they're always getting the same amount of electricity, they aren't. You've seen lights flicker. You've seen them dim. You've seen them flare up brightly and (often) burn out. All those pyrotechnics may be the result of irregularities in the power coming to your home. You can't do much about them; they're a fact of life.

Because these surges of power can be dangerous to electrical appliances, like computers, you should invest in a multi-outlet *surge protector*. Surge protectors come with a fuse that stands between the supply of power and your valuable equipment. If the power surges to dangerous levels, that fuse should burn out before a damaging power surge reaches your computer. If it's better "to light one candle than to curse the darkness," it's also better to blow up a $10 surge protector than to blow up thousands of dollars in computer equipment.

The multi-outlet type of surge protector can also be used to turn all of your computer equipment on from one switch. This saves you from having to mess with the switches on all of the various components—which, in itself, makes the surge protector worth the money.

Power "Conditioning"

Folks who live in areas that are subject to severe power irregularities—surges, brown-outs, or frequent power losses—may want to consider buying an *uninterruptible power supply* or UPS. This device is a big storage battery that intercepts the power before it gets to your equipment.

You plug the UPS into an outlet, and you plug your computer equipment into the UPS. If your power supply becomes weak (a brown-out), the UPS feeds extra battery power to your computer so you get a consistent supply. If the power surges, the UPS absorbs the excess or blows a fuse. If the power goes out, it supplies a few (from 8 to 45) minutes of power so you can save your data and shut down your computer properly, sparing it the stress of cutting the power abruptly.

To select the right UPS, you need to add up the power requirements (in watts) of *all* the devices you'll have plugged into it (that information should be readily available in the technical specifications chapter of your manuals). Buy a UPS that meets or exceeds your total system needs. One that exceeds your system needs is better, because you may add more peripherals later, and you don't want to have to buy another or larger UPS.

A UPS isn't for everybody, especially since it can cost from $300–500. But if you know your local power company isn't completely reliable, it's money well spent.

Ready to Roll!

Once you've got your act together in terms of furniture, accessories, and power, you're ready to bring home your new bundle of digital joy. The next three chapters will give you tips on setting it up and keeping it happy and healthy.

Chapter 6

It's Here!

I presume that you've already set up the area where you're going to use your computer. I also presume—how presumptuous—that you followed my advice and bought the computer locally (if you went the mail order route, see the sidebar entitled "Mail Order Tango"). So your computer was just delivered. Now where do you begin?

Before you start setting up the computer, give all of the surfaces of the desk (or whatever) a good going over with a dust cloth or damp wash rag. Hopefully, you won't be moving this equipment around too often, so start with a clean slate (so to speak).

You'll also find it useful to have a few tools handy: small and medium screwdrivers (both slotted and Phillips head), and a pair of long needle-nosed pliers or one of those claw-devices in case you drop a screw or some other tiny object into a crevice too small for fingers. (I do this *all* the time.)

The truly anal retentive may want some masking tape, a pen, some *more* masking tape or long twisty-ties (the kind you get with big trash bags). That's so you can bundle and label the snake-pit of cables and wires together into neat parcels, instead of a bunch of little vipers. (I keep saying I should do this, but never get around to it. "Should" is such a difficult word.) You won't need a hammer. If you find yourself wanting a hammer, something's really, really wrong. Stop. Take a break.

Check-Out Time Is Now

With your area prepared and your tools laid out, the first thing you should do is check out all of the cartons, boxes, and bags for signs of damage. Just a quick eyeballing will do to make sure nothing untoward happened in transit. You might also want to make sure you didn't leave anything in the car or back at the store. (I do this a lot, too—I'm such a goof.)

Once you're satisfied that everything looks okay, you can start to unpack. Don't go nuts. Open each box/bag/crate/whatever one at a time. Each one should have something like a packing list (either on a piece of paper or as part of a manual) telling you what should be in the box. Make sure everything's there, but also keep everything from one box together; you don't want to have to figure out later which cable goes with what component.

Mail Order Tango

The check-in process for mail order purchases is doubled. In addition to checking the individual pieces for signs of damage and missing parts, you should always give the shipping cartons a good once-over before you sign for them.

If you can, check the shipping boxes while the delivery person is still there. Just look for obvious signs of damage: water marks, which might indicate your computer was given a bath; broken and re-taped corners; footprints in the center of big crush marks; or anything else that indicates the cartons were mistreated. If the boxes were somehow damaged, indicate it on the form the driver wants you to sign—before you sign it. That way, it's officially noted that the packages were damaged *before* you received them. If something is broken inside, it's not your fault.

What if you can't be there when the delivery is made? (You've got a life, right?) If you ask a friend, neighbor, or your apartment manager to accept delivery, ask him or her to give the boxes a quick once-over before signing. It can save you a lot of hassle if problems develop later.

When you know (or at least think) you have everything you paid for, find the manuals. Gather them all together. Sit down. Read the assembly instructions completely before you begin, and then reread each step again as you proceed. Different computers go together differently, so this book will only help in the most general of terms.

Most likely, you'll begin by setting up the CPU, the box with the disk drives and so on. Once that's in position, you'll add the monitor, keyboard, and everything else that sits on or around the CPU. It will make your life easier if you have easy access to the back of the CPU (where all of the cables are connected). If your desk is against a wall or other obstruction that might make it difficult to plug the components in, you may want to assemble your computer so it's sideways or even backwards on the desk. Then just turn it around the right way when everything is together.

Speaking of cables . . .

Plugging In All Those Confusing Cords

Everything you attach to your computer is going to have at least two cords: a cable of some kind to connect it to the computer and a power cord. Work slowly and methodically. Add one thing at a time and cable it to the CPU. Most computer cables are designed so you can't plug them in the wrong way, so don't force anything. Make sure the end of the cable you're trying to plug in aligns nicely with the port you're trying to plug it into. Push firmly. Tighten any screws, finger screws, or clamps that hold the cables in place.

Run the power cord to the outlet or surge protector, but don't plug it in yet. You'll plug everything in at once when you're finished. That way you can move stuff around and jiggle things without fear of bending or breaking the plug and/or socket.

This would be the point where you would write the cable name and type on a piece of masking tape. You might also want to jot down where the cable will be plugged in (something like PRINTER/PARALLEL/LPT1 for a PC or PRINTER/SERIAL/PRINTER PORT for a Mac). Write big enough that you can read it easily, even from a distance. This will help later, when you have to undo/redo the cabling, or you need to replace a cable. Trust me.

So, where do things go? I can't help you too much there. Each item is connected differently on different makes and models of computer. Read your manuals carefully. I will say this, though: all Macs—and PCs by some manufacturers—have icons under the various ports (where you plug the cables in) so you can easily identify them. I wish more companies would.

When everything is cabled, you might want to take up most of the extra slack in the cables into neat bundles and tape or twist-tie them up. This is for two reasons. First, it's tidier than having all of those cables dangling all over the place (I should include a photo of the backside of my desk as an example of what *not* to do—what a mess). Second, it's safer. If you have a toddler who loves to climb/crawl into small, confined spaces and play with everything or pets (which do many of the same things), having the cables up and out of harm's way will make them less of a temptation. It also means less chance of you tripping over one or getting one caught in the vacuum cleaner. (I really should do this myself.)

Powering Up

Once everything is together and positioned on your desk, you can plug each piece into the surge protector and plug the surge protector into the outlet. Next, turn on each of the components. Check the manuals if you can't find the power switches; there is no standard location for them. Some companies seem to relish hiding them or making them inaccessible. Finally, turn everything on by turning on the surge protector. Your computer should hum to life. If it doesn't, don't panic.

Help! It Doesn't Work!

You're not panicking, are you? I distinctly said "Don't panic." If your computer doesn't start right up the first time, you probably missed a step in putting it together. Not a big deal.

Turn off the power, and then retrace your steps. Double-check everything you did against the instructions in the manual. The most obvious things are the ones most easily missed. Check them first:

◆ Is everything plugged in?

◆ Is it turned on?

◆ Is there power coming through the outlet you're using? Plug in a lamp or something to check.

◆ Are all cables and connections tight?

◆ Are all connections made to the right place/port?

If you hear the computer start up but don't see anything on the monitor, check to make sure the monitor is on and is getting power, and fiddle with the brightness and contrast knobs. It may be working fine, you just can't see it.

If the computer starts up, but doesn't seem to do anything, you may need to install your operating system on the computer's hard drive. Chapters 9, 10, and 11 talk about using (in order of appearance) MS-DOS, Microsoft Windows, and the Macintosh operating system. Chapter 15 talks about the most common ways software is installed; but check your manuals for specific installation instruction.

If all else fails, see Chapter 13 for coverage of the most common computer maladies and ways to fix them. You'll also find tips for getting the best service from companies' customer service and technical support departments. Likewise, computer manuals invariably include a section on troubleshooting. You might want to read that, too. It couldn't hurt. Most folks will find their trouble right away, solve it easily, and get on with their lives. I hope you're one of them.

Chapter 7

Keeping Your Computer Happy and Healthy

Since I'm determined to carry the choosing-a-computer-is-a-lot-like choosing-a-pet analogy through to its ugliest "poop-on-the-floor" extremes, let's talk about care and feeding. While a computer can't give you the unconditional love that a dog, cat, or other pet can, both will act up if you don't treat them right. I have a cat that likes to knock all the stuff off my dresser if he feels neglected. I have a computer that goes goofy if I use it during the steamy dog days of summer. Both are spoiled rotten.

Top 5 Things That Are Bad News for Computers

Just like chicken bones are bad for cats and chocolate can give dogs diarrhea (*yuck!*), there are things that are unhealthy for your computer. Here's a little list of the top five no-no's to have around your valuable computer equipment. We'll talk about some of them in a little more detail later.

5. Gravity. The force of nature that makes things fall down is the reason you don't want to set your computer up on a flimsy card table. It's also why you don't want, say, a 20-pound hanging plant dangling over it. Besides the dirt and water involved, the plant could fall down and go boom—you don't want it to take your computer with it.

4. Heat. When computers first hit the scene, they had to be kept in airtight, air-conditioned rooms or the heat would bollix them up. They're less sensitive these days, but if your computer gives you grief at the height of summer, the heat may be to blame. If you don't have air conditioning,

you may have to adjust your work schedule to work in the morning or at night when it's cooler.

3. Dust and other airborne crud. Dust is a big problem, and so are pet hair, food crumbs, and smoke. Crud that gets inside your computer can gum up the works. Moving parts can stop moving, or dust can form a layer of insulation that retains the heat produced by the machine (see number 4). Clean around your computer often, and keep the air vents clear. Whenever you have reason to pop the hood, dust inside the CPU with compressed air (the environmentally correct kind without chloroflouro-carbons—CFCs) or even vacuum carefully with one of those wand attachments (don't run your Hoover upright over it!).

2. Liquids. Most liquids you find around the house conduct electricity. They'll short out your computer if they come in contact with its electrical components. Additionally, beverages contain sugar-like substances that get sticky when they dry. Try typing when the keyboard is full of day-old cola. Not fun.

1. Magnets and magnetic fields. Very bad news. A simple refrigerator magnet or one of those magnetic paper clip holders can scramble all of the data on a floppy disk or hard drive in nothing flat. Your Great American Novel will read like you've got chronic dyslexia. *No magnets near the computer, ever.*

I just realized that the things that are bad for your computer include the Classical Greek's notion of the four basic elements: earth, air, fire, and water. Hmmm.

Playing It Safe

Granted, it sounds like you may as well have your computer in an airtight, air-conditioned room, where everyone wears scrub suits, surgical gloves, and hair nets. Not true. You don't have to be completely paranoid, but it helps. The following sections give you tips on some simple things you can do to prevent a major (or even minor) calamity. Once you get in the habit of doing them, they'll become second nature and will be no trouble at all.

Dealing with Dust

Dust happens. You can't stop it, but you can keep it from overwhelming your computer. Buy dust covers for your computer and peripherals, and keep those rascals wrapped when they're not in use. Buy a flexible keyboard cover that fits like a skin over the keys. This still allows you to type, but it doesn't let dust (or anything else) get between the keys. A keyboard cover is an essential purchase if children will be using your computer.

Set up a weekly maintenance schedule. For example, every Monday before you go to work on your computer, just wipe it down and dust around and under it. (Compressed air blown under the components will keep you from having to move everything.) If you smoke, have pets, or have any other special situations that can cause excessive crud to accumulate, you might want to do this more frequently.

Dealing with Disks

Floppy disks hold valuable programs and program data. If you follow the advice on backing up that's given in Chapter 12, everything you have on your hard drive will be backed up onto disks. You may also have some things on disk that aren't on your hard drive. That makes disks worth protecting.

Whether you use 5.25- or 3.5-inch disks, high density or low, they should be handled with respect. If the disks you use come in protective sleeves, use them. Store your disks in something: the little cardboard box they came in, a shoe box, even a solid gold file that plays the "Hallelujah Chorus" when you open it. Store disks out of direct sunlight and away from extremes of heat and cold. Disks are plastic: plastic melts when heated and cracks when frozen. That means you shouldn't leave them in your car when it's sunny and hot or freezing cold. Store them away from magnets/magnetic fields (that means don't anchor a disk to your refrigerator with a decorative magnet). Don't leave them in the disk drive when you turn off the computer (that leaves the protective shutter open on 3.5-inch disks, which isn't very protective), and put them away when you're done with them.

Don't touch the magnetic media inside your floppy disks. On 5.25-inch disks, it's exposed in the oval opposite the label area. On 3.5-inch disks, you have to slide a metal shutter to the side to see it. You can look, but don't touch. The oils and residue from your fingers can wreak havoc on the data on the disk, plus it can booger up the mechanism in your disk drives (technically speaking).

Please Don't Feed the Computer!

My mother's favorite rule of etiquette for her three kids was "Don't eat or drink in front your friends unless you have enough for everybody." It sort of applies to your computer, too. You don't want to share your food or drink with your computer, so don't eat or drink in front of it.

Apart from being rude, crumbs and spills are dangerous to the operating life of your machine. Besides, having to eat or drink is the perfect excuse to walk away from your computer. I don't care how pressured you feel or how tight your deadline is. You have to eat sometime; you can't work all of the time.

No Smoking

With the current trend of outlawing smoking everywhere, I hate to add another place in which you can't or shouldn't smoke. But here I go. Tobacco smoke is bad for your computer. It's full of particulate matter (bits of crud) that's every bit as bad for your machine as any other variety of dust. The already-bad badness of dust is compounded by the fact that the smoke particles are coated in tars that make them stick to the gizzards of your computer—you can't just blow it away like ordinary household dust.

You'll also develop a scum of nicotine on the plastic surfaces and on the monitor glass (which looks nasty). Not to mention that the sticky tar will also hold on to more run-of-the-mill dust, making that harder to get rid of, too. Looks like it's time to buy one of those obnoxious No Smoking signs to post nearby. Sorry.

If You Can't Stop

If you have to smoke at your computer, you can eliminate the tar and nicotine stains on the casing and monitor by cleaning them with a mild solution of white vinegar and warm water. Read the cleaning sections in this chapter before you try it, though.

Keep ashes out of your keyboard by buying one of the plastic keyboard covers I mentioned earlier. You can't, however, do anything about the crud that will collect inside the computer. That could still be hazardous to your system's health.

Cleaning Up Your Act

Dust isn't the only crud that affects computers: regular dirt affects them too. But you can clean your computer, if you do it correctly. All computer components can be cleaned on the outside, and most can (and should) be cleaned on the inside. If you own a peripheral that isn't discussed here, check its manual for cleaning instructions.

If you're the tidy sort, you may want to add some of these cleaning techniques to your weekly routine (like the dusting mentioned earlier) or less frequently. It's up to you.

Cleaning the Case and Monitor

The exterior housing of most computers, monitors, and keyboards is plastic. Some are coated metal. They can be cleaned with a mild solution of soap and warm water or a gentle commercial spray cleaner. The thing to remember when cleaning is that liquids aren't good for the insides of your computer. *Lightly* dampen your soft cloth with your cleaner of choice and wipe down the case. If you get the cloth too wet, you can always wring it out. It's hard to wring out a keyboard.

You can clean the glass part of your monitor with a glass-cleaning product— again moistening the cloth not the glass. The cloth you use to clean your equipment should be of the lint-free, non-abrasive variety. You can buy a 12-pack of washable cloths in office supply stores for $5 or less.

You may see special cleaning sprays for both monitors and plastic cases. They aren't necessary. The one nice thing about some monitor sprays, however, is their antistatic quality. They cut down on the amount of dust that gets stuck on your screen. Otherwise, there's nothing very special about them. And the pre-moistened towelettes that are available are very convenient, but expensive.

Cleaning the Disk Drives

Disk drives *do* require a special widget to clean them: a head-cleaner shaped like the appropriate disk. These come with "special" cleaning solutions made of isopropyl alcohol with a drying ingredient. If you buy the solution in a computer store, you'll pay a few dollars for a few ounces. You can buy half a pint of plain alcohol in the drug store for under a dollar. Don't waste your money.

Generally, you moisten the material inside the cleaning disk with a few drops of solution and insert the disk in your drive. When the computer tries to read the disk, it cleans the read/write heads of any accumulated gunk.

How often to clean your disk drives is a point of contention among users. Some say weekly, others say as little as once or twice a year. I split the difference: I do it whenever I remember. It isn't weekly, but it's more than twice a year.

Cleaning a Mouse

Mice need cleaning, too. When you roll one around on your desktop, whatever dirt it rolls over gets rolled up inside the mouse. It can make your mouse difficult to use.

There are special kits available to clean mice, too. They include foam-tipped swabs (like foam Q-Tips), lint-free wipes, and *another* cleaning solution. Don't waste your money. The solution is (what, class?) isopropyl alcohol again. Buy the foam-tipped cleaners and lint-free wipes separately (they're less expensive that way), and buy plain isopropyl alcohol. (Cotton swabs will work, but they may shed cotton fibers which will gum up the works as effectively as dirt.)

To clean the mouse, turn it over on its back. There's usually a locking ring around the hard rubber ball. Turn the ring to unlock it, and remove both the ring and the ball. Wipe the ball with a lint-free wipe and alcohol. Set it aside. Dip a foam swab in the alcohol. Shake off the excess and swab inside the cavity. Pay special attention to the rollers; a lot of junk can build up on them. The alcohol will evaporate. When it does, replace the ball and the locking ring. You're done. You can clean the mouse's casing as you would your computer's case.

The same method works for cleaning trackballs (which are just upside-down mice). Check your manual to see how to remove the ball, though.

The Great Debate: Turn It Off? Leave It On?

Turning your computer on has been likened to pouring hot water into a cold glass, starting a car on a cold morning, and other equally inventive metaphors. Essentially, the problem is that when you turn on the power to your computer, the initial jolt is stronger than the regular stream of power. It can stress the components inside your computer, causing wear and tear on the electronics. That's why PCs have Reset buttons and the Control+Alt+Delete key combination. Likewise, Macs have the Restart option under the Special menu. Each of these methods restarts your computer without that initial surge of power—without that stress.

The great debate, then, centers around whether it's better to turn your computer off and on as needed, to turn it on in the morning and off at night, or to leave it on all the time. I'm not going to take sides, since the argument has gotten almost as ugly as the "which way does the roll of toilet paper go?" feud. Here are some facts. You decide.

◆ Turning the computer on and off a few times in the course of a day inflicts stress on the components.

◆ Turning it on in the morning and off at night seems prudent, but a waste of energy if you only use it a fraction of the time.

◆ Leaving a computer on 24 hours a day is wearing in other ways. Besides wasting energy, hard drives spin and monitors burn all the time.

◆ Sparing your system the shock of being turned on and off will wear out your components.

What I do is this (I'm sharing with you, here, not telling you what you should do): I turn my computer on when I'm ready to work. I turn it off when I know I'm done for the day. That may be in ten minutes, or it may be in ten hours. If I don't know what my computing day will be like, I leave it on all day and turn it off before I go to bed. I aim for moderation.

Think of It As Car Care

Cleaning stinks. I hate to do it. However, I make an exception in the case of my computer equipment. Instead of thinking of it as "cleaning," I think of it as preventive maintenance. Just as you need to change the oil in your car every few thousand miles (to keep the engine running smoothly), you need to maintain your computer every few hundred hours. Head trouble off at the pass.

Computers haven't reached the point that some appliances (like VCRs) have, where it's cheaper to buy a new one than to get the old one fixed. Regular preventive maintenance will help keep you up and computing for a long time.

Chapter 8

My Computer, *My* Rules

This chapter is about setting up fair rules and schedules for two or more people to follow when using the same computer. If you're the only one who'll be using the computer in question, please feel free to skip merrily ahead.

People are territorial, just like all other animals. We use words like "yours," "mine," and "ours." Tempers flare when someone else crosses the boundary into territory that's "mine." (My pet peeve has always been my desk. You can snoop through my medicine cabinet until you *plotz* for all I care, but leave my desk and computer alone.) However, there are ways to negotiate computer use so that the primary user, or owner, doesn't feel like his computer has been commandeered, nor will other users feel like mere peasants trying to get an audience with the King.

Just how you do that depends on the reasons why you bought the computer and the reasons why individuals have come to rely on the computer after it's been with you awhile. Situations change, and the sharing schedules and rules may have to change to meet those new situations. Stay flexible. Stay calm.

Establish a Pecking Order

You may have bought a computer for one reason only: to start a home business, to let you do job-related work in the comfort of your own home, or to help your children in school. If that's the reason you bought the computer, that should be its primary use.

Your time-sharing schedule might be as free-form as saying "Anyone is free to use the computer as long as I don't have business to take care of with it or the kids don't have homework to do with it." To avoid clashes, the primary user should try to warn folks in advance: "I have a big project to do tonight.

I'll be on the computer right after dinner." Other users should ask the primary user before they start: "I wanted to use the computer tonight, do you need to use it?"

If you bought your computer for two or more reasons, you have to prioritize them. What reason gets priority? Which comes second, third, and so on? You should always be ready to negotiate when jobs collide if the schedules allow it; however, having a clear set of priorities should help avoid any hurt feelings. If too many conflicts arise, maybe you need another computer in your home.

Organic Scheduling

Home lives these days often look like the Venn diagrams we learned in grade school: two or more circles that only overlap in certain places, at certain times. Not everyone is home at the same time. These natural breaks in the day offer easy ways to schedule time for everyone to use the computer. While some users are at work or in school, other users should be able to get at the computer with minimal negotiation. If the primary user has a regular "night out," that's a time to set aside the computer for other users and uses.

When the computer is shared by two or more children, their respective bedtimes (if they vary) can serve as a guide: the one who has to be in bed first gets to use the computer first, and so on. If your children all go to bed at the same time, you'll probably need to work out and mediate a usage schedule that's fair for all the children and the grownups involved.

Getting all the different people who want to use the computer actually onto the computer shouldn't involve anyone jumping through hoops. Try to work with the natural rhythms that have already been established in your various lives.

Share the Rules

Everyone with access to a shared computer should know and follow the rules—especially (but not exclusively) children. Actually posting a set of rules by the computer may seem very controlling or authoritarian, but it makes good sense. It makes sense because people can't follow rules they don't know about or have forgotten. It also prevents conflicts over the dreaded "unwritten law," and short circuits the "I forgot" excuse.

Posted rules (especially for younger folks) can also work to the benefit of the user: you can't be called on the carpet over a rule that isn't on the list. The worst thing an infraction of an unwritten rule can bring about is a new rule.

Being Fair

When establishing a set of rules for your computer, mainly for the children in your household, be fair. Don't set a rule for children that you won't follow yourself. For example, don't say "No food or drinks at the computer," and then carry your cup of coffee in with you when you go to work. That's not fair. Instead of being a rule for using the computer, it becomes a rule for controlling the children. It sets a double standard (and aren't there enough of *those* around as it is?).

Try to phrase the rules so the kids don't feel like they're the target of all this in-house legislation. Come up with the rules together, discuss them together so everyone understands what they mean and why they exist, and let the children help you print them up and post them. Kids can be difficult and intractable, but try to use "Because I said so" only as a last resort.

For infractions of the rules, mete out justice equally. Be just as lavish with your praise for following the rules as you are with your punishment for breaking them.

Suggested Rules

These are only suggestions. Every household is different, just like every child is different. Tailor these to suit your needs, or ignore them completely—it's your computer after all.

You may:

◆ Trade or share your computer time with someone else.

◆ Give your computer time to someone else.

◆ Play a game if your homework or work is finished.

◆ Negotiate new rules or permanent schedule changes if the majority agrees.

◆ Ask someone else to settle an argument.

You may not:

◆ Have food or drinks near the computer. No exceptions.

◆ Smoke near the computer.

◆ Use magnets near the computer.

◆ Use the computer during someone else's time without asking permission.

◆ Play games on the computer unless your homework or work is finished.

◆ Let friends use the computer unless you ask permission and tell them the rules.

◆ Install software on the hard drive without permission.

◆ Open, alter, or delete files (other than your own) without permission.

◆ Logon to an on-line service without permission and/or supervision.

The "You may" rules are to keep the list from being a litany of NO's. Most of the "You may not" rules are to protect the computer and to avoid arguments. Others, like the rules about playing games, are pretty self-explanatory. The rules about installing software, deleting files, and using on-line services are about protecting you and your child, and giving you both a chance to work together.

Having a child ask permission to install software gives you a chance to look at the software before you let your child use it. It should be legally obtained (more about that in a minute), and you should see some value in the child using it. Some people find the content of some software, mainly games, objectionable (see the article "Fun and Games" in Part V for more information). This rule gives you a chance to say "No."

The rule about on-line services has similar goals: children shouldn't be allowed to run wild on-line any more than anywhere else. They could get an eyeful of adult material, be disruptive in areas not meant for children, and otherwise get into trouble. Besides that, kids should be supervised because they'll be running up your phone bill and on-line charges whether they get into trouble or not.

The rule about not opening, altering, or deleting any files but your own is to protect all users' data. Whenever people share a computer or data, there are questions of privacy and security. Both are very important (see Chapter 12 for more details on this topic).

Depending on the ages and abilities of the children involved, you may want to put an older child or adult in charge of turning the computer on and off for younger ones. You may also want to name an older child as first stage "technical support" for when younger children run into problems. Then if she can't solve the problem, she can get an adult.

Sharing Software

People share things. It's a nice concept, and one that should be encouraged with things that are legal to share. Sharing software, however, is in most cases illegal. The folks who use your computer should know that. Generally speaking, when you buy software, you're buying the right to use it on one computer. If you copy software and give it away (or receive it or, worse, sell it), in most cases you're breaking the law.

Regardless of who put the software on the computer, if you own it, you're the one who will be held responsible if the Software Police show up. If you need more detailed information, the article "Avast There Maties! Software Piracy" in Part V is devoted to the finer/grayer points of software piracy.

The Bottom Line

Rules and down-to-the-second schedules aren't any fun for children or grownups, but they are necessary. You can be as free-form and open about them as you care to be. But, however you mediate and/or moderate computer use, everyone should know what's expected of them up front. It will protect your computer and everybody's nerves from rough handling.

Part II

A Computing Survival Guide

In your average survival course, you may be dropped in the middle of a wilderness area with nothing more than a piece of string and a bent pin suitable for fishing. If you're lucky, you may get a compass and a pocket knife, too. You'd be expected to survive for three or more days, feeding yourself, fending off wild animals, and avoiding poison ivy—all while finding your way out of God's country and back to civilization.

For our computer version of a survival course, all you'll get is this section. Armed with these informative pages (covering topics as diverse as MS-DOS, Windows, the Mac environment, and computer safety), you will be dropped off in the digital wilderness. You are expected to find your way through the operating system of your choice and back to the real world. Your goal is to survive (don't forget to eat and take breaks) and to get out with your computer intact—which is why you aren't given a sledge hammer as basic equipment for this course.

On your mark. Get set. *Go!*

Chapter 9

A Short Course in DOS

Computers don't have any brains—they can do only what the software tells them to do. Without instructions, a computer can't even start itself up! The instructions a computer needs to start up (and to be ready to accept your commands) are contained in a handy bit of software called an *operating system*.

Most IBM-compatible computers use an operating system called Microsoft Disk Operating System, or MS-DOS. There are other versions of DOS (DR-DOS and PC-DOS, for instance), but they all work roughly the same, and most people just call whatever version they have "DOS" and leave it at that.

When you turn on your computer, it goes through some grinding and whooshing noises while DOS loads itself. When it's done with the preliminaries and is ready to accept your commands, you'll see a DOS prompt on-screen. It looks something like this:

    C:\>

What's Your Version?

MS-DOS started out back in the early '80s with version 1.0. It is improved every few years, and a new version number is slapped onto it. We're up to version 6.21 at the time of this writing. You can tell what version you have by typing **VER** at the DOS prompt and pressing **Enter**.

DOS provides dozens of commands that let you manage your files, directories, and disks. In this chapter, you'll meet a few of the most important ones. If you want to know more, you'll be pleased to hear that Alpha Books has published an outstanding book called *The Complete Idiot's Guide to DOS*, by Jennifer Fulton. It'll satisfy your craving for DOS know-how.

A Word About Typing Commands

This note may be beneath some people's dignity, but if we don't include it, there will invariably be some irate reader who'll write to us. To enter a DOS command, type the command on the keyboard. It doesn't matter whether the letters are upper- or lowercase. When you're finished, press the **Enter** key to execute the command.

Working with Disks

A *disk* is a physical storage unit that holds files and directories. (You'll learn about files and directories later in this chapter.) It would be easy to tell you more than you ever wanted to know about how disks hold data; instead, let's just say it works by magnetizing tiny particles on the disk with positive and negative charges. The computer translates these patterns into useful information.

There are two kinds of disks: floppy and hard. They work the same way, but are fairly dissimilar.

◆ **Floppy disks**   Small, thin wafers encased in plastic. They're removable, portable, and don't hold very much data. They're fairly fragile and prone to damage.

◆ **Hard disks**   Large, clunky cartridges with thin metal platters sealed inside. They're usually not removable (without disassembling your computer). They hold lots of data (sometimes thousands of times more than a floppy disk), and are seldom damaged.

Your floppy drives are usually called A: and B:. Your hard drive is usually C:. (If you have more than one hard drive, the others are probably called D:, E:, F:, and so on.) The colon is important: it tells DOS that the letter stands for a drive, and isn't part of a command you're typing.

Changing the Active Drive

Even if you have several disk drives, only one of them can be active at any time. "Active" in this case means something like "default"—it's the drive DOS assumes you are referring to unless you specify otherwise. If you type a command and don't say which drive letter you mean, DOS will use the active drive.

When you first start your computer the active drive is usually your main hard disk, C:. To change the active drive, just type a different drive letter (and a colon) and press Enter. For example:

> A:
>
> B:
>
> C:

The DOS prompt shows which drive is active. For example, if you changed to the A: drive (by typing A: and pressing Enter), the DOS prompt would change to something like this:

> A:\>

Formatting Disks—FORMAT

Most floppy disks you buy in the store are unformatted. That's because it's cheaper for the manufacturers to make them that way, and also so people who have non-DOS computers can format them their own way.

You must format a disk before you can use it. DOS, being the logical program that it is, provides a command called FORMAT for this purpose. To format a floppy disk, place the disk into your floppy drive (A:) and type

> FORMAT A:

(If you place the disk in drive B, substitute B for A in the above command.) You see the following message:

> Insert new diskette for drive A:
> and press ENTER when ready...

Press **Enter** to format the disk. When the formatting process is complete, DOS asks the following question:

> Volume label (11 characters, ENTER for none)?

Just press **Enter** or, if you want to give the disk a name, type the name and press **Enter**.

Other Disk Commands

Here are a few other disk commands you might find useful:

◆ **VOL** tells you what the name of the disk is, if it has one.

◆ **LABEL** enables you to assign a name to a disk.

◆ **CHKDSK** (pre-DOS 6.2) or **SCANDISK** (DOS 6.2) checks a disk for errors.

Managing Directories

A disk can contain thousands of files—an organizational nightmare. Luckily, the files on your disk can be arranged into directories and subdirectories, making your hard disk a kind of electronic filing cabinet. The top-level directory is called the *root directory*; it holds all the other directories, like a file cabinet holds drawers and folders. Within the root directory are other *directories* (drawers), which in turn sometimes hold *subdirectories* (drawer dividers). A *file* can reside anywhere you want to put it—in the root directory itself or in any other directory or subdirectory. The filing system is yours to use any way you want.

Alternative Analogy

So you don't like the filing cabinet analogy? Okay, here's another. A root directory is like the main lobby of a building, with lots of rooms opening up from it. Each room is a directory. Some rooms (directories) have closets inside them (subdirectories). What could be simpler?

Every directory has a unique name—except the hard disk's root directory. It's nameless. When you type a directory name, it's customary to add a backslash (\) before it, so DOS will know you're referring to a directory. When you refer to the root directory, you use the backslash by itself. Here are some examples:

C:\

C:\WORD

C:\EXCEL

Notice that the drive letter (C:) is included before the directory name. If you don't specify the drive letter, DOS will assume you mean the active drive (which you learned about a few sections ago). DOS supplies several commands for handling directories, which you'll learn about in the following section.

Listing the Contents of a Directory—DIR

When you first start your computer, you'll probably wind up in your hard drive's root directory. You can tell because the DOS prompt looks like this:

C:\>

To see the names of the files in your root directory, type **DIR** at the DOS prompt and press **Enter**. You then see a list of files something like this:

DOS	<DIR>	12-10-93	5:25p
DPAINT	<DIR>	12-10-93	6:23p
MOUSE	<DIR>	01-30-94	3:45p
QUICKENW	<DIR>	12-10-93	6:16p
STACKER	<DIR>	12-10-93	6:06p
WINDOWS	<DIR>	12-10-93	5:35p
WINWORD	<DIR>	12-10-93	6:21p
TSENG	COM	4,080 08-18-92	2:53p
COMMAND	COM	54,619 09-30-93	6:20a
CONFIG	SYS	399 03-10-94	4:37p
AUTOEXEC	BAT	795 03-11-94	11:01a
	11 file(s)	59,893 bytes	
		193,143,040 bytes free	

Items in the list that have <DIR> following them are directories. Other items in the list are names of files located in the root directory. Each item in the list shows its name and size, and the date and time it was created.

The Handy /P Switch

If your directory list is too long to fit on the screen, the first part of it will scroll up out of sight. To avoid that, you may want to use the command DIR /P. DOS will then display your directory one screen (or page) at a time. Just press **Enter** to see the next part of the list.

At the end of the list, DOS shows you the total amount of space taken up by the files in the list and the total amount of space left on the disk. Note that the total size of the files does not include files inside other directories—only the files in the root directory itself. (In the above example, that would be the last four files in the list.)

To see the contents of a different directory, use the name of the directory you want to examine. For example, to see the contents of the directory WINWORD, you would type:

> **DIR \WINWORD**

Another way to see the contents of a different directory is to make the other directory active—to "change to it" or "move to it," as you'll learn in the next section.

Moving to a Directory—CD

Just like with drives, only one directory can be active at a time. When you're referring to a directory other than the active one, you have to specify its name in the command, as you just saw in the DIR example.

To avoid a lot of extra typing, it is often easier to change to the directory you're going to be working with, so you don't have to keep specifying the directory name. You do this with the CD (change directory) command. For example, to move to the WINWORD directory, you would type:

> **CD \WINWORD**

Don't confuse the backslash (\) with the regular slash (/). The regular slash will only annoy your PC and provoke an error message. CD tells DOS that you want to change to a new directory. The second part of the command (\WINWORD) is the name of the directory you want to access. After you type this command on most computers, the DOS prompt will look like this:

> C:\WINWORD>

Now, suppose you had a subdirectory called LETTERS in the WINWORD directory. The command

CD \WINWORD\LETTERS

moves you to the LETTERS subdirectory.

To Slash or Not to Slash?

Sometimes DOS will let you get away with typing the directory name after DIR without the backslash (\), and sometimes it won't. The key is this: if you're in a directory directly "above" the one you want (for example, if you're in \WINWORD and you want to change to \WINWORD\LETTERS), the backslash isn't needed. But if you want to hop around to other directories, DOS requires the backslash.

Creating Directories—MD

When you install a program, it usually creates a directory for itself and installs all the files there. You may find that you want to make your own directories, though, to set up your own individual filing system.

To make a directory of your very own, use the MD (make directory) command. If you wanted to create a LETTERS subdirectory in your WINWORD directory, you'd type:

MD \WINWORD\LETTERS

The MD command tells DOS to create a new directory. The second part of the command tells DOS where to put it and what to call it. In this case, the location is the WINWORD directory, and the name of the new directory is LETTERS.

Still More on Slashes

Again, the necessity for the backslash (\) before the directory name varies. It's easiest to use it all the time so you don't have to memorize the rules for when it's needed.

Deleting a Directory—RD

To remove a directory, use the RD (remove directory) command. In order to help you avoid deleting files unintentionally, DOS will allow you to delete a directory only after you delete all files in the directory. (I'll explain later how to do that.) To delete the LETTERS subdirectory you created in the previous section, you would type:

RD \WINWORD\LETTERS

The first part of this command tells DOS to delete a directory. The second part of the command is the location and name of the directory to delete. In this example, the location is the WINWORD directory, and the name of the subdirectory to remove is LETTERS.

Express Directory Removal with DELTREE

If you use DOS 6.0 or above, you also have a command available called DELTREE. It works just like RD except it allows you to remove a directory that contains files and destroy the files in that directory all in one step. Type **DELTREE**, followed by the name of the directory you want to remove. *Be careful with this command!*

Handling Files

Your computer stores everything you do in files. When you save a letter to Uncle Ned, your word processor stores it as a file. Every file has a name, too, and (in most cases) you're the one who gets to name it. When you save that letter to Uncle Ned, for example, you might give it a name like NEDLETTR.DOC, to remind you that it's a letter to Uncle Ned, not Aunt Mildred.

Since all computer data is stored in files, you need to know the DOS commands to tinker with those files. The following sections show you the most important of these commands.

Copying a File—COPY

One thing you'll do regularly is copy files. Therefore, DOS provides the COPY command. As an example, suppose you wanted to copy the file

NEDLETTR.DOC, which is in the directory C:\LETTERS, to the directory OLDLETTR on a floppy disk in drive A. At the C:\> prompt, you would type the following command:

COPY C:\LETTERS\NEDLETTR.DOC A:\OLDLETTR

The word COPY tells DOS what you want to do. The next part of the command gives the location and name of the file you want to copy (the *source*). The last part of the command gives the new location to which you want to copy the file (the *destination*).

Notice that both the source and destination parts of the command include full location names (the drive letter and the directory name). If either the source or the destination is the active directory, you can leave out the drive and directory specs for that part, and DOS will figure it out. For example, if the active directory is C:\LETTERS, you can get away with typing

COPY NEDLETTR.DOC A:\OLDLETTR

Or, if A:\OLDLETTR is the active directory, you could use

COPY C:\LETTERS\NEDLETTR.DOC

Notice that the destination drive and directory is completely left off! DOS assumes you mean the active directory unless you specify otherwise.

Deleting a File—DEL

When you have used your computer for a while, you will have accumulated a lot of files, many of which you no longer need. Don't be a digital pack rat— get rid of them. To trim away the dead wood, use DOS's DEL (delete) command. Want to get rid of that letter to Uncle Ned? You'd use the following command:

DEL C:\LETTERS\NEDLETTR.DOC

The first part of this command tells DOS to delete a file. The second part of the command is the path name of the file to delete. If the file is in the active directory, you can leave off the drive and directory specs. For instance, if C:\LETTERS is the active directory, you could just type

DEL NEDLETTR.DOC

Be forewarned: The DEL command gives you no chance to change your mind. Once you type the command and press **Enter**, DOS erases the file from your disk. If you make a mistake, you can try using the UNDELETE command to bring back the file, but it doesn't always work. You will learn about UNDELETE later in this chapter.

A Walk on the Wild Card Side

There will be times when you will want to delete many files simultaneously. You can do this using *wild cards*—symbols that stand for "any character." An asterisk means "any number of characters," while a question mark means "any single character." For example, to delete every file with a .DOC extension, use DEL *.DOC. To delete every file in a directory, type DEL *.*.

Moving a File—MOVE

When you copy a file, the original file stays where it was, and a brand-spanking new copy appears in the destination directory. So what do you do if you just want to move a file from one place to another? You move it.

How you move a file depends on which version of MS-DOS you have installed on your computer. If your version of MS-DOS is 5.0 or earlier, you must move a file by copying it to its new location and then deleting the original file. Just use the COPY command you've already learned, and then the DEL command. For example, type

COPY C:\LETTERS\NEDLETTR.DOC C:\OLDLETTR

DEL C:\LETTERS\NEDLETTR.DOC

If you have MS-DOS version 6.0 or later, you can use the spiffy new MOVE command, which works exactly like the COPY command, except it deletes the source file after making the new copy. To move Uncle Ned's letter, you'd type

MOVE C:\LETTERS\NEDLETTR.DOC C:\OLDLETTR

Just as with the COPY command, if you're already in the source directory, you can simply type

MOVE NEDLETTR.DOC C:\OLDLETTR

MOVE: The Type-A Personality Command

The MOVE command is very fussy about knowing the drive and directory for the destination. Even if the destination directory is the active one, you still must type out its whole name.

Renaming a File—REN

When you christen a file, you're not stuck with that name forever. With the REN command (no, not like Ren and Stimpy!), you can change any file's name to anything you like—as long as the new name follows the file naming rules (see "Rules to Name By" in the sidebar). For example, to rename NEDLETTR.DOC to NED.DOC, you would use the following command:

REN C:\LETTERS\NEDLETTR.DOC C:\LETTERS\NED.DOC

The first part of this command is the word REN, which tells DOS that you want to rename a file. The second part of the command is the location and name of the file you want to rename. The third part of the command is the new file name.

As usual, if the directory where NEDLETTR.DOC resides is the active one, you can skip much of the hoopla and simply type

REN NEDLETTR.DOC NED.DOC

Rules to Name By

When naming a file, there are only a few rules you must follow. The part of the name before the period can't have more than eight characters. The part after the period can't have more than three characters. You can choose these characters from the letters A–Z and the numbers 0–9. (There are also some special characters like # and & that you can use, but you'll rarely, if ever, need them.)

Three DOS Commands That May Save Your Life Someday

While the fear of doing something wrong or having something bad happen to your data should never ever stop you from trying and learning new things, you really need to plan for the day that something screwy does happen. Trust me, it will. Even ancient geeks who cut their teeth on DOS 1.0 sometimes zig when they should zag, and then poof! Pop goes the directory. It could happen.

While the temptation is strong to just chuck the darn thing out the window, don't do it yet. First, check out three simple DOS commands that might help you avoid trouble in the first place, or might bail you out when trouble happens (in spite of all your caution).

Undeleting Files—UNDELETE

Eventually, you're going to delete a file and immediately regret it. Everybody does. When that happens you can try using DOS's UNDELETE command to bring the file back. Be warned: UNDELETE will only be successful if you use it immediately after you delete the file. The longer you wait, the slimmer your chances are of recovering the file. To undelete a file, type the following command:

UNDELETE *FILENAME.EXT*

Here, UNDELETE is the command that tells DOS to restore an erased file. The *FILENAME.EXT* part of the command is the name of the file you want to restore.

When you type the command, DOS looks for a deleted file that matches the name you requested. If it finds the file, DOS displays it on-screen and asks if this is the file you want. Because of the way DOS deletes files, the first character of the file name will be a question mark. After you tell DOS you want to restore the file, DOS asks what the first letter of the file name should be. When you respond, DOS tries to restore the file, and then displays a message letting you know whether or not the restoration was successful. It isn't always. (The world just isn't that simple.)

Getting DOS Help—HELP

If you've looked through your DOS manual, you know that DOS is chock-full of commands. It's almost impossible for anyone to remember all the different commands, much less how they all work. Because human memory isn't perfect, DOS has the HELP command. It lets you request help on most any DOS-related topic. It's easy to remember: to get help, type **HELP** at the DOS prompt. In DOS 6.0 and above, this command brings up DOS's Help system (shown in Figure 9.1), which lists dozens of topics you can explore on-screen. (In DOS 5.0 it brings up a less friendly but still usable version.)

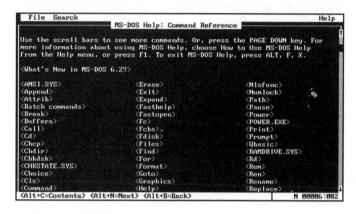

Figure 9.1   *The DOS Help system.*

To search for the information you need, simply use your mouse to click on a topic, or use the arrow keys to move the blinking cursor to the topic you want and then press **Enter**.

If you know the DOS command you want to use, but have forgotten how to use it, you can use the HELP command by typing **HELP *COMMAND***. In this case, HELP is the DOS command, and *COMMAND* is the subject for which you want help. For example, if you wanted help with the FORMAT command, you'd type **HELP FORMAT**. You would then see the help screen shown in Figure 9.2, displaying information about FORMAT. Of course, you can also find this information in your DOS manual, if you'd rather dig it out than type **HELP**.

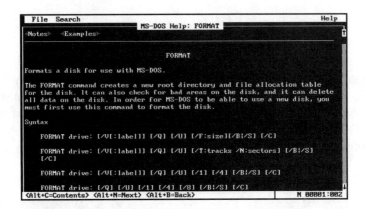

Figure 9.2   *More of DOS's Help system.*

If you use DOS 6.0 or above but you prefer the faster, less friendly help that DOS 5.0 provides, use the command FASTHELP instead (with or without a command name), or type the command name followed by /?. This brings up a briefer help screen.

Alternatives to DOS

If you don't like typing a lot of strange commands into your computer, you do have a few alternatives. For example, MS-DOS versions 4.0 through 6.0 come with a handy utility program called the DOS Shell that you can load by typing **DOSSHELL** at the DOS prompt. DOS Shell enables you to manipulate files and directories with your mouse, and choose commands from menus, rather than having to remember a lot of commands to type (see Figure 9.3).

Another alternative is Microsoft Windows, a *graphical user interface* or GUI (pronounced "gooey") that resembles a very fancy DOS Shell. Using Windows, you can do everything from copying files to running programs—and that's just the beginning. In fact, you can use Windows to do almost anything you can do with DOS and much more. You'll read more about Windows in the next chapter.

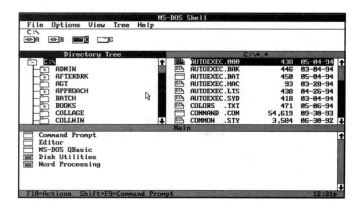

Figure 9.3   DOS Shell's main screen.

Although Windows is the most popular GUI on the market, it doesn't have the scene all to itself. If you have a real zippy machine—say, a 486 with 16 megabytes of memory—you could also opt for OS/2, IBM's entry into the GUI race. If you have an un-zippy machine (like a 286 with 1 megabyte of RAM) that can't handle Windows or OS/2, you could opt for GeoWorks Ensemble, which runs on almost anything. However you decide to run your computer, though, it's wise to know how your machine does what it does. Understanding DOS is the first step toward attaining that knowledge.

Chapter 10

A Look Through (Microsoft) Windows

In the last chapter, you learned some of the important DOS commands that help keep your computer running properly and enable you to manipulate programs and files on your disks. While you were typing all of those DOS commands, though, you may have thought, "There's got to be an easier way!" Why should you have to memorize a barrelful of cryptic text commands just to use a computer?

You'll be delighted to know that computer programmers all over the world have been working long and hard to make using computers simpler. As a result, they've developed many *graphical user interfaces* (GUIs). A GUI allows you to use your mouse to manipulate the programs and files loaded on your hard disk, without having to type all those text commands. Moreover, most GUIs adopt a desktop metaphor (like the Macintosh's), which means that they use familiar office concepts like clipboards, file cabinets, and files that you can shuffle around the "desktop" (screen).

The most popular GUI is Microsoft Windows, or Windows for short. These days, almost every new IBM-compatible computer comes with Windows installed. Because Windows is so popular, and because your home computer probably has Windows on it (whether you use it or not), this chapter gives you a brief overview of this popular GUI.

Starting Microsoft Windows

Once you have Windows installed on your computer (if you've just bought a new computer, Windows is probably ready to go), getting Windows started is easy—on some computers, Windows even starts automatically.

If you need to start Windows yourself, you can do so by typing **WIN** at the DOS prompt (and, of course, pressing **Enter** after you type it). When you do, you'll see the Windows title screen followed by the Windows desktop, which, when Windows is newly installed, looks something like Figure 10.1.

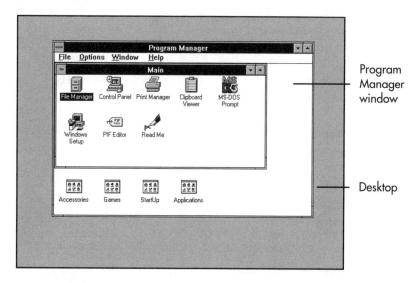

Figure 10.1   *The Windows desktop.*

What If It Doesn't Work?

Most of the time, typing WIN at the DOS prompt gets Windows up and running. However, if this command doesn't work on your computer (and you're sure you have Windows installed), try switching to the WINDOWS directory by typing **CD\WINDOWS** and pressing **Enter**. Then try the **WIN** command again. If Windows doesn't start this time, there's definitely something wrong with your Windows installation. Check your Windows manual for help re-installing it.

Using a Mouse with Windows

When you learned about DOS, you typed commands to manipulate files and programs. With Windows, however, you can toss all those DOS commands into the garbage can along with today's junk mail. In Windows, you use your mouse to issue almost every command. You can perform five actions with a mouse: point, click, double-click, drag, and drop.

◆ To *point* to a screen object, move the mouse so that the on-screen pointer points to the object.

◆ To *click*, quickly press and release the left mouse button. A click (a.k.a. a single click) usually selects, or highlights, the object.

◆ To *double-click*, press and release the left mouse button twice quickly. You usually double-click to activate Windows to carry out a command.

◆ To *drag* an on-screen object, first point to the object with your mouse. Press and hold down the left mouse button and move the mouse in the direction you want to move the object. If the object to which you pointed is draggable, its outline follows your mouse pointer as you move the mouse.

◆ To *drop* the object, drag it to its new location and release the left mouse button. When you do, the object's outline disappears, and the object appears in its new location.

Don't be dismayed if you have trouble getting the mouse to move the pointer just where you want. All it takes is practice and a little eye-hand coordination.

Learning how to handle your mouse is only a small part of learning Windows. In the sections that follow, you'll discover how to make Windows work for you.

Working with Windows

A *window* is just a rectangular area on-screen that contains some sort of data. Microsoft Windows has one large, main window called Program Manager. All the other windows are contained inside it.

When you look at Program Manager's window in Figure 10.2, you can see a smaller window, labeled Main, inside. "Main" is the name of a *program group*. The programs you can run are arranged in groups to make it easier to find them. Notice the little pictures inside the Main program group? Those are *icons* that represent programs you can run.

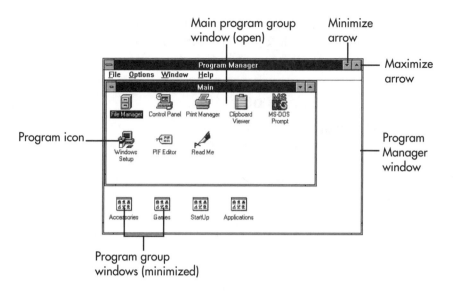

Figure 10.2   *Windows, windows, windows—and icons.*

There are several other program groups you can see in the figure (Accessories, Games, Startup, and Applications), but they are *minimized* (shrunk down to icons). The size of a window is flexible—it can be minimized, *maximized* (enlarged to fill the whole screen), or some size in-between the two extremes, as Main is here.

Changing the Size of a Window

To open a minimized window, double-click on its icon. For example, to open the Accessories window, you would double-click on the **Accessories** icon at the bottom left corner of the Program Manager window.

To maximize an opened window, click on the maximize (upward-pointing) arrow in its top right-hand corner. This expands the window to fill the whole screen. When you maximize a window, the maximize arrow turns into a restore arrow (a double-arrow, pointing both up and down). Clicking on the restore arrow takes the window size back to its un-maximized state.

You can resize any unmaximized window by dragging its borders with the mouse. Point to a border, hold down the left mouse button, and move the mouse. When you release the mouse button, the window changes size.

Viewing Different Parts of a Window

Sometimes after you have resized a window, you can no longer see everything in it; there's more to display than can fit in the space you've allotted for that window to take up. In that case, *scroll bars* appear on the right and bottom edges of a window. Scroll bars help you change the view to see different parts of the window's contents.

Each scroll bar has *scroll arrows* on each end. Click a scroll arrow to move the view slightly in the direction of the arrow, or click and hold to move (scroll) quickly. Drag the *scroll box* to move quickly to a different area. Click on the scroll bar above or below the scroll box to move one windowful at a time. Figure 10.3 shows all the important scroll tools.

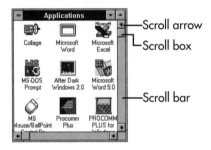

Figure 10.3   Scrolling around the neighborhood with scroll bars.

Running Programs

To run a program (sometimes called an "application"), just double-click on its icon. Program icons are located in program groups, as you learned in the last section. (You may have to open and close a few program groups before you find the program you're seeking.) The program opens up in its own window.

You can have many programs running at once (see Figure 10.4); the only limits are your computer's memory and your own sanity. However, only one program window can be active at once. You can spot the *active program* because its title bar is different from the others (it's usually darkened).

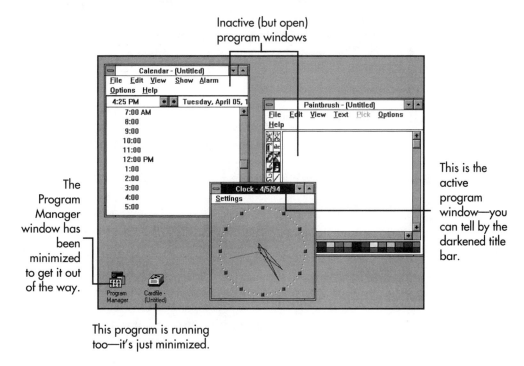

Figure 10.4 Programs, programs, programs.

Most programs create a useful printed product, such as a spreadsheet or letter. These products are generically referred to as *documents* in computerese. Most programs allow you to have more than one document open at once, and (not surprisingly) each one has its own separate mini-window within the program window. These mini-windows can be minimized or maximized just like the program group windows in Program Manager. Figure 10.5 shows a program with multiple documents open.

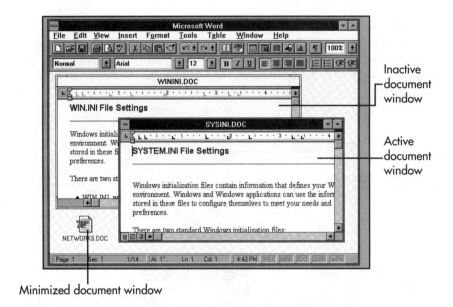

Figure 10.5   *A single program window can have lots of smaller document windows inside it.*

Closing a Program

As long as a program is running, it is using up your computer's resources. Unless you have an unlimited supply of memory in your computer (which is very unlikely) and an endless tolerance for clutter (also unlikely), you will want to close programs when you are finished using them.

The easiest way to close a program is to double-click the Control-menu box in its window's top left-hand corner. (It looks like a little gray box with a minus sign in it. See Figure 10.6.) Another way is to use the program's menu system to select the Exit command. (You'll learn about menus in the next section.)

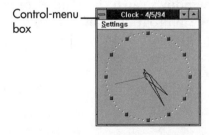

Figure 10.6   *Closing a program the easy way: the Control-menu box.*

A Saving Safeguard

If you have not saved the document you were working on, the program will ask you if you want to do so. If you click on No, the program shuts down without further ado. If you click Yes, a box will appear asking for the name you want to assign to the document. Type a name, and press **Enter** or click the **OK** button.

Using Menus

Clicking on icons and buttons is only half of what it takes to work in Microsoft Windows. The other half involves using the menu system.

Notice that there is a white bar with several words on it running directly under Program Manager's title bar. This is the *menu bar*. To open a menu with the mouse, just click on any of the words. For instance, to open the File menu, click on the word File. A menu of commands drops down, as shown in Figure 10.7.

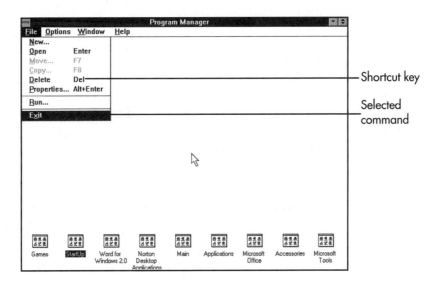

Figure 10.7   Menus drop down from above.

Once the menu is open, you can select a command by clicking on it. For instance, to exit Windows, click on the Exit command.

The Mysterious Underlining Explained

Why do commands and menus all have one letter underlined? That's for the convenience of poor souls who don't have a mouse. Another way to open a menu is to hold down the **Alt** key and press the key that corresponds to the underlined letter in the menu name you want. Once the menu is open, a command can be selected by pressing the key that corresponds to the underlined letter in the command name.

Notice that some commands have the names of keyboard keys beside them. These are *shortcut keys* you can use instead of the menu system. For instance, instead of opening the **File** menu and selecting **Delete**, you can press the **Del** key. This is just a shortcut that helps people without a mouse.

Some commands have an ellipsis (three dots) after them. An ellipsis indicates that when you select that command, a box will appear, asking for more information before the command is executed.

Managing Your Files

Back in the DOS chapter (Chapter 9), you learned all about moving, copying, and deleting files, plus some other handy disk and file management tricks. Windows—wonderful program that it is—offers the same sorts of capabilities, but without the tedium of typing. All the power you seek can be found in a program called File Manager.

To run File Manager, open the **Main** program group and double-click on the **File Manager** icon. File Manager opens in its own window (see Figure 10.8).

Across the top of the window is File Manager's menu bar. You can select commands from it, as you learned to do in the last section. Inside the File Manager window is a smaller window representing the active drive (usually C:). Below the menu bar is a group of icons representing all the drives in your system. To view the contents of a different drive, just click on its icon.

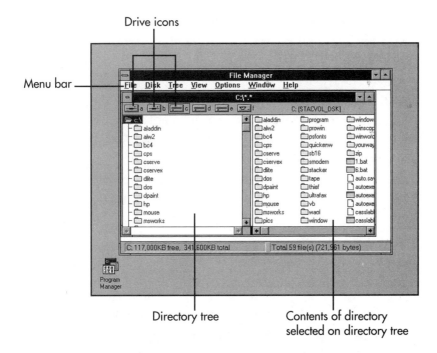

Drive icons

Menu bar

Directory tree

Contents of directory
selected on directory tree

Figure 10.8   *File Manager's main window.*

On the left side of this window is a *directory tree,* a diagram that shows all the
directories on the drive. On the right is a list of all the files and subdirectories
in the selected directory. (The selected directory appears as a highlighted
open folder in the directory tree on the left.) To see the contents of a different
directory, just click on it on the directory tree, and its contents appear in the
file list on the right.

Moving and Copying Files Between Directories

To move or copy a file from one directory to another on the same disk, just
drag the file from the file list, and drop it on the appropriate directory in the
directory tree. Plain-old dragging without any keys pressed moves the file. If
you want to copy the file, hold down the **Ctrl** key on the keyboard as you
drag.

Moving and Copying Files Between Disks

To move or copy a file onto another disk, drag the file from the directory tree to the appropriate drive icon at the top of File Manager's window. Just drag the file icon to copy the file; hold down **Alt** and drag to move the file.

The above method puts the file in the root directory of whatever drive you dropped it into. If you want to put the file in a different directory, open a second drive window and drag between windows, as described here:

1. Double-click (not single!) on the drive icon for the drive to which you want to copy. Now you have two drive windows open: one for the drive where the file currently resides, and one for the drive where you want it to reside.

2. Open the **W**indow menu and select the **T**ile command. This arranges the drive windows so you can see both of them clearly at once (see Figure 10.9).

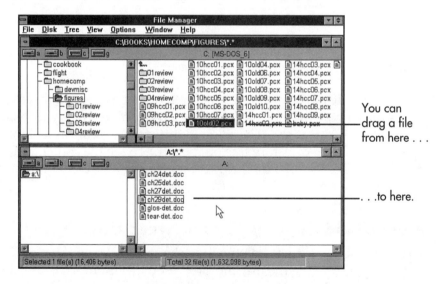

Figure 10.9   With two drive windows open at once, you can drag files between them to move and copy.

3. Make the source and destination directories active on their respective directory trees by clicking on the directory names on the trees.

4. Drag the file from its current home to the file list for the destination directory. To move the file, simply drag. To copy it, hold down the **Alt** key as you drag.

Another way to move or copy is to open the File menu and select the **Move** command or the **Copy** command. A dialog box appears asking what you want to copy or move, and to where you want to move it. Type in the information, and then click the **OK** button. This method requires as much typing as using clunky old DOS, though. I find the drag-and-drop methods much easier.

Ctrl Versus Alt

No, it's not a typo in the book. To copy between directories on the same disk, you hold down the Ctrl key. To copy between drives, you use the Alt key instead.

Deleting Files

Sooner or later, you'll accumulate files on your disk that you no longer want or need. To delete a file, click its name once to highlight it, and then press your keyboard's **Delete** key. (Remember, you saw on the File menu that the Delete key is a shortcut for opening the File menu and selecting **Delete**.)

Renaming Files

You can also rename files with File Manager. First, click the file to highlight it. Then select the Rename command from File Manager's **File** menu. When the Rename dialog box appears, type the new file name and press **Enter**.

Working with Several Files at Once

All of the commands you've learned so far can be performed on more than one file at once. All you have to do is select the files you want, and then issue the command. To select files:

◆ For files that are contiguous (all together on the list), click the first file, hold down the **Shift** key, and click the last file. All the files between the two (including those two) are selected.

◆ For files that are non-contiguous (not together on the list), click the first file, hold down the **Ctrl** key, and click each of the other files you want.

There's lots more you can do with File Manager—more than fits in a brief introduction like this. Once you get the hang of copying, moving, deleting, and renaming files, read about File Manager in your Windows manual.

Changing the Colors

The first thing most people want to know after they've mastered the basics in Windows is how to change the colors. The gray and blue color scheme that Windows starts with isn't exactly attractive, after all.

Follow along with these steps, and you'll be coloring your world in no time.

1. Open the **Main** program group, and double-click on the **Control Panel** program to open it.

2. Double-click on the **Color** icon. You'll see the Color dialog box (see Figure 10.10).

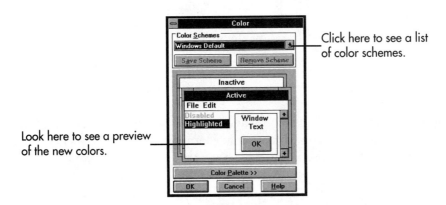

Figure 10.10   The Color dialog box lets you customize your world.

3. Click on the down arrow next to the Color **S**cheme box, and a list of color schemes drops down.

4. Pick a color scheme from the list and click the **OK** button. Presto, your colors change to the scheme you chose.

Shutting Down Windows

As with any computer program, it's important that you exit from Windows properly. This ensures that all data is updated and stored correctly. If you just turn off your computer, a wide variety of bad things could happen.

To shut down Windows, double-click Program Manager's **Control-menu box**. Windows displays the Exit Windows dialog box, giving you a chance to change your mind. To exit, click the **OK** button.

Chapter 11

A Short Course in Using a Mac

M acs are so easy to use, it really will be a *short* course. There's barely a handful of skills for you to master before you'll be using your Mac like a pro.

Considering this is a short introduction to Macintosh computing, it won't give you all the answers you need. Heaven forbid, it may even leave you with more questions than you started with. Don't panic: you can always consult the set of manuals that came with your Mac—or better yet, get *The Complete Idiot's Guide to the Mac*, published by Alpha Books.

Starting Up

The only real secret to starting up your Mac is this: you should turn on all the necessary peripherals before you turn on the Mac itself. By peripherals, we mean your monitor (if your Mac isn't a compact model with a built-in monitor), your printer (if you're planning to use it), and your modem and/or external hard drive (if you have either).

The reasons are simple. Whenever you turn on a peripheral that's attached to your Mac, you could be sending a little jolt of electricity to the computer. There's a slim chance that that little jolt could damage an expensive piece of hardware. The other reason applies only to external SCSI devices, such as a hard drive, CD-ROM drive, or scanner. In order for your Mac to know that there's a SCSI device attached, the device has to be on and running before the Mac is fired up.

The other great secret to starting a Mac is determining where the heck the ON/OFF switch is hiding. On some models it's on the back; on others, it's on the front. Some Macs can even be turned on and off from the keyboard. Likewise, different peripherals put them just about anywhere they please. If you can't find one of your power switches, check your manuals.

Startup Routine

After you power up your Mac, you'll hear a bell-like tone, a chord, or some other Mac sound (Apple likes to introduce a new sound for each new line of Macs). Your hard drive will churn for a second or two, while the startup information (the System software) is read from it. You'll see a friendly smiling Mac followed by the "Welcome to Macintosh" greeting. Then a group of little pictures (icons) will probably pop up, one at a time, across the bottom of your screen.

Those icons represent little bits of software called *extensions* and *control panels* that are being loaded into your Mac's memory. They add extra functions and capabilities to your Mac. Consult your manual for more information on these fun and helpful add-ins. Once the show is over, your desktop will appear.

No Happy Mac?

When you start your Mac for the very first time, if you don't see a happy Mac, but see instead a picture of a floppy disk with a question mark on it—don't panic! That means your Mac can't find your System software. Either somebody goofed and forgot to install it on your hard drive, or it was installed and was somehow damaged in transit. You should be able to fix it by re-installing your System software. Chapter 15 talks you through installing almost any software, including the System variety.

If you see or hear anything else at startup, you may have a problem. You might want to check out Chapter 13 (of course, it *would* be thirteen) for tips on diagnosing and correcting the problem.

It's All *Gooey!*

No, some naughty kid didn't run his sticky fingers all over your Mac. The Mac's interface is gooey—actually GUI (for graphical user interface), but it's pronounced the same. Just as those little icons popped up across the bottom of your screen as a graphical representation of something your computer was doing, most things you do on your Mac are represented by graphics (pictures) that you move around, click on, or otherwise manipulate with your mouse and cursor. You'll find it's a whole lot easier to remember what to do with an icon than it is to remember a long string of obtuse commands you have to type exactly right to get anything done.

The overall Macintosh metaphor is that of a desktop, which is something like a physical desktop you might have worked on. The Mac's desktop is shown in Figure 11.1.

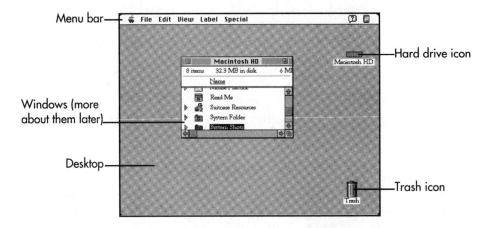

Figure 11.1   *The desktop.*

Since it's a metaphor, the Mac's desktop is only *something* like a regular one. On the Mac's desktop, you'll find file folders. In those folders, you may find files or more file folders (also containing files and folders). There's even a trash can for throwing away stuff you no longer want or need. However, on the Mac's desktop, you'll also find icons and windows—things you don't normally find as part of run-of-the-mill office furniture.

Desktop icons are like filing cabinets: opening one gives you access to a storage area (like a disk or your hard drive) containing a lot more folders and files. Windows, like their real-life counterparts, enable you to view the information stored in these filing cabinet-type icons, and make it possible for you to work with the individual files stored in them. To open a window and get at its contents, you need to use your mouse.

It's So Nice to Have a Mouse Around the House!

The mouse is an integral part of operating a Mac. While you can substitute keyboard commands for many mouse-generated actions, until you learn the keyboard commands, you'll be relying heavily on your mouse. Treat it nice. Give it some cheese. (Sorry, I had to get that out of my system.)

There are two basic mouse actions: pointing and clicking. Then there are fancier variations on those themes. In a nutshell, you need to be able to do the following things (if you're sitting at your Mac, feel free to play along):

◆ **Point**   To move the mouse so the on-screen cursor (which, on the desktop, will usually be an arrow) is pointing at an icon, window, or menu item with which you want to do something. This is one of the few instances when it really is polite to point.

◆ **Click**   To press and release the mouse button once quickly. Clicking usually selects an icon or pushes a button while you're at the desktop. It also does other things in other applications.

Once you've pointed at an icon, you can click on it. If the cursor is actually touching the icon when you click on it, it will appear darkened to show that it's been selected. Now what? Now you can get fancy.

If you point at the selected icon and click and hold the mouse button down, you pick up that icon. As long as you hold down the mouse button, you can drag the icon all over your desktop. When you release the mouse button, the cursor will drop the icon wherever the cursor is pointed. That's called *drag and drop*, for obvious reasons.

To get at a menu item in the menu bar (shown back in fig 11.1), you'd point at the menu heading—let's say **File**—and click and hold down the mouse button. The menu will drop down, and it will remain open as long as you're pressing the mouse button. While it's open, you can drag the cursor down the list of menu items (each one will turn black as the cursor touches it) to select the item you want or the operation you want to perform.

If you want to open an icon (like your hard drive) to get at its contents, you point at it and click twice quickly. That's called a *double-click*. It opens icons, launches applications, and opens documents (and the application that created the document).

In applications (word processors, for example) you can click, double-click, and sometimes even *triple*-click to do things to your documents. Check your application manual(s) for the click details.

Anatomy of a Window

When you double-click on an icon or folder (or even a document) your Mac will open the item and present you with its contents in a window. An icon's window will be full of files and folders. A folder's window will look very much the same. A document's window will contain whatever data is in the document (words for a word processor, numbers for a spreadsheet, and so on).

You're going to be using windows a lot. You may as well get familiar with one. Figure 11.2 shows you the common parts of a window.

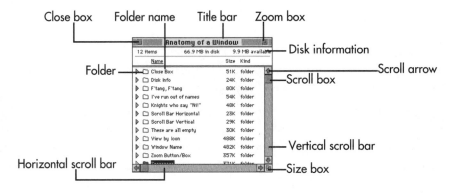

Figure 11.2   Anatomy of a window.

The window in the figure is one I made up. Any hard drive or folder's window will look almost exactly like it—only the names will be changed to protect the innocent. Starting at the upper left corner of the window, you'll see a little box labeled "Close box." Click in that box to close the window.

Keyboard Shortcuts and Menu Items

You'll discover that there are usually two or three ways to do any one thing on a Mac. For example, holding down the ⌘ key and pressing **W** (typically shown as ⌘**-W** in books and manuals) is the command-key equivalent of clicking on a window's close box. Likewise, selecting the **Close** option from under the **File** menu will also close the window. (Notice that the shortcut ⌘-W is listed after the Close command in the File menu as a reminder that you can do it either way.)

You'll also find that once you've learned how to use a function (close a window, or whatever), it will work the same in most any application you use. That's one of the reasons Macs are so easy to learn to use.

The striped bar that the close box sits on is called the title bar. It contains the name of the folder (or icon) you're working with. This one's cleverly called "Anatomy of a Window."

On the opposite end of the title bar (the upper right corner) is the zoom box. Clicking here will zoom the window out to a larger size, or in to a smaller one. This kind of button is called a toggle, because it does the opposite of whatever it did the last time you clicked it. If the last click made your window big, the next click will make it small.

Under the title bar there is a row of disk information: how many files/folders are in the window (it doesn't include what's inside folders), how much space is used on your disk, and how much space is left.

Under the disk information, there's heading information, such as file name, file type, and so on. It tells you what type of information is displayed in the columns below. This line only appears when you view your window information by name. (How information is displayed in windows on the desktop is controlled by the Views menu and the Views control panel. Check your manual for details, or just play around with the options. It won't hurt anything.)

Along the right side and across the bottom of the window are the scroll bars. These allow you to shift the window's display up/down or left/right, so you can see everything that's in the window. Sometimes information hides in the corners out of sight, and you have to go looking for it. If the scroll bars are plain gray, with no scroll boxes, there's nothing more to see in either direction.

Clicking on the arrows at the end of the scroll bars will move the display one line in that direction. Clicking in the gray area to either side of the scroll box will move the display one page in that direction. You can also click and drag the scroll boxes to position them wherever you'd like.

In the bottom right corner of the window there's a box with two little boxes drawn inside it. This is the size box. Click and drag on this box and you can resize the window to the exact dimensions you want.

When you have more than one window open on your desktop, you can only work with (or in) the active window. The *active window* is usually foremost (it's in the front), and all of it's details (the stripes in the title bar, the dot-pattern in the scroll bars, etc.) will appear as shown in the figure above.

If a window is inactive (meaning you can't work in it), all of those details will turn gray. To make a window active, just click on it somewhere, and it will pop to the front (if it isn't already) and come to fully detailed life.

Other windows you encounter in applications may add other things to the basic window anatomy, but on the whole, these features are a constant no matter what.

Starting Applications

As we mentioned earlier, you launch an application by double-clicking on its icon. (You may also click on its icon once to select it, and then use the ⌘-**O** (for OPEN) shortcut or select **Open** from the **File** menu.)

Let's try it out. Somewhere on your Mac's hard drive is an application called TeachText. It's a very simple word processor that comes with every Mac. When you find its icon, double-click on it, and TeachText will start.

You can also start it up by locating a TeachText document (a text file created with TeachText) and double-clicking on that. This will launch TeachText and open the document at the same time. Pretty cool, huh. Most ReadMe files you'll see (there's probably one on your hard drive now) are TeachText files.

Once you have TeachText open, you can fiddle with the ReadMe file, create a new file, or just stare wildly at the screen in admiration. The first two are probably better for you in the long run, though. Play around, you can't hurt anything. When you're done playing, quit TeachText by selecting **Quit** from the **File** menu.

The Party's Over

When you're done playing with your Mac for the day, you need to shut it down. This is important: there is a right way to shut down, and, therefore, a wrong way too.

Before you shut down your Mac, you should save the files you were working on (if you want to keep any changes you made), and quit any applications (like TeachText if you're still using it).

You save files with the ⌘-**S** (for SAVE) key combination or by selecting **Save** from the application's **File** menu. If it's a brand-new file, you'll be asked to name it and to tell your Mac where you want it stored. If the procedure puzzles you, consult your manual—it's easy, though.

Once your open files are saved, quit your open applications. To do so, use the ⌘-**Q** (for QUIT) key combination or choose **Quit** from the application's **File** menu.

When your applications are closed, you can turn off your Mac. But *don't* reach for the power switch yet! You should use the **Shut Down** option under the **Special** menu instead of just cutting the power. Here's why.

First of all, using the Shut Down command will shut down the Finder, the part of the Mac's System software that gives you the desktop. In the process of shutting it down, your Mac will memorize exactly where everything is on your desktop: icons and any windows. The next time you start up, they'll be just where you left them.

Second, and most importantly, you may not be aware of it but your Mac might be doing something behind the scenes. It may be reading or writing a little snip of information to your hard drive. If you just cut the power, you may damage (sometimes called *corrupting*) a vital bit of information that your Mac needs to work. The next time you power up, instead of a smiling Mac and a "Welcome to Macintosh," you may get a sad Mac and then nothing. You'll have to re-install your System software, and you may lose some important data.

When you tell your Mac to shut down, it will think about it for a second. Then the screen will go black, and there will be a message saying that it's safe for you to turn off your Mac (it also gives you a chance to restart it, if you've forgotten to do something). When that message is on-screen, it's safe to cut the power to your Mac. Then you can turn off all of your peripherals, too.

By the Way . . .

With some of the modular Macs (like the Quadras, for instance), you can turn the Mac on and issue the shut down command from the Mac's keyboard. Check your manuals for details.

When in Doubt

This has been a very brief, simplistic introduction to Macintosh. (Really cool people don't say "the" Macintosh or "the" Mac, just Macintosh or Mac.)

For brevity's sake, a lot of important information has been ignored, omitted, or otherwise snubbed: copying files, formatting disks, using the Save and Open dialog boxes, and more. It's all important stuff, but we would need a couple of chapters to cover it properly.

Before you continue with your Mac experimentation, read your manual. Read a book (like for instance *The Complete Idiot's Guide to the Mac*). Learn the basics. The computing life you save may be your own.

Chapter 12

CYA = Cover Your dAta

Even if you choose to do all of the things discussed earlier under the heading of "preventative maintenance," bad things can still happen to your computer. A child may forget the "No magnets" rule, and data may get scrambled; you may go on a hot writing streak and forget to save your file until just *after* the power goes out; plugs may be unplugged accidentally. Stuff happens.

While you can't really prevent some bad things from happening, you can certainly prepare for the eventuality and cover your data in advance of the disaster. Then when disaster comes, you can laugh in its face.

Reality Check

There is no absolutely foolproof method for protecting your data from prying eyes, accidental or willful destruction, or human fallibility. A person who knows what he's doing and has the right tools can get around any protection scheme, given the time and patience.

Most security protection is aimed at deterring the common snoop by making it too difficult or time-consuming for him to get at your data. For most folks, that will be enough. However, if you're still extremely paranoid or you deal with especially sensitive data, you may want to consult a computer security specialist for other options.

Be warned, though, that protecting your data is a lot like carrying an umbrella when you think it may rain: it often ensures that it won't rain. The day you leave it at home is the day the flood comes. Protecting your data can have the same effect.

If you take the time to prepare for trouble, the trouble may never arrive. Don't let it make you sloppy or careless. As soon as you stop protecting your data: crash, boom! There it goes—not with a bang but a whimper.

Protecting Sensitive Data from Prying Eyes

"Sensitive data" doesn't have to be military or industrial secrets. It only has to be something you'd rather keep private. Your checking account balance is sensitive, and so are the spreadsheets that track your home business's profits (or losses). Here are some simple guidelines you can follow to help keep other people from knowing your business.

◆ If it's practical, restrict physical access to your computer by locking the room it's kept in.

◆ Don't store sensitive files on your hard drive. Store them on floppy disks that you can lock away.

◆ When you delete a sensitive file from your hard drive, it isn't really gone until it's replaced by another file. Be sure to use a disk optimizing utility or file "shredding" utility (like those discussed in Chapter 28) to make sure the deleted file cannot be retrieved with a file recovery utility.

◆ You can password-protect files, hard drive partitions, or an entire computer system with security software. Many utility packages offer various security options. Shop for one that suits your needs. (See Chapter 28 for more details on utility programs.)

If security is a prime concern, you may want to invest in a utility or stand-alone security package that offers not only password protection, but also *data encryption*. Data encryption takes data and jumbles it according to specific rules so it can only be decrypted by someone who has the same "key." It's the stuff of spy thrillers, but it's effective for keeping the curious from snooping. The only danger is that if you lose the key, you lose your data too.

Protecting Valuable Data from Playful Kids

Children (and child-like adults) like to play around with computers. They like to play the old "what happens when I do this?" game. Sometimes what happens is that a file disappears in a puff of smoke or gets scrambled beyond recognition. If you aren't prepared, it could mean spending long hours trying to reconstruct important data. There are ways to protect yourself. In addition to those listed in the previous sections, you can:

◆ Teach children to respect and not mess around with other people's files.

◆ Arm yourself with a utility package that recovers deleted files. NOTE: Not all files can be recovered, so this isn't the only step you should take.

◆ Insist that children (and other users) using your computer only use floppy disks to save data.

◆ Set aside a separate hard drive or a partitioned area of the logical drive for the kids' exclusive use. Password protect the adult hard drive/ partition as discussed above. A utility package will make the process of partitioning and protecting easier.

◆ Back up your hard drive regularly (more about that shortly).

People are naturally curious, and young people are doubly so. You don't want to crush a child's impulse to explore and discover, but you don't want that impulse to crush your hard work either.

Protecting Data from Your Own Silly Mistakes

To err is human, right? You're human, right? So you're going to make a mistake sooner or later. Be prepared.

Even if you use every method outlined above to keep other people from messing with the files on your computer, you will still have access. A mistake by you, a power failure, or an act of God could wipe out your data in short order. The only sure-fire method of protecting yourself against the heartbreak of lost data is to back up (or make a spare copy of) your files on a regular basis.

You can back up your data files simply by saving them twice: once to your hard drive and once to a floppy disk that you put in a safe place when you're done. That's a good habit to get into, but it doesn't do anything to protect the program files and system software that you may have customized extensively.

The most comprehensive form of backup protection involves getting a utility package (like one of the ones reviewed in this book) that will copy every last shred of information from your hard drive(s) to a series of floppy disks or other storage media (like those discussed in the add-ons section of Chapter 2). Most backup utilities allow you to make full or incremental backup copies. *Full* backs up everything on the drive; *incremental* backs up only files that have been created or altered since the previous backup, and adds them to the existing full backup.

Ideally, you should do a full backup first, and then do incremental backups daily or weekly (depending on how you work). Once a week or month (also depending on how you work), you should start the process over by doing another full backup. New incremental backups would be tacked on to the latest full backup.

Store your backup copies in a safe, fireproof, natural-disaster-proof place. Some people keep their backup copies in a fireproof box or safe. Others put them in a safe deposit box in a bank vault as insurance against a major home-destroying calamity. Let your level of paranoia be your guide.

A Cautionary Tale

I'll tell you this story just so you can appreciate the full magnitude of a sudden data emergency.

In the months that followed the last big earthquake in San Francisco, I recall reading somewhere that novelist Amy Tan (author of *The Joy Luck Club* and *The Kitchen God's Wife*) lost the complete manuscript of an entire unpublished novel because she did not keep backup copies (or she didn't keep them in a safe place, I forget which).

Imagine that: a complete novel. Years of work. Gone. Poof! My head hurts just thinking about it. My heart goes out to her, but I bet she keeps backup copies now—and in very safe places.

Protecting your data from the various misfortunes that can befall it doesn't take a lot of effort once you get into the habit. The benefits are peace of mind and nearly effortless recovery when accidents do happen. Don't say I didn't warn you.

Chapter 13

When Bad Things Happen to Good Computers

These words of wisdom should be tattooed in reverse on the forehead of every person buying a computer. (In reverse so they can be read reflected in the mirror as suicidal users are in the bathroom, eyeing their wrists and the box of razor blades, after hair-raising sessions with their digital imps of the perverse.):

Computers are *soooo* stupid!

These are words to live by (and stay sane by). Computers are so stupid (How stupid are they?), that they'll try to do anything you tell them to, whether it's possible or not. A computer will sacrifice its digital mind trying to accede to your slightest whim. In short, it would rather self-destruct than disappoint you. How's that for loyalty? This blind, selfless devotion can cause a lot of problems: system crashes, fatal errors, and error messages for the computer (and chronic heartburn for the user).

Some Common Problems

Regardless of what kind of computer you're using, there are some horrors common to all kinds of systems. All computers tend to go *pffftt* in similar ways. Here's a few.

Error Message

You make a simple request of your machine and/or software, and the computer sticks out its digital tongue in the form of a cryptic error message: "Bad F-line Instruction," "Unimplemented Trap," "Incorrect DOS version," "What are you, crazy?" Okay, I made the last message up, but it's every bit as helpful as the others. Whenever you receive an error message, the first thing you need to do is write it down.

Right after you receive an error message, you may be able to proceed on your merry way—or your application may quit or freeze on you. You may have to restart your computer and try again. If you keep getting the error message, call the software company's technical support line and let them decipher the error message. (More about calling technical support, shortly.)

Crash

Let's say you're plugging away with an application and all of sudden it just quits—no error message, no warning. It just quits. The application has *crashed*, or *bombed*. Sometimes computers crash for unknown reasons (possibly too much confusion in their electronic brains or a badly written application). Simply restarting your computer may fix whatever's wrong. But it may not. Be prepared to call technical support.

Freeze

Like an early killing frost, you get no warning: suddenly your application freezes up. The cursor stops blinking, the mouse won't move the pointer, and you can't type anything. It's like everything is locked. Your only option may be to restart your computer and try it again.

Like crashes, *freezes* sometimes happen because of an odd, unseen convergence of operations inside your computer (like the moon is in the seventh house, and Jupiter is aligned with Mars). It may never happen again or in quite the same way. If it does keep happening, call technical support.

Out Of Memory

Some crashes, freezes, and error messages occur because the application has run out of memory. If you know you have plenty of RAM installed to run that particular application, you may want to quit any other applications you have open and close extra windows in your shell program (or the Mac's Finder or Windows) to free up some extra memory.

PC owners running DOS 6.x may want to take a stab at reconfiguring their memory by running the Memmaker application. Consult your DOS manual for details on optimizing memory. Mac owners may want to allocate more memory to the troublesome application. Your Macintosh User's Guide will give you the details.

Another possible solution would be to install more RAM. Applications are getting very greedy in the RAM department. But you can add memory in a number of different ways on different computers. Consult your system manual for details on how to add memory to your particular computer model.

Other Hardware Won't Cooperate

You go to print, and you get an error message saying that your computer can't find the printer. You want to play a CD-ROM game, but it can't find that drive. What do you do?

Before you panic, make sure that the peripheral in question (the printer, the CD-ROM, or whatever) is plugged in, turned on, and connected properly to your computer. Sometimes cables jiggle loose merely because of the vibrations caused by pounding on the keyboard, people walking past, or traffic. Then make sure you installed the proper driver software for the peripheral. Most hardware add-ins also require software add-ins to tell the computer how to deal with the hardware. Make sure that you installed that software and installed it properly. Check the peripheral's manual for details.

Diagnosing Simple Problems

Computer problems happen for a reason, no matter how oblique or obscure. Tracking down the problem is a process of elimination. So put on your deerstalker cap, and light your Meerschaum pipe. You're going to play Sherlock Holmes in the *Case of the Cranky Computer*.

Playing Problem Sleuth

To diagnose any computer problem, you need some basic information before you can do any deductive reasoning. Try to gather the following bits of information first.

◆ What happened *exactly*? Was it a freeze, a crash, an error message, or something completely bizarre?

◆ When did it happen? Had you just turned on the computer or started an application? Were you doing something in an application (saving a file, for example) or quitting an application?

◆ What did you do just before it happened? What keystrokes, commands, menu selections, or mouse movements did you make? If you just installed new hardware or software, that's the most likely culprit.

Assumptions, Assumptions . . .

This section is written as if the problem has happened to you. If, by some chance, the problem happened to the love of your life, a child, or a stranger, your first step is to try to duplicate the problem. You duplicate the problem so you can gather your trouble-sleuthing information firsthand. The truth is, inexperienced computer users will panic first and pay attention later. The person who had the problem probably won't remember what he did just before it happened, or what the error message said, or anything else useful.

If you can't duplicate the problem, it probably isn't a problem. Just chalk it up to the user's inexperience, and tell whomever it is to pay close attention the next time something goes wrong.

The answers to these questions may point your investigation in several different directions. Problems that occur while you're starting up your computer are most often related to problems with incorrect hardware installations, operating system problems, conflicts between different driver software, or a conflict with new hardware.

Problems that occur while starting and/or using a particular application may be related to memory (not enough RAM), a badly written application, or a conflict with another open application. Or the software may not be compatible with your system (maybe some functions require a math coprocessor, and you don't have one).

If a problem happens, for example, while you're trying to save a file to disk, your disk might be full. A badly written program may not know how to cope with that common situation and may crash (believe me, I've seen it happen). If a problem happens when you're trying to open a file, it might be that something is wrong with the file—and not with the application at all. Try opening a different file to see.

Once you think you know when the problem is occurring, you can try different steps to see if you can resolve the problem on your own. You should write down each thing you try, and what happened when you tried it. (There are some flow charts coming up to help you keep track of these steps.) You need to write things down for a few reasons: 1) so you won't try the same thing twice; 2) so you can undo things that don't work; and 3) if you wind up calling technical support, you can save time by telling them what you've already tried.

Short of technical support, your best resource is the troubleshooting section of the manual for the suspicious piece of hardware or software. Start there, and then widen your search. If you can't fix it yourself (or you don't feel confident trying), there are tips for getting good technical support at the end of this chapter.

A Macintosh Troubleshooting Guide

Here's a chart that summarizes the steps to take with your Mac, in very general terms. If you don't know how to do some of the suggestions, don't worry about it—just skip this step and call tech support. This all gets easier with practice.

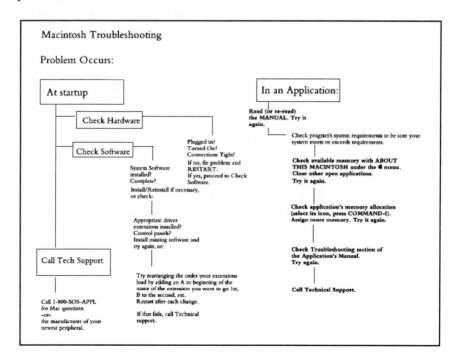

An IBM-Compatible Troubleshooting Guide

If it's a PC on the blink, use this chart to start diagnosing the problem. If you don't know enough about a suggested step to handle it (for example, if you don't know about drivers or memory), go ahead and call tech support. This all gets easier with practice.

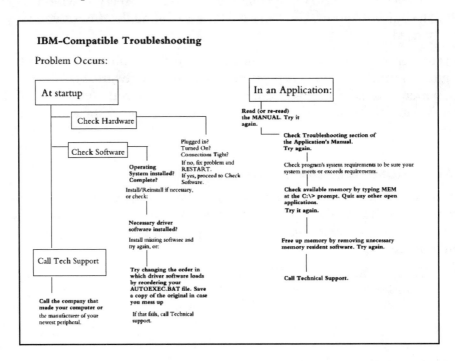

Getting Technical Support

When you've tried everything you care to try to resolve the problem on your own, your next sure step for getting help is to call the technical support number provided by the manufacturer of the software or hardware in question. You'll usually find the phone number in the troubleshooting section of the manual, or on a "How to Contact Us" page.

Before You Call

Before you even pick up the phone, you need to have the following information handy (you should have the first four items on your shopping list from Chapter 3, if you kept it):

◆ The make and model of your computer (some manufacturers may want your serial number too)

◆ The amount of RAM you have installed

◆ The peripherals (extra toys) you have attached

◆ The version of your operating system (DOS 6.2, Mac System 7.1, and so on)

◆ A list of the things you already tried in your attempt to resolve the problem (you did write it down, didn't you?)

In addition to the above items, which are basic for any computer, the tech support person may need information that's specific to your particular type of computer. Therefore, it will be helpful if you also have the following information:

◆ PC owners: They may want to know what your CONFIG.SYS and AUTOEXEC.BAT files say. You can open and print copies with any word processor or DOS's Editor.

◆ Mac owners: They may want to know what extensions and control panels you have loaded. You can print a list of each by opening each folder and using the **Print Window** command under the **File** menu.

You'll want to have a pencil and paper handy, so you can write down the tech-person's suggestions *exactly* (read them back so you know you got them right). You should also call from a phone within reach of your computer. The techie may want you to try various solutions—which you can't try if you're in another room or part of town.

Finally, before you pick up the phone, you should calm down a little. Take a break. Have a beverage. Calling while you're in a fit of pique won't help.

And remember one other thing: the person who answers the phone is not responsible for your problem. He's trying to help you, so calm down and let him.

Talking Techie

When you're ready to pick up the phone, have that pencil poised and ready to write. Usually, the technician who answers the phone will introduce himself by name. Write it down in case you need to call back later. Introduce yourself and state your problem briefly but completely. You might say something like: "Hi, my name's John. I'm having trouble with your Whiz-Bang 2000 graphics converter. I'm running it on a Mac Quadra 660AV with System 7.1 and 12MB of RAM. When I try to turn a PICT file into a GIF file, the application crashes." (Remember to breathe.)

The technician will then ask relevant questions. (Like what are you wearing?—Just *kidding*.) Actually, here's where you'll need some or all of the information you gathered in the last section. He will then make suggestions; try them. If they don't work, be prepared to say *exactly* what you did and what happened. Keep your cool. Remember that this is a process of elimination, and it may take some time. You've been struggling with the problem for hours or days, but this is the first time he has encountered your particular problem.

Give the technician a fair chance to help you. Nine times out of ten, the problem will be resolved with a minimum of fuss. If he can't help (or if you suspect he's just reading from a manual that you've already exhausted—and that does happen), you can ask to speak to a supervisor. Asking to speak with someone else means starting the process all over again: taking a name, describing the problem and the steps you've taken, and so on.

You can keep going up the chain of command until you get satisfaction or the head of the company. The CEO probably won't be able to help, but you can certainly tell him what you think of his product and technical support team.

Good luck.

Part III

Software You Can Really Use

If Part II was a computing survival guide, this section is a variation on that theme—sort of a field guide to software. Software has to enter the picture somewhere, otherwise, you've just got a pretty expensive paperweight.

In this section, you'll learn to navigate the trenches of your local software store or favorite mail order company. The *modus operandi* is the quick strike: get in, find what you need, make sure it will run on your computer, and get out.

You'll learn how to select applications for your computer, how to install them, and how to get through some important operations. You'll also find a round-up of the major software categories, and reviews of the more popular packages for your computer.

Like the Audubon Society's field guides, you'll be able to use this section to familiarize yourself with the various species of software before you encounter them in the wild. Instead of knowing a red-throated hummingbird, you'll be able to spot a nimble-fingered word processor at a hundred paces.

Chapter 14

Making Intelligent Software Decisions

If you've used computers before (and, more importantly, if you haven't), you should know that buying the right software is every bit as important as buying the right computer. Without the right software for your needs, your computer is just about as useful as a bicycle with square tires.

The first time you pop into your local software emporium, you may be flabbergasted to find an incredible range (both in price and performance) of software to choose from. How do you make important software decisions? Can you be sure the software you buy will perform as you expect it to? How do you decide between an inexpensive software and a more expensive professional package? How can you tell whether the software will even run on your computer? This chapter will help you find the answers to these questions.

What Types of Software Are There?

The first step in choosing software is deciding what you want or need to do with your computer. Every job you want to tackle probably has at least one kind of software associated with it.

For example, if you want to write letters and reports with your computer, you'll need a word processor. If you want to keep track of your CD collection or the phone numbers and addresses of business associates, you need some sort of a database. There are literally thousands of tasks you can do with your computer, and each task requires a particular type of software.

Luckily, you have this wonderful book. The following section not only gives you something to read when your boss isn't looking, but also gives you some idea of what kinds of software you can buy, and what each kind can do for you.

Word Processors

Word processors (like the one in Figure 14.1) are probably the most commonly used computer software. It's probably safe to assume that 99.999% of home computers have some kind of word processor installed on them. Every Mac comes with TeachText; every IBM-compatible with Windows has Write.

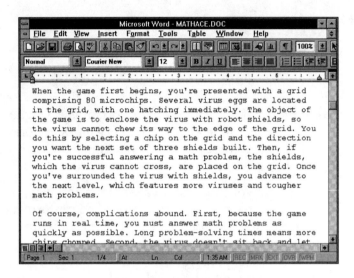

Figure 14.1   *A word processor.*

Word processing software makes your computer like a space-age typewriter. With it you can create all kinds of text documents: letters, reports, articles, and even brochures. Unlike a typewriter, a word processor allows you to manipulate your text in dozens of ways. You can delete text, copy text, paste text, and more—all without having to pick up an eraser or a bottle of Liquid Paper.

Most word processors also enable you to format documents. You can add headers and footers, insert footnotes, use different fonts, and change normal text to **bold**, *italic*, or <u>underlined</u> text. More sophisticated word processors also let you add graphics (from boxes, rules, and other simple line graphics, to charts and tables, as well as digitized photos and artwork) to documents.

Databases

Another common use for computers is for organizing large amounts of information, or data. Database software (like what's shown in Figure 14.2) is a good choice for this sort of task. Whether you want to keep track of your CD collection, or you want to store a list of everybody you know with everything you know about them, a good database program will be up to the challenge.

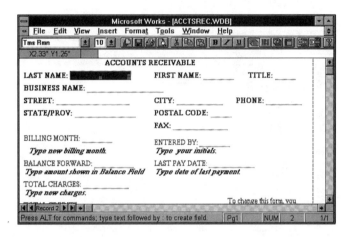

Figure 14.2   A database program.

There are two major types of databases: dedicated and programmable. Dedicated database programs, such as computerized address books, are designed to store only one type of data. The advantage of a dedicated database is that they tend to be less expensive than the programmable variety.

Programmable databases, on the other hand, can handle virtually any data-organization task. While it'd be tough (okay, impossible) to store information about your videotape library in a dedicated address database, a programmable database will accommodate both tasks handily. It's up to you to tell the program what kind of data you want to manipulate and how to display it on the screen. When you want to see a different kind (or set) of data, you just load the appropriate file.

Spreadsheets

For number crunching there's nothing like a spreadsheet program (see Figure 14.3). Using a spreadsheet, you can create sophisticated tables of calculations that update themselves each time you change a value in the table. For example, you could set up a table that shows your monthly loan payments, and then see how raising and lowering payments affects the total interest paid and the length of repayment.

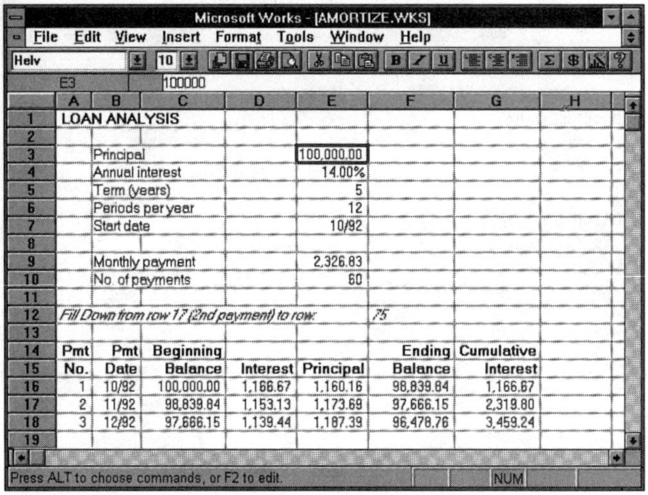

Figure 14.3   A spreadsheet program.

A spreadsheet is a perfect tool for many tasks, from setting up and maintaining your household budget to creating your company's annual financial report.

Graphics Applications

When home computers first became available, they could do little more than display text and draw a few colored lines. These days, computers can display photographic-quality images with millions of colors.

Of course, as computer graphics have become more sophisticated, so have the related software packages. There are now many different types of graphics software from which to choose. The most common are paint programs (Figure 14.4), which allow you to use your mouse to draw pictures on the computer screen.

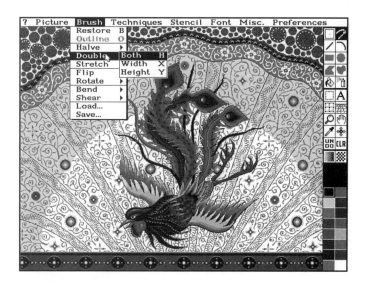

Figure 14.4   A paint program.

With most paint programs you can draw all kinds of shapes using different lines and a choice of colors. You can copy one part of the screen and paste it in different places. You can even zoom in for a closer look at the work in progress. Many paint programs also allow you to add graphic text, and to save your creations in a variety of picture-file formats for use in other applications.

Other types of graphics software include technical drawing programs, computer-aided design (CAD) programs, image-processing programs, presentation programs, charting and graphing programs, and many more.

Desktop Publishing Software

A desktop publishing (DTP) program, shown in Figure 14.5, takes up where a word processor leaves off. While a word processor lets you create various types of text documents, you can use a DTP program to transform those text documents into professional-quality documents that are ready to be duplicated and distributed. With DTP software you can create everything from simple documents like flyers, invoices, and newsletters, to major projects, such as fully illustrated brochures and even full-length books.

113

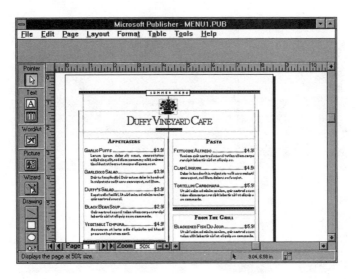

Figure 14.5   A desktop publishing program.

DTP programs are sophisticated graphics and text layout tools that enable you to set up pages of any size and move text and graphics around on the pages just as you would if you were working with scissors and glue.

The more expensive DTP programs provide all the tools a professional needs to create virtually any type of text- and graphics-based document. In fact, DTP programs are used to produce many of the newspapers and magazines you find at your local book store.

Communications Software

If you've been keeping up with the news lately, you've surely heard the term "information super-highway," which refers to the vast amounts of data being transferred through computer networks.

If your computer has a modem and a communications program (see Figure 14.6), you can access that super-highway to transfer data to and from other computers. You can browse an on-line encyclopedia, bank electronically, make airline reservations, follow the stock market, shop for gifts, send electronic mail, chat with people all over the world, and much, much more.

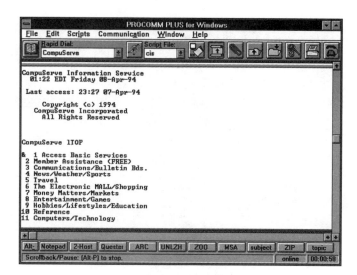

Figure 14.6   A communications program.

Educational Software

Computers are wonderful tools for learning. You'll find your local software store's shelves bursting with educational packages that help you learn to type, speak Spanish, solve math problems (as Figure 14.7 shows), and even prepare young children for reading. With educational programs, you can travel around the world or take a rocket ride into space. You can study anatomy, geometry, environmental issues, art, medicine, architecture, and a rapidly growing list of other fascinating topics.

Some educational programs drill you with questions, while others hide the learning inside clever games. The best part is that there are educational programs for just about every member of your family, from the smallest child to the oldest adult. You can even get complete reference works for your computer, including dictionaries, literature, and even full encyclopedias.

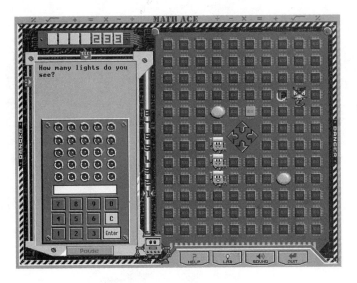

Figure 14.7   *The educational game Math Ace.*

Games

More games are bought for home computers than any other kind of software. One popular type is the adventure and role-playing game that plunges you into the middle of an interactive story. You control the characters; you decide what to do. Using clues you find throughout the game, you solve puzzles and make wondrous discoveries that send shivers up your spine. Sometimes you die a horrible death, but you only have to restart the game to get a second (or fifth, or hundredth) chance. Life should be so amenable.

If fantasy worlds aren't your cup of tea (and, after all, reality is only a crutch for those who can't handle fantasy), there are other more "serious" games. For example, flight simulators imitate an environment in which you pilot a plane, and "Sim" programs let you build and manage SIMulated farms and cities— or whole planets (see Figure 14.8). You'll quickly discover that games can also be serious business.

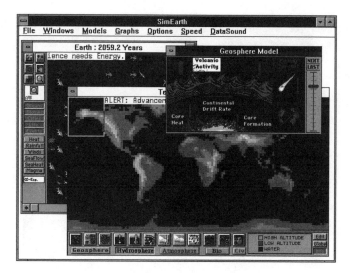

Figure 14.8   *The simulation program SimEarth.*

Special Interest Software

Although the categories of software already covered are the most popular, there are thousands of other specialized packages. For example, there are programs that help you design a house (see Figure 14.9), plan a trip, plan a diet, and track investments. No matter what your special interests, you're almost certain to find software that covers it.

Choosing the Right Package

Just like anything else in life, software packages vary in quality. And, as with everything else, you get what you pay for. That isn't to say that the most expensive software package is necessarily the best one for you. You need to balance the cost of the software—and the features it offers—against your needs. If you'll only use a word processor to write simple letters, why spend gobs of money on a program that can also create graphics, format text into multiple columns, and generate an index?

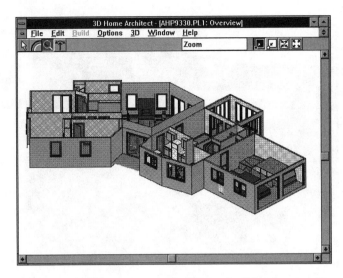

Figure 14.9   *The home design program 3D Home Architect.*

On the other hand, always think ahead before you lay down that green stuff for software. Cheaper software may be perfect for you today, but will it fit your needs tomorrow, or next year?

As you see all of the options available in software packages, you may wish that you'd gone with a more expensive product that does more. It's almost always cheaper to buy the more expensive package the first time around than to replace an inexpensive package later. As you do when you buy kids' clothes, you should buy software that leaves you room to grow.

When you go to the software store, discuss your needs with the salesperson and see what he recommends. Read the back of the box for a description of the software. Better still, ask the salesperson to demonstrate the software. Some stores demonstrate software; others don't. Many major software chains (like Babbages and Electronics Boutique) go one step further and let you return software if it doesn't meet your needs. If you're not sure what software you want, you might want to shop at a store with a generous return policy.

Software Requirements

All of your software choices will be governed by the type of computer equipment you own. If you have an IBM-compatible, you can't shop in the Macintosh aisle, and vice versa. But many programs come in both Macintosh and IBM-compatible versions.

Different software packages, though made for the same type of computer, will also vary in hardware and software requirements. Some will require that you have a particular version of your operating system, other have strict memory needs, or need particular peripherals.

To make sure your computer meets the minimum requirements for the software you select, read the software box carefully. There's usually a small label somewhere that lists the minimum requirements. The list probably includes most of the following topics.

Processor

Every computer has a microprocessor. Generally, the better the processor, the faster the computer runs. IBM-compatible computers have processors with numbers like 286, 386, and 486. Macs have 68030 and 68040 processors, and the Macintosh PowerPCs have 601 processors. Generally speaking, the higher the number, the better the processor. (Currently, the best IBM-compatible microprocessor is called the Pentium processor. It doesn't have a number, but some folks call it the 586.)

If the software you're looking at requires a 386, you're out of luck if you have a 286. Conversely, if the software requires a 386 and you have a 486, you're all set, because a 486 is a better processor than a 386. It works the same for Macs, too, although most software companies cut to the chase and name specific Mac models rather than chip numbers.

Processor Speed

Although it's generally true that all 486 processors are better than all 386 processors (and 68040s are better than 68030s), not all processors of the same type are equal in speed. The speed of a processor is measured in megahertz (MHz). Processors runs at speeds like 16MHz, 20MHz, 33MHz, or 40MHz. Again, the higher the number, the better—and faster—the processor. If a software package requires a 33MHz 386 and yours is 20MHz 386, the program will probably run sluggishly on your machine. If the software requires a 33MHz 386 and you have a 40MHz 386, the program should zip along quite nicely, thank you. Since processor speeds don't vary too much for individual Mac processors, you won't often find a speed requirement.

Operating System Version

Over the years, DOS and the Mac OS have undergone many changes. For this reason, most software packages specify a certain version of the appropriate operating system. The higher the version number, the newer the version. (As of the time of this writing, the latest version of DOS is 6.2; for the Mac it's version 7.5.) If a software package requires Mac System 6.0.8 or higher and you have 7.1, you're in the clear. But if you have a version older than 6.0.8, you'll probably run into trouble. You should either upgrade to a newer version of your operating system or buy a different program.

Memory Requirements

All computer programs take up space in memory. To run a program, you need at least as much memory in your computer as that program requires, though more is usually better. Memory is measured in megabytes (millions of bytes, abbreviated as M or MB) and kilobytes (thousands of bytes, abbreviated as K or KB). If a program requires 550KB (550 kilobytes, or 550x1024 bytes, which equals 563,200 bytes), and you have 2MB (two megabytes, which equals two million bytes), you're probably okay.

Graphics

IBM-compatible computers can run in various graphics modes, including CGA, EGA, VGA, and SVGA (listed in order of quality, lowest to highest). If you have an SVGA system, you can run programs that require SVGA or any of the lesser display modes. (If you have a VGA system, you can run programs in VGA, EGA, or CGA. You get the idea, right?) It doesn't work in reverse, though—you can't run a software package that requires better graphics modes than what you have on your computer.

These days, your home computer should have at least VGA graphics. If it doesn't, you should upgrade. Otherwise, your software choices will be severely limited. Most new IBM-compatible computers come with SVGA graphics.

Mac video requirements are generally stated in terms of the size of your monitor (13-inches or better) and the number of colors you're able to display (256 colors). Be sure you at least meet the stated requirements.

Hard Drive

Almost all computers today have hard drives, so many software packages require them. If a software package requires a hard drive and you don't have one, don't bother buying the software. You can't use it. Some boxes specify a minimum amount of free space required on your hard drive. For example, it may say that you need 10 megabytes (maybe it's written as 10M or 10MB) of free space on your hard disk. That means if your hard disk is full of other programs and there isn't 10MB of free space, you can't install the program. Most programs require you to install them onto your hard drive: you can't run them from the floppy disks they come on.

Mouse

Some programs you can control with either the keyboard or the mouse; some you can use with just one or the other. Of course, everyone has a keyboard on their system, but everyone may not have a mouse. If a software package requires a mouse and you don't have one, you can't use the software—unless, of course, you have a trackball or other device that takes the place of a mouse. It's that simple.

Sound

Most IBM-compatible software packages support some sort of sound card, which is a circuit board you can add to your computer that enables sound and music to come out of speakers you attach (sold separately). The most popular sound cards are Sound Blaster, Ad Lib, and Pro Audio Spectrum.

"Support" versus "Require"

In most cases, you can use a software package that supports sound cards even if you don't have a sound card. The key word here is supports. If the software package *supports* a certain sound card, that means it'll use that card if you have it. But if a software package *requires* a sound card, you must have the right sound card to use the software. Macs come with built-in sound support, so Mac owners don't have to sweat it.

Disk Format

The last thing to look for is the type of disk the software comes on. The most common disk formats are 360KB 5.25", 1.2MB 5.25", 720KB 3.5", 1.44MB 3.5", and CD-ROM. 360KB and 720KB are double-density disks; 1.2MB and 1.44MB are high-density ones. The sizes refer to the diameter of the round disk that's encased in the square plastic shell.

These days, most computers can handle 1.44MB 3.5" disks; the 5.25" disks are virtually obsolete. The newest format is CD-ROM (compact disk read-only memory), which look just like a music CD. To use CD-ROMs, you must have a CD-ROM drive.

MPC-Compatible?

Some CD-ROM-based games may require an MPC-compatible computer. MPC stands for Multimedia PC; it's a set of minimum standards for sound cards and CD-ROM drives. If the program requires an MPC computer, that means you need a 16-MHz 386SX or better with 4MB of RAM, a 1.44MB floppy drive, VGA, a 2-button mouse, a CD-ROM drive that transfers data at a rate of at least 150KB per second, and a 16-bit sound card. Whew! MPC should stand for Mighty Pricey Computer.

Putting It All Together

At first, it may seem like there's too much to remember—that it'd be easier to bench press an ox than to buy a piece of software. Don't panic. You'll get the hang of it fast enough. To make the task easier, write down your computer's vital statistics and take the list to the store with you. A typical list might look something like this (PC first, Mac alternatives in parentheses):

Computer: IBM compatible (Macintosh Quadra 660AV)

Processor: 386 (68040)

Speed: 40 MHz (25MHz)

Operating System: MS-DOS 6.0 (System 7.1)

Memory: 4MB (8MB)

Graphics: VGA (14-inch monitor/thousands of colors)

Hard drive: yes (yup)

Mouse: yes (yup, yup)

Sound: Sound Blaster Pro (yup again)

Disks: 1.44MB 3.5" and CD-ROM (ditto)

Off to the Store

After you've given some thought to the kinds of software you need and what that software should do, and you've put together a list of your computer's specifications, you should have no difficulty choosing the right software. Your local software store or favorite mail order catalog should have everything you need.

Happy shopping!

Chapter 15

Installing Almost Any Application

My first computer (back in the computer equivalent of the Jurassic period) didn't come with a hard drive. Instead, it came with two 5.25-inch floppy drives. You ran the application you were using from the A drive, and you saved your files to a blank floppy in the B drive. Those days are long, long gone. Today, computers come standard with hard drives, which gives programmers the freedom to soup up applications to sizes and capabilities that were heretofore unimaginable.

The good news is that the programmers have taken advantage of that freedom: applications have become very, very cool and very powerful. The bad news is that they've gotten so complex that you can't just pop in a program disk and be on your merry way. You have to install the software on your hard drive before you can use it. It isn't difficult or complicated, it's just another set of steps to move through before you can get to work.

"Install Sez Me"

The first step in installing software is finding the proper command to get the installation under way. There are several, fairly standard installation routines for Macs, IBM-compatibles, and PCs running Windows.

Naturally, the easiest way to get good information on how to install your new software treasure is to read the Installation section of its manual. That way there's no guessing involved, and, hopefully, there are no ugly surprises.

Installing on Macs

Some Macintosh software requires special installation; such programs generally come with a small Installer application that you access with an icon (see
Figure 15.1).

Figure 15.1   *A Macintosh Installer icon.*

The Installer application will be on the first (or only) disk, and there will be
other files there, too. You won't have to bother with most of them.

Read the README

If there is a README file, you should read it before you install the program. This
file often contains late-breaking and important news about the software you just
purchased. Read the README file by double-clicking on its icon to launch
TeachText. You can read it on-screen or print out a copy to read, whichever you
prefer.

You launch the Installer like any other Mac application, by double-clicking on
its icon. You'll usually get some kind of welcome screen that congratulates
you on your keen software-buying skills, followed by an installation window
(see Figure 15.2). The Installer will give you step-by-step instructions on how
to proceed, including any custom options you may have available.

Most Mac Installers give you two or more installation options; the one shown
here gives you three. Easy Install installs all the various software that comes
with the application, which sometimes includes extensions and control panels
that you may already have. If you know you already have some of those
extensions and control panels, you can select the Custom Install option.
Custom Install lets you select only the functions and software you think you
need. Most users will choose the Easy Install option. You can always delete
any unwanted bits of software later.

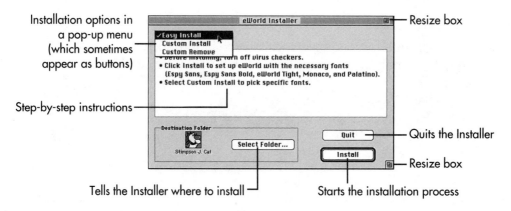

Installation options in
a pop-up menu
(which sometimes
appear as buttons)

Resize box

Step-by-step instructions

Quits the Installer

Resize box

Tells the Installer where to install

Starts the installation process

Figure 15.2   A typical Installer window.

The Installer in Figure 15.2 is unusual because it gives you a Custom Remove
option. Since some install programs place software not only in the chosen
folder but also in the System Folder and other locations, you sometimes have
the option of removing specific bits of software from these locations without
having to search for them.

Once you've decided whether to do an Easy or Custom installation, all you
need to tell the Installer is where you want it to put the software. The default
selection is the drive where your System software is located (often called the
startup disk). If you want to put it somewhere else, click the **Select Folder**
button (as shown in Figure 15.2; some Installers have a Switch Disks button
instead). Then just click on the **Install** button or press **Enter**, and the installation will get under way. If the software comes on multiple disks, your Mac
may spit one out and ask for another. Just plug them into the drive as they are
requested.

When the installation is complete, the install program may give you the
option of quitting or installing another copy somewhere else. Choose whichever is appropriate for you. Some software requires that you restart your Mac
before you can use it. If you need to, the Installer will tell you and will probably give you the option of doing a restart immediately or later. If you choose
to do it later, use the **Restart** command under the **Special** menu.

You're done!

Installing with DOS

Installing an application on an IBM-compatible that isn't running Windows or a shell program (like GeoWorks or the DOS Shell) can be a simple affair. As with Macintosh installations, you should read the manual's installation instructions first just to be sure there isn't some funky variation coming your way. You should also look on the disk to see if there are any README files, and read them. These often contain information that isn't contained in the manual—and sometimes it's even important.

To peek at the contents of the disk, insert it in your A: or B: drive (if you have two), type the appropriate drive letter followed by a colon (:) at the C:\> prompt, and press **Enter**. The C: prompt will change to an A: (or B:) prompt. Type **DIR** and press **Enter**. That will give you a list of the files on the disk.

Installer program——

A README file!——
You should read it.

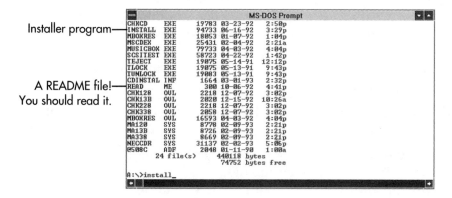

Figure 15.3   *Typing DIR gives you a list of the files on the disk.*

Scrolls Away Too Fast?

If there are more files on the disk than can be displayed on the screen at once, they scroll off the top of the display too fast for you to read them. Slow them down by adding a /P or /W to the end of the DIR command. The command DIR/P shows the files one page at a time; the command DIR/W shows the files in several columns on-screen.

127

If the application uses an installer program, it will appear somewhere on that list (in Figure 15.3, it's called **INSTALL.EXE**). If you don't see an INSTALL.EXE, look for another program that ends in .EXE and has a likely name. For instance, SETUP.EXE, HDINSTAL.EXE (short for "hard disk install"), or any variation of the word setup or install are all good bets.

Just type **INSTALL** or whatever command you've decided must be the installation program. (If you're still at the C:\> prompt, you'll need to type the appropriate drive letter too: **B: INSTALL**.) If you've chosen the right command, the installation program will start up and give you step-by-step instructions for whatever you need to do next. If you get a message like "Bad command or filename" or if some other program starts, you've chosen the wrong command, and you need to try again.

Installation programs vary widely in the information they ask of you. You usually must tell the installation program where you want the program to be installed. It will usually give you the option of naming the subdirectory it is creating or using a default name. Do whatever makes you happy. Many programs will also ask you for the type of printer and monitor you have, and may ask you to type in a serial number from the box or from a disk.

In a multidisk installation, the installer will ask you to swap disks in and out of the drive. Be sure to give it the disk it's asking for.

When it's finished, the installer may ask you to restart your PC. If it asks you to restart, that means it altered your startup files, and you need to restart before you can use the software. Press your PC's **Reset** button or the **Control+Alt+Del** key combination to restart if the installer doesn't restart your computer automatically for you.

Installing in Windows

To install software made to run under Microsoft Windows, you'll use the **Run** command under the **File** menu in the Program Manager. Figure 15.4 shows you the window that will appear. Insert the first (or only) disk in the appropriate drive. In the command line, you'll usually need to type **A:\INSTALL.EXE** (if the disk is in your A: drive), and press **Enter** or click **OK**. Sometimes the Windows installation routine is called SETUP, in which case you'd type **A:\SETUP.EXE**. If you aren't sure what it's called for the application you're installing, you can check the manual (best idea) or click on the **Browse** button to scan through the contents of the disk.

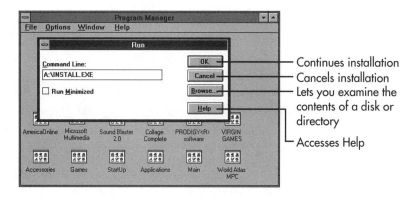

*Figure 15.4   The Windows Program Manager's **Run dialog box.***

Once you've got the installation routine going, you will probably be asked to tell the installer where you want the software installed, and perhaps to name the folder or subdirectory into which it will be installed. If you need to swap disks out of the disk drive for a multidisk application, insert them as requested.

When the installation is complete, you may need to restart your PC before you can use the software. If you do, the manual and/or installation program will let you know.

Stuff Me? Zip You!

Once in a while, whether you're dealing with Mac, IBM-compatible, or Windows software (usually of the freeware and shareware varieties), the files you need may come *compressed*. Compression squeezes computer data so that it takes up less space—which means you can fit more on a floppy disk, and you spend less time downloading the files from an electronic bulletin board.

Before you can use compressed software, you must *decompress* or expand it using the appropriate software. The most common compression utilities are StuffIt (for the Mac) and PKZip for DOS and Windows. StuffIt is a commercial product that you can purchase in a software store under the name of StuffIt Deluxe. It provides more compression utilities than an average user will ever need. StuffIt Lite is a less powerful freeware version you can get from most on-line services. All it does is stuff and unstuff files. PKZip is the PC standard for

continues

129

continued

file compression. You can find the full shareware version of it on most on-line services. If you don't need all those compression options, there is a "lite" version called PKUnzip, too.

Compressed files usually have 3-letter extensions added to their file names to indicate that they are compressed. Mac files compressed with StuffIt have the extension .SIT added to their names. PC files compressed with PKZip have the extension .ZIP. Still other files will have the extension .SEA, which stands for self-extracting archive. Self-extracting files will decompress themselves, and require no other software.

Compression utilities are also handy when you start running out of space on your hard drive. You can compress little-used files so they take up less space, and then decompress them on the rare occasions that you do need them.

Simple Answers to Simple Questions

Generally, no matter what software you're installing and no matter what computer you're using, an installation program will only ask you a few questions. And the program often provides the most common answer to that question by telling you what the *default* is. The default is the answer that the installer will use if you don't have a preference.

The location default is generally the hard drive where your operating system is installed (your *boot disk* or *drive*). If you have no other hard drives or logical drive partitions, don't sweat it. If the installer asks you to name the folder or subdirectory the software is going to be installed in, you can usually accept the default name, unless you already have a folder or subdirectory with the same name. If you do already have a folder or subdirectory by that name, you need to either change the name for the folder you're installing to or quit the installer and rename the existing folder or subdirectory (your operating system manual will tell you how, if you don't already know).

Lastly, after the installation is complete, the installer may ask you questions to configure the new application for your computer (this is generally for IBM-compatibles). For instance, it may ask about your monitor and printer type, whether or not you have a mouse or joystick, and so on. If you're not sure, guess. The installation program sometimes makes a guess for you, which is right about 90% of the time. If the guess is wrong, you can always reconfigure with the help of the application's manual.

Common Installation Woes

In my experience, there are only two things that often go wrong with any installation procedure. (This is, of course, *my* experience. You may run into some new and completely bizarre installation woe. If you do, your best bet is the troubleshooting section of the software's manual.)

The first problem is that if you have any virus protection software installed that constantly scans your system for suspicious activity, it can often booger up the installation of new software. Check the virus software's manual for instructions on how to temporarily deactivate it. Turn the software off, install your new application, and then remember to turn the virus software back on when you're done.

The second most common installation woe is the dreaded "Not enough room to install XYZ application" (on the Mac) or some variation of that in Windows. In DOS you might see a helpful message similar to that or a more cryptic one like "Write error on drive C:." No matter how it's said, it means you've run out of room on your hard drive. There are a couple of things you can do to remedy that situation:

◆ Delete unused or unneeded files and/or software from the drive to free up space.

◆ If you have another hard drive, install the application to it, to a logical drive, or to a partition that has enough room.

◆ Invest in a hard drive compression utility like StuffIt SpaceSaver for the Mac or Stacker or DoubleSpace (part of DOS 6.0 and 6.20) for the IBM-compatible PC. See the sidebar entitled "Stuff Me? Zip You!" earlier in the chapter for more information.

◆ Buy another hard drive.

If you're already running short on hard drive space, buying a second big fat hard drive is probably the best (if most expensive) option. Applications aren't getting smaller. Sooner or later, you'll need the space.

Help! There's No Install Program!

Calm down. That's no reason to panic. All that means is that the software you want to install hasn't reached the monolithic proportions of, say, Microsoft Word yet. All you have to do is copy the application file(s) from the floppy disk to a new home on your hard drive.

On a DOS machine without Windows or another shell program, that means using the COPY command. It's discussed in Chapter 9, along with other handy-dandy DOS commands.

I've never run into a Windows application that didn't have an install routine. You can, however, use Windows File Manager (or the similar feature of any shell program) to copy the files from a non-Windows program disk to your hard drive. Check your Windows (or other) manual for details.

On a Mac, it's just a question of opening the disk's window (by double-clicking on its icon) and dragging the appropriate file(s) onto the hard drive or folder icon/window where you want to store the new software. (Chapter 11 gives you some scoop on clicking and dragging with a Mac; or you can refer to your Mac Users Guide for even more information.)

Happy installing!

Chapter 16

Surviving in Almost Any Software Program

O ne of the great secrets of computing is this: once you've mastered one application for your particular computer, you've got a fairly good start toward mastering all of the software for your computer.

This is especially true of Macintosh applications, since Apple has a strict set of interface guidelines that many companies follow to the letter. The guidelines standardize core operations (like opening, closing, and quitting applications, to name a few) so they work the same way in all applications. That really cuts down on the learning curve.

Folks who use Windows and Windows-based applications have a similar (if not as far reaching) continuity between applications. It was DOS users who, for the longest time, had the hardest time of it: there were no set standards, and no two applications did the same thing the same way. Lately, however, as even non-Windows applications have started using graphical interfaces, that's changed. More and more plain DOS applications are being modeled after their Windows cousins. This gives DOS applications at least an ersatz sense of standardization.

Wherever there is command standardization between applications, you can spend less time re-learning the basic stuff, and more time learning what's different about your new application. This chapter will focus on the general similarities within Macintosh, Windows, and DOS-based applications.

Survival Skills 101

In my opinion, the most important survival skill you can develop is a sense of what's the same from application to application, especially for the functions that you'll use all of the time. We're talking real basic basics here: how to open, close, and save files and how to copy and paste. No matter what kind of application you're using, you will use these commands.

In menu driven programs, you generally find the most important suite of survival commands under the File and Edit menus. These menus are cross-platform and cross-application standards. They're everywhere.

File Me!

The File menu, oddly enough, is where you'll usually find commands that are file-specific: New file, Open, Save, and Close your file(s). Figures 16.1 and 16.2 show four different file menus. In order of appearance they are: the Macintosh Finder's File menu, the File menu from the Mac version of Microsoft Word, the File menu from Windows Program Manager, and the File menu from the Windows version of America Online's software.

Figure 16.1   The File menu in Macintosh Finder and in the Mac version of Microsoft Word.

If you compare the Mac menus and the Windows menus, you should notice two things: they contain a similar set of file commands, plus different file commands that are specific to that application. In any application you use, the same sort of commands should be grouped under the file menu.

Figure 16.2   *The File menu in Windows Program Manager and in the Windows version of America Online.*

The second thing you'll notice, particularly between the Macintosh menus, is that each command is followed by its command-key equivalent. To open a file on a Mac, you can select the Open command from the menu, or you can press the ⌘-O key combination as a shortcut. Note that this is true in any Macintosh application: ⌘-O always opens a file, just as ⌘-S always saves a file.

Save Me!

Anytime you're working on your computer, you should save the file you are working on every few minutes. This is especially true when you're working with a new application that you haven't quite gotten the hang of yet. Saving regularly spares you the heartbreak of having to re-create work that was lost because you hit the wrong key, accidentally quit the program, or made any of a number of other typical embarrassing mistakes.

Save every time you get up to take a break, go to the bathroom, or answer the phone. You should also save after each page of a document and before you make any editing changes—basically, whenever you can without breaking your chain of thought. Saving your files will save your sanity, too.

Unfortunately, the keyboard shortcuts in Windows aren't as standardized as those in Macintosh applications. There are keyboard shortcuts after the menu commands, but they aren't always the same (or even similar) from program to program.

Because of the standardization of the File menu, you can approach any new application, even on a system other than the one you're used to, and know where to locate the file-related commands. If you aren't sure what a particular command does... well, we'll cover some helpful resources in a bit.

Edit Me!

The Edit menu of most applications contains a set of commands with which you copy, cut, and paste selected file data from one spot to another in the same document or another document. There is also usually an Undo command with which you can cancel the last command you issued. This can be extremely useful when you change your mind about an editorial change and want to return to the original version. Figure 16.3 shows the Edit menus from both the Windows version of Microsoft Word and the Mac version of Microsoft Word.

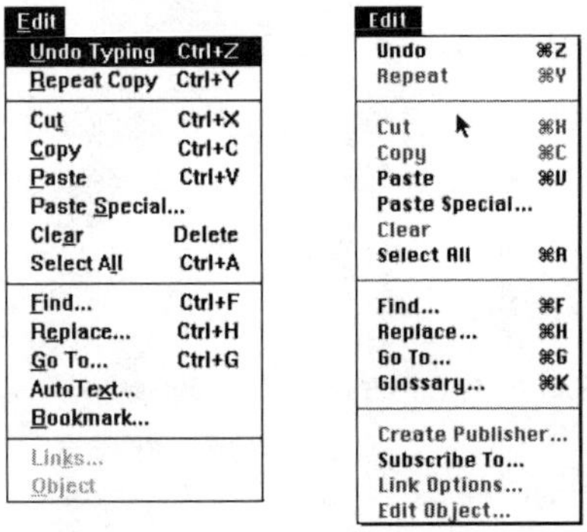

Figure 16.3   *The Edit menu in Microsoft Word for Windows and in the Mac version of Microsoft Word.*

Feature for feature, these two menus are pretty well matched—even the keyboard shortcuts are fairly similar. If you aren't sure what these commands do, help is right around the corner.

Surviving in Cranky Old DOS Programs

If you're dealing with some odd DOS-based program (maybe an older one) that doesn't use the normal kind of menus, you may have to resort to reading the manual. If you don't have the manual, try some of these tricks:

◆ If you are working with Lotus 1-2-3 or some other Lotus product, the menus are a little different: you activate them by pressing the slash key (/). The top line that appears lists the main menu names, and the words below that are the commands that are available on the menu that's highlighted. Confusing? You bet. Read the manual.

◆ Watch the screen and press each function key (the "F" keys). Observe what each function key does and take notes. Try each function key alone, and then in combination with Shift, Ctrl, and/or Alt.

◆ If function keys don't work, try other keys. Start with number keys and then letter keys, trying each separately and in conjunction with Alt, Ctrl, and/or Shift until you find something that changes the screen in some way. Keep notes.

◆ Press the Esc key. A menu or message might appear.

◆ Click or click-and-hold the left mouse button on an item. Many times this will give you an explanation or call up a menu. Try the right mouse button if that doesn't work.

◆ To exit, try pressing Esc, Ctrl+Esc, or Ctrl+Break. Press Ctrl+Alt+Delete as a last resort to exit a program.

Help Me!

Even if you master the menu basics of all your software, you still may run into features that are unfamiliar to you, or you may forget what a particular command does.

Naturally, the best source of help is the application's manual or a good book devoted to that application. However, it isn't always convenient for you to drop what you're doing, go find a manual, and look up the information. By the time you get back to work, you could easily have forgotten what you were trying to do in the first place. Understanding that manuals are a necessary evil, programmers have begun to include more easily accessible sources of help (known as *on-line help*) that are available at your computer.

On-Line Help

As I mentioned in Chapter 15, many software packages come with README files that contain important information that isn't contained in the manual. Most README files can be opened and read with any word processor; you don't have to leave your computer.

Many more complex applications come with tutorials that walk you through a simple project using your new software. Generally, they're in small, easily digestible chunks. Each stage of the tutorial builds on the features and functions you learned in the last stage. By following along, you learn what the program's major (and minor) features are and how to use them. A good tutorial is worth a dozen dense manuals.

If you have already read the manual, done the tutorial, and gotten down to work, you can often get a quick refresher using other methods. The standard method for Windows and Windows applications is a stand-alone Help menu (like the one shown in Figure 16.4) that gives you these options: a table of contents in which you can browse for a certain topic; search capability; help about using the Help system; and information about the particular application.

Figure 16.4   The Help menu from the Windows version of America Online.

Macintosh applications have double-duty help. If you turn on the **Show Balloons** option in the Balloon Help menu (Figure 16.5), every time your cursor touches a screen element that has even a brief help-file associated with it, that information will appear on your screen in a balloon. If you need specific or more detailed help, you'll also find the application's help system available under the Mac's Balloon Help menu (for example, the Microsoft Word Help command appears on the menu in Figure 16.5). Either way, you can get help whenever you need it.

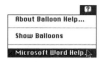

Figure 16.5   *The Balloon Help menu in the Mac version of Microsoft Word.*

Help! Help! Help!

Sometimes, in the course of human events, you run into a problem so huge that no on-line help, help balloons, or manuals can dig you out from under it. Then it's time to call in the big guns.

User groups and computer clubs (like those discussed in the article "Computer Clubs" in Part V) are a fabulous source of help. Since the groups have members at all levels of computing experience, from the newest newbie to thundering geeks, you can probably find someone who has encountered and corrected your problem before.

Many hardware and software companies maintain technical support lines that you can call to get help (Chapter 13 covers this in greater detail). In addition, many companies run their own electronic bulletin board services, and even more have message areas on the major on-line services (also discussed in Part V). These are all sources of heavy-duty help.

If you learn your system's basic commands, learn the ones that remain standard for all your applications, and maintain a willingness to get help when you need it, you should be able to survive learning any application that's thrown your way.

About the Reviews

T he reviews in this part of the book are pretty self-explanatory, but there are a few things you need to know about the "shorthand" we've developed to keep the book from turning into a 1000-page brick.

System Requirements

In the reviews listed here, system requirements are given for various platforms (Mac, Windows, and so on.) Because such a list of specs could be quite long if we covered the software thoroughly, we've decided to make certain assumptions about your equipment. For example, a machine that can run Microsoft Windows must meet certain minimum requirements, including EGA or better graphics, a hard drive, and two megabytes (2MB) of RAM. Instead of listing all these requirements for each Windows program reviewed, we may simply say "Minimum" for the software's hardware requirements.

For software that requires more than the minimum, we've listed the requirement that differs. For instance, if a Windows program requires 4MB of RAM instead of the minimum of 2, the review's specifications will say something like "4MB RAM."

The following list gives you what we consider to be the minimum requirements:

Windows Minimum Requirements   286 or better microprocessor, Windows 3.1, DOS 3.1 or later, 2MB RAM, mouse, hard disk, and EGA or better graphics.

DOS Minimum Requirements Any IBM-compatible computer, DOS 2.0 or later, 640KB RAM, and CGA or better graphics.

Macintosh Minimum Requirements A Mac Plus or later, System 6.07 or later with 2MB RAM (4MB for System 7), and a monitor.

Keep in mind that you must also have the correct type of floppy drive in order to install the software after you purchase it. These days, most software is shipped on 3.5" high-density (1.44MB) floppy disks. If you do not have a high-density floppy drive, you should seriously consider adding one.

Any software that's listed as "multimedia" requires a CD-ROM drive and some kind of sound card. Check out the article "Multimedia" in Part V to learn the nitty-gritty details about multimedia equipment.

Prices

Never pay the manufacturer's suggested retail price (MSRP) for a software program. You can buy it cheaper in stores, and even cheaper by mail. How much cheaper? Anywhere from 10% to 50% off—a substantial chunk of change when you're talking about a $500 program!

To avoid getting bogged down in the exact prices of software, we've broken the programs into several price categories based on the MSRP:

$ - $1 to $50
$$ - $50 to $150
$$$ - $150 to $275
$$$$ - $275 to $500
$$$$$ - $500 and up

Word Processing Programs

It'd be pretty safe to say that 99.9% of all home computers have word processors installed on them. After all, word processing is the #1 task for which home computers are used. With a word processor, you can create all kinds of documents, including everything from a quick note to a huge, complicated report.

Today's word processors can do a lot more than just cut and paste; they can also format text into multiple columns, import pictures, and use different fonts and text attributes. A good word processor can even check your spelling and grammar. The following reviews will help you choose the right word processor for you.

Microsoft Word

Manufacturer: Microsoft Corporation
Platforms: Windows, DOS, Macintosh
System requirements:
    Windows—4MB RAM
    DOS—286 recommended, DOS 3.0 or later, hard disk
    Mac—Minimum
Price range: $$$$

The Windows version of Word is a favorite of serious writers. This is because of its ease of use, its full supply of state-of-the-art word-processing features, and its extra goodies (which include a graph maker, an equation editor, a dialog editor, and WordArt, a mini-application that generates text special effects).

To make many document-creation tasks easier, Word for Windows includes *Wizards*, automated templates that lead you step by step through the creation of a document. Word includes Wizards for awards, calendars, fax cover sheets, newsletters, and more. Word also ships with 12 regular templates, as well as 15 prewritten business letters.

Word, of course, features the usual spell checker and grammar checker, along with customizable toolbars and menus. But Word really shines in its capability to predict what you want to do. Word can correct spelling errors as you type, format documents, and add numbers to lists automatically. With Word's drag-and-drop editing, you can move a block of text by dragging instead of having to use slow cut-and-paste operations. Word also handles all kinds of special formatting chores like adding drop caps, borders, graphics, and tables to a document.

The Mac version of Word is very similar to the Windows version in terms of power and features. However, the DOS version is not as easy to use or nearly as powerful. Most DOS users look to WordPerfect as their word processor of choice.

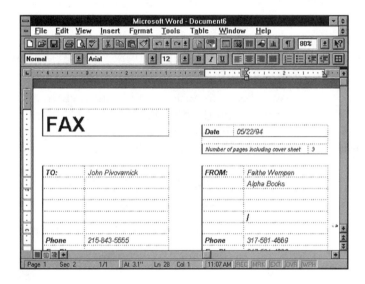

Microsoft Word for Windows 6.0

WordPerfect

Manufacturer: WordPerfect Corp.
Platforms: Windows, DOS, Macintosh
System requirements:
    Windows—4MB RAM
    DOS—DOS 3.1, 386 or better processor, hard disk, VGA graphics.
    Mac—Minimum (4.5MB RAM on a Power Mac).
Price range: $$$$

WordPerfect is probably the most popular word processor of all time. Although it lost some ground when Windows came on the scene, the DOS version of WordPerfect 6.0 is still one heck of an impressive DOS application. In fact, the DOS version looks and acts deceivingly like a Windows application, eschewing the usual DOS text-based screens and opting instead for its own graphical interface.

Although it was slow coming out of the gate, WordPerfect for Windows has since become a serious contender for top place. It includes all the features found in a top word processor, including customizable button bars, automated templates, mail merge, spell checker, drawing, charting, and more. WordPerfect especially shines when it comes to document management. You can find, copy, move, delete, print, and rename files all from within WordPerfect. You can even create or delete directories. Moreover, the program's QuickList feature lets you assign descriptive names to file paths so you can jump instantly to any directory. Another powerful feature is Reveal Codes, which enables you to see exactly what formatting codes are in effect.

Finally, WordPerfect's tables feature superior spreadsheet capabilities. In fact, WordPerfect's tables—which can include named ranges, fills, and up to 100 formulas—may be powerful enough to replace your regular spreadsheet program. With WordPerfect, you can even place floating cells, which display the result of a spreadsheet calculation on another page, into a paragraph of text.

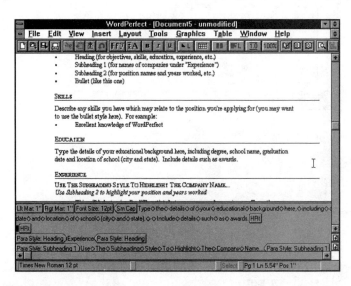

Microsoft Word for Windows 6.0

Ami Pro

Manufacturer: Lotus Development Corp.
Platform: Windows
System requirements: Minimum
Price range: $$$$

Although Ami Pro is not as popular as Word for Windows and WordPerfect for Windows, it's the easiest to use of the major Windows word processors—especially when it comes to complex tasks like page layout. Using Ami Pro, for example, it's especially easy to create newsletters and documentation, thanks to its graphics frames and ready-to-use templates.

Ami Pro's superior graphics-handling capability helps set it apart from its competitors, as does its lightning speed, especially when it comes to printing and mail merge. Like most modern word processors, Ami Pro's uncluttered screen also includes a button bar at the top and a status bar at the bottom from which you can select fonts and styles.

WordPerfect for Windows 6.0In addition to the usual spell checker and grammar checker, Ami Pro sports handy tools for customizing the program. For example, its SmartIcons, icon editor, and powerful macro recorder all work together to enable you to customize Ami Pro to your tastes. Just create a new icon, place it on the toolbar or floating toolbox, and assign a macro to the icon.

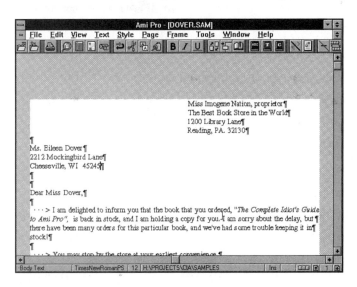

Ami Pro 3.0 for Windows

MacWrite Pro

Manufacturer: Claris Corp.
Platform: Macintosh
System requirements: Minimum
Price range: $$$

Although MacWrite Pro's predecessor, MacWrite II, was not serious competition for many other high-end Macintosh word processors, it had a solid reputation for being easy to use. MacWrite Pro has built upon that solid foundation, adding a slew of new features that bring the package almost up to the state of the art, while retaining its simplicity and clean design.

One welcome addition is MacWrite Pro's new page-layout features, such as column formatting, document sections, and various types of frames. Using these new features, MacWrite Pro can create sidebars and graphical objects that fit anywhere in a document, automatically causing text to flow around them. The program also features a superior table tool that enables you to insert and delete rows and columns, as well as sort and merge cells. In addition, MacWrite supports style definitions that you can define and apply to different paragraphs of a document, by selecting the defined styles from the program's Styles palette.

In spite of the many improvements, however, MacWrite Pro has serious competition, even from Claris's own ClarisWorks (see the Integrated Software review section), which includes not only a word processor similar to MacWrite Pro, but also other handy applications. Moreover, MacWrite Pro is missing such high-end features as an outliner, an equation editor, an index/table of contents generator, and splittable windows (all of which are found in major applications such as Microsoft Word). Still, if ease of use is your most important criteria, MacWrite Pro delivers the goods.

Q&A Write 3.0

Manufacturer: Symantec Corp.
Platform: Windows
System requirements: Minimum
Price range: $$

Q&A Write demonstrates the you-get-what-you-pay-for principle of software purchasing: you get a limited, but reasonably useful, product at a low price. Although Q&A Write boasts few amenities like automated templates, macros, and indexing, it does provide a solid, simple interface for creating short documents like letters, reports, memos, and résumés.

The program comes with 11 templates that you can use to start a document, or you can create your own templates for more specific uses. However, templates in Q&A Write are really nothing more than basic documents; the templates cannot prompt you for needed information as they can in more sophisticated word processors like Word for Windows. Q&A Write does allow you to create and save custom text styles that you can later apply to any part of a document. In addition, it includes an easy-to-use mail merge function for creating form letters.

With Q&A Write, you can import graphics into a document and create tables that support a few built-in functions like sums and averages. You cannot, however, move and size graphic frames by dragging them with the mouse pointer; instead, you must reposition frames by editing their coordinates in a special dialog box. Because of its slow performance and limited features, Q&A Write cannot handle long documents well. But if you're looking for an inexpensive, competent word processor for everyday use, this package may be just right.

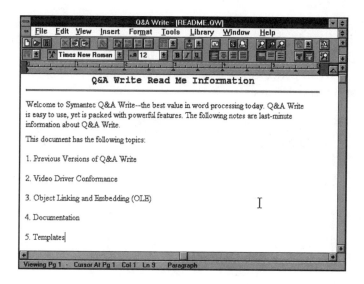

Q&A Write

Professional Write

Manufacturer: Software Publishing Corp.
Platforms: Windows, DOS
System requirements:
    Windows—Minimum
    DOS—286 or better, DOS 3.1 or later, hard disk
Price range: $$$

Professional Write has been around for a long time, fulfilling the needs of people who don't require a lot of fancy options to get their documents done. The DOS version jumps you right into the editing screen where you can get to work. The menu bar across the top gives you quick access to the commands you need, and the on-line help system incorporates Hypertext-like links with which you can jump easily from one topic to another related topic.

The program supports a host of text styles and fonts, makes document layout easy, and enables you to edit documents while still in layout mode. Moreover, the preview mode enables you to view your documents exactly as they will look when printed. And you can zoom in and out from a document in layout view in order to view it in various levels of detail.

As with most modern word processors, Professional Write comes packed with a spelling checker, an on-line thesaurus, and even a grammar checker (Grammat-ik IV). In addition, the program recognizes file formats of many other popular word processors, including WordPerfect, Microsoft Word, WordStar, and OfficeWriter.

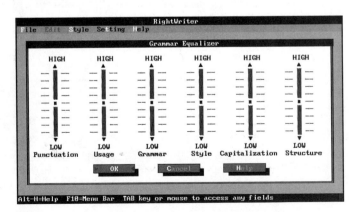

Professional Write

RightWriter

Manufacturer: Que Software
Platforms: Windows, DOS, Macintosh
System requirements:
   Windows—Minimum
   DOS—DOS 3.0 or later, 286 or better, 1MB RAM, hard disk
   Mac—Minimum
Price range: $

Nothing can do more to ruin a report, letter, memo, or other document than poor grammar. And, while you may have learned grammar well in school, professional-level writing requires knowledge of many rules you may have long since forgotten. That's where programs like Que Software's RightWriter come in handy. RightWriter is a grammar checker that scans your documents, much like a spelling checker, and can find a variety of grammar errors.

When RightWriter finds an error, it immediately gives you a suggestion for improving the writing and lets you make the correction before moving on to the next error. Or, if you prefer, you can avoid the interactive correction feature and instead have the program produce a marked-up copy of the document that you can review using your word processor or send to your printer.

RightWriter can handle a variety of writing styles, including business, technical, and fiction writing. Moreover, by using RightWriter's Grammar Equalizer, you can create your own custom writing styles by varying how your documents are analyzed. You can set the sliders on the Grammar Equalizer to control the number of comments generated for punctuation, usage, grammar, style, capitalization, and structure.

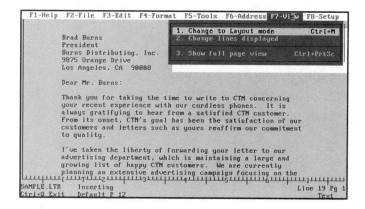

RightWriter

Spreadsheets

A spreadsheet is a grid of rows and columns that intersect to form cells. You can store text, numbers, or formulas in cells. (Formulas perform calculations on numbers.) Spreadsheets can show the sales figures for a sales department, a financial projection for a company, or even something as simple as a home budget. If you have ever worked with a ledger before or done any bookkeeping, you are probably already familiar with the spreadsheet concept.

In a computerized spreadsheet program, you can enter data in a number of formats, as well as edit the table's contents at any time (much as you would edit a document in a word processor). The real power of a computer spreadsheet, however, lies in the way the values in the spreadsheet relate to each other. When you change one value, all values that depend on the edited value are automatically updated to reflect the change.

The average home computer user's need for a spreadsheet is minimal, so we won't review every spreadsheet on the market. But let's look at the top contenders and see what sets each one apart.

Microsoft Excel

Manufacturer: Microsoft Corp.
Platforms: Windows, Mac
System requirements:
    Windows—EGA graphics, 4MB RAM
    Mac—Minimum
Price range: $$$$ (Competitive upgrades much cheaper)

Microsoft Excel, one of the Windows spreadsheet biggies, has recently undergone an extensive facelift. Borrowing from Quattro Pro, Excel now features three-dimensional page-tabbed worksheets, with which you can switch between data views just by clicking on a named tab at the bottom of the screen.

To help you find data in a large worksheet, Excel includes powerful and intelligent database-type functions that can extract and sort lists of data. Helpful commands such as AutoSum, which automatically calculates totals, and AutoFilter, which helps you build custom lists of data from a larger set, are just a couple of the new ease-of-use features added to Excel. Excel also supports object linking and embedding (OLE), which enables you to quickly and easily edit objects inserted into a worksheet.

Excel also includes a powerful macro language based on Visual Basic. In addition, its powerful charting module can create many types of 2D and 3D charts that automatically change to reflect changes in the data upon which they're based. As with all Microsoft high-end products, automated templates and tasks called Wizards abound. Microsoft Excel is for power-users who like their applications to be easy to use.

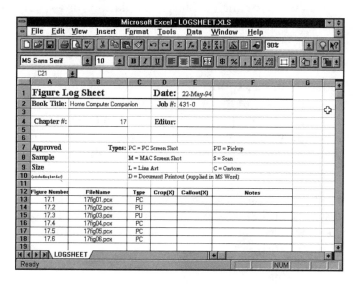

Microsoft Excel

Quattro Pro 5.0

Manufacturer: Borland International Inc.
Platforms: Windows, DOS
System requirements:
   Windows—386 or better, 4MB RAM
   DOS—DOS 3.3 or later, 286 or better, hard disk
Price range: $

Quattro Pro has long been a top contender among Windows and DOS spread-sheet programs. It was the first spreadsheet to incorporate the page-tabbed notebook metaphor for managing multiple worksheets, and it continues to be one of the easiest to use, thanks to its extensive help system. Quattro Pro's help system includes on-line training sessions, Experts (automated tasks), and ObjectHelp (which displays message balloons in response to a request for help about a specific on-screen object).

Like most full-featured spreadsheet programs, Quattro Pro includes a huge library of functions: not only the usual mundane functions like sums and averages, but also date-and-time, text, financial, and engineering functions. There are even functions for such esoteric calculations as exponential smooth-ing, moving averages, and descriptive statistics. As an extra bonus, Quattro Pro's array formulas enable you to represent myriad data with a single formula.

Quattro Pro can, of course, produce a wide variety of charts and graphs (although you can only zoom in for a closer look at data with the DOS ver-sion). You can drag and drop pages, ranges, and even single cells to new locations. The Windows version of the program can locate various types of errors such as circular references, but falls short in this area when compared with the DOS version.

Quattro Pro's biggest weakness is its slow recalculation speed, which is only half the speed of some other spreadsheet programs. Still, it's one of the best and most powerful spreadsheet programs available, and at its incredibly low price, it's an absolute steal.

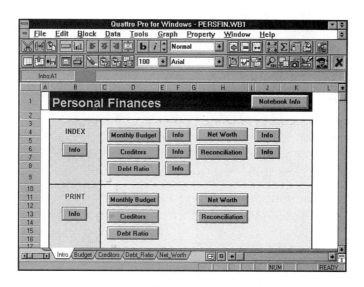

Quattro Pro for Windows

Lotus 1-2-3

Manufacturer: Lotus Development Corp.
Platforms: Windows, DOS, Macintosh
System requirements:
    Windows—386 or better, 4MB RAM, VGA graphics
    DOS—286 or better, DOS 3.0 or later, 1MB RAM, hard disk
    Macintosh—Minimum
Price range: $$$$

Lotus 1-2-3 has a long history of playing catch-up with its competitors. And although the latest Windows version is a big improvement over previous versions, it's still lacking in several areas. For example, although Lotus 1-2-3 has now adopted the popular 3D-tabbed worksheets, the tabs really act only as selection icons. You can't rearrange pages with the tabs, nor can you select ranges of pages with the tabs. Further, you can't adjust margins from within page preview, hide rows, or name expressions, as you can with other high-end spreadsheet programs.

The program does, however, offer some ease-of-use features like customizable button palettes and a control bar from which you can select formats and fonts. You can also edit a worksheet by dragging and dropping cells and ranges to new locations, and you can perform in-cell editing instead of having to edit a cell's contents in the formula bar. Lotus 1-2-3's chart handling, though, is a bit clumsy, forcing you to create a group object from a chart and its associated text boxes and arrows. To regain access to the Chart menu, you must ungroup the chart object.

Like its competitors, Lotus 1-2-3 includes a large function library, along with easy on-screen function selection. Function lists feature descriptions and syntax examples. Unfortunately, the manual offers no function reference, forcing you to learn about the function library from the on-line help system.

The bottom line is, if you've been using a previous version of Lotus 1-2-3, you'll probably be thrilled with the improvements in the new version. If you're looking for your first spreadsheet, you're better off looking elsewhere.

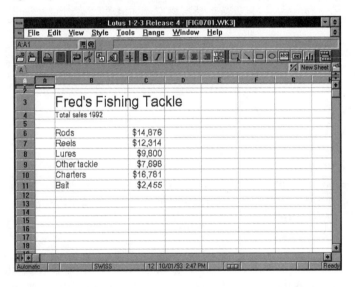

Lotus 1-2-3 for Windows

Database Programs

A *database* helps you organize large amounts of information. For example, you could think of a phone book as a database for phone numbers. Database programs store collections of data and organize them on your computer. You can use a database program to organize a CD collection, to create an address book for business contacts, or to handle accounts receivable.

Database programs store data in *records*; each record is an entry. For example, in a phone book, all the information about one person (Name, Address, and Phone Number) comprises a record. Each type of information is a *field*—for example, Phone Number is one field, and Name is another.

There are different kinds of databases. The simplest kind is a *free-form database*, which is like a random pile of post-it notes. In a free-form database, you don't necessarily have to have the same fields in each record. In a *flat-file database*, you set up fields that pertain to every single record. Then you fill in the fields for each record so that every record has the same structure. The third kind of database is the *relational database*, which is the most powerful and expensive kind. It's like a fancy flat-file database. It can combine the contents of two or more databases into a separate file, and perform other advanced functions. Free-form and flat-file databases are probably the best choices for casual home users.

Data Manager

Manufacturer: Timeworks International
Platforms: Windows, DOS
System requirements:
  Windows—Minimum
  DOS—Minimum
Price range: $$

This flat-file database offers plenty of helpful features, without overwhelming the inexperienced database user with powerful features he'll never use. Setting up a new database is a simple matter of displaying the Data Field Definition (DFD) editor and entering the information for the various fields each record will contain. When you've saved the new database definition, you're ready to start entering data.

A Data Manager database can contain many types of information, including textual data, numeric data, dates, pop-up notes, and even pictures. In addition, you can use different fonts and colors in your layouts. Finally, Data Manager's Report Designer enables you to create custom reports that display your data exactly as you like. Reports can contain graphics, tables, calculations, and many other types of data, formatted according to your specifications. If you've got simple database needs, a program like Data Manager may be just right.

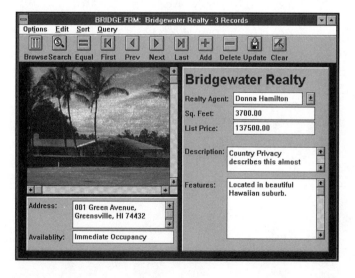

Data Manager for Windows

Q&A

Manufacturer: Symantec Corp.
Platforms: Windows, DOS
System requirements:
Windows—386 or better, DOS 3.3 or later, 4MB RAM, VGA graphics
DOS—Hard disk
Price range: $$$

Q&A is one of the simpler flat-file database programs available, but its simplicity is often also its strength. It can't build the type of powerful databases that a relational database can build, but Q&A's ease-of-use and strong mail merge capabilities may make the difference for people with more modest needs. For the novice, one of Q&A's biggest strengths is that you can build a database application without knowing how to program databases.

Q&A is actually both a database program and word processor in one, since it includes Symantec's Q&A Write (reviewed under "Word Processing Programs") in the package. In fact, it's that link between the database and Q&A Write that gives Q&A its powerful mail merge feature. Q&A also features a spreadsheet view for easy editing of data, a simple report generator, and a Ditto function that makes entering repetitive data a breeze. In addition, the DOS and Windows versions can work with each other's files, as long as you spring for the optional compatibility disk.

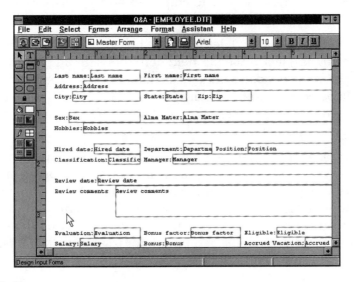

Q&A for Windows

When it comes to creating database queries or macros, few packages are easier to handle than Q&A, which includes what it calls the Intelligent Assistant (nicknamed DAVE). Using the Intelligent Assistant, you can generate complex queries by simply choosing syntactically correct terms from a series of menus. You can build macros the same way, after which you can assign the newly created macro to its own button. Power users may find Q&A to be somewhat limited, but for the average database user's needs, Q&A may fit the bill perfectly.

FileMaker Pro

Manufacturer: Claris
Platforms: Windows, Macintosh
System requirements:
    Windows—3MB RAM, VGA or better graphics
    Mac—Minimum
Price range: $$$$

FileMaker started out as a popular database program for Macintosh users, but it's now also available for use under Windows. Although FileMaker is a flat-file database, it does allow you to link databases in a way that simulates a relational database. For example, suppose you had a payroll list that included payroll data along with an employee ID number. You could use FileMaker's Lookup Files to link these records to employee addresses in another file, as long as that file also contained the employee ID.

Starting a new database with FileMaker is a breeze. A special dialog box (shown in the figure) lets you enter field definitions for all types of data, including text, numbers, dates, times, calculations, and even pictures. Most of the setup can be performed by clicking a few buttons and typing appropriate field names. Once you have created your database form, entering data is just a matter of typing information and tabbing between fields.

To help you along, FileMaker includes such handy functions as automatic data entry (for repeated or common data) and scripts (for performing complicated tasks with a click of a button). In addition, FileMaker features a complete set of tools for creating database layouts. You can draw various types of shapes and fill those shapes with different fill patterns. You can even tell FileMaker to use a drawn shape as a button for triggering a script or performing other types of commands.

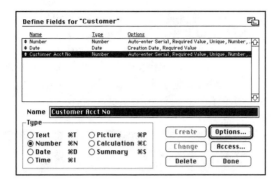

FileMaker Pro's Define Fields screen

Approach

Manufacturer: Lotus Development Corp.
Platform: Windows
System requirements: Minimum
Price range: $$$$

PC/Computing magazine recently called Approach "the most usable Windows relational database ever," so if you need a sophisticated database program, Approach just may be your best bet. Unlike flat-file database programs, a relational database program like Approach can cross-reference records in different databases in order to come up with more complete reports. For example, using Approach you could create a database of teachers and another database of students, and then ask Approach to find all students who have Ray Brown for a teacher.

Thanks to Approach's validation options, entering data into a database is as easy and error-free as possible. Objects like radio buttons, check buttons, and pull-down lists can all be utilized in a database form, enabling you to select data with the mouse. In addition, Approach's PicturePlus fields make it possible for you to include pictures, charts, and even sounds in a database record. Just click on any of these objects, and the application that created it appears. You can then edit these objects directly from within Approach.

To add to its power, Approach can generate professional-looking reports, forms, and mailing labels, and using Approach's mail merge option, you can quickly generate form letters. Finally, Approach features powerful macro capabilities that enable you to automate tasks and assign those tasks to on-screen buttons. However, because Approach is a complex program, you should consider it only for heavy-duty database needs.

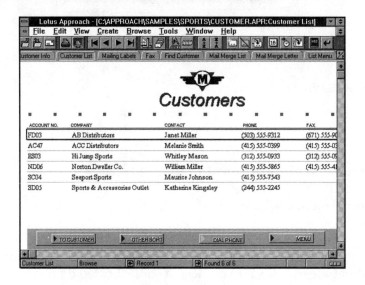

Approach 3.0

Microsoft Access

Manufacturer: Microsoft Corp.
Platform: Windows
System requirements: 386 or better, 6MB RAM, EGA or better graphics
Price range: $$$$

Access is Microsoft's entry into the Windows database fray, and like most Microsoft programs, it's one of the best. Access is easy to use thanks to auto-mated tasks called Wizards, an extensive on-line help system, and a slick interface. The ease of use is even more amazing when you consider that Access is a relational database—not just the simple flat-file type.

In Access, you create your databases as tables, and then you enter your data. As with any full-featured database program, you can edit data in various ways, such as changing the text and assigning text attributes and styles. Once you have created your tables, you can view your data in the table, or one record at a time by creating forms (which can contain not only text fields, but also handy controls like list boxes). You can also view data by constructing *queries*, which combine the data in your tables in various ways. As with other program features, constructing a query can be a quick and easy process with Access's help.

For printing data, you can design custom reports or even print mailing labels. Access handles charts and graphs, too. If you need a powerful database system, it'd be hard to go wrong with Access.

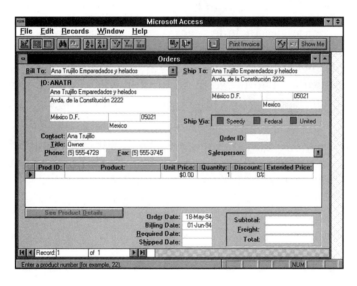

Microsoft Access 2.0

Integrated Software

The best software packages work seamlessly together, allowing you to share data easily. For example, a good word processor should allow you to easily import a table from a spreadsheet program. Windows programs make it easy to share data. But another option that makes it easy to share data—and save a heap of cash—is to purchase one of the products reviewed in this section.

Integrated software packages include several applications in one: usually a word processor, database, and spreadsheet, with a couple of extras (like a graphics or communications module) thrown in. By purchasing the "works," you get all the basic applications you need to get started with your computer. And because the different application modules are designed together, data sharing is a snap.

The only disadvantage of an integrated package is that the individual programs it contains are not as full-featured and powerful as the higher-priced programs you might buy separately. However, most home users don't need the high-powered features that make the expensive programs so expensive. They just need to get by with the basics, and an integrated package works great for that purpose.

Microsoft Works 3.0

Manufacturer: Microsoft Corp.
Platforms: Windows, DOS, Macintosh
System requirements:
   Windows—VGA graphics
   DOS—DOS 3.0.
   Mac—Minimum
Price range: $$ ($$$ Mac)

When it comes to integrated software, Microsoft Works for Windows is clearly the favorite. The easy-to-understand interface, coupled with

Microsoft's famous *Wizards* (automated macros for completing complicated tasks), make Works a good package for someone just dipping into the waters of integrated software. To further assist you, Microsoft's cue cards provide context-sensitive help, and the more than 40 templates quickly get you started creating your own documents.

Works for Windows includes word processor, spreadsheet, database, and telecommunications programs all rolled into one powerful application that enables easy communication between the modules. In addition, Works comes with Microsoft Draw (a drawing program) and WordArt (a text-effect creator). The included clip-art library, spell checker, and thesaurus also help you create professional-looking documents.

Works' word processor is much like Word for Windows 2.0, featuring toolbars and capabilities for easy text editing, multiple columns, bulleted lists, borders, hyphenation, wrapping text around objects, envelope printing, and more. The spreadsheet program supports over 75 statistical and mathematical functions and offers powerful charting capabilities, while the flat-file database features a sophisticated query tool that enables you to use Boolean operators like AND, OR, and NOT to extract data. Finally, the telecommunications program makes it a snap to connect with on-line services such as CompuServe. All versions of Works are similar, but the DOS version lacks such graphics extras as Microsoft Draw and WordArt.

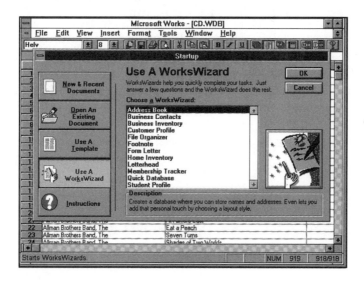

Microsoft Works for Windows

Claris Works

Manufacturer: Claris Corp.
Platforms: Windows, Mac
System requirements:
   Windows—386 or better, VGA graphics
   Mac—Minimum
Price range: $$$ ($$$$ Mac)

Claris Works for Windows may not be as powerful as Microsoft Works for Windows, but its lower hard-disk space requirements (only 3.8MB for a full installation) and its amazing integration help make up for most differences. Claris Works allows you to piece together a document using only a single window instead of having to switch from one module to another. To do this, you select database, spreadsheet, and graphics tools from Claris' palette.

Claris Works includes word processor, spreadsheet, database, and graphics modules. The word processor supports the creation of title pages, multiple columns, linked text frames, and footnotes. It also sports spelling and thesaurus tools, which are available to all the modules. The spreadsheet module offers 100 functions for calculating values, although it lacks many formatting features. The database module, on the other hand, allows fairly sophisticated forms (thanks to Claris' tool palette) and provides easy searching and sorting. Although Claris Works has no telecommunications package, you can access Windows' Terminal applet from Claris' menu.

Claris Works is particularly strong in the graphics department—so strong, in fact, that you can use the graphics module as a mini desktop-publishing program. The graphics tool includes the capability not only to create shapes in various colors and patterns, but also to rotate, align, and flip objects. You can even group many objects into a single object for easier manipulation. All in all, if simple integration is more important to you than power, Claris Works may be the best choice.

PFS:WindowWorks

Manufacturer: Softkey International
Platform: Windows
System requirements: 386, DOS 5.0 or later, 4MB RAM, VGA Graphics
Price range: $$

PFS:WindowWorks ships with a wide range of integrated modules, including not only the usual word processor, spreadsheet, and database, but also address book, charting, communications, and label-maker modules. Delrina Corp.'s WinFax Lite is even thrown in to round things out. You can select any of the seven modules from the start-up screen, and you can have as many modules open simultaneously as you like. Although PFS:WindowWorks does not have a graphics module, the word processor does feature a simple drawing tool.

Simple data sharing among PFS:WindowWorks' modules is as easy as cut and paste. For more sophisticated data sharing, the program supports Windows' object linking and embedding (OLE), with which you can double-click on a database table in a document in order to call up the module that created that table. The data sharing works especially well between the word processor and other modules.

PFS:WindowWorks' word processor includes all the usual editing features, as well as features for creating outlines, styles, text and graphic frames, multiple columns, and templates. The spreadsheet module supports only 46 functions and has limited formatting features. However, simple black-and-white charting is available, including the capabilities to add titles and legends and to automatically update values. With the flat-file database you can create simple queries for extracting data, and you can view data as a card file or a table. The communications module is much like Windows' Terminal applet, except it has a toolbar and supports scripting, which allows you to automate certain communications tasks.

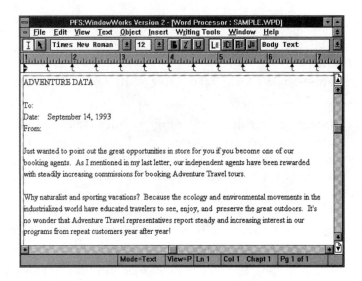

PFS:WindowWorks

PushButton Works for Windows

Manufacturer: PushButton Software Inc.
Platform: Windows
System requirements: 286 or better
Price range: $

If PushButton Works for Windows has anything going for it, it is its incredibly low price. Although PushButton Works can't create fancy documents containing multiple columns and sophisticated custom graphics, its word processor, spreadsheet, and database enable you to add charts and tables to a document, as well as create form letters from a database. Unfortunately, the program is not always particularly easy to use (depending on the task) and lacks an on-line tutorial and context-sensitive help.

PushButton Works' word processor is capable of creating most basic documents and includes 15 templates to get you started. The word processor includes features for wrapping text around inserted objects and the creation of custom text styles, but lacks outlining, envelope printing, and multi-column formatting features. The spreadsheet module can format cells in a variety of ways and offers approximately 50 functions, several of which are selectable from a toolbar. Simple charting is also available.

166

The flat-file database module enables you to handle many types of data. However, while the database supports simple queries using operators such as Greater Than and Equal To, searching for data entries is not an intuitive process. Finally, the limited graphics module features several drawing tools, but is used mainly for charting tasks. PushButton Works includes no communications module, nor does it provide direct access to Windows' Terminal applet. Still, although PushButton Works boasts limited features, it's well worth the low price.

Graphics Programs

In the early days of their existence, home computers displayed only text. Any graphics that appeared were really just characters in the computer's text character set. These days, however, computers are capable of displaying photographic-quality images in millions of colors. With all that graphical power under the hood, it's not unreasonable that you should add some sort of graphics program to your software arsenal. The type of program you choose depends, of course, on what graphical tasks you want to perform. The programs reviewed in this section will give you a good idea of what's available.

There are two basic kinds of graphics programs: drawing and painting. They create different kinds of images, so it's important to know which kind you want. A paint program gives you an on-screen "canvas" made up of thousands of little dots. You can change the color of each dot with the tools of the program, creating a picture. A draw program creates lines and shapes with the same types of tools, but it keeps track of the shapes as mathematical equations instead of as dots. These equations make it much easier to modify and resize the image in a drawing program without distorting the image. This is sometimes referred to as "object-oriented" graphics.

If you want to work with scanned images or photographs, or if you have children and want a program they can play with, a paint program is best. If you want to make technical drawings that may need to be resized, go with a draw program.

PC Paintbrush

Manufacturer: Softkey International
Platforms: Windows, DOS
System requirements:
    Windows—VGA or better graphics
    DOS—DOS 3.0 or later, hard disk
Price range: $$

The DOS version of PC Paintbrush was one of the first paint programs ever released for IBM-compatible computers. In fact, it was PC Paintbrush that first used the .PCX picture-file format, which has now become a standard. The Windows version of PC Paintbrush follows in its predecessor's footsteps, providing a top-quality, yet reasonably priced, graphics program for Windows.

PC Paintbrush features a toolbox chock full of useful graphics tools, including not only the usual collection of shapes and lines, but also tools that simulate real-world objects like crayons, pens, colored pencils, charcoal, paint brushes, and chalk. In addition, the clone tool paints one area of a picture with the pixels found in another area, the tint tool changes the colors of a small area of a picture, and various types of erasers do everything from bleaching an area to erasing it completely.

As if that weren't enough, you can apply various special effects to your pictures. For example, you can make a picture look like a mosaic, an embossed surface, or a motion blur. Other special effects include Crumple, Crystallize, Fisheye Lens, Sharpen, Outline, Twist, and Pixelate. You can also transform a picture in various ways, changing its contrast, brightness, orientation, or size. For the price, PC Paintbrush is an amazing value.

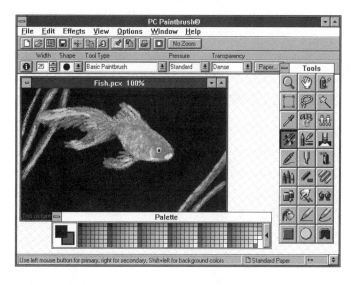

PC Paintbrush for Windows

Fractal Design Painter

Manufacturer: Fractal Design Corp.
Platforms: Windows, Macintosh
System requirements:
   Windows—386 or better, 4 MB RAM, 256-color VGA graphics
   Mac—Mac II or better
Price range: $$$$

Fractal Design Painter is one of the most unusual paint programs available. Although it lets you draw using the typical drawing tools found in most paint programs, that's only the tip of the iceberg. Fractal Design Painter contains many paint tools (like colored pencils, pens, watercolors, chalk, and charcoal) whose drawing on the screen looks almost exactly like their real-world counterparts. In addition, you can draw on many different paper grains, which also affects how images look. In short, Fractal Design Painter uses your computer to simulate actual artists tools.

After drawing an image, you can apply various special effects. For example, color overlays tint and texture an image, and lighting effects create highlights and shadows. You can also easily modify an image's contrast, brightness, and tone. You can even distort images or flip-flop them in any direction you like. The soften effect gives images a fuzzy look, or you can add blobs, which are miniature bubbles formed from the picture's main image. There are many other effects available, too.

Fractal Design Painter

Unfortunately, as one of the most fascinating paint programs you're likely to find, Fractal Design Painter comes with a hefty price tag. If you can afford the price of admission, you'll have one of the best paint programs you can buy.

CorelDRAW!

Manufacturer: Corel Systems Corporation
Platform: Windows
System requirements: 386 or better, 8MB RAM, VGA or better graphics
Price range: $$ to $$$$$ (depending on version)

CorelDRAW! 3.0 was the state-of-the-art drawing program several years ago. It's still a great package—so great that version 3.0 is still being sold, even though CorelDRAW! 4.0 has been released and contains still more features and power. By the time this book reaches the stores, CorelDRAW! 5.0 will be out, once again raising the stakes.

Because there are three version numbers on the market, the oldest of the three, CorelDRAW! 3.0, is being sold very cheaply. Therefore, home users who ordinarily would not be able to afford a powerful graphics package can own CorelDRAW! 3.0 for less than $200. This makes CorelDRAW! 3.0 one of the best deals around.

What do you get for your money? For tough graphics tasks, CorelDRAW! offers a complete range of power functions, from standard drawing tools all the way up to some sophisticated desktop-publishing features. With CorelDRAW!, you can do everything from generate a new company logo to design a simple brochure. In addition, CorelDRAW! can generate complex curves, fills, and special effects.

CorelDRAW! also comes with a suite of accessory programs, including CorelPHOTOPAINT (a paint program that complements the drawing features in CorelDRAW!), plus a screen capture program, a tracing program (which turns "paint" images into "draw" images), and several other handy tools. The strongest of the group is PHOTOPAINT, which looks and acts like many of the expensive paint programs sold as stand-alone products.

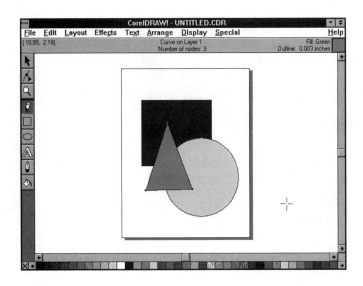

CorelDRAW!

Doodle-mation

Manufacturer: ScreenMagic, Inc.
Platforms: Windows, Macintosh
System requirements:
    Windows—386 or better, VGA or better graphics
    Mac—Classic or better, System 7.0
Price range: $

Doodle-mation is probably one of the most unusual graphics programs ever written. Except possibly for its ability to create screen savers, this combination graphics and animation program is really little more than a good time. But don't let its lack of seriousness stop you from dipping in. Doodle-mation will have your creative juices flowing as you create one awesome graphical animation after another.

Basically, the idea is to choose a shape and then tell it how to move around the screen and multiply itself. Of course, you have complete control over how the shape duplicates, grows, and rotates, as well as how fast it moves and how it changes colors. Other options include bounce paths, rainbow colors, fill colors, video controls (start, pause, and stop), and sound. When you create an animation worth viewing again, you can save it to disk—or you can even install it as a Windows screen saver or wallpaper.

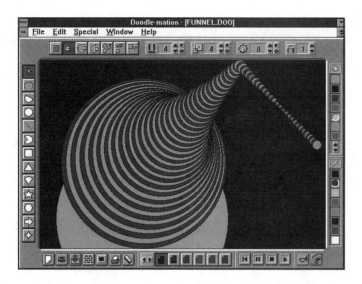

Doodle-mation

Visio

Manufacturer: Shapeware
Platforms: Windows (Macintosh forthcoming)
System requirements: 386 or better, 4MB RAM, VGA or better graphics
Price range: $$ to $$$ (depending on version)

Visio is a drawing program that enables you to create drawings by dragging and dropping predefined shapes onto a drawing window. By clicking on the shapes' connection points, you can connect them into various types of charts. For this reason, Visio is perfect for constructing network charts, organizational diagrams, flowcharts, and other types of displays that you can draw using the drag-and-drop method.

Visio's shapes are stored in stencils that you load and display on the screen. The stencils that come with the program include Block Diagram, Border, Connector, Electrical, European Map, Flowchart, Network, Space Planning, and more. You can combine shapes from any number of stencils on a single drawing, and, because the shapes know how to draw themselves, they can be resized and moved easily with a mouse.

Visio can also organize shapes in a drawing in various ways. The snap-to-grid option, for example, helps keep shapes lined up, whereas other options can center shapes, equally space groups of shapes, and align shapes. If you can't find the shapes you want, you can create your own by defining the rules that tell a shape how to act. Most importantly, Visio is so easy to use, you'll hardly need to look at the manual. In addition, a six-minute, on-line tutorial shows you the ins and outs of drag-and-drop graphics the first time you run the program.

Several versions of Visio are available; home users will probably get the most use from Visio Home, which provides specialized palettes of shapes for home design.

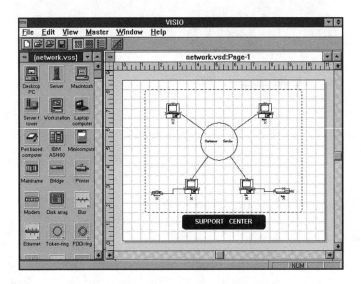

Visio 2.0

Home and Landscape Design

There are many specialized drawing programs that enable you to draw up your own home and yard plans. Some can even be used to design businesses! Visio, which we just looked at, comes with several groups of landscaping and home-design shape palettes, but it is also good for making organizational charts and flowcharts. The programs in the Home and Landscape Design category focus solely on helping you plan the space around you.

3D Home Architect

Manufacturer: Broderbund
Platform: Windows
System requirements: 386 or better, 4MB RAM, VGA graphics
Price range: $$

3D Home Architect is a versatile home-design program that can help you do anything from adding a room to your existing home to building a new mansion in the south of France. Creating your plans is a snap. Simply open a new window and start dragging objects from the palette, which includes not only standard objects like walls, windows, stairs, and doors, but also a full selection of appliances and furniture.

Having so many objects at your beck and call makes it easy to create perfect plans. For example, after designing your on-screen kitchen, you can fill it with a table and chairs, cabinets, sinks, a stove, a refrigerator, and other kitchen-type things. Not enough room between the table and the stove? Looks like you'll have to make the kitchen a little bigger. Furnishing your rooms in this way gives you a better sense of space.

After you've got plans drawn, you can view your work either as a traditional two-dimensional drawing or as a fully realized three-dimensional object that you can view from any angle. You can even zoom yourself through a door and into a room to see how different areas will look when completed. When the design is just the way you want it, 3D Home Architect can generate a list of materials so you know exactly what you need to build the project. If the idea of designing an entire house intimidates you, you can just modify one of the 30 beautiful house plans included with the program.

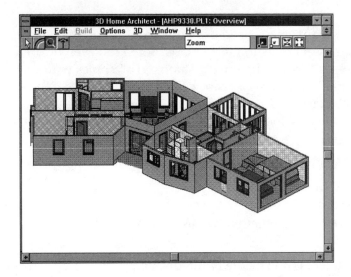

3D Home Architect

Autodesk Home
Autodesk Deck
Autodesk Kitchen & Bath

Manufacturer: Autodesk
Platform: DOS
System requirements: DOS 3.0 or later, hard drive, mouse
Price range: $$

For folks who like to dig in deep when it comes to home design, Autodesk has a series of products that take the detailed and complicated CAD (computer-aided design) approach to designing plans. With Home, Deck, and Kitchen &

Bath, you don't create your plans by simple dragging and dropping functions. Instead, you draw plans much like a blueprint. Boasting accuracies within 1/16 of an inch, the Autodesk design programs are probably more appropriate for professional designers.

Although the majority of your plan is drawn, these programs do include drag-and-drop symbols for such objects as furniture, appliances, doors, windows, and other odds and ends you need to fill out your design. In addition, you can view your design as either a 2D flat image or a 3D image that you can view from different angles. But unless you have a fairly good computer (at least a fast 386 with a math coprocessor), you can expect to do a lot of waiting while the program calculates and draws 3D images. Even something as simple as a color change can stall the program for a minute or two.

Once your plans are complete, the Autodesk programs, like many of the home design programs, produce a complete shopping list that you can take with you (along with your wallet) to the building supply store. You can also print your plans, of course, in both the 2D and 3D views. Finally, CAD experts will appreciate the programs' capability to export data so that it can be loaded into other CAD programs.

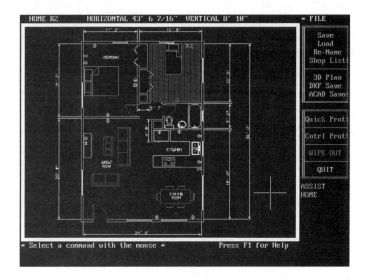

Autodesk Home

Interiors
Landscape
Kitchen & Bath

Manufacturer: Synergistic Software
Platform: DOS
System requirements: 386 or better, DOS 5.0 or later, 2MB RAM,
    VGA graphics, hard disk
Price range: $

If you're looking to spruce up your house or yard, one of these three programs can help you organize your plans by enabling you to create rooms and landscapes right on your computer screen. The first program, Interiors, provides the tools you need to design a room for your home. Using simple drag-and-drop procedures, you add windows, doors, staircases, and furniture to your developing room. You can even change the colors of any of over 450 different objects included in the program, as well as look at the room from different angles.

The Kitchen & Bath program is very similar to Interiors, except it concentrates on—guess what—the kitchen and bathrooms. As with Interiors, you create your room by using your mouse to drag objects into place. The more than 300 objects included with the program include everything from tables and chairs to stoves, refrigerators, sinks, tubs, cabinets of various styles, and much more. After you've sized the room and filled it with objects, you can try different colors and floor designs in order to find the best combination.

The last program in the group, Landscape, does for the outside of your house, what Interiors and Kitchen & Bath do for the inside. With this program, you can design the perfect surroundings for your home, selecting from over 400 objects like trees, bushes, patio furniture, flowers, fences, decks, and fountains. You can even add a hot tub or swimming pool. Want to see what your new yard will look like in the fall? Just change the season in the Seasons menu.

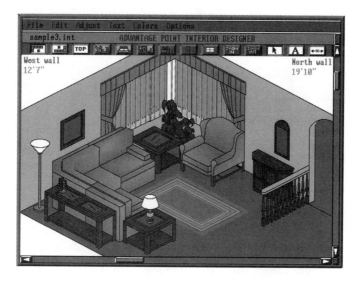

Interiors

Key Home Designer

Manufacturer: Softkey
Platform: Windows
System requirements: 386 or better, 256-color VGA graphics, CD-ROM, sound board
Price range: $

Key Home Designer is actually two programs in one. Before you start designing your own home, the main program takes you through the basics of home design, giving you an overview of why architects make the decisions they make. You'll learn about choosing materials, using space, fitting a home in with its environment, and other topics, all while touring the designs of actual homes and listening to real-voice narration.

Key Home Designer also features a special tutorial on designing kitchens and bathrooms. In this section of the program, you learn many details you need to know to make your designs a success. Although the multimedia aspect of the program is limited, including only sporadic narrations, the photographs and sample plans offer many ideas from which you can work when you get started on your own designs.

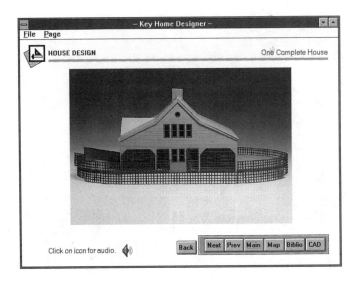

Key Home Designer

Once you know a little about home design, you can crank up Key Home CAD, which is a CAD (computer-aided design) program with which you can create your dream house. First you use the program's tools to draw the basic plan, including walls, windows, doors, and other objects. Then you can load one of the many included libraries from which you can add objects like furniture, appliances, sinks, and cabinets to your design. Key Home CAD is a nicely engineered CAD program but, unlike some of the other home-design programs, it cannot display the final plan as a 3D image, nor can it generate a materials shopping list.

Expert Landscape

Manufacturer: Expert Software
Platforms: Windows, DOS, Macintosh
System requirements:
    Windows—386 or better, 4MB RAM, VGA or better graphics
    DOS—DOS 3.0 or later, 286 or better, EGA or better graphics, hard disk
    Mac—Minimum
Price range: $

Creating the perfect landscape plan is just a matter of dragging and dropping with Expert Landscape. The program includes over 200 resizable landscape objects (trees, plants, pools, fences, decks, furniture, and more) that you can use in your landscape plan. Using a full set of graphical tools, you can easily draw special items not included in the object libraries.

Expert Landscape lets you view your landscape at any of four scale settings, and you can zoom in and out at will. In addition, you can examine your design using the side elevation view or the top view. The on-screen grid and measurement display ensures that objects are placed exactly where you want them.

Thanks to Expert Landscape's many tools, you can manipulate objects in a number of ways, rotating, flipping, and grouping them with ease. Once you're finished with your design, Expert Landscape features a Material Estimate window that you can use to produce a detailed materials list showing prices and quantities of all the items in your plan.

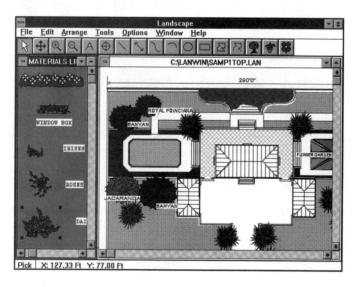

Expert Landscape

Desktop Publishing Programs

Desktop publishing (DTP) programs help you create your own text-and-graphics masterpieces. True, you can combine text and graphics with most word processing programs, but DTP programs are specially designed to do it, and offer extra features.

Some high-end desktop publishing programs are super word-processors—they enable you not only to enter and edit text, but also to design sophisticated documents like brochures, catalogs, and even full-length books (depending on the program). There are also some inexpensive general-purpose DTP programs that produce results comparable to the fancy, high-priced DTP programs. (We're not covering any of the top-of-the-line DTP programs here because they're overkill for a home user's basic needs.)

Other DTP programs are more specialized, giving you tools specifically designed for banners, greeting cards, signs, and other graphics-oriented projects. Such programs are lots of fun for the whole family, and they make a nice supplement to your word processing program. In this section, we will also review a couple of clip art packages, which provide ready-made art you can insert into most DTP programs.

Microsoft Publisher

Manufacturer: Microsoft Corp.
Platform: Windows
System requirements: 286 or better, 4MB RAM, VGA or better graphics
Price range: $$

Microsoft Publisher is one of those rare applications that can please both novices and professionals. Microsoft's Page Wizards are one reason it's so easy to create documents with Microsoft Publisher. These automated templates, which guide you step by step through the document creation process, enable you to quickly assemble a basic document design by answering a few questions. Once the basic document is created, you can customize it any way you like.

In addition to the 17 Page Wizards, Microsoft Publisher ships with 35 templates for common documents, making it easy to create anything from an invitation to a newsletter. Just load a template and then modify it to your needs. Using Microsoft Publisher's text and graphics tools, you can quickly add lines, borders, and other shapes to the page. You can even add shadows and patterns to areas of your document, as well as create bulleted or numbered lists.

Publisher's other capabilities include text-wrapping around graphics, creating fancy logos, importing graphics, creating custom styles, resizing graphics, automatic kerning (controlling the space between letters), checking spelling, and much more. Although Microsoft Publisher can't handle long documents, it's the perfect program for casual publishing needs.

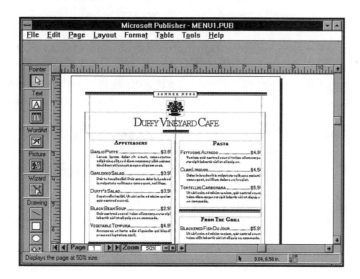

Microsoft Publisher

Publish It!

Manufacturer: Timeworks International
Platforms: Windows, DOS, Macintosh
System requirements:
  Windows—Minimum
  DOS—EGA graphics, hard drive
  Mac—Minimum
Price range: $$

Novice desktop publishers who don't want to get buried in a feature avalanche—and don't want to empty their wallets for the privilege—might want to take a look at Publish It!, which contains many powerful DTP tools, yet remains basically easy to use. Publish It!'s low price tag, however, means you'll have to do without some amenities, such as automated tasks like Microsoft Publisher's Wizards or even an on-line tutorial.

Some advanced features you'll find in Publish It! include the capability to import graphics (although color graphics are converted to black and white), and the use of master pages for repeating text and graphic elements on every page, text frames that can flow around graphical images, and PowerText for creating special text effects. In addition, the program's toolbar provides quick access to many program features, such as the built-in spell checker and thesaurus, and gives you convenient access to various formatting commands.

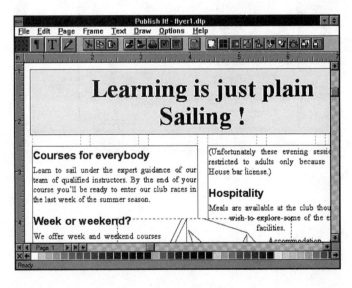

Publish It! for Windows

Although Publish It! doesn't have an on-line tutorial, the manual features a quick-start tutorial that will get most people up and running in an hour or two. Moreover, the manual's reference section provides clear instruction for all the program's features. However, you may find that some tasks (such as creating tables or applying paragraph styles) can be a bit clumsy. For this reason, experienced DTP folks will probably want a more powerful program; this one is for novices only.

PFS:Publisher

Manufacturer: Spinnaker
Platform: Windows
System requirements: Minimum
Price range: $$

When you set out to purchase a desktop publishing program, you may be stunned by the cost, which can reach street prices of well over $500 depending upon which program you run into first. Luckily, there are some cheap yet reliable packages—like PFS:Publisher. Although PFS:Publisher can't compete with the big boys (such as PageMaker or even Microsoft Publisher), its simple tools and easy-to-handle interface make it just about right for anyone jumping into DTP for the first time.

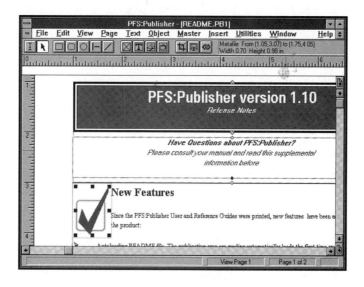

PFS:Publisher

Creating a document can be as easy as choosing a template from the thumbnail browser, putting text and graphic frames into place, and then filling those frames with words and pictures. When it comes to the text, you can compose it from within PFS:Publisher (and use the built-in spelling checker and thesaurus) or you can bring the text in from disk, including files created by Word for Windows, Ami Pro, WordPerfect, and WordStar. When it comes to text effects and drawing tools, PFS:Publisher supplies only the minimum. It's also lacking some helpful features like undo and object alignment.

Still, PFS:Publisher does boast some advanced features like automatic index (or table of contents) generation, master pages (pages containing objects that should appear on every page of the document), text wrap around nonrectangular objects, and the use of Windows' OLE (object linking and embedding) mechanism to add to a document objects created by other applications. This is a competent package for a budget price and just may be the best of the low-end DTP programs.

The Print Shop Deluxe

Manufacturer: Broderbund Software
Platforms: Windows, DOS, Macintosh
System requirements:
   Windows—286 or better, 4MB RAM, VGA or better graphics
   DOS—DOS 3.0 or later, 386 or better, 1MB RAM, VGA or better graphics, hard drive
   Mac—System 7
Price range: $

The Print Shop is one of the best-selling computer programs of all time, and when you consider how easy and fun it is to use, its success is not surprising. Using this scaled-down desktop publishing program, you can easily produce professional-looking greeting cards, banners, signs, calendars, and more. The Print Shop comes packed with everything you need, from a large graphics library to a supply of paper and envelopes.

Because most people aren't professional graphic artists, The Print Shop lets you design documents by piecing together various predesigned elements. For example, you first select a project type: greeting card, letterhead, sign, calendar, or banner. You then can add backgrounds, titles, text, borders, and other objects by selecting them from lists. At each step, The Print Shop shows you what your project looks like so far.

Because attractive layouts are so important to a well-designed document, The Print Shop offers dozens of ready-to-go designs that you can use by simply adding your choice of text and graphics. However, you can also take off on your own and change a design to suit any need that might arise. Although The Print Shop can't handle large projects like books or fancy pamphlets, for everyday use, it's one of the finest programs of its type.

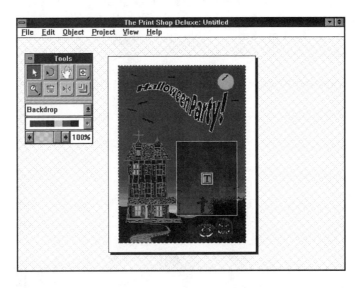

The Print Shop Deluxe

BannerMania

Manufacturer: Broderbund Software
Platforms: DOS, Macintosh
System requirements:
   DOS—Minimum
   Mac—Minimum
Price range: $

Coupled with your creativity, BannerMania can create some truly dazzling banners. Whether you want to advertise a garage sale or decorate for a party, you can choose from dozens of different fonts, shapes, and special effects to create the perfect banner for your occasion. Or, if you want to get the job done ultra-fast, you can choose a design from the forty ready-made banners and print it out immediately. Depending on the type of printer you have, BannerMania can produce banners in black and white or in full color.

If you decide to design your own banner, you select the layout, type a message, select a font, apply any special effects you'd like, add color, choose a shape, and then print. When the printing's done, just piece the pages together (if necessary), and you're done. The whole process is fast and fun.

Although Broderbund's premiere product, Print Shop, can also create banners, BannerMania costs significantly less since it doesn't do greeting cards, signs, calendars, and other types of printed objects. So if you're not interested in that other stuff, BannerMania will keep your printer busy for what almost amounts to pocket change.

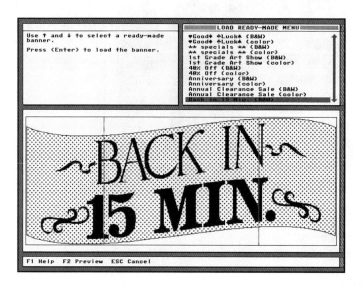

BannerMania

ClickArt: Incredible Image Pak 2000

Manufacturer: T/Maker
Platforms: Windows, DOS, Macintosh
System requirements:
   Windows—Minimum
   DOS—286 or better, hard disk
   Mac—MAC SE or better, System 7.0 or later
Price range: $$$ ($$$$ for DOS)

Desktop Publishing programs can create fancy documents, but to get that professional look, you need the correct tools. One of those tools is a good selection of clip art. The Incredible Image Pak contains over 2,000 pieces of clip art—in such categories as animals, arrows, holidays, fitness, foods, clothes, and business—that can spruce up your documents with that professional graphics look.

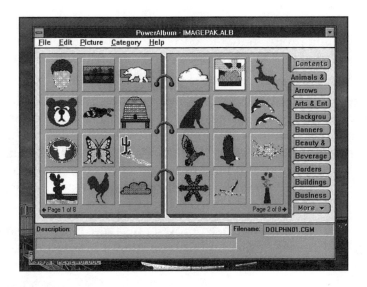

Incredible Image Pak 2000

Along with the clip art images, the Incredible Image Pak also includes 40 fonts that you can add to your desktop publishing system. In addition, the image browser presents thumbnail images of all the clip art, enabling you to easily find exactly the right image for your current project. Also, because different desktop publishing systems require clip art images in different file formats, the Incredible Image Pak comes packed with a program that can convert images from one file format to another. Finally, because the type of paper you choose for a DTP project is as important as any other element, the Incredible Image Pak provides a 25-sheet paper sampler.

If you're serious about desktop publishing, you can never have enough clip art. But with 2,000 images, the Incredible Image Pak comes pretty darn close to providing everything you need.

Presentation Task Force

Manufacturer: T/Maker
Platforms: Windows, DOS, OS/2
System requirements:
   Windows—Minimum
   DOS—Minimum
   OS/2—Minimum
Price range: $$

Presentation Task Force is a huge collection of clip art you can use in any desktop publishing program that imports .CGM (color graphics metafile) format pictures (that includes Microsoft Publisher and Publish It!). Presentation Task Force includes 3500 images to choose from.

The strength of this clip art package is its versatility. The installation program lets you pick which types of images you want to install, so you don't have to clog your hard disk with images you will never use. You can also pick whether you want the images installed in color, grayscale, or black-and-white format, based on whichever you use the most. (If you don't have a color printer, there's no point in installing color clip art.) A wide variety of images, from businesspeople to animals, is included in this package.

There is no friendly Windows-based browser (as there is with the Incredible Image Pak), but in terms of sheer number of images available, Presentation Task Force is the winner.

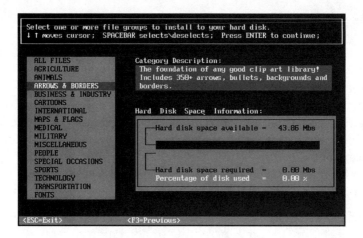

Presentation Task Force (Installation program)

PhotoLibrary

Manufacturer: Softkey International
Platforms: Windows, Macintosh
System requirements:
   Windows—386 or better, 4MB RAM, 256-color VGA or better
   graphics, CD-ROM drive
   Mac—Macintosh Classic or better, 4MB RAM, CD-ROM drive
Price range: $$

Thanks to today's high-resolution graphics, most computers can now display photographic-quality images. Such images can be used in desktop publishing or for presentations, or can just be added to your collection of Windows wallpaper for desktop backgrounds. Whatever you use digitized photos for, PhotoLibrary is likely to have exactly the photo you want. You do, after all, have 2,500 photos in almost 100 categories from which to choose!

Whereas the ClickArt 2000 Incredible Image Pak provides scalable, object-oriented drawings, PhotoLibrary provides "paint" type images. They don't resize very well, but they are as clear and sharp as photographs in their original size.

PhotoLibrary

The two CD-ROMs included with PhotoLibrary are compatible with either a DOS or Macintosh machine, with the photos saved in .TIFF and .BMP file formats. Finding a particular photo is easier than rolling a ball downhill thanks to the included PowerAlbum application, which enables you to look through thumbnail representations of the pictures. You can also use PowerAlbum to put together your own collections of photos.

Communications Programs

These days computers talk to each other over the phone lines almost as much as humans do. In order for your computer to do this, you need a *communications program*, which not only connects you to another computer, but also allows you to transfer data back and forth between machines.

The most common use for a communications program is to connect with commercial on-line services like CompuServe, GEnie, or Delphi. (Some on-line services, such as Prodigy and America Online, provide their own software.) Another use for a communications program is to connect to a friend's computer and chat with him by typing on your keyboard. (Sure, calling is easier—but it's not as much fun.) With a communications program, you can also call bulletin board services or BBSs, which are like small privately owned on-line services within your community.

Communications programs vary in the options they provide. The ones reviewed here are all pretty much full featured. However, there are simpler ones (such as Terminal, which comes with Windows 3.x) available as part of other programs. Many integrated packages also come with a communications program.

White Knight

Manufacturer: The Freesoft Company
Platform: Macintosh
System requirements: Minimum
Price range: $$

White Knight, formerly known as Red Ryder, is one of the most popular communications programs for Macintosh owners. This program supports all the usual features found in communications programs, including the capability to capture incoming text to a file, to send or receive files using any of a full set of file-transfer protocols, and to use "phonebooks" for quick logons to on-line services and BBSs.

White Knight also offers many high-end features. For example, the BASIC-like script language includes over 200 commands that you can use to automate your on-line sessions. For those who are shy of programming, White Knight can automatically generate simple scripts by recording activities as you work. In addition, the screen buffer lets you read text that has already scrolled out of view, and the on-screen display keeps you posted on how much time you've spent on-line and how much that time is going to cost you.

Because White Knight works with all modems (as long as they're connected to a Mac), you're unlikely to have installation or hardware problems. And to keep your modem hopping at its highest rate, White Knight can handle data speeds up to 57,600 baud. Moreover, the 30 user-definable macro keys ensure that you can perform common tasks requiring multiple actions with just a press of a key or a click of your mouse. In short, White Knight offers a complete set of communications features for a reasonable price.

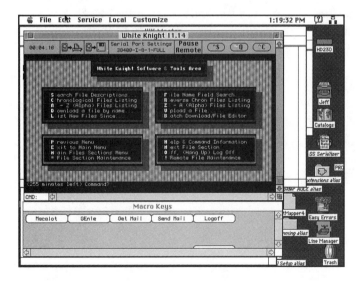

White Knight

PROCOMM PLUS

Manufacturer: Datastorm Technologies, Inc.
Platforms: Windows, DOS
System requirements:
   Windows—Minimum
   DOS—Minimum
Price range: $$$ ($$ for DOS)

When it comes to telecommunications programs for IBM compatibles, PROCOMM PLUS is a long-time favorite. This program provides a complete set of file-transfer protocols (including Xmodem, Ymodem, Zmodem, and CompuServe B+), as well as a comprehensive C-like script language for those who don't mind programming. And, like many other communications programs, PROCOMM can generate scripts automatically by watching the actions you take during an on-line session.

The program is so easy to install that you will be logging on to your first service (which will probably be Datastorm's automatic on-line registration) in a few minutes. Still, in spite of its easy startup, the program is rich with advanced features like macros that can be assigned to on-screen buttons, a fully implemented dial directory, the capability to look back to previous screens of text, and over thirty different terminal emulations.

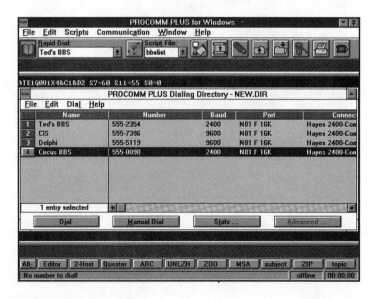

PROCOMM PLUS for Windows

Unfortunately, although the script language is impressive, PROCOMM PLUS doesn't come with many ready-to-run scripts for popular on-line services. In fact, the only one included is for MCI mail. Still, generating basic scripts is easy enough, and, when you consider the reasonable price, PROCOMM PLUS is a real bargain.

QmodemPro

Manufacturer: Mustang Software Inc.
Platforms: Windows, DOS
System requirements:
    Windows—386 or better
    DOS—Minimum
Price range: $$

When it comes time to jump on-line with your computer, you have a lot of communications software packages from which to choose. One you might consider is QmodemPro. QmodemPro's DOS version built up a faithful following thanks to its ease of use and comprehensive features. QmodemPro for Windows now builds upon its DOS cousin's reputation by supplying fax support and a scripting language similar to BASIC.

QmodemPro for Windows

QmodemPro can handle most of the popular file-transfer protocols, including Xmodem, Kermit, CompuServe B+, and Zmodem. In addition, a built-in .GIF file viewer displays picture files as they're downloaded. QmodemPro is also one of the first programs to support RIP (Remote Imaging Protocol) for viewing graphical screens on BBSs that support them.

The program's script language draws upon the popular BASIC programming language, enabling you to write your own log-on scripts (automated tasks for logging onto a system) and other automated functions using a familiar syntax (familiar, that is, if you know BASIC programming). If you're not into writing your own log-on scripts, QmodemPro can make its own by recording your log-on process. One of the most inexpensive Windows communications programs, QmodemPro will get you on-line quickly and easily.

Crosstalk

Manufacturer: Digital Communications Associates
Platforms: Windows, DOS, Macintosh
System requirements:
    Windows—Minimum
    DOS—286 or better, hard disk
    Mac—MAC SE or better, System 7.0 or later
Price range: $$$ ($$$$ for DOS)

If you want a communications program that you can grow into, Crosstalk may be a terrific choice. Getting started with Crosstalk is a speedy and almost automatic process. But once you get used to the basics, there are a lot of goodies to dip into. In fact, Crosstalk turns out to be the power-user's choice, thanks mostly to its immense scripting language and its wide assortment of transfer protocols.

One of Crosstalk's dandiest features is its QuickPads, which are button bars customized for specific on-line services. When you load the configuration for a particular on-line service, the button bar changes appropriately, creating a custom interface for the service. Other power features include dialing queues that dial a list of numbers until a connection is made, and the ability to hold 256 pages of data in the scrollback buffer. For folks just starting out, Crosstalk comes with pre-written scripts for the major on-line services.

In reality, Crosstalk offers more features than many users will ever need. And all those features come with a price, both in the cost of the software and in the Windows resources the program consumes. If you have modest communications needs, Crosstalk may be more than you need. But if you want to start out with one of the best, Crosstalk is an excellent choice.

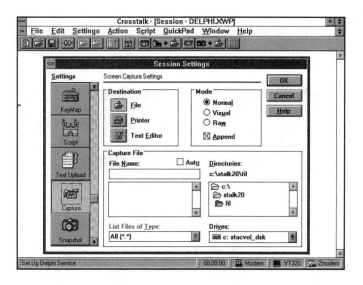

Crosstalk for Windows

WinFax PRO

Manufacturer: Delrina Corp.
Platform: Windows
System requirements: 386 or better, 4MB RAM
Price range: $$

The other communications programs reviewed in this book connect you to remote computers. WinFax PRO, on the other hand, takes the place of a fax machine, letting you send or receive fax documents on your computer. WinFax PRO also features a number of extra fax enhancements—such as the capability to convert faxes to word-processor files or to create your own cover pages—that make it one of the most complete fax packages available.

WinFax PRO's phonebook keeps tabs on all your fax contacts and enables you to just click on a number to dial. In addition, you can send a fax to a whole group of people at once, as well as attach a group of documents from different applications to be faxed all at once. You can even schedule your fax sessions at low-rate times in order to save money.

You can receive faxes in several ways: directly to your printer, to disk, or on the screen. WinFax notifies you of incoming faxes and can even automatically forward those faxes to other fax machines. Finally, WinFax comes packed with over 100 ready-to-use fax cover sheets, everything from serious business to whimsy. All in all, you can be sure that WinFax PRO can handle almost all your faxing needs.

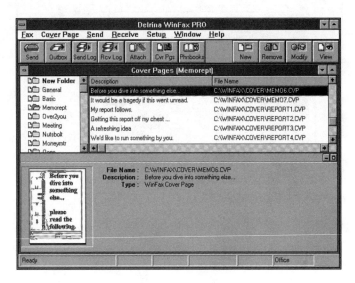

WinFax PRO

Personal Information Managers

Y ou don't have to have a business to have a busy schedule. Even in a
small family, there is a huge amount of information you must organize, including phone calls that need to be made, errands that must be
run, and events to go to (preferably on time!). Trying to keep track of all this
information in a regular notebook can be an almost impossible task.

That's where personal information managers (PIMs) come in. A PIM provides
you with all the computer tools you need to keep track of your family or
business activities. While most PIMs are designed primarily for business use,
you can adapt them easily for home use too. They provide modules for recording important reference information, printing to-do lists, and generating
graphical calendars that you can tack up to remind everyone of his schedule.

What Are You Doing Today, Charlie Brown?

Manufacturer: Individual Software Inc.
Platforms: Windows, DOS, Macintosh
System requirements:
   Windows—VGA or better graphics
   DOS—286 or better, DOS 3.3 or later, VGA or better graphics
   Mac—Mac SE or better
Price range: $

For those who don't take their daily planning too seriously, Individual Software offers What Are You Doing Today, Charlie Brown?, a very simple PIM
with humor. This program offers a daily planner, a to-do list, and a calendar,
but lacks other modules (such as a phonebook) found in more expensive
PIMs. However, it does provide a large collection of Peanuts cartoons.

While this program probably isn't suitable for business use, all the folks in your home can get their lives in order, by taking advantage of Charlie Brown's simple calendars to record appointments, tasks, special days, and other items they want to remember. To get an overview of upcoming events, the calendar can show daily, weekly, monthly, and even yearly views. In addition, you can view or print events by the group. For example, you might want to produce a sheet showing all the upcoming music lessons, complete with a Peanuts cartoon at the bottom.

What Are You Doing Today, Charlie Brown?

Lotus Organizer

Manufacturer: Lotus Development Corp.
Platform: Windows
System requirements: VGA or better graphics
Price range: $$

Lotus Organizer is one of the nicer of the middle-priced PIMs, offering a lot of options under a simple and elegant interface. In fact, Organizer's notebook metaphor is almost as intuitive to use as a real old-fashioned organizer. But its simplicity belies a wealth of powerful features, such as the capability to cross-reference information between sections, import data from other sources, and search for specific periods of free time.

Organizer features a "fold-out" appointment scheduler and notepad, as well as a full-featured button bar across the top and a toolbar on the left. You can drag-and-drop an item between text fields or into the trash can, where the item bursts into flames and burns away. Adding appointments, events, and tasks is as simple as clicking on the appropriate notebook page and filling in the dialog box that appears.

The sections included in the notebook are Calendar, ToDo, Address, Notepad, Planner, and Anniversary. To switch from one section to another, simply click on the notebook's labeled tabs. In this way, you can quickly find the information you need, without having to fiddle with menus or other hidden commands.

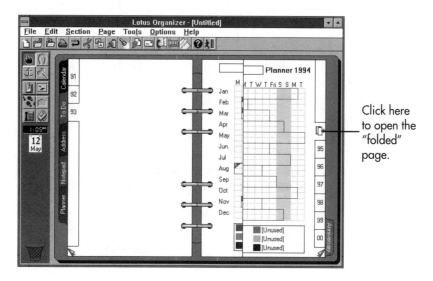

Lotus Organizer 1.1

AnyTime

Manufacturer: Individual Software
Platforms: Windows, DOS
System requirements:
   Windows—Minimum
   DOS—hard disk
Price range: $

Like Lotus Organizer, AnyTime uses a notebook metaphor that makes the program easy to use right out of the box. If you're at all familiar with Windows software, you probably won't even need to read the manual to get started. Included in the package is a calendar, day planner, and address book. The calendar can be viewed as a daily, weekly, or yearly display, showing appointments and tasks in various ways—as text or graphics—depending on the view.

If you're not familiar with Windows applications and how they work, you can get immediate help by running the on-line Quick Tour to get a brief overview of the program. (Complete on-line help is also available.) Once you get started, you'll discover that entering appointments and tasks is as easy as clicking on the notebook and typing your entry. You can even assign priority levels to tasks, add alarms to appointments, or attach notes to Day Planner entries.

Whereas you can find many PIMs that do more than AnyTime, you're not likely to find many that are as easy to use or for such a low price. Also, AnyTime doesn't gobble up huge amounts of disk space (it requires only 3MB), so you can save plenty of space for other applications. If you don't require a lot of fancy functions, AnyTime is an excellent choice for a personal information manager.

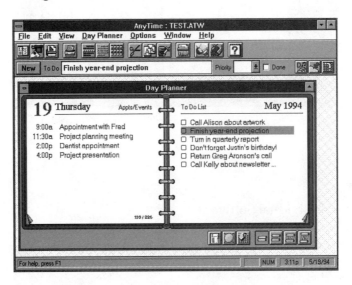

AnyTime for Windows

OnTime

Manufacturer: Campbell Services, Inc.
Platforms: Windows, DOS
System requirements:
  Windows—Minimum
  DOS—286 or better, EGA or better graphics, hard disk
Price range: $$

With OnTime, you'll never again have to worry about missing an important meeting or forgetting to complete a critical task. This electronic appointment and task manager can handle anything from displaying a day's appointments to printing calendars and sounding alarms to warn you of impending events.

OnTime's well-organized display presents your schedule by the day, week, or month, and can track your activities up to the year 2079. Recurring events need be entered only once, and OnTime fills them in for the future. Moreover, OnTime can display your time allotments graphically, so you can see at a glance what time slots are open.

Although OnTime does a fine job of handling appointments and task lists, it lacks some features of other fancier PIMs. For example, there's no provision for storing names and addresses, nor is it possible to dial a phone from within the program. Still, if you don't need these extra features, OnTime's simple and understandable approach to time management may be just right.

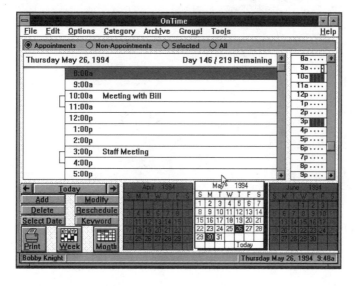

OnTime for Windows

Ecco Professional 2.0

Manufacturer: Arabesque Software
Platform: Windows
System requirements: 386 or better, VGA or better graphics
Price range: $$$ (Simplicity version $$)

Most personal information managers incorporate some sort of form-based database to keep track of meetings and appointments. Ecco, though, organizes information into outlines, much like those created in a word processor. Because of this unusual organization, Ecco may be harder to use at first than other PIMs. But the outline metaphor actually offers extra flexibility not found in software using the more conventional approach.

Because each line of an outline is a single object (such as a task, phone call, or meeting), you can easily rearrange the objects using drag-and-drop operations. More importantly, this drag-and-drop flexibility enables you to quickly cross-reference outline objects by dragging multiple copies into different folders. Then when you change the outline, all the copies change automatically. In addition, to add data to an outline item, you can create additional columns, making the outline similar to a database list display.

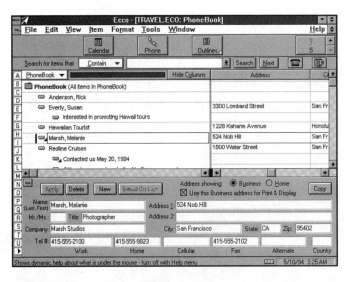

Ecco Professional 2.0

Ecco's phone book and calendar look a little like those found in other PIMs. Although the phone book is really an outline, each entry in the outline brings up a form containing the associated data. The calendar display can be viewed by the day, week, or month. Finally, Ecco's Shooter function can instantly copy information between applications. For example, you can highlight text in a word processor and then shoot it straight into your Ecco calendar without bothering with Windows' Clipboard.

Polaris Advantage

Manufacturer: Polaris Software
Platform: Windows
System requirements: 386 or better, 4MB RAM, VGA or better graphics
Price range: $$

Polaris Advantage is a complete personal information manager that includes not only the usual phone book, appointment scheduler, and task list, but also extra features like the capability to start other applications from within the program, as well as to print sheets perfectly formatted for paper-based organizers such as Franklin Day Planner, DayTimer, and DayRunner. But, in spite of its power, Advantage is surprisingly easy to use, thanks to careful organization of modules, plenty of function buttons, and tabs for switching between views.

Advantage's phone list can store all the information you need about any contact. In addition, you can schedule phone calls by dragging phonebook entries into the Contact List window. And when you make the call, you can record notes about your conversation. Advantage even keeps a log of all calls, including the time and duration of calls.

As for appointments and tasks, Advantage lets you view your schedule by the day, week, or month. You can also assign alarms to important events. As with many PIMs, Advantage enables you to check off tasks as you complete them and marks overdue tasks so they catch your attention. Finally, Advantage's Document Manager acts as a filing cabinet and organizer for important documents related to your work.

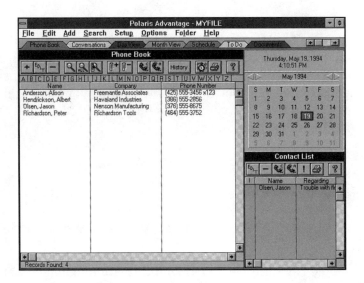

Polaris Advantage

WordPerfect InfoCentral

Manufacturer: WordPerfect Corp.
Platform: Windows
System requirements: 386 or better, 4MB RAM
Price range: $$

InfoCentral is a personal information manager (PIM) that takes the object-oriented approach to information management. That is, every item entered into the program is considered an object that can be linked to any other object. You can, for example, link a person in your employee list with the project he's working on, or you can link a document to a meeting.

The information entered into the PIM is displayed as an outline (not unlike the way Ecco, another PIM reviewed in this book, displays information) with lines connecting objects and showing how they relate to each other. In addition, notebook tabs at the bottom of the window enable you to switch between different information groups with just the click of a mouse button.

Besides all its object-oriented power, InfoCentral handles any of the other information management tasks that other PIMs do. You can record contacts, appointments, tasks, and schedules, as well as bring up a notebook-like calendar that can display information by the day, week, or year. You can even dial your phone directly from the program. And, to get you started, InfoCentral comes with four ready-to-go information bases listing top consumer product companies, software and hardware companies, world business travel information, and wines of the world.

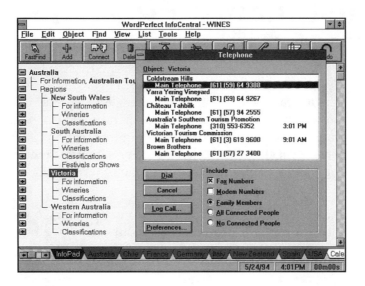

WordPerfect InfoCentral

Home Finance Programs

C omputers are fantastic number crunchers. So it should be no surprise that they are wonderfully equipped to handle your personal finances. The home finance managers reviewed in this section can do everything from balance a checkbook to track a portfolio of investments. Some even let you pay your bills by computer, relieving you of writing checks and addressing envelopes.

The home finance programs reviewed here are very similar, so you'll need to make your choices carefully. Once you read about these programs, you may even want to go down to your local computer store and get a demonstration.

Quicken

Manufacturer: Intuit Inc.
Platforms: Windows, DOS, Macintosh
System requirements:
    Windows—VGA graphics
    DOS—DOS 3.0 or later, hard drive
    Mac—Minimum
Price range: $$

When it comes to home finance programs, Quicken pretty much rules the roost. It's been around forever and has a large, loyal following. More importantly, it's one of the most powerful packages of its type, but is still easy to use. Using Quicken you can do everything from balance your electronic checkbook to pay your bills by computer and track your portfolio of investments.

Quicken handles your money by setting up various types of accounts. For example, a typical person might have one account set up for his checkbook and one for cash transactions. A more advanced user could have many more accounts, including accounts for credit cards, investments, assets, and liabilities. The accounts all work together to track the user's money. To help provide a clear picture of one's financial status, Quicken can generate many different types of reports based on the accounts that have been set up.

Of course, as with most financial software, Quicken lets you set up a list of budget categories to which you can apply your transactions. If you're careful in setting up your categories, come tax time, one quick report will list just about everything Uncle Sam wants to know. Quicken also boasts such advanced capabilities as transferring money between accounts, using the CheckFree system to pay bills electronically, printing checks, generating graphs, scheduling automatic transactions, and much more.

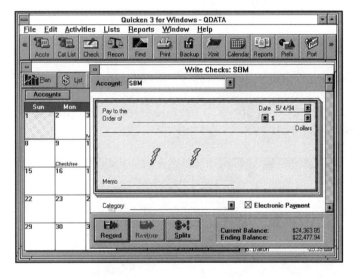

Quicken for Windows

Microsoft Money

Manufacturer: Microsoft Corp.
Platform: Windows
System requirements: VGA graphics
Price range: $

When Microsoft Money was first released, it couldn't compete with some of the biggies like Quicken. However, with the release of version 3.0, Microsoft Money has been tuned and polished until it hums like a new Rolls Royce. As long as you're working with the program's checkbook or budgeting functions, few programs are easier to use, thanks to Microsoft Money's step-by-step on-screen instructions.

Getting a handle on the program's cash, credit card, investment, asset, and liability accounts requires a bit more studying of the manual. Still, Microsoft Money is a delight to use. When you complete a transaction, for example, you hear a cash register ring. Also, the on-screen checks feature scenic backgrounds like those fancy paper checks you can buy from your bank. That's not to say that Microsoft Money doesn't take financial considerations seriously. Its financial calculators are among the best, and the program's Financial Wizards guide you step by step through such complex tasks as planning your retirement and evaluating mortgages.

Like many home finance programs, Microsoft Money lets you pay your bills electronically and download stock quotes. In addition, you can opt for on-line banking through First National of Chicago, U.S. Bank, and Michigan National Bank. Using this service, you can use your computer to retrieve up-to-date information on savings, checking, and credit card accounts, as well as to transfer funds between accounts. If on-line electronic banking is important to you, Microsoft Money may be your best buy.

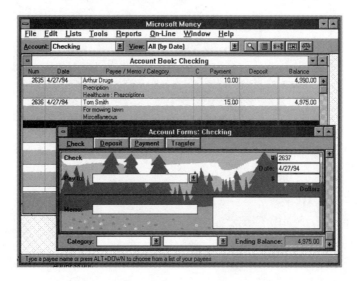

Microsoft Money

CA-Simply Money

Manufacturer: Computer Associates International Inc.
Platform: Windows
System requirements: 4MB RAM, VGA graphics
Price range: $

One of CA-Simply Money's claims to fame is its easy setup. Accounts for savings, checking, investments, and credit cards are ready to go after the program is installed, making it easy for you to get right to work organizing your finances. Moreover, CA-Simply Money's icon buttons let you perform common tasks with simple drag and drop actions. For example, to pay a credit card bill, you can just drag the appropriate button to the checkbook icon. You can even create your own buttons for specific tasks.

CA-Simply Money does more than just record your financial transactions, though. It can also provide various types of financial advice. For example, if your loan debts start getting too high in relation to your income, CA-Simply Money suggests ways to get your cash back under control. The program also provides helpful usage hints. Other little niceties include the capability to memorize repeated transactions.

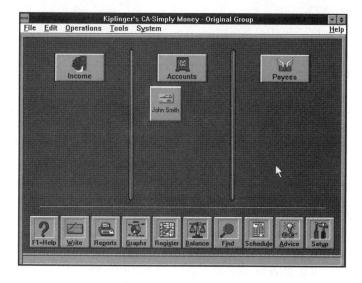

CA-Simply Money

211

When it comes to more sophisticated financial matters, however, CA-Simply Money cannot keep up with packages like Quicken. Its report capabilities, for example, are much less flexible, as is the program's portfolio management. In addition, CA-Simply Money offers no electronic bill paying and little tax-preparation help. Still, if you're jumping into finance programs for the first time, CA-Simply Money's lack of sophistication may actually be a plus, especially when you consider its quick and easy setup.

Managing Your Money

Manufacturer: MECA Software Inc.
Platforms: Windows, DOS, Macintosh
System requirements:
   Windows—386 or better, VGA graphics
   DOS—DOS 3.0 or later, EGA or better graphics, hard disk
   Mac—Minimum
Price range: $

If you're serious about managing your money, especially when it comes to investments, this software package (especially the DOS version) provides the most power of the currently available financial programs. In spite of its power, though, Managing Your Money contains plenty of helpful shortcuts and excellent on-line help.

When you use Managing Your Money for the first time, the program helps you create your starting accounts and assists you in entering financial data. Once you get going, the program's many automated features continue to make the program easy and convenient to use. For example, you can recall past payees, memorize transactions, and schedule repeated transactions with a couple of keystrokes. Managing Your Money is so smart that it can even help you find problems when you reconcile your account.

Where Managing Your Money really beats out the competition, though, is in its portfolio management, financial planning, and tax help. The program even includes a 1040 worksheet to assist you in planning for the dreaded tax day. When you add to this the capability to pay bills electronically, download stock quotes from on-line services, and create detailed budgets, Managing Your Money turns out to be one the best programs of its type.

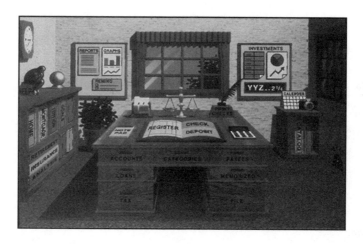

Managing Your Money

WealthBuilder

Manufacturer: Reality Technologies, Inc.
Platforms: DOS, Macintosh, (Windows forthcoming)
System requirements:
  DOS—286 or better, DOS 3.3 or later, EGA or better graphics, hard disk
  Mac—Minimum
Price range: $$

Unlike Quicken and Microsoft Money, which help you manage your finances, WealthBuilder, created by Money Magazine, concentrates on planning for future financial scenarios. You give the program your complete financial profile, including how much investment risk you're willing to take and your long-term objectives, and WealthBuilder constructs a complete financial plan that'll help you get where you want to go.

Using various charts and graphs, you can get an instant look at any aspect of your financial plan, including your asset allocation, purchasing strategy, and current and projected financial position. You can even conduct "what if" experiments to try out and compare different investment strategies. Finally, to keep you up to date, WealthBuilder can tap into Rueter's Money Network, an on-line service from which you can download the latest information on all types of investments. You can even buy and sell investments while on-line. (The on-line service requires an additional monthly fee.)

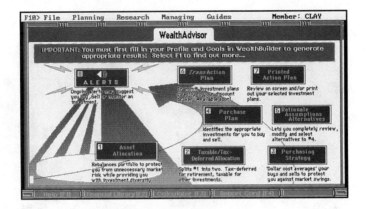

WealthBuilder

Legal Programs

There are certain legal papers no one should be without—a will, for instance. But working with a lawyer can be expensive, so many people put off their legal needs until it's too late. With the legal software available today, you can draw up your own legal papers for routine situations. The disclaimers in the box will warn you, however, that you should consult a real attorney to make sure the contracts that the program creates are legal in your state.

WillMaker 5.0

Manufacturer: Nolo Press
Platforms: Windows, DOS, Macintosh
System requirements:
    Windows—Minimum
    DOS—DOS 3.0 or later
    Macintosh—Minimum
Price range: $

If you've been putting off writing your will, WillMaker might help you get started. Despite its unusually spartan Windows interface, you can easily draw up a will or create a living will and final arrangements. To make the task of creating such important legal documents easier, WillMaker employs the interview method to take you step by step through the process, asking questions that are tailored to your specific circumstances.

For example, during the process of creating a will, WillMaker asks if you have any living children. If you select the Yes box, WillMaker takes you through the process of providing for those children in your will. Otherwise, the program skips ahead to the next section. Wherever possible check boxes and lists are used to speed data entry.

Although it's always a good idea to have a lawyer look over any legal documents you draw up, Nolo Press guarantees that you can create your complete will without consulting a lawyer. The thorough on-screen instructions and the well-organized manual ensure that you create the will properly. Moreover, the manual includes a comprehensive legal guide in which you can look up areas of the law that may apply to your specific situation.

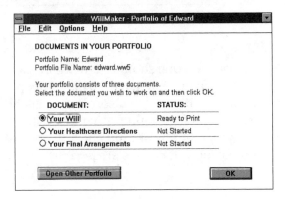

WillMaker

Living Trust Builder

Manufacturer: JIAN Tools for Sales, Inc.
Platforms: Windows, DOS, Macintosh
System requirements:
   Windows—Minimum
   DOS—Minimum
   Mac—Minimum
Price range: $$

Like JIAN's BizPlanBuilder, Living Trust Builder is a collection of documents that you can use by filling in the information specific to your situation. In doing so, you can create a living trust that will ensure that your estate is handled the way you want it handled.

Because the documents are plain text files, you can easily import them into most word processors. Then, to customize a document, you need only replace insertion codes, which are text strings like ***Q1***, with the appropriate information (such as your name, the name of the trust, the state of residence, and so on).

The Living Trust Builder package includes a manual that explains how to use the various on-disk forms, as well as a worksheet for listing the correct information that'll replace the insertion codes in a document. Also included with Living Trust Builder is the book *Understanding Living Trusts*, by Vickie and Jim Schumacher.

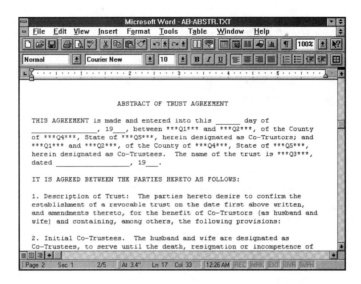

Living Trust Builder

It's Legal

Manufacturer: Parsons Technology
Platforms: Windows, DOS
System requirements:
  Windows—Minimum
  DOS—Minimum
Price range: $

Most people can't afford to have a lawyer at their beck and call. Thankfully, programs like It's Legal can help you through many of the more mundane legal matters with which you may be presented, as well as some other more hefty matters. Using It's Legal, you can create dozens of legal documents, including wills, premarital agreements, powers of attorney, living wills, credit report challenges, real estate leases, bills of sale, confidentiality agreements, and many more.

Creating a legal document is simply a matter of starting a new document and filling in the blanks. As you work, the program displays instructions for the area of the document on which you're working. In addition, a drop-down list on the menu bar lets you jump instantly to any part of the document. When the document is complete, you can use the print preview to see how the printed version will look, after which you can print the final version.

The short manual that comes with It's Legal includes not only operating instructions, but also quick explanations of each document, including what the document is and who should use it. Although It's Legal can't replace the need for a lawyer in every instance, it sure helps to get you started. One warning: Installing It's Legal can take an absurdly long time, over an hour on even a fast machine.

It's Legal

Small Business Programs

S ince so many people are starting their own small businesses at home, we're covering a few of the most popular small business accounting packages here. By and large, they're not suitable for keeping the family finances in order; for that purpose, you'll want a personal finance program (reviewed a few pages back).

The biggest difference among small business/accounting software is the amount of hand-holding it does. Some packages walk you step by step through the process of setting up accounts and entering transactions, whereas others assume some knowledge of accounting principles. Choose the software that best matches your accounting abilities.

Peachtree Accounting

Manufacturer: Peachtree Software
Platforms: Windows, DOS, Macintosh
System requirements:
   Windows—Minimum
   DOS—DOS 3.3 or later, hard disk
   Mac—Minimum
Price range: $$$

When it comes to accounting software, Peachtree Accounting is the granddaddy of them all. A recent recipient of *PC Magazine*'s Editor's Choice award for best accounting software, Peachtree offers more features than you can shake a journal at. From the general ledger to accounts receivable to inventory to payroll to business analysis, Peachtree does it all.

Moreover, Peachtree strikes a good balance between ease of use and power. For example, the account setup procedure (often the most difficult part of setting up accounting software) is a breeze for those familiar with accounting practices. But novices aren't left out in the cold either. A setup checklist guides beginners through this critical task, while SmartGuides (pop-up hint windows) keep you on track. There's also a special Getting Started manual, as well as copious on-line context-sensitive help.

Jumping between modules is as quick as clicking on one of the notebook tabs at the bottom of the screen and selecting a task from the pop-up window that appears. A full menu bar and toolbar are also provided for selecting program functions. Finally, Peachtree features 75 types of reports that you can customize at will. Add the Cash Manager, Collections Manager, and Payments Manager, which provide graphical analyses of those parts of your books, and you've got a complete package suitable for just about any small business.

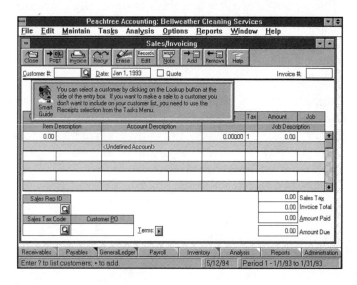

Peachtree Accounting for Windows

Microsoft Profit

Manufacturer: Microsoft Corp.
Platform: Windows
System requirements: 386 or better, DOS 3.1 or later, 4MB RAM
Price range: $$$

If the words "credit" and "debit" give you shivers of dread, you may want to use Microsoft Profit to keep your company's books. Microsoft Profit takes the non-accountant approach to accounting, providing fun interactive tutorials and the famous Microsoft Wizards (automated tasks) to help with your accounting. The Wizards guide you step by step through the dreaded account setup process, producing a set of accounts for your business that you can tailor to your needs. The Wizards can also handle such tasks as billing, budgeting, reconciling a bank account, and closing a period.

Profit's File Cabinet offers six drawers that access the Transactions, Cardfile, Reports, Wizards, Profit Signs, and Accounting modules. Throughout the accounting process, Profit offers plenty of smart help. For example, when you are entering transactions, Profit brings up the correct form (check, purchase order, invoice, deposit or withdrawal slip) based on the transaction type. When you complete a transaction, Profit automatically updates journals, inventory, and other related data. Finally, Profit's Profit Signs give you a graphical overview of your business in six categories.

Other extras include a report generator and the Cardfile, which keeps track of business contacts and inventory. However, the current version of Profit doesn't include the sophisticated payroll capabilities that M.Y.O.B. has, although such a module will be available soon. Regardless of this deficiency, if accounting isn't your cup of tea, you may find Microsoft Profit easier to swallow.

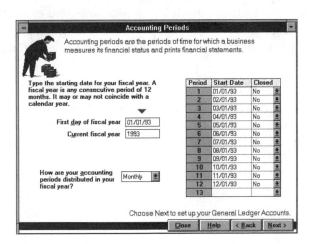

Microsoft Profit

CA-Simply Accounting

Manufacturer: Computer Associates International, Inc.
Platforms: Windows, DOS, Macintosh
System requirements:
   Windows—Minimum
   DOS—DOS 3.0 or later
   Mac—Minimum
Price range: $$

Unlike Microsoft Profit, which makes accounting easy for non-accountants, CA-Simply Accounting assumes that you have at least a nodding acquaintance with credits and debits. This can be an advantage if you employ an accountant, who may find too much computer hand-holding annoying. On the other hand, CA-Simply Accounting is user-friendly enough that anyone can learn it if he's willing to learn a little about accounting. (A manual of basic accounting is included with the program.)

Like many other accounting programs, CA-Simply Accounting groups its accounting activities into several modules that are accessible from control icons. Setting up your initial accounts is fairly easy. Just select the chart that best matches your type of business, and then customize the accounts to fit your specific needs by adding and deleting accounts and entering starting balances. Once you get started, CA-Simply Accounting keeps everything up to date for you: each transaction automatically updates all related journals and ledgers.

Graphically, the displays with which you must work, including checks, invoices, and other forms, look like their paper counterparts. And entering transactions is a breeze, thanks to easy-to-follow forms with drop-down lists and other amenities. CA-Simply Accounting also handles inventory, payroll, and report generation.

M.Y.O.B.

Manufacturer: Best!Ware
Platforms: Windows, Macintosh
System requirements:
   Windows—386 or better, DOS 5.0 or later, 4MB RAM (6MB with payroll)
   Mac—4MB RAM (6MB with payroll)
Price range: $$

If you prefer your mouse over your keyboard, you'll probably be delighted with M.Y.O.B. (Mind Your Own Business), a full-featured accounting package from Best!Ware. All of M.Y.O.B.'s modules are available as icons on its Command Center. Just click a button, and you're off. The Command Center features direct access to the General Ledger, Checkbook, Sales, Purchases, Payroll Inventory, Card File, and Administration modules, each of which displays its own set of buttons. For example, when you select the General Ledger module, the program displays buttons for accessing a chart of accounts, working with the general ledger, analyzing the balance sheet, and analyzing profits and losses.

In addition to its wealth of accounting features, M.Y.O.B. features contact-management functions that let you track contacts in a card-file type database. M.Y.O.B. also offers a to-do list that helps you remember to act on such tasks as overdue receivables and payables, running recurring transactions, and pending purchase orders. The Business calendar shows at a glance the number of days in the current work week, indicating the days the business is closed and reminding you of important dates.

M.Y.O.B. can also handle payroll tasks with ease, as the transactions are linked to the general ledger. The program can handle everything from creating wage categories to printing checks, creating W-2s, itemizing employer expenses, and analyzing the payroll. On top of everything, M.Y.O.B. comes with the capability to handle many inventory tasks, including not only reporting on inventory, but also setting item prices, making adjustments, and counting inventory.

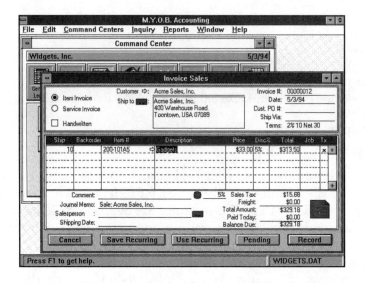

M.Y.O.B.

BizPlanBuilder

Manufacturer: JIAN Tools for Sales, Inc.
Platforms: Windows, DOS, Macintosh
System requirements:
  Windows—Minimum
  DOS—Minimum
  Mac—Minimum
Price range: $$

When you're ready to put together a serious business plan, BizPlanBuilder will prove to be an invaluable tool. Providing templates for over 90 pages of word processing and spreadsheet documents, BizPlanBuilder gets you started quickly by providing ready-to-use forms that you simply need to update with your business's specific data.

Because the documents are available in a number of different file formats, you'll have little difficulty importing them into your own word processor or spreadsheet application.

Some of the directly supported applications include Microsoft Word for Windows and DOS, Microsoft Works, WordPerfect for Windows and DOS, Professional Write, Q&A, MacWrite, WriteNow, Lotus 1-2-3, Microsoft Excel, and Quattro Pro. Most applications not directly supported by BizPlanBuilder can easily import the included files. The documents provide plenty of help in entering your own data. For example, word processor documents include suggestions for the type of material you need to supply, as well as incomplete sentences that you can customize by filling in the blanks. In this way, you can simply edit the business plan documents provided by BizPlanBuilder instead of writing your own from scratch.

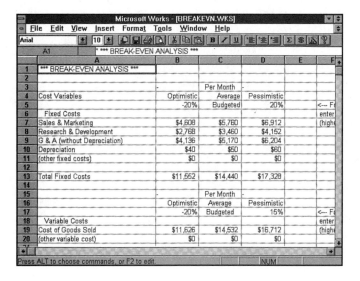

BizPlanBuilder

Tax Software

E ach year, prior to the dreaded date of April 15th, millions of Americans get busy on their tax returns. What many of these people may not know is that a home computer can make tax day a heck of a lot easier because tax preparation software can provide them with complete on-screen forms with detailed instructions. In addition, many tax programs enable you to file your taxes electronically instead of having to mail them the old-fashioned way—which means a faster refund (assuming, of course, you're entitled to a refund).

TurboTax

Manufacturer: Chipsoft
Platforms: Windows, DOS, Macintosh
System requirements:
   Windows—Minimum
   DOS—DOS 3.0 or later, hard disk
   Macintosh—Minimum
Price range: $

Of all the tax programs, TurboTax has the biggest following. Like other programs of its type, TurboTax allows you to enter data in three ways. Its EasyStep option uses a question-and-answer format to get you started on your taxes, whereas the File Cabinet option matches your tax documents up with the appropriate forms. Finally, the Classic option lets you enter data directly into the tax forms.

After finishing your return, you can activate the Deduction Finder to see whether you may have missed some possible money-saving deductions. The Final Review feature searches out incomplete entries and alerts you to data that could possibly trigger an IRS audit. In addition, the tax graphs clearly illustrate your tax analysis, income, deductions, and cash flow.

TurboTax's on-line help includes the complete original IRS instructions, as well as a Help icon that brings up additional instructions on the currently active tax form. When necessary, TurboTax can refer you to other IRS publications that may help your tax preparation. All in all, TurboTax is a well-rounded, easy-to-use tax helper.

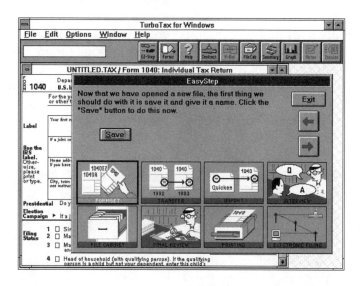

TurboTax

Andrew Tobias' TaxCut

Manufacturer: MECA Software Inc.
Platforms: Windows, DOS, Macintosh
System requirements:
   Windows—Minimum
   DOS—DOS 3.3 or later, hard disk
   Macintosh—Minimum
Price range: $

Flexibility is the name of the game with the top tax programs, and TaxCut is no different, offering three ways in which to complete your taxes. The easiest method employs TaxCut's Navigator, which leads you step by step through the process of gathering tax data by interviewing you for the information the program needs. As you go through the process, TaxCut's Assistant, who offers extra instructions, is always only a mouse click away.

If you'd prefer a more self-guided approach to your taxes, you can choose TaxCut's ShoeBox or direct-entry methods. The ShoeBox enables you to select tax documents (for example, a W-2 or a 1099) from a list, and TaxCut then jumps you to the correct form and line on which to enter the data. With the direct-entry method, on the other hand, you enter data directly into the appropriate forms.

No matter what tax-preparation method you choose, there's plenty of help to be had in TaxCut. You can call up the IRS's instructions for any form, get a list of new tax laws for the year, or access an index of tax topics. Choose a topic from the list, and you can jump directly to the relevant form or part of the Navigator. Other helpful features include on-line worksheets, an auditor that checks for errors, and a review function that displays on a single sheet all data you've entered so far.

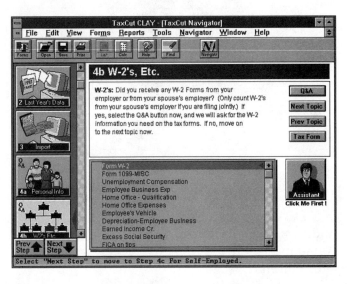

Andrew Tobias' TaxCut

Personal Tax Edge

Manufacturer: Parsons Technology, Inc.
Platforms: Windows, DOS
System requirements:
   Windows—Minimum
   DOS—DOS 3.0 or later, hard drive
Price range: $

For the last couple of years, Personal Tax Edge was kind of an also-ran when compared with other tax packages, but the 1993 Windows package closed the gap significantly. The simple interface may be the least confusing of all the tax packages, and while Personal Tax Edge doesn't always offer the same detailed guidance that TaxCut does, following each step in the tax-preparation process is easier.

Like the other tax programs reviewed here, Personal Tax Edge lets you tackle your taxes via a question-and-answer process that guides you through each step, popping up the appropriate forms when they're needed. You can also use the Organizer, which matches tax documents like W-2s and 1099s to the appropriate form. Or you can skip all the guidance and enter data directly into the tax forms.

Personal Tax Edge's help tools include the complete text of the IRS instructions, as well as standard program help and Tax Tips, which display helpful hints from within the IRS instructions. A Tax Law Update, which covers the specifics of the current year's tax law changes, is also included in the package. Other helpful features include The Bookkeeper, which itemizes data; a note feature for attaching extra information to forms and data; a depreciation calculator; and easy menu-bar access to Windows' calculator applet.

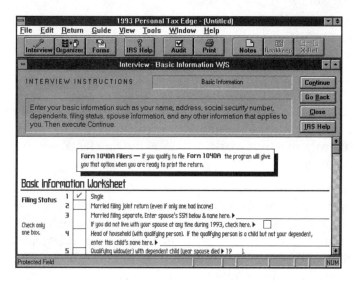

Personal Tax Edge

Utility Programs

Just as you need tools to take care of a garden or to repair a sink, you also need tools to keep your computer running smoothly. Some tools, such as a hard disk backup program, are essential, while others, such as a disk compression utility, are just nice to have. But all of the tools reviewed here will make your computing experience more pleasurable by ensuring that you're reasonably protected against disaster or that you can perform complex tasks easier.

MS DOS 6.x

Manufacturer: Microsoft Corporation
Platforms: DOS, Windows
System requirements:
   Windows—Minimum
   DOS—Minimum
Price range: $ (utilities free with purchase of MS-DOS)

You might not think of MS-DOS as a utility program. It's an operating system, after all. But DOS versions 6.0 and above come with an impressive suite of simple utility programs that work as well as the fancier programs sold separately for most users.

The utility programs included with versions 6.0 and above include Defrag, a disk defragmenting program; MS Antivirus, a virus detection and cleaning program; ScanDisk, a disk diagnostic and repair program; MS Backup, a disk backup program; Undelete, a file protection program; and MemMaker, a memory optimization program. These are simple programs with few options, but they are as reliable as the more expensive programs and, in many cases, have been licensed from the manufacturers who made the features famous, such as Central Point's PC Tools and The Norton Utilities.

Some of the utilities have Windows versions too; DOS provides both DOS and Windows versions of the Antivirus, Undelete, and Backup programs.

If you have DOS version 6.0 or 6.2 (not 6.21 or 6.22), you also have DoubleSpace, a disk compression program that enables you to fit more information on a hard disk. A maintenance program is also included to help you care for your compressed disk.

A quick note is in order about the compression programs that you'll see reviewed here. There are two kinds of space-saving programs for DOS files: *file compression programs* (which compress individual files, making them unusable until you uncompress them) and *disk compression programs* (which compress an entire disk that is still usable in its compressed state). Programs like PKZip are file compression programs; programs like Stacker and MS-DOS's DoubleSpace are disk compression programs.

PKZip

Manufacturer: PKWare
Platform: DOS
System requirements: Minimum
Price range: $

PKZip was the only shareware program chosen to be included in these reviews. That fact alone should tell you how important this program is. When it comes to file compression utilities, PKZip is the standard. Yes, there are other programs that compress files, but PKZip rules.

PKZip is a *file* compression program: it shrinks files for storage. When you want to store ("archive") a file, use PKZip on it. Then when you need the file again, you restore it to its original size with the companion program PKUnzip (included with PKZip).

This process of compressing and uncompressing may seem like a lot of hassle, but when used correctly, PKZip is perfect for archiving files (storing them for long periods of time) or for reducing the size of files you are uploading to or downloading from BBSs and other on-line services. In fact, if you're active on any on-line services, you'll quickly discover that you can't get by without PKZip. Virtually every file available to be downloaded from professional

231

on-line systems is compressed using PKZip. When you add to that the fact
that PKZip can compress multiple files into a single file, as well as create self-
extracting files (files that can automatically uncompress themselves), you've
got a software tool that's tough to do without.

```
C:\>pkzip batch.zip *.bat

PKZIP (R)   FAST!   Create/Update Utility   Version 2.04g   02-01-93
Copr. 1989-1993 PKWARE Inc.  All Rights Reserved.  Registered Version
PKZIP Reg. U.S. Pat. and Tm. Off.   Patent No. 5,051,745

  ■ 80486 CPU detected.
  ■ XMS version 2.00 detected.
  ■ DPMI version 0.90 detected.
  ■ Using Normal Compression.

Creating ZIP: BATCH.ZIP
   Adding: WORD.BAT       Storing   ( 0%), done.
   Adding: MARTHA.BAT     Deflating (58%), done.
   Adding: AUTOEXEC.BAT   Deflating (36%), done.

C:\>
```

PKUnZip

PC Tools

Manufacturer: Central Point Software
Platforms: Windows, DOS
System requirements:
   Windows—Minimum
   DOS—Minimum
Price range: $$$

PC Tools provides just about any tool you need to fend off problems or
correct them when they occur. PC Tools is a complete suite of utility programs
that can do everything from back up your hard disk drive to eradicate viruses.

Included in the package are tools for backing up data, handling computer
viruses, recovering damaged data, and even restoring a crashed system. In
addition, PC Tools for Windows features an alternative desktop for Windows
that enables you to use Windows in a whole new way. Windows enhance-
ments include a classier file manager, an icon editor, multiple desktop con-
figurations, a scheduler for automatically running applications, and a dialog
box editor.

In addition, PC Tools for Windows' System Consultant offers a cornucopia of information about how your system is configured. This information includes hardware, DOS, Windows, and system data. System Consultant can even offer advice on how to improve your system's performance. All told, PC Tools is one of the most comprehensive products of its type.

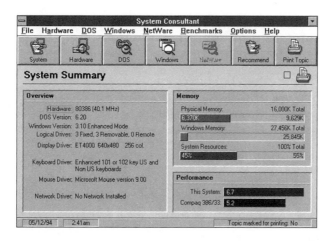

PC Tools for Windows

Norton Utilities

Manufacturer: Symantec Corp.
Platforms: Windows, DOS, Macintosh
System requirements:
 Windows—386 or better, 4MB RAM, VGA or better graphics
 DOS—DOS 3.3 or later, 286 or better, hard disk
 Mac—Minimum
Price range: $$$

Norton Utilities has long been a favorite system-utility suite. Its menu-driven programs can handle such tasks as undeleting files and reconstructing damaged data. In addition, Norton Utilities' famous Disk Doctor program can analyze your hard drive and search out many common types of disk problems, including lost and cross-linked clusters. Once problems are identified, Disk Doctor does its darnedest to get things back to normal.

When it comes to recovering deleted files, Norton Utilities is tough to beat. For example, you can view the contents of a deleted file before trying to restore it. In addition, Norton's SmartCan TSR tucks deleted programs away in a safe place for a limited period of time, guaranteeing that they can be restored should you change your mind.

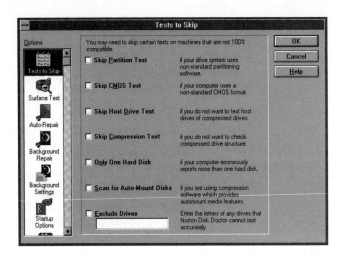

Norton Utilities

Unfortunately, one utility missing from this otherwise comprehensive package is an anti-virus program (although you can purchase Norton AntiVirus separately). Except for virus protection, when it comes to keeping your system up and running, Norton Utilities does as good a job as its biggest competitor, PC Tools. However, if virus protection is important to you, you may prefer PC Tools.

Stacker

Manufacturer: Stac Electronics
Platforms: Windows, DOS
System requirements:
   Windows—Minimum
   DOS—DOS 3.2 or later, hard disk
Price range: $$

Although hard disks get bigger and bigger every day, so do the programs that fill them. If you've been running out of space on your hard drive lately, you might want to consider a disk compression program like Stacker, which can more than double your hard drive's capacity. Stacker performs this seeming miracle by compressing all the data on your hard drive. Then, when you select a file, Stacker automatically uncompresses the data. But you never even know Stacker is working; it performs all its magic while completely invisible to you.

If you have DOS 6.0 or 6.2 (not 6.21 or 6.22), you have a disk compression program called DoubleSpace. DoubleSpace works similarly to Stacker, but currently Stacker is the only disk compression program that can more than double the capacity of a hard drive. Other similar programs, including DoubleSpace, typically give you 1.8 to 1 compression ratio, whereas Stacker can give you a ratio of 2.2 to 1 or better.

Stacker includes a handy toolbox utility that enables you to keep an eye on how Stacker is working, as well as to change various Stacker options. Using the toolbox, you can check your hard disk's integrity, optimize your hard disk for speed, and configure how you want Stacker to work. The bottom line is, if you're willing to pay the price, Stacker is currently the best disk compression program on the market.

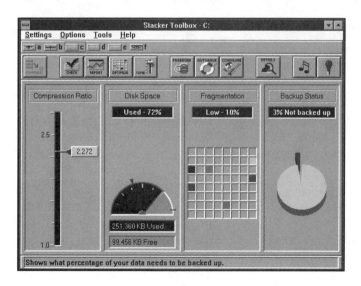

Stacker 4.0

QEMM

Manufacturer: Quarterdeck Office Systems, Inc.
Platform: DOS
System requirements: 386 or better, DOS 3.0 or later, 1.5MB RAM, hard disk
Price range: $$

As DOS programs get bigger and bigger, it becomes more and more likely that you'll run into memory problems on your computer. If you have programs that give you "out of memory" errors, a program like QEMM may be able to help. QEMM (Quarterdeck Expanded Memory Manager) is a memory utility that uses all the tricks known to man to free up as much memory as possible on your PC. Having extra memory means you can run bigger programs or programs that need extra space to operate.

The best part is that you don't have to be a rocket scientist to figure it all out. QEMM is smart enough to do the driving and let you enjoy the ride. Just start the program and watch it perform its magic. On the other hand, if you understand how your computer's memory works, and you've a hankering to customize the memory manager yourself, QEMM will let you dig in and get your hands dirty. In either case, by the time QEMM is done analyzing your system and shuffling around device drivers, TSRs, and other memory gobblers, you'll be amazed at how much extra memory you have.

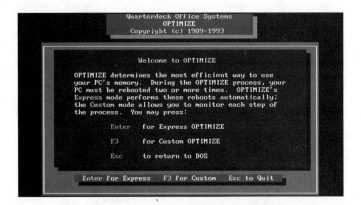

QEMM 7.03

386MAX

Manufacturer: Qualitas, Inc.
Platform: DOS
System requirements: 386 or better, DOS 3.3 or later, hard disk
Price range: $$

Although you can count on DOS 6.0's MemMaker program to squeeze some extra memory out of your system, nothing does the job quite so well as a full-featured memory manager like 386MAX. And, although 386MAX is slightly more difficult to use than its biggest competitor, QEMM, it provides just as much free memory. In addition, it includes such Windows tools as a new PIF editor (if you don't know what that is, you probably don't need it) and the capability to run DOS programs under Windows with extra memory.

Getting 386MAX set up on your computer is a snap. Just run the install program and follow the instructions on-screen. If you don't understand much about the way your computer handles memory, you can let 386MAX go about its business, configuring your system with a default memory setup. If you want to get a few extra bytes of memory, you can help 386MAX along by telling it which drivers and TSRs must be run in a specific order and then letting 386MAX try to rearrange the others. Even with the default setup, though, you'll probably have a lot less trouble getting larger DOS programs to run once 386MAX optimizes your memory usage.

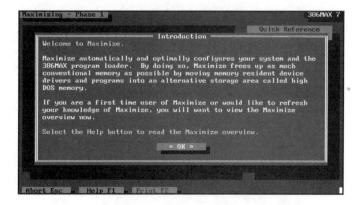

386MAX

The Norton AntiVirus

Manufacturer: Symantec
Platforms: Windows, DOS, Macintosh
System requirements:
   Windows—Minimum
   DOS—DOS 3.1 or later
   Macintosh—Minimum
Price range: $$

If you've had your computer for any time at all, you know about computer *viruses*, sneaky and often dangerous programs that can infect your computer system. Luckily, there are many programs that can help you keep your system free from viruses; The Norton AntiVirus is one of the best.

With The Norton AntiVirus, you can check your system for digital trouble-makers in a number of ways. For example, you can set up the program so that it provides automatic protection whenever you start your computer. In addition, because you regularly place new floppy disks in your drives, you can scan drives, directories, or files at any time. You can even have AntiVirus look for suspicious activities, like a running program attempting to change a program file on your disk.

The Norton AntiVirus provides a heap of options so that you can configure the program to run exactly as you like. In addition, the well-written manual provides all the information you need to understand, eliminate, and avoid computer viruses. You can even get descriptions of over 100 viruses. With a program like The Norton AntiVirus on your system, you'll be able to breathe a little easier, knowing your valuable data is safe from meddling.

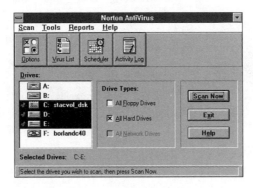

The Norton AntiVirus

Norton Desktop

Manufacturer: Symantec Corp.
Platforms: Windows, DOS
System requirements:
   Windows—386 or better, 4MB RAM, VGA or better graphics
   DOS—DOS 3.1 or later, hard disk
Price range: $$$

One of the best-known alternative desktops for Windows is Norton Desktop, which lets you work with Windows in an easier-to-use environment. It replaces Program Manager and, in the process, improves upon several parts of Windows that are not as intuitive as they could be.

The Norton Desktop offers several benefits over Windows' Program Manager. The most impressive is its improved File Manager that is integrated into the desktop: you don't have to open a separate program to manage your files, as you do with Windows by itself. You can drag copies of your most-used program icons right out onto the desktop and launch them from there. And a complete suite of utilities is included: AntiVirus, Backup, Undelete, SpeedDisk (a defragmenter), Norton Disk Doctor (a disk diagnostic program), and a calendar/day planner.

When compared with the alternative desktop included with PC Tools for Windows, Norton Desktop scores extra points for its Smart Groups and Daily Planner. However, Norton Desktop does not allow virtual desktops (a way to switch quickly between different desktop configurations) like PC Tools for Windows does. In addition, PC Tools boasts a better replacement File Manager.

There is also a DOS version: The Norton Desktop for DOS. This program offers many of the same features as the Windows version but hasn't sold as well. Perhaps this is because people who stubbornly cling to DOS and shun Windows are not people who want the graphical interface that the DOS version provides.

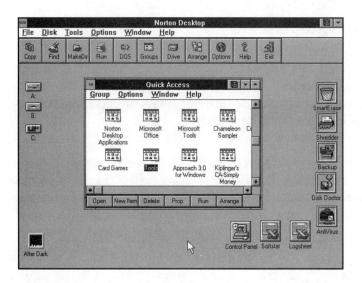

Norton Desktop for Windows

MacDisk

Manufacturer: Insignia Solutions, Inc.
Platforms: Windows, DOS
System requirements:
  Windows—Minimum
  DOS—Minimum
Price range: $$

Every day it becomes more and more important to be able to transfer files between IBM-compatible and Macintosh computers. Because the disks used on these two machines are incompatible, you need special hardware or software to read them. That's where MacDisk comes in. It enables you to use your IBM-compatible to read and write files from and to a Macintosh disk.

MacDisk is a TSR (terminate-and-stay-resident) program that works invisibly to enable you to handle Macintosh disks exactly like you would MS-DOS disks. Just load it into memory and forget about it. You can then use DOS's DIR command to get a directory of a Macintosh disk or even read Macintosh files from within your favorite DOS and Windows applications. The package also includes DOS and Windows utilities for displaying Macintosh files along with the converted DOS file names.

VirusScan

Manufacturer: McAfee
Platforms: Windows, DOS
System requirements:
   Windows—Minimum
   DOS—Minimum
Price range: $$

VirusScan includes a suite of programs that can both detect and remove computer viruses. And because new computer viruses are constantly unleashed, VirusScan also comes with a full year of free updates. This program, like most sophisticated virus utilities, can sense not only conventional viruses, but also polymorphic viruses (viruses that can change themselves in order to avoid detection). So even the sneakiest of computer infections can be stomped out.

The Scan program automatically searches memory and disks for virus programs, while the memory-resident VShield program constantly watches your system for any evidence of viral activity (such as attempts to write to an executable file). Moreover, VShield can provide its protection with no noticeable degradation in system performance. Finally, the CleanUp program restores virus infected disks and files to their original state and destroys all virus programs that it detects.

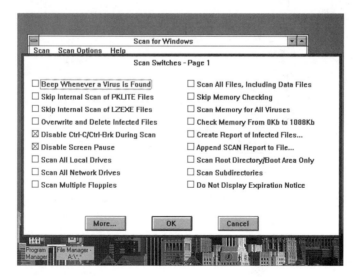

VirusScan

XTree Gold

Manufacturer: Central Point Software
Platforms: Windows, DOS
System requirements:
   Windows—Minimum
   DOS—DOS 3.1 or later, hard disk
Price range: $$

The DOS version of XTree gives you a barrelful of disk management functions that help you handle DOS more easily. You even get extra goodies like file viewers, a full-featured text editor, and a file transfer program. XTree is like a super DOS Shell that can handle everything from displaying the contents of a directory to creating a menu from which you can run any of your applications.

XTree's file viewers can handle graphics files in many formats, including .PCX, .TIFF, and .EPS. In addition, you can view word processor, database, and spreadsheet files just as they would look if you viewed them from within the application that created them. The included DOS-management utilities feature the usual DOS functions like copy and delete, as well as ZIP file compression, file searching, undeleting files, searching for duplicate files, and much more.

XTree Gold

Screen Saver Programs

I n the early days of computing, if a computer was left on and idle too long, the computer's display could burn into the screen, leaving a permanent ghost-like image. To guard against this problem, programmers developed screen savers, which automatically change the screen display every few minutes whenever the computer is left idle.

These days, screen burn-in isn't likely to occur (because of higher quality monitors), but screen savers are more popular than ever before, thanks to the ingenious ways these programs have of changing your computer's display. While the early screen savers rarely did anything more complex than change the screen colors, today's screen savers are full-featured graphics and sound marvels. The screen savers reviewed here are all top products, differing mostly in the themes used for the displays.

T2: The Screen Saver

Manufacturer: Sound Source Unlimited
Platform: Windows
System requirements: VGA graphics
Price range: $

If you're a "Terminator" fan and are in the market for a new set of Windows screen savers, you'll probably get a kick out of this collection, which includes 10 modules all based on the famous T2 movie. Not only will you be treated to visual delights, but each module also includes full sound effects—as long as you have a Windows compatible sound card. (The sound card is optional.)

The modules run the gamut from simple animations to full-screen displays that rival the graphics found in top-notch computer games. If you turn on the

Gunshot Morphs module, for example, shotgun blasts blow self-healing, liquid-metal holes in your Windows desktop. The Desktop Morphs module causes the icons on your Windows desktop to metamorphose into terminators that then strut off the screen.

The full-screen modules include Terminator Factory, in which you can watch terminators under construction, and Skynet World Clock, which displays the current time in various locales around the world. Although the T2 screen savers aren't as customizable as some other collections, they are guaranteed to turn an idle computer into a fascinating graphics demo machine.

T2: The Screen Saver

After Dark

Manufacturer: Berkeley Systems
Platforms: Windows, DOS, Mac
System requirements:
    Windows—Minimum
    DOS—Minimum
    Mac—Minimum
Price range: $

After Dark was the first screen saver to capture widespread attention. The famous "flying toasters" screen saver, in which winged toasters and slices of toast sail across the screen, has become an industry icon. That original set of screen savers also included many other clever and colorful screen saver modules, including a customizable aquarium.

Since the success of the original After Dark, Berkeley Systems has released More After Dark (more of the same), Star Trek: The Screen Saver, and After Dark Presents: The Disney Collection. These thematic modules each feature over a dozen animated modules, from Star Trek's Sickbay gauges to a Fantasia sequence featuring Mickey Mouse.

The strongest feature of After Dark and its related modules is their customizability. You can change nearly every aspect of a module's operation, from the number of toasters flying across your screen to the amount of brownness on the accompanying bread slices.

After Dark

Opus and Bill Brain Saver

Manufacturer: Delrina
Platforms: Windows, Macintosh
System requirements:
　　Windows—Minimum
　　Mac—Minimum
Price range: $

Delrina's first foray into the screen-saving business, Opus and Bill is a real treat for Bloom County and Outland fans. Opus the Penguin, Bill the Cat, and their friends are featured in over a dozen adventures, including Bill the Cat bungee jumping and toaster-hunting, in which Opus takes rifle shots at propellered toasters flying by (in a tip of the hunting cap to After Dark, the makers of which are not amused). As Opus says in one ad for this product, "Them's good eatin'."

Opus and Bill Brain Saver

The only problem with these screen saver modules is that they lack customization capabilities. The user can choose whether or not to hear the sound effects that accompany the modules, but the modules are nowhere near as rich in changeable features as the After Dark products. One module in particular that cries out for customization is the module in which Opus "moons" the White House. Users can't display their own messages on Opus's rear; they must be content with Delrina's ideas of appropriate messages. Because of this, users may get bored with Opus and Bill after playing all the modules a few times.

Johnny Castaway

Manufacturer: Sierra
Platform: Windows
System requirements: Minimum
Price range: $

The premise of this screen saver is simple: our hero, Johnny, is stranded on a small island in the middle of the ocean, with a palm tree and a few rocks. All day long, you can watch Johnny's day pass on the island. He catches and cooks fish, jogs, bathes, takes naps, interacts with seagulls, and repeatedly comes very close to getting rescued. (Sounds like "Gilligan's Island", doesn't it?)

It's a silly premise, of course, but it's fun. The programmers have built in little surprises along the way that keep the user watching: shamrocks spring up on the island when your computer's internal clock indicates that it's the week of St. Patrick's day, for instance, and a tree appears for Christmas. Johnny has an ongoing correspondence via message-in-a-bottle with a ladyfriend, dons a native mask to perform a rain dance, meets mermaids and sharks, and builds a raft for his escape.

There is no customization and there are no options for this screen saver, and there is only one module. But the module is so rich and full of surprises that special options are not sorely missed.

Johnny Castaway

Games

Almost as long as there have been computers, there have been computer games. Little in the world of computing can capture the imagination so thoroughly, which is probably why more games are bought for home computers than any other kind of software.

Computer games range from simple arcade contests to fully rendered worlds (like those found in the famous Ultima games) in which you must complete some quest. Although there are literally thousands of games to choose from, the games reviewed in this section are among the best currently available. Pick a couple that appeal to you and watch the hours fly by.

Dracula Unleashed

Manufacturer: Viacom New Media
Platforms: DOS, (Macintosh forthcoming)
System requirements: 386 or better, DOS 5.0 or later, 4MB RAM,
   VGA graphics, CD-ROM, sound board, mouse
Price range: $$

In Dracula Unleashed, a CD-ROM adventure game that's billed as "an interactive horror movie," you take on the role of the vampire hunter Alexander Morris as he investigates his brother's mysterious death. One thing's for sure: from the movie-like opening credits with their spooky soundtrack, to the professionally acted, full-motion video sequences, Dracula Unleashed will keep you squirming in your chair and looking over your shoulder.

In this eerie adventure, you'll have to do more than just explore the streets of London for clues. Because much of the game's action takes place in real time, you must be sure to be in the right places at the right times, or you may miss out on important information. Luckily, the game's journal screen can supply summaries of video sequences that you can peruse, looking for clues that may have slipped past you.

Although Dracula Unleashed is not quite as interactive as it could be (in the video sequences, you just watch for clues as the scenes unfold), it still provides an impressive computerized tale. Each new scene features a detailed image of the location, and the buttons near the bottom of the screen let you access various game commands. The clean interface and the spooky story work well together to provide a rewarding computer-adventure experience.

Dracula Unleashed

Star Trek: Judgment Rites

Manufacturer: Interplay Productions, Inc.
Platform: DOS
System requirements: 386 or better, DOS 3.1 or later, 2MB RAM, 256-color VGA graphics, hard disk
Price range: $$

Judgment Rites is a series of eight space adventures based on the stories of Captain Kirk and his loyal crew's explorations of the galaxy. These adventures include action space-battle sequences (which you can skip if you don't care much for arcade-style game play), as well as galactic missions that must be completed. Your task is to take on the character of Captain Kirk and guide your crew as they try to complete their assignments.

The missions are presented much like episodes of the famous TV show. For example, each episode begins with title and credit screens, after which the

Starfleet Command notifies the Enterprise of its current mission. Before you're done, you'll command such missions as "Light and Darkness," "Void," "Though This Be Madness," and "Museum Piece." Throughout the adventures, you'll confront a slew of cosmic calamities, including evil computers, Klingons, and mysterious alien civilizations.

Judgment Rites features detailed and well-rendered graphics, as well as lots of sound effects taken directly from the original show. Even though the eight adventures may go by fairly quickly, Judgment Rites is the best Star Trek game available.

Star Trek: Judgment Rites

Myst

Manufacturer: Broderbund Software
Platforms: Windows, Macintosh
System requirements:
   Windows—386 (486 recommended), Super VGA, 4MB RAM, CD-ROM, sound card
   Mac—System 7.01 or higher, 4MB RAM, 256-color graphics, CD-ROM
Price range: $$

Probably one of the most graphically gorgeous adventure games ever written, Myst drops you on a mysterious island that is a gateway to other worlds. This game's graphics are so detailed and carefully rendered that you'll swear you're looking at photographs instead of computer images. Moreover, Myst is loaded with digital music and sound effects that combine with the graphics to plunge you head-first into Myst's surrealistic universe.

If all Myst had to offer was its wonderful graphics and sound, it would still be worth the money. However, the game, too, is computer adventuring at its finest, featuring an original plotline that avoids clichés and presents a fresh storyline with carefully crafted puzzles. As you explore the island, you learn more and more about why the island is empty and where the inhabitants have gone. If you think hard (or buy the clue book), you may even discover surprising secrets about the man who created the island.

Unlike other computer adventure games, Myst's player interface doesn't get in the way of the game. In fact, most screens show only the current location and the mouse pointer. Using only your mouse, you'll explore underground passages, abandoned buildings, strange machinery, and much more. If you can afford only one adventure game (and have the equipment to run it), Myst should be the one.

Myst

Return to Zork

Manufacturer: Activision
Platforms: DOS, Macintosh
System requirements:
   DOS—386 or better, VGA or better graphics, CD-ROM drive, hard disk.
   Mac—LC III or better, System 7.0 or later, 256-color graphics, CD-ROM
   drive
Price range: $$

Way back in the early days of home computing, there was an immensely
popular all-text adventure game called Zork. This simple game was so well
written that it captured the imaginations of hundreds of thousands of people
and launched a new software company called Infocom. These days Infocom is
owned by Activision, who recently released a new Zork adventure on CD-
ROM. This time, however, the text has been replaced by vivid graphics, action
video, digitized sound, and a professionally produced soundtrack. In fact,
Return to Zork is so cutting edge, that it's probably the only game that can
currently stand up to Broderbund's masterpiece, Myst.

Return to Zork

As you explore the underground world of Zork, you'll use only your mouse
to interact with the world. Moreover, a built-in "tape recorder" preserves
important conversations, and a "pholobloid" camera retains snapshots of

game scenes. With this game's slick interface, you'll never even miss the keyboard (although you can use the keyboard if you like). With its state-of-the-art presentation and professionally acted scenes, there's no doubt that Return to Zork is top-shelf computer gaming.

The Seventh Guest

Manufacturer: Virgin Games, Inc.
Platforms: DOS, Macintosh
System requirements:
   DOS—DOS 5.0 or later, 386 or better, 2MB RAM, super VGA graphics, CD-ROM, hard drive, sound card, mouse
   Mac—LC III or better, system 7.0 or better, 256-color graphics, CD-ROM
Price range: $$

The Seventh Guest was the first computer game to be designed especially for CD-ROM. In this horror adventure game, you explore the haunted Stauf mansion, trying to discover its secret and learn why people keep disappearing from there. As you move through the mansion's 22 rooms, you must solve 23 quirky puzzles. Along the way, you'll be delighted by the game's eerie atmosphere, created by sensational super VGA graphics and an other-worldly soundtrack.

While exploration is a main element in most adventure games, in The Seventh Guest exploration takes a second seat to puzzle solving. The game's puzzles are cleverly integrated into the mansion, and you must solve a puzzle before you're allowed to move on to other rooms in the mansion. Luckily, you can get puzzle help from the Book of Clues, which is found in the mansion's library.

Although The Seventh Guest doesn't provide the in-depth adventure-game experience you find in a game like Myst, it is one of the most stunning interactive computer games available today.

Ultima Underground II: Labyrinth of Worlds

Manufacturer: Origin
Platform: DOS
System requirements: DOS 3.3 or later, 386 or better, 2MB RAM, 256-color VGA graphics
Price range: $$

Ultima Underworld II: Labyrinth of Worlds is a spectacular role-playing game (RPG), in which you take on the persona of a mighty hero known only as the Avatar. In this adventure, Lord British's castle has been completely enclosed in a huge blackrock gem, and it's up to you to explore beneath the castle to find a way to release the castle's occupants from their terrifying captivity.

Ultima Underworld's claim to fame is its 3D first-person viewpoint, which is among the best in the industry. In Ultima Underworld's world, you can look in any direction, including up and down, and see a realistic representation of the current scene from your new angle. In addition, all the locales in the game are well populated with all manner of life, from human allies who can teach you important skills to horrible monsters who would like nothing better than to reduce you to scrap meat and bone.

As with all RPGs, your character has attributes—including strength, dexterity, intelligence, and vitality—that change as you play. Each of these basic attributes affects your character's abilities and the way he acts in specific situations. Besides his attributes, your character has a number of skills that you can improve throughout the game, including spell-casting, combat, lock-picking, swimming, bartering, and repairing broken items. There are several other dungeon-exploration games on the market, but the Ultima Underworld series is the cream of the crop. You'll be amazed at how realistic a computer-generated fantasy world can be.

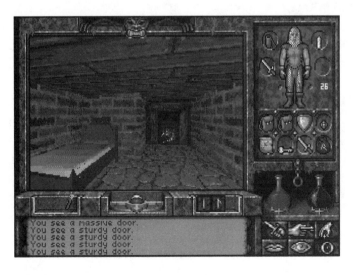

Ultima Underground II: Labyrinth of Worlds

Links 386 Pro

Manufacturer: Access Software
Platform: DOS
System requirements: DOS 3.3 or later, 386 or better, 2MB RAM, super VGA
Price range: $$

There's a good reason Links 386 Pro has been a top seller for over a year. Not only does this golf simulation feature some of the best graphics seen in a sports game, but it also plays an extremely realistic game of golf. The ball responds to the terrain just as a real ball would, rolling down hills, bouncing on pavement, getting stuck in sand. In addition, the game's interface carefully duplicates the difficulty of real golf.

To add to the realism, you can change your point of view on the course to whatever angle you like, with all the scenery changing to reflect the new angle. You can even split the screen into multiple views, including golfer's eye and aerial views, with each window showing a different perspective. For those who like to brag, if you make a particularly tough shot, Links 386 Pro can replay the shot or save it to disk. You can even save an entire game to disk, send it to another player, and let him play against you, just as if you were there.

IndyCar Racing

Manufacturer: Virgin Games
Platform: DOS
System requirements: 386 or better, DOS 3.5 or later, 4MB RAM, VGA
   graphics
Price range: $

IndyCar Racing has garnered a reputation as one of the most realistic racing games ever released. Just as if you were racing a real car, you must handle the controls with finesse, taking into consideration the effects of decreasing fuel, wearing tires, and even the wind turbulence caused by nearby cars. The racing experience is so realistic that you can even get in behind an opponent and use his car as a wind break to save on energy.

If you like to tinker under the digital hood, IndyCar Racing offers several ways to customize your car before you roll out onto the track. You can also choose from many different tracks, including Portland, Long Beach, Toronto, and Laguna Seca. Moreover, like many simulators, IndyCar Racing sports 3D textured graphics with plenty of details like signs, towers, vegetation, walls, and fences. Also, the digitized sounds of racing engines and squealing tires add depth to the racing experience.

Because of the game's detailed 3D graphics, though, you really need a speedy 486 processor in your machine to keep things chugging nicely. Moreover, although the game will run in four megabytes of memory, you need eight megabytes to load many of the tracks provided with the game.

SimCity 2000

Manufacturer: Maxis
Platforms: DOS, Macintosh
System requirements:
   DOS—386 or better, DOS 3.3 or later, 4MB RAM, super VGA, hard disk, mouse
   Mac—LC II or better, System 7.0 or later, 256-color graphics
Price range: $$

SimCity, the original game upon which SimCity 2000 is based, has won a slew of awards, and in spite of the fact that the game has been around for years, it's still a top seller. SimCity 2000 updates the original game with more detailed graphics, new types of buildings, and myriad other objects that you use to construct your perfect city.

When you play SimCity 2000, it's your job to build up a successful city that can pay its bills, and keep its population happy at the same time. At the start of a game, you have nothing but a bare stretch of land upon which to zone residential, commercial, and industrial areas, but once you get comfortable with your mayoral duties, your tiny town may spring up into a massive metropolis.

As emergencies arise, you must carefully parcel out the funds you earn from taxes, yet be sure that you keep enough money to run your police department, fire department, road crews, and other important city services. Let your city start to go downhill, and the citizens move out faster than rabbits fleeing a forest fire. The best thing about SimCity 2000 is that it's not only fun, it's also educational. Maxis also publishes other fascinating and award-winning games including SimEarth, SimLife, SimAnt, and SimFarm.

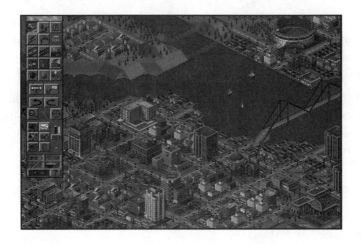

SimCity 2000

Strike Commander

Manufacturer: Origin
Platform: DOS
System requirements: DOS 5.0 or later, 486, 4MB RAM, 256-color VGA
graphics, hard disk
Price range: $$

Origin struck gold with their space-combat game Wing Commander, which featured state-of-the-art graphics and hot action space flying. That program was soon followed by Strike Commander, which is the same sort of flight simulator/combat game, but rather than being set out in the far reaches of the galaxy, Strike Commander's scenarios take place on good-old Earth in the year 2011. As a pilot for a band of mercenaries called the Wildcats, it's your task to fly an F-16 jet in strikes against massive corporations and other forces who have come to rule most of the world.

Although Strike Commander is essentially a flight simulator, the focus is more on action than on realistic flying. Still, there's a lot to learn if you want to get off the ground and into battle. To help you get started, the program includes a training mode that lets you practice flying in combat. After your training, you jump into the game's main plot, which features a storyline with intervening cinematic sequences. The graphics throughout are surprisingly detailed, even while you're flying.

Strike Commander may be a cutting-edge air combat game, but all that technology doesn't come without a price. You'll need a fast computer system (a 486) to keep Strike Commander cranking. In addition, the game takes up an unbelievable 27 megabytes of hard disk space. When you add in the optional speech pack, the total reaches over 40 megabytes! Is it worth it? You bet!

Strike Commander

X-Wing

Manufacturer: LucasArts
Platform: DOS
System requirements: 386 or better, 256-color VGA graphics, hard disk
Price range: $$

Star Wars fans will have a blast as they join up with the rebel forces to do battle against the evil empire. This space-combat epic features stunning graphics, awesomely realistic sound, and game-play so hot it could melt your mouse. In short, X-Wing takes up where Origin's Wing Commander left off, providing a vivid space combat experience.

Of course, as a rebel rookie, you can't expect to jump right into combat. First, you must do your time in the Pilot Proving Ground, where you learn to handle your battle craft. After basic training, you can try your hand at the Historical Missions simulations that are provided to get rookies up to speed on different spacecraft as quickly as possible. When your skills are honed and your nerves are steeled, you're ready for your Tour of Duty, in which you get your chance to earn hero status in the battle against the empire.

Unlike some space-combat simulators, X-Wing gives you control over how you choose to use your ship's systems. Specifically, you can select how much power to apply to your shields, engines, and weapons. For example, if you need a little extra fire power, you can take power away from your shields long enough to get the shot off. No matter how you decide to run your ship, though, you can expect a series of thrilling and challenging space missions.

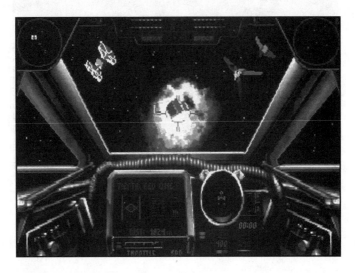

X-Wing

Wing Commander: Privateer

Manufacturer: Origin Systems
Platform: DOS
System requirements: 386 or better, 4MB RAM, VGA graphics, hard disk, sound card
Price range: $$

Take a good helping of space-merchant simulation and add in an equal measure of action, and you'll come up with something like Origin's Wing Commander: Privateer. Like the original Wing Commander game, in Privateer a trip into space can be a dangerous proposition, resulting in attacks by enemy craft and maybe even an untimely death. But such are the risks you must take if you're to be a successful space merchant, transporting supplies between planets.

If you like, you can forget merchanting, instead making money by performing such services as defending bases or patrolling nav points. You can even try your hand at illegal activities like trafficking in slaves or drugs. If you do, though, you'd better be prepared to deal with the authorities, who immediately attack any craft they suspect of shady dealings. However you decide to make your living, as you earn money, you can upgrade your craft in a number of ways, adding various types of weapons, shields, and drives—or even buying a whole new ship.

Wing Commander: Privateer

Chessmaster 4000

Manufacturer: Software Toolworks
Platform: Windows
System requirements: 386 or better, 4MB RAM, 256-color VGA graphics
Price range: $$

Chess has always been the classic computer game, and it still is. Chessmaster 4000 advances the state-of-the-art of computer chess by providing a variety of beautifully rendered boards, along with real-voice advice and background music (for systems with a compatible MIDI device). Of special interest are the creative sets of playing pieces, which include everything from undersea creatures to dinosaurs. Most important of all, Chessmaster 4000 plays one mean game of chess.

Chessmaster 4000's screen display can manage as many as nine different windows, containing the playing board, a chess clock, a list of moves, a list of captured pieces, and other information. If you like, you can have the playing board fill the entire screen. And, when it comes to controlling the game, drop-down menus make it easy to select commands and options.

Although the computer opponent can be a challenge for even expert players, you can opt to play another human player via modem. Or if you're not yet ready to take on an opponent, Chessmaster 4000's tutorial system can transform a chess novice into a reasonably good player. No matter what your skill level, Chessmaster 4000 can provide you with a well-matched opponent.

Chessmaster 4000

Microsoft Arcade

Manufacturer: Microsoft Corp.
Platform: Windows
System requirements: 386 or better, VGA graphics
Price range: $

Back in the early days of video games, programmers didn't have a lot of fancy graphics and sound to work with, so they put their imaginations to work instead. The result was some of the best games that have ever been written, regardless of how old they are. Microsoft has now rescued five of these classic arcade games and released them for play under Windows.

Included in this omnibus edition are the classic favorites Missile Command, Asteroids, Tempest, Battlezone, and Centipede. Microsoft has done a commendable job restoring these games for play under Windows, providing a nostalgic thrill for those who remember the originals, and a look at a creative past for those who missed these titles the first time around.

Also featured in this package is a history of the games and the developers who wrote them. Just as no library is complete without a few literary masterpieces, no software library is complete without these digital classics.

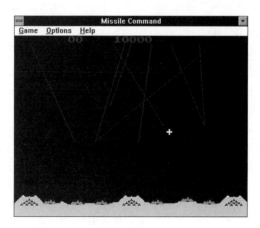

Microsoft Arcade

Reference Software

W hile it's true that nothing can replace the feel of a good, hefty book in your hands, it's also true that nothing can locate information for you faster than a computer. For this reason, computerized references have become all the rage, especially in these days of multimedia.

Computer reference works from dictionaries to encyclopedias can find any item you're looking for in a flash. But just as importantly, today's multimedia references like Compton's Interactive Encyclopedia or Microsoft's Bookshelf can enhance the learning experience with video clips, animations, color graphics, and recorded sound. When's the last time an old-fashioned encyclopedia talked to you or showed you a movie of a rocket blasting off?

Great Literature Plus

Manufacturer: Bureau of Electronic Publishing, Inc.
Platform: Windows
System requirements: 386 or better, VGA or better graphics, CD-ROM drive, sound board
Price range: $$

Great Literature Plus is a CD-ROM collection of 1,900 works, plenty of reading for even the most faithful of library hounds. Included on this packed disc are short stories, poems, historical documents, novels, religious documents, and more. In addition, the collection sneaks in multimedia features like pictures, narrations, musical excerpts, and animations (although the animations are unimpressive and add little to the program).

Finding your way around this massive library is as easy as clicking the screen with your mouse. To start off, you can search for works by subject, author, or title. Click on the appropriate topic, and an illustrated list appears from which you can make your final selection. In addition, the Find command enables you to search for specific words or phrases throughout the entire collection.

Along with the literary works, you can bring up mini-biographies of authors, complete with pictures and vital statistics, such as birth and death date and a list of works. Finally, many screens contain "hot spots" on which you can click to get additional information like definitions and biographies. Some hot spots link directly to a literary work, enabling you to bring it up on the screen with a single mouse click.

Great Literature Plus

The Library of the Future 3.0

Manufacturer: World Library, Inc.
Platforms: Windows, DOS
System requirements:
   Windows—VGA graphics, CD-ROM
   DOS—DOS 3.3 or later, 286 or better, VGA graphics, CD-ROM
Price range: $$

If you want a room full of classic literature, you could go out and buy thousands of books. On the other hand, you could save a lot of space and money by picking up this one CD-ROM product that includes over 3,500 pieces of literature written by 205 different authors. Although short essays and poems are part of the mix, there are also plenty of full-length novels, as well as other long works like Shakespeare's plays. The CD even includes 12 video clips and 297 illustrations, not to mention religious works, historical documents, and scientific works.

Finding what you're looking for is a snap with Library of the Future's search features. You can list contents by title or author, or you can even quickly search the entire CD for specific words. How many works on the disc use the word "lion"? Only 259! In addition to the regular search features, you can use the Strategies dialog box to find information by category, region, age, era, century, and country. Moreover, when you finish reading, you can save your place with bookmarks that you can recall the next time you run the program.

Although Library of the Future's Windows interface is somewhat non-standard, you'll barely need the on-line manual to find your way around. The DOS version includes all the same features, but runs quite a bit zippier than the Windows version. In either case, this CD is a gold mine of important writings from down through the ages.

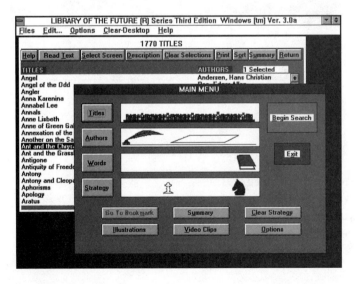

The Library of the Future

Microsoft Bookshelf

Manufacturer: Microsoft Corp.
Platforms: Windows, Macintosh
System requirements:
  Windows—386 or better, 4MB RAM, VGA or better graphics, CD-ROM
  drive, sound card
  Mac—256-color graphics, System 7, CD-ROM drive
Price range: $$

Nothing can replace a good set of reference books, and Microsoft has taken seven of the best and converted them into a multimedia CD-ROM that contains the answer to just about any question. Included on this omnibus reference work are *The American Heritage Dictionary, The Original Roget's Thesaurus, The Columbia Dictionary of Quotations, The Concise Columbia Encyclopedia, Hammond Intermediate World Atlas, The People's Chronology,* and *The World Almanac and Book of Facts.*

So that your references are always available, Bookshelf loads its QuickShelf button bar whenever you start Windows. The button bar is always visible on-screen and can take you to the book of your choice with a single mouse click. Amazingly, you can find information on any word in any application in which you happen to be working. Just highlight the word and click on a button in the QuickShelf button bar. Bookshelf springs into action and presents you with a list of places the word appears in all of the books.

But Microsoft Bookshelf is much more than a text-based reference. You can hear the spoken pronunciations of over 80,000 words and listen to 40 audio clips of famous people like John F. Kennedy and Dylan Thomas. In addition, you can listen to over 160 national anthems and watch animation sequences on dozens of subjects. The fast search functions make it easy to find material in any book, and the Gallery list gives you direct access to all of Bookshelf's multimedia objects. Microsoft Bookshelf is a complete and easy-to-use computerized reference. What more could you ask for?

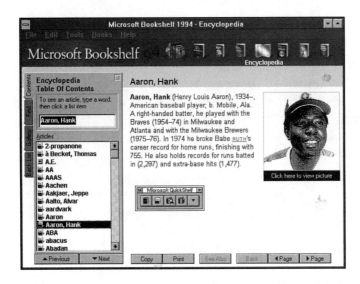

Microsoft Bookshelf

The American Heritage Talking Dictionary

Manufacturer: Softkey International, Inc.
Platforms: Windows, Macintosh
System requirements:
    Windows—386 or better, 4MB RAM, CD-ROM drive, sound card
    Macintosh—CD-ROM drive
Price range: $$

The American Heritage Talking Dictionary from Softkey is a complete electronic dictionary that can give you not only the spelling of any word, but also the definition and a real-voice pronunciation. In addition, for extra convenience, many applications (such as Word for Windows and Ami Pro) let you install the dictionary right into the application's menu bar, so it's instantly available whenever you need it.

The program contains five main modules that'll delight any word aficionado. The first module, the main dictionary, can display the definition of any word you type. The built-in thesaurus can find the perfect word for any situation; the word hunter, on the other hand, finds all the definitions that contain any word you specify. Finally, The American Heritage Talking Dictionary can create anagrams or find words that match incomplete words using wild cards.

You can also search for words by using Boolean operators such as AND, OR, and NOT. For example, enter "large AND cat," and the program finds leopard, lion, mountain lion, panther, and tiger. Also the program can find words by using special search categories, such as citations, etymology, and idioms. One thing's for sure, having a dictionary on your computer can save you a lot of time finding words. Note that non-talking versions of the dictionary (including one that'll run under DOS), which require no CD-ROM drive, are also available.

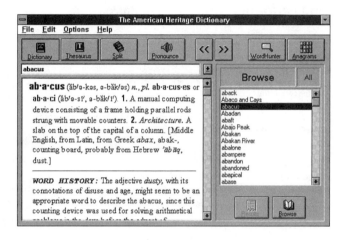

The American Heritage Talking Dictionary

The Columbia Electronic Dictionary of Quotations

Manufacturer: AAPEX Software Corp.
Platform: Windows
System requirements: Minimum
Price range: $$

Nothing bolsters a piece of writing quite so much as a profound quotation from some literary master. With The Columbia Electronic Dictionary of Quotations, your search for quotations can be as simple as a couple of mouse clicks. This dictionary of quotations, which claims to have "six pounds and 1,500 pages of wisdom packed into 5.5MB of disk space" offers more than 18,000 quotations from 3,500 authors on 1,500 subjects.

Although the program's interface is simplistic, it allows you to search for quotations based on subject, author, source, text string, and more. The database is fully indexed by author, source, biography, citation, life span, subject, and quotation, and you can view any of the indexes by selecting them from the menu bar. In spite of the immense amount of text included with the program, the search mechanism is almost instantaneous.

Once you locate your quotation, you can highlight it on-screen and copy it to Windows' Clipboard, from which you can paste it into your document. The mark command lets you mark a series of quotations and copy them all to the Clipboard simultaneously. In addition, the program's simple toolbar provides buttons for moving backward and forward through quotations, as well as for selecting fonts and performing other general tasks.

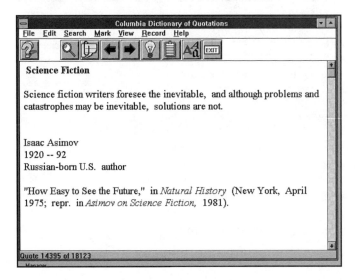

The Columbia Electronic Dictionary of Quotations

Twain's World

Manufacturer: Bureau Development Inc.
Platform: Windows
System requirements: 386 or better, DOS 3.3 or later, VGA graphics, CD-ROM, sound board suggested
Price range: $

In spite of the title's terrible pun, Twain's World is a serious piece of software for folks who are into this famous American author's writings. One of the least-expensive CD-ROM titles available, Twain's World includes over 300 unabridged pieces of Mark Twain's work, including not only novels and short stories, but also speeches, essays, and even letters.

This multimedia presentation also features myriad photos, as well as narrated slide shows and even short video clips, including a short film of Twain that is reputed to have been taken by Thomas Edison. Although the disc features many works, you can find specific titles easily by checking the table of contents or by performing different types of searches, all accessed from the program's button bar. For students wishing to get more insight into Twain's work, Twain's World also includes critical essays by other authors.

Because older children tend to be fascinated by books like *The Adventures of Tom Sawyer*, it doesn't take much to get them to explore Mark Twain's writings further. Twain's World, with its multimedia presentation, may be just the boost your kids (and you) need.

Twain's World

Microsoft Encarta

Manufacturer: Microsoft Corp.
Platforms: Windows, Macintosh
System requirements:
Windows—386 or better, 4MB RAM, VGA graphics, CD-ROM, sound board
Macintosh—Color Mac II or better, System 7.0 or later
Price range: $$

Although Encarta is not as well-aimed at the young student as Compton's
Interactive Encyclopedia, when it comes to multimedia presentations, Encarta
can't be beat. For example, Encarta features seven hours worth of sound,
including music, animal sounds, and word pronunciations. There are also
plenty of videos, photos, animations, and interactive charts. Moreover,
Encarta's expertly produced animations and videos tend to be longer than
those in other CD-ROM encyclopedias, sometimes lasting over two minutes.
The video segments use a much larger screen, although they do run slower.

Microsoft Encarta is also the easiest to use of the CD-ROM encyclopedias,
featuring a carefully designed interface. You can find your way around using
topic lists that display thumbnail sketches of photos, a Find function for
searching the encyclopedia's text, and a full table of contents. In addition, the
Gallery Wizard guides you step by step through locating specific pictures,
sounds, animations, maps, and videos. And the Find Wizard makes it a snap
to compose text search criteria.

To add to the program's value, Encarta comes with an on-line dictionary,
thesaurus, and atlas. Encarta also includes the educational game MindMaze in
which you explore a castle by answering questions based on the encyclopedia's contents. If you're not concerned about the slightly higher reading
level of the articles, Encarta is almost the perfect CD-ROM encyclopedia.

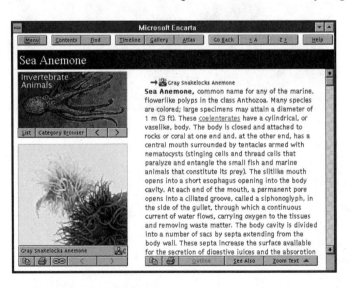

Microsoft Encarta

Compton's Interactive Encyclopedia

Manufacturer: Compton's NewMedia Inc.
Platforms: Windows, Macintosh
System requirements:
    Windows—386 or better, 4MB RAM, VGA graphics, CD-ROM,
    sound card
    Macintosh—LC or better, 4MB RAM, color graphics, CD-ROM
Price range: $$$$

If you're looking for a good student's reference work, Compton's Interactive Encyclopedia may be exactly what you need. This CD-ROM program is easy to use, and its writing level is precisely aimed at readers between the ages of 8 and 15. Boasting 32,000 articles comprising nine million words—not to mention 13,000 images, maps, and graphs; 50 minutes of sound, music, and speech; 90 multimedia sequences; 5,000 charts and diagrams; and the complete Merriam-Webster's OnLine Dictionary—this reference book was designed for one-stop shopping.

Compton's supplies various ways for you to hone in on information. The Idea Search function lets you type in plain-English queries like "How do rockets work?" The program then generates a list of topics from which you can choose. If you click on the Contents button, the table-of-contents window appears, from which you can select a topic. Typing the first few letters of a topic jumps you instantly forward in the list. The Topic Tree, on the other hand, lets you start by selecting a topic like Law, which generates a list of subtopics and articles.

Although Compton's video-sequence screens are small (only about two inches square), they feature many interesting, voice-annotated presentations. The slide shows, too, include not only near photographic-quality images, but also music and voice. Unfortunately, the multimedia presentations tend to be very short, typically less than 30 seconds each. In any case, it'll be many, many hours before your family runs out of things to learn about with Compton's Interactive Encyclopedia.

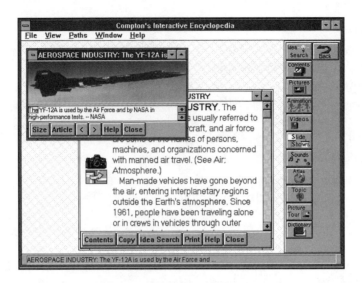

Compton's Interactive Encyclopedia

The New Grolier Multimedia Encyclopedia

Manufacturer: Grolier Electronic Publishing
Platforms: Windows, DOS, Macintosh
System requirements:
    Windows—386 or better, DOS 3.3 or later, 4MB RAM, VGA graphics,
    CD-ROM, sound card
    DOS—386 or better, DOS 3.1 or later, VGA graphics, hard disk
    CD-ROM, sound card, mouse
    Macintosh—Color graphics, 4MB RAM, CD-ROM
Price range: $$ ($$$ for DOS)

Although The New Grolier Multimedia Encyclopedia is somewhat lacking in
the multimedia department when compared with Compton's and Encarta, it
contains the most information, featuring all the text from the 21-volume
Academic American Encyclopedia. In addition, of the encyclopedia's 23,000
contributors, many are well-known experts in their fields. For the serious
academic, then, Grolier's may be the best choice.

The New Grolier does feature plenty of photos, music, speeches, video clips,
and animations. (The animations are not available in the DOS version.) All
told, there are over 3,000 photos, 35 minutes of sound, 34 animations, and 53

video clips. An atlas boasting 250 maps also comes on the CD-ROM, with the maps linked to appropriate articles in the encyclopedia.

Finding information is fairly easy with Grolier's, thanks to its Knowledge Tree, which leads you down through topics and subtopics until you find the article you want. You can also access an alphabetical list of articles or use Boolean operators to search the entire encyclopedia for specific text. When one considers its comprehensive text and authoritative articles, for college-age and up, The New Grolier Multimedia Encyclopedia should be able to stand up to just about any informational need.

Speed

Manufacturer: Knowledge Adventure, Inc.
Platform: DOS
System requirements: 386 or better, DOS 3.1 or later, VGA graphics,
    hard disk, CD-ROM, sound card
Price range: $

Speed is unique among the CD-ROM titles reviewed in this book in that it features a 28-minute interactive motion picture. The movie, entitled "Speed," traces up through the ages man's need to go fast, from prehistoric man to modern-day space travelers. You can watch the movie from beginning to end or use it to choose speed topics in which you're interested. To choose a topic, you pause the movie and click on the screen. This action places you into a sort of multimedia encyclopedia called the Speed Reference that offers more information about the topic in the movie.

The Speed Reference also lets you easily select various topics. You can click on the program's speed bar in order to select a topic that best matches the chosen speed. In this way, you can go from learning about the first bicycle to discovering whether man will ever go faster than the speed of light—all with a click of your mouse. You can also click on areas of the displayed globe in order to discover speed topics related to the selected area. The Speed Reference itself displays images and text along with a real-voice narration.

Speed also includes simulations, games, and the Extended Learning Module. In the simulations, you see various film clips about speed, including a roller coaster ride and a running track star. The games challenge you to match an object to the correct speed, brush up on your speed reading, and make your way as fast as possible through a pseudo-3D maze. Finally, the Extended Learning Module suggests experiments for learning about speed in the real world.

Speed

Microsoft Dinosaurs

Manufacturer: Microsoft Corp.
Platforms: Windows, Macintosh
System requirements:
  Windows—386 or better, 4MB RAM, VGA graphics, CD-ROM,
  sound card
  Mac—4MB RAM, Color graphics, CD-ROM
Price range: $$

If you can afford only one dinosaur program, Microsoft Dinosaurs ought to be the one. Although it lacks the 3D images and movie found in 3D Dinosaur Adventure, its slick interface, stunning visuals, professional narrations, and awe-inspiring movies more than compensate.

Microsoft Dinosaur's interface allows you to learn about dinosaurs in various ways. You can take a guided tour, in which your narrator takes you through one of sixteen topics, describing each screen as you go. Or, if you like more free-form exploration, you can chart your own path through the life of the dinosaurs by clicking on buttons to hear narrations about the current topic, selecting highlighted words to bring up definitions, and clicking on jump words to branch immediately to a related topic.

Microsoft Dinosaurs also features six almost full-screen movies complete with music and voice. The professional quality of these films is surprising. In fact, the three-minute movie entitled "The Chase" is absolutely gripping, as harrowing as a scene from Spielberg's *Jurassic Park*. Add the program's illustrated index and its Timeline and Families screens that enable you to quickly find the facts you need, and you have a fascinating resource that's hard to beat.

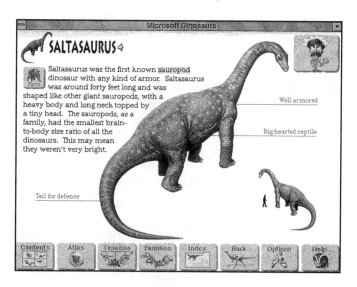

Microsoft Dinosaurs

Grolier Prehistoria

Manufacturer: Grolier Electronic Publishing Inc.
Platforms: Windows, Macintosh
System requirements:
    Windows—DOS 5.0 or later, 386 or better, 4MB RAM, 256-color VGA, CD-ROM, sound card
    Mac—LC II or better, 4MB RAM, 256-color graphics, CD-ROM
Price range: $$

Almost as graphically stunning as Microsoft Dinosaurs, Grolier Prehistoria covers a much wider range of material. Although there is plenty of information about dinosaurs, you can also learn about other prehistoric creatures, going back 250 million years before the dinosaurs and going forward all the way to early man. Prehistoria's Gallery enables you to browse through the creatures by selecting ever-narrowing groups until you single out the creature of your choice. The Creature Show, on the other hand, offers a slide show of prehistoric creatures.

One of Prehistoria's biggest strengths is its strong multimedia presentation. With a total of over 60 minutes of multimedia, this package features dozens of audio-visual essays and narrated movies, including movies that are also included with Microsoft Dinosaurs. The multimedia presentations cover such topics as fossils, extinction, prehistoric earth, the lives of dinosaurs, baby dinosaurs, and more. If you prefer mini-movies to static graphics, this package may be the one for you.

Grolier Prehistoria

Discover Space

Manufacturer: Broderbund Software
Platform: DOS
System requirements: 386 or better, VGA or better graphics, hard disk
Price range: $

Blast off with Discover Space and explore the universe, learning fascinating facts about such cosmic topics as planets, stars, constellations, moons, and asteroids. To help you find the information you want, the program is divided into six sections covering the sun, star maps, deep sky objects, the planets, space exploration, and comets and asteroids. Just click on a topic, and the appropriate screen appears.

All the screens are rendered in awe-inspiring detail. In addition, sound effects and music add to the program's overall atmosphere. Moreover, in order to illustrate some more complex ideas, Discover Space features a number of short animations of such events as solar eclipses, sun flares, and the rotation of the earth. In the star viewer, you can watch the stars from different positions and times of the year, including a celestial sphere or a skyline. In addition, you can turn on and off the associated constellations.

InfoNation

Manufacturer: Software Marketing Corp
Platform: DOS
System requirements: DOS 3.3 or later, 386 or better, VGA or better graphics, hard disk, mouse
Price range: $

InfoNation is a program that provides maps and information about all areas of the United States (the "Nation"). Whereas Broderbund's PC USA can run on just about any computer system, InfoNation requires a more state-of-the-art machine. But if you can meet the hardware requirements, and you have the extra space on your hard drive, InfoNation is a much more graphically pleasing program than PC USA. InfoNation's maps use 3D satellite imagery to ensure stunning realism. In addition, the program's Windows-like interface is both attractive and a snap to use.

You can easily customize InfoNation's main map to show different kinds of data. By simply clicking a few buttons, you can have the map display states, metropolitan areas, cities, roads, national parks, Indian reservations, military bases, and more. Moreover, you can view the map in any of four different magnifications.

Using InfoNation, you can gather information in any of ten general categories, including people, housing, money, crime, health, education, the arts, sports, transportation, and environment. Each main topic leads to a lengthy list of subtopics. For example, click on Housing, and you get a list of almost fifty housing subtopics. Choose a subtopic, and the information you requested is displayed on the screen. Because both PC USA and InfoNation can supply similar information, you should choose which program to use based on your computer's configuration.

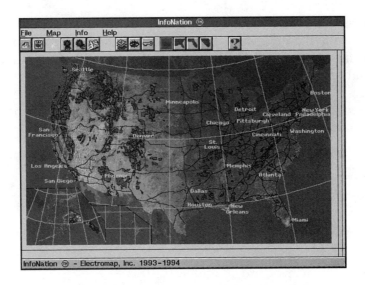

InfoNation

PC Globe Maps 'n' Facts

Manufacturer: Broderbund Software
Platform: DOS
System requirements: 386 or better, VGA or better graphics, hard disk
Price range: $

Maps 'n' Facts is sort of a super version of PC USA, which is also reviewed in this book. But rather than being limited to only the United States, Maps 'n' Facts covers the entire world, although not in as much detail as PC USA does. Maps 'n' Facts' Windows-like screen contributes to a slick and easy-to-use interface. By clicking on buttons displayed on the left side of the screen, you can quickly change the current map view. In addition, clicking the map itself enables you to zoom in to different areas of the world.

Maps 'n' Facts can display six basic types of maps: political, physical, statistical, group, time zone, and custom. The type of map you choose determines the type of data displayed on the map. In addition, you can call up detailed information on countries, cities, rankings, and currency, to name a few topics. For example, the rankings information screen lists, from highest to lowest, continent sizes, river lengths, city populations, and other similar data. The city information screen displays facts for each of the 4,839 cities in the database—including population, time zone, and phone codes.

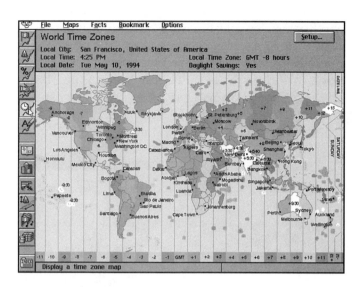

PC Globe Maps 'n' Facts

Automap Road Atlas

Manufacturer: Broderbund
Platforms: Windows, DOS, Macintosh
System requirements:
    Windows—Minimum
    DOS—DOS 3.3 or later, EGA or better graphics
    Mac—Classic II or better
Price range: $$

Planning a trip can be a real stumper if you're not familiar with the country's roads. You could join AAA, or you could do your own trip planning by buying Broderbund's Automap Road Atlas. Using Automap Road Atlas, you can display detailed road maps of any part of the United States. You can even zoom in for a closer look at specific areas. Locating cities is as easy as typing in a name. In addition, to identify roads and cities on the map, you need only click on a map marker.

You can customize the map display in a number of ways, by turning on or off such details as places, names, roads, routes, and coastlines. Moreover, you can change the types of graphics used to display various map elements. Once you have the map looking just how you like it, Automap Road Atlas can send the display to your printer.

One of Automap Road Atlas's best features is its ability to plan trips for you. Just mark your starting and ending points on the map, and the program can show you the quickest, shortest, preferred, or alternate routes. The detailed travel instructions, including the length of the trip in miles, the approximate travel time, and the cost of gas, appear in a table that you can immediately print out to take with you on your trip. Best of all, you can have Automap Road Atlas suggest interesting sights to see along your route.

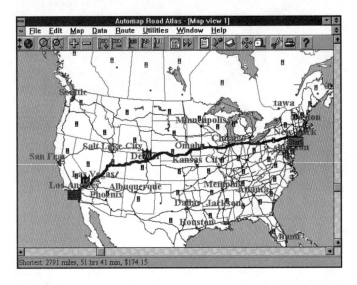

Automap Road Atlas

PC USA

Manufacturer: Broderbund
Platforms: DOS, Macintosh
System requirements:
   DOS—Minimum
   Mac—Minimum
Price range: $

PC USA is an interactive atlas that provides a wealth of information about the United States. Using the drop-down menus and your mouse or keyboard, you can select regions of the U.S., groups of states based on several criteria, or individual states, and then view information about everything from a state's population to crime statistics and living conditions.

In fact, so much information is available for any selected state that the program is useful for more than just the casual student. Anybody, including business people and travelers, who needs to know detailed state data can benefit from PC USA. You can quickly find information on population, age distribution, ethnic groups, education, resources, agriculture, taxes, average pay, government, history, climate, and even ZIP codes and area codes. In addition, various bar charts let you compare data.

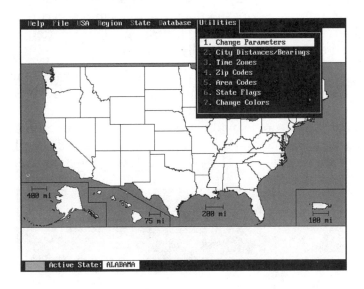

PC USA

MovieSelect

Manufacturer: Paramount Interactive
Platforms: Windows, Macintosh
System requirements:
  Windows—386 or better, 4MB RAM, 256-color VGA graphics, sound card
  Mac—LC or better, 4MB RAM, 14" color monitor
Price range: $

Sometimes it seems as though there are more movies than there are stars in the galaxy. So when it's time to rent that Saturday night video, you may have a tough time narrowing down your choices. But don't despair. MovieSelect is an electronic movie critic that can convert your mood and tastes into a list of recommended movies. Just tell the program what movies you've seen and liked, and it generates a "highly recommended" and "recommended" list from which you can choose your weekend entertainment.

Once you get your recommendations, you can filter them by movie type or thematic content. For example, you can select movie genres like Action/Adventure, Comedy, Drama, Sci-Fi/Fantasy, and Horror/Suspense, just to name a few. Or if the genre doesn't matter, select a movie according to such styles as Triumph of the Spirit, Dark/Disturbing, Light Hearted, Off-Beat, Fast-Paced, and even…ahem…Sexually Charged.

Before you run off to the video store with your list, you can get further information about any of the listed films. Just click the film's title, and a complete description of the movie appears on-screen. You can also use the search functions to find every movie made by a particular actor or all the movies made by a particular director. Finally, the Hollywood Guide displays alphabetized lists of all the videos, actors, and directors in the database.

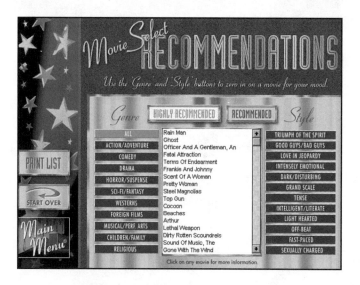

MovieSelect

Mega Movie Guide

Manufacturer: INFOBUSINESS Software
Platforms: Windows
System requirements: 386 or better, VGA or better graphics, CD-ROM drive, sound card
Price range: $$

Mega Movie Guide features reviews of over 60,000 films (from films of the early 1900s through such current flicks as *Jurassic Park*, *The Firm*, and *Sleepless in Seattle*), as well as major Academy Award winners and nominees for all years since the start of the awards. In addition, you can view almost two hours worth of video clips showing important scenes from major films, and examine over 50 movie stills. There are even biographies of major motion picture stars.

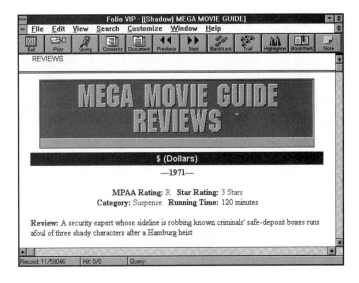

Mega Movie Guide

Mega Movie Guide's interface is a bit unusual and may take some getting used to. For example, the major sections of the guide are all combined into one huge document that you can scroll through, as opposed to being separate entries in a database. But once you get the hang of it, you can use the search functions to find just about any piece of information (every word in the guide

285

is indexed). In addition, buttons in the reviews lead to video clips, movie stills, and other related displays. Moreover, key words are linked to other sections. Click on an actor's name, for example, and you can use the Next and Previous buttons to jump to all references to that actor.

If Mega Movie Guide has a weak point, it's the length of time it takes to run a search. Even something as simple as scrolling through a table of contents list is very slow, requiring that the next screen be read from the CD-ROM before it can be displayed. Still, Mega Movie Guide offers a lot of information for a reasonable price.

Microsoft Cinemania '94

Manufacturer: Microsoft Corp.
Platforms: Windows, Macintosh
System requirements:
    Windows—386 or better, VGA graphics, CD-ROM, sound board
    Mac—System 7.0, 256-color graphics, CD-ROM
Price range: $$

Movie buffs will go bonkers over Microsoft Cinemania '94, which features not only reviews of over 19,000 movies, but also biographies of thousands of stars, as well as movie stills and even film clips. The program's fast search functions can locate any topic you want in a flash, and the highlighted words in the text provide links to related subjects. Just click a word, and you instantly branch off to the new topic.

Cinemania's main control looks a lot like a VCR remote, containing buttons that let you select reviews from as many as four different sources (Roger Ebert, Leonard Maltin, Pauline Kael, and Baseline), select movie stills and film clips, check a movie's credits, list a star's complete filmographies, and more. The program's Gallery displays a complete list of all the stills, portraits, film clips, dialog, and music on the disc, making selection easy and quick.

Finally, you can get a complete list of all the Academy Award winners and nominees for every year since the awards started. Movie links in the awards list let you jump immediately to any movie listed. And, if you like lists, you can use Cinemania's easy ListMaker function to create a shopping list for the next time you drop into the video store. No excuses for missing those movies now!

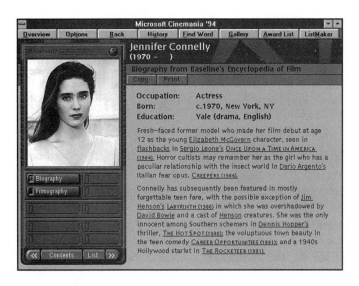

Microsoft Cinemania '94

Microsoft Art Gallery

Manufacturer: Microsoft Corp.
Platforms: Windows, Macintosh
System requirements:
   Windows—386 or better, 4MB RAM, 256-color VGA graphics,
   CD-ROM, sound board
   Mac—4MB RAM, 256-color graphics, CD-ROM
Price range: $$

Microsoft Art Gallery takes a much more restrained approach to multimedia than do most of their other CD-ROM titles, utilizing only dignified narratives and simple animations to describe many of the pieces in this worthwhile collection. From the Contents window, you can opt to learn about the artists lives, explore the art of a particular location on the map, browse through art based on its type, explore the general reference, or take one of four guided tours.

It's in the guided tours that you can hear the real-voice narrations, as well as view simple animation sequences that illustrate how many of the artists work. The guided tours' topics are Composition and Perspective, Making Paintings, Paintings as Objects, and Beneath the Varnish. In the illustrated general reference, you can locate subjects by first clicking on the starting letter and then choosing the subject from the index that appears.

Art Gallery's interface is easy to understand, providing interactive buttons that enable you to navigate through the program with ease. For example, when following a path through a subject, you can use the Go Back button to move back to the previous screen or the Next Page button to move forward. In addition, the Help, Options, See Also, and Contents buttons give you quick access to other program functions.

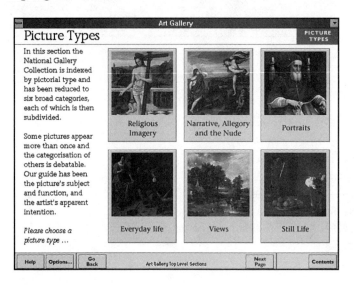

Microsoft Art Gallery

MediaClips

Manufacturer: Aris Multimedia Entertainment, Inc.
Platforms: Windows, Macintosh
System requirements:
   Windows—386 or better, 4MB RAM, super VGA graphics, CD-ROM, sound card
   Macintosh—System 7.0 or later, 256-color graphics, CD-ROM
Price range: $

Nothing can spruce up a computer screen quite so much as some photographic-quality images. A little music and sound doesn't hurt to improve the computer experience, either. With Aris Entertainment's MediaClips, you can add hundreds of fabulous sights and sounds to your computer system. Each disc in the set contains 100 photographic-quality images, 25 videos, and 100 music clips, all of which you can use for your own purposes, royalty free.

Whether you're just setting up some wallpaper for your Windows screen or putting together a business presentation, MediaClip's slick interface will get the job done fast. You can select any of the images from a series of thumbnails, activate the program's slide show, or look through the images using the VCR-style controls. To keep things interesting, each image is accompanied with a music sound clip. Once you've found the picture or music clip you need, MediaClip's copy function transfers the files to your hard disk for you.

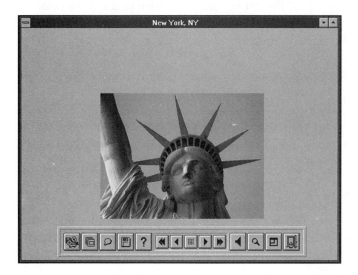

MediaClips

Adult Education and Self-Improvement

T he software in this category helps you become smarter or better informed. Maybe you're studying for a college entrance exam or trying to get through a literature course. Maybe you want to learn another language or look for a new job. Whatever your needs, there is a software to fill them. Check out the following reviews, and also the reviews in the "Reference Software" section.

Your Personal Trainer for the SAT

Manufacturer: Davidson & Associates, Inc.
Platforms: Windows, Macintosh
System requirements:
Windows—3MB RAM, VGA or better graphics
Mac—System 7.0 or later
Price range: $$

Getting good scores on the SAT (Scholastic Aptitude Test) can make a difference for your child's future, so it makes sense to be prepared. Your Personal Trainer for the SAT is a computer program that teaches your child how to take the SATs and tests the child's abilities in the many areas of skills covered by the typical SAT test. In fact, Personal Trainer includes as many sample questions as a student is likely to find on five full SAT tests. In addition, test booklets that are packed with the program feature two complete tests in the actual SAT format.

But this is more than a test-taking program. Personal trainer actually creates a training schedule for each individual and tracks that person's results in order to improve SAT scores. The student's progress is charted on colorful three-dimensional graphs, showing scores for verbal, math, analogies, sentence completion, and other SAT test categories. Finally, to break up the work, the program includes an SAT Game, which lets your student practice SAT questions while competing against the clock.

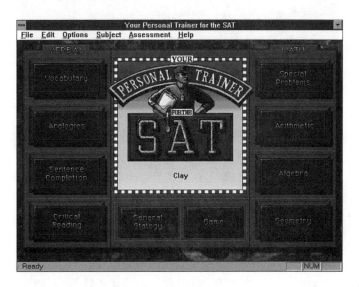

Your Personal Trainer for the SAT

Cliffs StudyWare for the SAT

Manufacturer: Cliffs Notes, Inc.
Platforms: DOS, Macintosh
System requirements:
   DOS—VGA graphics, hard disk
   Macintosh—Minimum
Price range: $

If one of your kids is facing SAT tests this year, you might want to check out Cliffs StudyWare for the SAT, which turns your home computer into an online SAT study hall. Cliffs Preparation Guide, a 440-page book included in the package, provides a complete introduction to each test topic and focuses on strategies (such as effective use of time, how to avoid wrong answers, and knowing when to skip questions) for obtaining the highest possible SAT scores. The book also features three full-length sample tests.

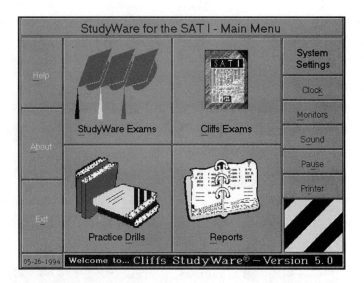

Cliffs StudyWare for the SAT

The computerized side of the package enables a student to practice and refine SAT test-taking skills. Because the program can track the student's performance, it can direct the student toward the best use of his study time. In addition, various reports, including a personalized study program and score graphs, can be viewed on-screen or sent to a printer. The program also features an on-screen clock, sound options, full on-line help, and an easy-to-use graphical interface.

Score-Rx for the SAT

Manufacturer: Xenon Educational Systems, Inc.
Platforms: Windows, DOS, Macintosh
System requirements:
  Windows—Minimum
  DOS—DOS 3.3 or later, hard disk
  Mac—Minimum
Price range: $$

Score-Rx for the SAT is probably the most graphically visual of the SAT programs reviewed in this book. Its on-screen 3D graphs, scoring charts, and question-and-answer sections are all attractively laid out and often resemble screens you'd see in an application like a spreadsheet. The program covers both the PSAT and SAT tests, and includes three sample test booklets, as well as various on-screen tests that you can take to improve your test-taking skills.

Score-Rx for the SAT runs in two modes: test and tutor. In the test mode, you answer a test section's questions, after which the test is scored and stored in your personal database. In the tutor mode, you are immediately informed whether the answer you chose was correct. A comprehensive menu bar and toolbar provide easy mouse or keyboard access to all the program's functions.

Although the program's manual offers only minimal strategies for increasing test scores (unlike Cliffs StudyWare for the SAT, which includes a 440-page book), Score-Rx for the SAT I displays and prints extensive charts and graphs showing your progress and the analyses of tests. Despite the program's tendency to crash now and then, it provides a solid foundation upon which to build SAT skills.

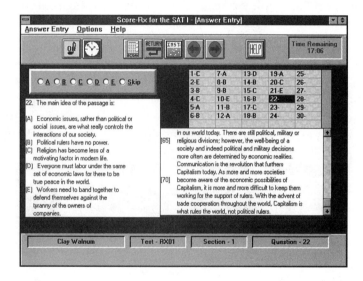

Score-Rx for the SAT I

Monarch Notes

Manufacturer: Bureau of Electronic Publishing
Platforms: Windows, DOS, Macintosh
System requirements:
    Windows—386 or better, VGA or better graphics, CD-ROM drive
    DOS—DOS 3.1 or later
    Mac—CD-ROM drive
Price range: $$

This program features the full text of 256 Monarch guides—every one that's ever been published. You can learn about such literary classics as Daniel Defoe's *Robinson Crusoe*, Thomas Paine's *Common Sense*, Jane Austen's *Pride and Prejudice*, Charles Dickens' *A Tale of Two Cities*, and Ray Bradbury's *The Martian Chronicles*. In fact, the works covered in this CD-ROM edition cover periods from Oral Tradition all the way to the twentieth century.

In addition, the program includes photographs, narrated passages and quotations, videos, and animations. However, like Great Literature Plus (which is also reviewed in this book), the animations are fairly crude, being little more than hastily drawn cartoons. Still, Monarch Notes is a powerful resource of literary criticism. For example, the program's "hot spots" enable you to click on highlighted text to display pop-up definitions, and the search function can find every occurrence of a word in all the works covered.

Added to the mix is a complete glossary of literary terms, an index showing not only the included topics but also the number of references for the topic, and pop-up lists that let you choose new topics related to the current screen. Finally, the Gallery provides quick access to all the program's multimedia features. The bottom line is that any literature student will find Monarch Notes to be an invaluable guide to writings down through the centuries.

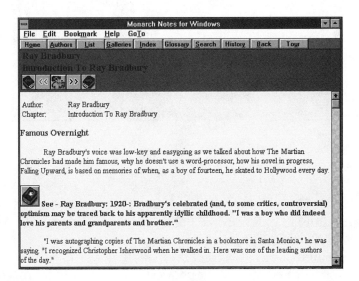

Monarch Notes

Translate It!

Manufacturer: Timeworks International
Platforms: Windows, DOS
System requirements:
   Windows—386 or better
   DOS—386 or better, DOS 5.0 or later, hard disk
Price range: $$

Translating text from one language to another is a long, painstaking process. Luckily, if you have to perform such tasks, Translate It! can do the grunt work, leaving you with only some text-polishing chores. Basically, Translate It! is a program that can translate text files between English and some other language. The three versions of the program cover Spanish, French, and German bi-directional translation.

Translate It! couldn't be easier to use. Just load the document you want to translate and click the translate button. The program starts chugging, translating text at a rate of over 300 words a minute and boasting accuracies of between 90 and 95 percent. Of course, no machine can provide a perfect translation so, during translation, the program marks unknown words with error flags. You can then edit the flagged words and, if you want, add them to the program's dictionary for future use.

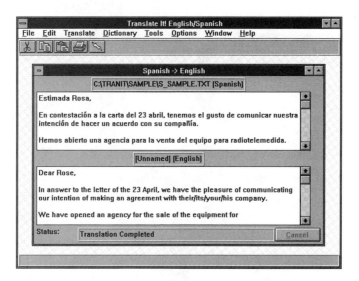

Translate It! for Windows

When the translation is complete, you can save the new text to its own file. Then you can use your own word processor to put the finishing touches on the document. Translate It! can save you an immense amount of time if you regularly need to translate documents. It doesn't, however, eliminate the need for foreign-language skills. You still have to know how to correct the translated text, especially if the translation is from English to another language.

Learn to Speak Spanish 4.0

Manufacturer: HyperGlot Software
Platforms: Windows, Macintosh
System requirements:

Windows—33MHz 386 or better, 4MB RAM, super VGA, CD-ROM, sound card

Mac—LC III or better, System 7.0 or later, 256-color graphics, CD-ROM

Price range: $$

Learning to speak a foreign language can be a challenge, but Learn to Speak Spanish on CD-ROM from HyperGlot Software helps make that challenge more surmountable. Providing 30 lessons that teach you to communicate in many practical situations, the program covers not only verbal skills, but also important reading skills. In fact, when you've finished all the lessons, you'll have taken the equivalent of a two- to three-year high-school Spanish class.

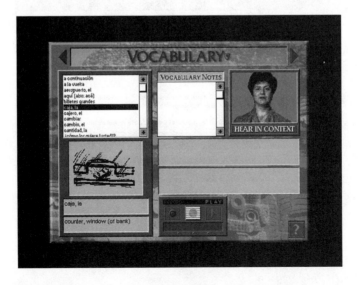

Learn to Speak Spanish

The structure of the lessons enables you to concentrate on different aspects of the language. For example, you can choose to listen to a conversation between two people, or you can opt for a vocabulary drill or work on your grammar. Each lesson also features appropriate customizable tests and quizzes. Although the program requires a CD-ROM drive, the addition of integrated speech removes the need for external cassette players or other sound devices that cannot be linked directly with the program.

To help you use your new skills in real situations, Learn to Speak Spanish features video movies, as well as an extensive workbook. If you have a microphone, you can even record yourself speaking in your new language. If you can't meet the stringent hardware requirements for version 4.0, version 3.0 (which includes no movies and is about $50 cheaper) is also still available.

French Assistant

Manufacturer: MicroTac Software, Inc.
Platforms: Windows, DOS, (Macintosh forthcoming)
System requirements:
   Windows—386 or better, 4MB RAM
   DOS—Hard disk
Price range: $$

Not only can French Assistant translate documents between English and French (in either direction), but its reference tools can also help you brush up on your own French. In order to make document translation as easy as possible, the program supports many file formats, including Word for Windows, WordPerfect, Microsoft Write, and Ami Pro. Doing the actual translation is as easy as clicking a button, and two types of translations, automatic and interactive, give you control over the final translation's accuracy.

In the automatic mode, the program simply reads the original file and translates it accordingly. However, exact translations of this type are never 100% accurate. The interactive mode increases translation accuracy by allowing you to choose from a list of meanings for words that are ambiguous in their current context. The program also includes a searchable French dictionary (to which you can add or delete additional words and phrases), as well as grammar help and conjugations of over 3,000 verbs.

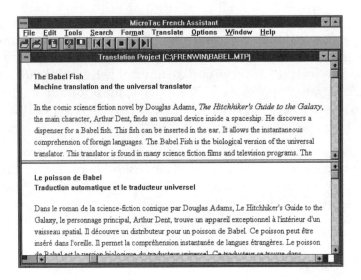

French Assistant

Typing Tutor 6

Manufacturer: Que Software
Platforms: Windows, DOS, (Macintosh forthcoming)
System requirements:
    Windows—Minimum
    DOS—286 or better, DOS 4.0 or later, hard disk
Price range: $

Learning to type may be easier than you think, and with a program like Typing Tutor, it can even be fun. Typing Tutor leads you through each lesson, providing feedback on your improvement and monitoring your abilities so that each lesson is geared specifically for you. You'll begin by learning the location of the keys, and then you'll practice common letter combinations until you graduate to typing passages from best-selling books.

But it isn't all work and no play. Typing Tutor also features a number of simple games that not only help you with your typing skills, but also train you to use a mouse. In Letter Invaders, for example, letters float down from the top of the screen singly and in groups. Your task is to blast them before they hit the ground by typing the correct letter combinations. Mouse Invaders, on the other hand, charges you with keeping the cheese safe, by clicking and double-clicking invading mice into oblivion. Other games include RRiibbit, Keyrobics, and Mouserobics.

After each typing session, you can see graphs depicting your progress or you can print reports. In addition, the program can be configured to perfectly match your current typing skills, providing just enough challenge to ensure improvement. Whether you're just a beginner or an accomplished typist, Typing Tutor has plenty of help to offer.

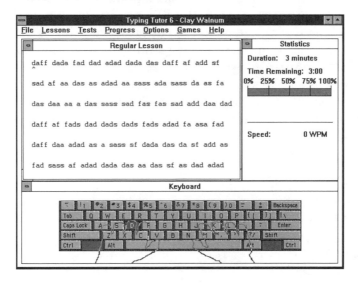

Typing Tutor 6

The Miracle Piano Teaching System

Manufacturer: The Software Toolworks
Platforms: DOS, Macintosh
System requirements:
   DOS—DOS 3.1 or later, serial port
   Mac—Mac Plus or later with a serial port
Price range: $$$$

If you've never played a music synthesizer, a piano-like keyboard that enables you to simulate a number of instruments as you play, the Miracle Keyboard that ships as part of this package will amaze you. Even if you have plenty of practice with such keyboards, the software that accompanies this particular synthesizer will hold many surprises.

The Miracle Piano Teaching System is designed to teach just about anyone how to play the piano. Plug the Miracle Keyboard into a serial port on your computer, install the software, and you're ready to begin playing. In the Classroom, you are led through interactive lessons that begin with how to play single notes with your right hand and how to follow a metronome and that progress to levels that will challenge some intermediate piano players.

In addition to the Classroom, you can visit a practice room to review what you've learned or to practice any of the 40 songs provided with the program. When you feel ready, you can go to the performance hall and play along with a full orchestra or head for the recording studio to record and playback your own performance. An arcade room offers three arcade-style practice games, plus a "jukebox" that plays pre-recorded songs. Although the program has a few annoying features (such as the time it takes to move from one screen to the next), this is a powerful teaching tool for anyone wanting to learn more about playing the piano.

Speed Reader

Manufacturer: Davidson & Associates, Inc.
Platforms: Windows, DOS
System requirements:
   Windows—Minimum
   DOS—Minimum
Price range: $

In this information-intensive world we live in, anything that can get more data into our brains faster is well worth looking into. Speed Reader can help you accomplish that goal by fortifying existing reading skills, while building new ones. Speed Reader claims it can double, triple, or even quadruple your reading speed with no loss in comprehension. In fact, you may even increase your comprehension!

When you start the program, you create an individualized program by first taking a reading test and then selecting the topics you'd like to read about during your training. Then you begin to learn about such important reading techniques as controlling eye movement and better utilizing peripheral vision.

In each lesson, you work in up to six different training modules, including Reading Warm-ups, Eye Movement, Newspaper Reading, Paced Reading, and Timed Reading. And, as you advance, you can view your progress as a training report or as a graph.

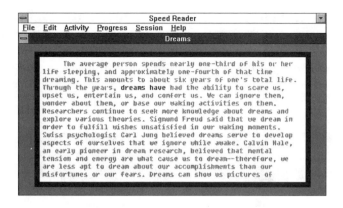

Speed Reader

PFS:Resume & Job Search Pro

Manufacturer: Spinnaker Software
Platforms: Windows, DOS
System requirements:
    Windows—VGA graphics
    DOS—DOS 3.1 or later
Price range: $

Creating a résumé is a challenging task, but with PFS:Resume & Job Search Pro, you can not only get that résumé cranked out quickly and easily, but you can also effectively organize your job search. The program offers many different styles of résumés that you can select with the click of a button. Moreover, its control bar enables you to change fonts, apply text attributes, and set text alignment. In fact, when you come right down to it, PFS:Resume is a full-fledged word processor—but with brains!

When you start a résumé, the program brings up a general form on the screen. You then use the Tab key to move from one section of the résumé to another. When you select a section, it becomes highlighted, and what you type replaces the general text in the form. All the fancy formatting chores are handled automatically by the program; all you do is type. However, you can easily modify the basic résumé forms by adding and removing sections or changing the document as you would with any word processor.

Once you have your job search started, the Job Search Manager keeps you on track. This mini-database lets you store important information about each of your job contacts, including not only names and addresses, but also notes about discussions and a list of activities. In addition, the weekly and monthly calendars show what job-search activities you've completed and which are coming up. To round out the package, the word processor module comes stocked with over a dozen sample letters, guaranteed to impress prospective bosses.

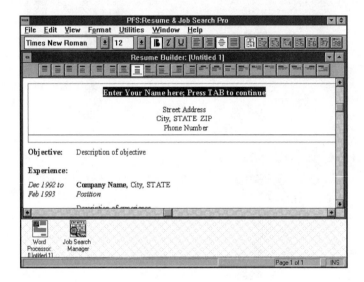

PFS:Resume & Job Search Pro

Job-Power Source

Manufacturer: INFOBUSINESS
Platform: Windows
System requirements: 386 or better, VGA graphics, CD-ROM, sound card
Price range: $

Job-Power Source is an information-packed guide to finding a job in the '90s. In fact, when you consider the number of career books, video clips, sample documents, and worksheets included on this disc, you've got a complete course in the art of job hunting. Employing a three-stage approach to finding a career, Job-Power Source guides you from identifying your abilities and choosing a career to creating résumés and letters. It also focuses on how to handle the nerve-wracking interview process.

From Job-Power Source's main screen, you select the stage with which you want to work, and then choose the specific resource. For example, after selecting Stage Two, you can choose from among the four books *Job Search Letters That Get Results*, *Dynamite Resumes*, *Dynamite Cover Letters*, and *High Impact Resumes & Letters*. To drive home the more important topics, the program includes almost two hours of video clips from lectures by Pat Sladey, an award-winning communications professional. The video clips alone are worth the price of the package.

To help you analyze your abilities and goals, Job-Power Source offers dozens of interactive worksheets. In addition, a button bar features controls that let you move back to previous screens, set bookmarks, highlight text, print the current screen, and more. In short, Job-Power Source includes everything you need to get a job—except the job itself.

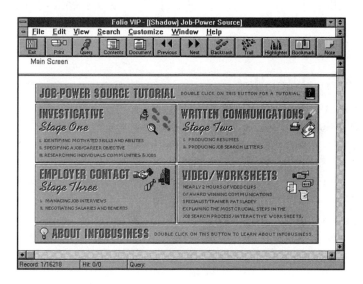

Job-Power Source

Home and Family Software

These days, you can find all kinds of home-oriented software that will do everything from explaining how to fix the kitchen drain to helping you plan a dinner party for 20. You can chart your genealogy, learn about drug interactions, even get parenting advice. Most of the home software on the market is relatively inexpensive, too, making it a great value.

Home Survival Toolkit

Manufacturer: Books That Work
Platform: Windows
System requirements: VGA or better graphics
Price range: $

If you've got a dripping faucet that drives you nuts or a door that gets stuck every time you close it, you could probably use a program like Home Survival Kit, a multimedia "how-to" book of home repairs. The program features twelve chapters on such subjects as Emergencies, Tools, Plumbing, Electrical, Windows and Doors, and Painting that show you how to keep your home repairs up to date. And, thanks to the zippy search functions, finding the information you need is as easy as typing a word and clicking a button.

Of course, you can't solve every repair problem yourself; sometimes you need professional help. At those times, the program's built-in list of toll-free phone numbers can get you in touch with the appropriate company quickly. In addition, three special Estimators help you solve such problems as the amount of paint to buy or how many bags of concrete you need for that new sidewalk. If you don't mind getting your hands dirty, Home Survival Toolkit can save you thousands of dollars in unnecessary repair bills, as well as provide valuable training in home repair.

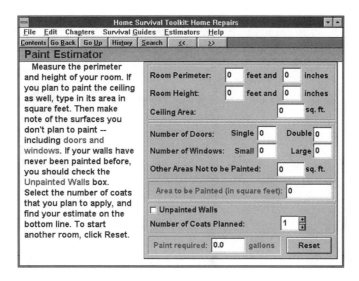

Home Survival Toolkit

Micro Kitchen Companion

Manufacturer: Lifestyle Software Group
Platforms: Windows, DOS, Macintosh
System requirements:
  Windows—Minimum
  DOS—DOS 3.0 or higher
  Mac—Minimum
Price range: $

Lifestyle Software Group has a huge selection of electronic cookbooks, as well as a slew of other types of software. Their Micro Kitchen Companion comes packaged with two on-line recipe books totaling over 500 dishes. The "A Taste for All Seasons" cookbook includes recipes for everything from Amaretto Mousse to Zuppa Di Cozze, including traditional favorites like Barbecued Chicken Wings, Caesar Salad, and Meat Loaf. The "New Currents in American Cuisine" also features many favorites, along with more experimental dishes.

The interface for the Windows version of the program is a bit hard to handle, often leaving you confused for a moment or two. But once you get the hang of it, you'll be able to quickly find the recipes you need, add to your own recipes, or edit existing recipes. A great convenience is the program's capability to group recipes under one heading like "Christmas Dinner." And, once you've got your meals planned out, you can print a shopping list of the ingredients, list nutritional information, resize a recipe, and print the recipe.

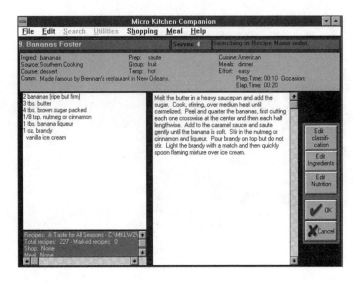

Micro Kitchen Companion

Micro Cookbook

Manufacturer: Pinpoint Publishing
Platform: Windows
System requirements: 386 or better, DOS 5.0 or later, VGA or better graphics
Price range: $$

Micro Cookbook features over 1,000 recipes organized into twelve cookbooks with titles like "The Low Fat Good Life Cookbook," "Culinary Hearts Cuisine," and "Fresh Ideas: Make It Meatless!" When you select one of the cookbooks, an alphabetical listing of all its recipes appears. You can then either pick your recipe from the list or use the program's search function to find entries that match the word you enter. You can even find recipes that will use the leftovers in your refrigerator.

Creating your own cookbook and entering your own recipes into the database is also possible, although the process is somewhat clumsy. In addition, you can plan menus (including recipes, course descriptions, and complete nutritional summaries) for days, weeks, and months. Menus can be scaled to serve more or fewer people and can be printed out so that you have a handy reference when working in the kitchen. Once you have your recipes organized, Micro Cookbook can print out a complete shopping list, with foods ordered by category.

If you're looking for a good assortment of recipes to try out on your family, Micro Cookbook surely fits the bill. However, if editing existing recipes or adding your own is something you'll want to do often, you might have better luck with another product.

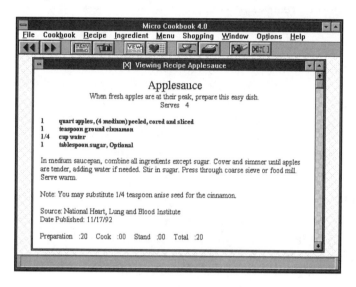

Micro Cookbook

Better Homes & Gardens Healthy Cooking CD Cookbook

Manufacturer: Multicom Publishing
Platforms: Windows, Macintosh
System requirements:
 Windows—386 or better, 4MB RAM, 256-color VGA graphics, CD-ROM, sound card
 Mac—256-color graphics, 4MB RAM, HyperCard Player 2.0 or later, CD-ROM
Price range: $$

If you're a cooking novice, you can now give up TV dinners and learn to prepare your own healthy and tasty dishes. This CD cookbook assumes nothing on the part of the would-be chef, explaining everything from what a colander is to how to make Apple Slaw. To help you find your way around the kitchen, the Healthy Cooking CD Cookbook includes a photo and definition for almost every food-preparation tool, and video clips demonstrate actions like slicing tomatoes and shaping meatballs.

To pick a recipe, you first select a group, such as pork and lamb, beef dishes, or main-dish salads. You then get a list of recipes from which you can choose. After you select your recipe, a picture of the dish appears on the screen, accompanied by one of the 60 music selections included with the program. When working on a recipe, you can view a list of ingredients, cooking instructions, nutritional information, or even a list of videos that show how to perform the tasks needed to prepare the recipe.

If you have a lot of leftovers growing green coats in your refrigerator, you can have the program select recipes that can put those aging ingredients to good use. Just enter the ingredients and have the program search for recipes that use them. You can even specify a limit on calories, fat, cholesterol, and salt that the dish should contain. Although other computer cookbooks may have more recipes, few offer such complete instruction.

Family Ties

Manufacturer: Individual Software Incorporated
Platform: DOS (Windows version forthcoming)
System requirements: DOS 2.1 or greater
Price range: $

Family Ties makes genealogy easy by offering a clean interface that's so intuitive you can probably get by without even looking at the manual. The various data-entry screens are virtually self-explanatory, with important keystrokes shown on-screen. Even configuring the program for your system is a snap, requiring only a minimal amount of information before Family Ties is up and chugging.

Genealogical data is organized into two types of screens: Family Cards and Individual Cards. A Family Card shows one set of parents and their children, including birth, marriage, and death dates, as well as other vital information. Individual Cards show more detailed information on each person in your family, such as the person's last-known address, phone number, occupation, and religion.

Jumping forward or backward through your family tree is just a matter of pressing a key or two. Moreover, you can access any individual's data simply by finding that person in the Index of Names, a handy list that shows every person's name and birth date. To help you keep hard-copy records of your family research, Family Ties prints several types of reports, including graphical family trees, as well as various lists. All in all, if you want to avoid complicated genealogy programs like Personal Ancestral File, Family Ties may be perfect for you.

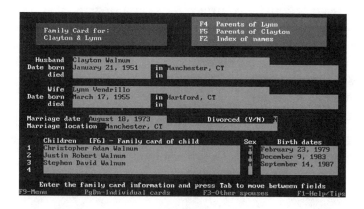

Family Ties

Personal Ancestral File

Manufacturer: The Church of Jesus Christ of Latter-day Saints
Platforms: DOS, Macintosh
System requirements:
    DOS—Minimum
    Mac—Minimum
Price range: $

The Mormon church takes their genealogy seriously, so it's not surprising that they have their own genealogy program. But, although the program is a complete genealogical data managing and organizing package, don't expect anything too fancy. This software was designed to run on even the oldest computers, so it takes the old-fashioned text-screen approach to data entry and display. Still, it's probably the most complete program of its type, capable of everything from organizing family data to printing various types of charts and reports.

Personal Ancestral File is extremely configurable. For example, you can have the program request that you retype all data for verification, or you can turn this feature off. There are dozens of similar options you can set, such as screen colors, whether the program requires a carriage return after menu selections, whether you'll allow changes to records, how many generations should be printed on charts, and more. Obviously, setting the program up the first time you use it requires some time in front of the computer with the manual.

The program itself is equally complex, including dozens of editing features and the capability to link to your communications program so you can transfer GEDCOM (Genealogical Data Communication) files between computers. For those who don't own a communications program, Personal Ancestral File includes its own simple one called PAFCOM (Personal Ancestral File Communications).

If you want the official genealogy program of the Mormon church, Personal Ancestral File is your only choice. However, if you want an easy-to-use graphical program, you should look elsewhere.

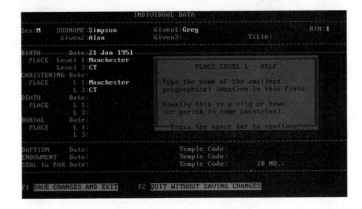

Personal Ancestral File

Family for Windows

Manufacturer: AbleSoft
Platform: Windows
System requirements: 386 or better, VGA graphics
Price range: $

Family for Windows is a family-tree program that can handle databases containing up to 2,500 people in 1,200 families. Adding new people and families to the database is a simple matter of filling in a form comprised of edit fields, check boxes, and drop-down lists. You can add people to the database and then later link them to the appropriate family tree, or you can start by filling in a new family form, which provides direct access to the Add Member function.

The program displays family trees in a variety of ways. You can get a standard family tree display, or you can view family members on a time line, which shows bars for the years they were living and shows their lives in relation to important events (such as the American Revolution or the Civil War). Finally, you can display a list of special family events like birthdays and anniversaries, or bring up an age/date calculator.

Of the family tree programs reviewed in this book, only Family for Windows enables you to add digitized photographs to the database. Photos can be displayed individually along with the full record for that family member, or the photos of an entire family can be grouped into one display. More importantly, like Personal Ancestral File, Family for Windows can take advantage of the Mormon church's Genealogical Data Communication (GEDCOM) data format, which enables you to share family information with other people.

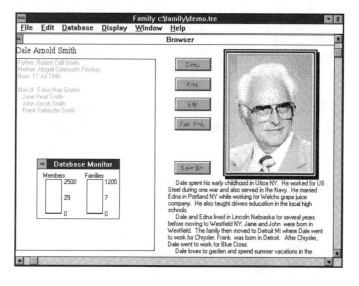

Family for Windows

B.A.B.Y.

Manufacturer: Software Marketing Corp.
Platform: DOS
System requirements: DOS 3.3 or later, VGA graphics, mouse
Price range: $$

Pregnant parents may want to dip into B.A.B.Y. (which stands for Birth and Baby Years) to learn all they can about their forthcoming big event. Using B.A.B.Y., you can study the subject of pregnancy, covering everything from conception to the actual birth. After you come home from the hospital, you can rely on B.A.B.Y. to help you record important events in your baby's first months.

B.A.B.Y. presents its information as text accompanied by pictures and animated sequences, all organized within a Windows-like interface that features drop-down menus and interactive buttons. The course of study includes not only the obvious topics like fetus development and the birthing process, but also important subjects like diet, exercise, and genetics.

While most of the program is informational in nature, you can use it to keep track of certain aspects of a pregnancy, including tracking the mother's weight gain and calculating a due date. You can even use B.A.B.Y. to record doctor's appointments or to choose your baby's name.

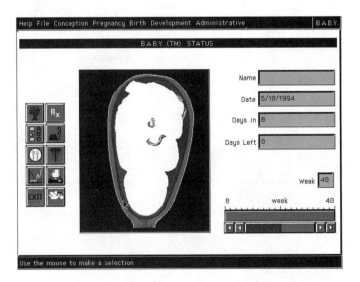

B.A.B.Y.

Home Trainer

Manufacturer: The Dumbbell Press
Platform: DOS
System requirements: Minimum
Price range: $

If pumping iron is your route to physical fitness, you'll appreciate Home Trainer, a weight lifter's program that can design, regulate, and track your regular workouts. More important than designing your workout, however, Home Trainer will keep you working. One of the program's main thrusts is avoiding boredom (a primary reason people quit exercise programs) by creating a varied set of daily workouts.

The program can be used in conjunction with home equipment or with equipment at a gym. Free weights and machines, such as Soloflex, Universal, and Nordicflex Gold, are all supported. Moreover, the program takes into consideration the muscle groups on which you want to concentrate, including shoulders, chest, back, thighs, calves, hamstrings, biceps, and triceps.

The software is surprisingly easy to use, even for folks not wholly attuned to computers. In addition, the manual is well-written and easy to understand. Add the on-line help and the included instructional video, and you're not likely to get stuck. The best news is that future versions of the program that will include cardiovascular training, as well as sports, are already in the works. Although Home Trainer can't take the sweat out of working out, it can make the experience as rewarding as possible.

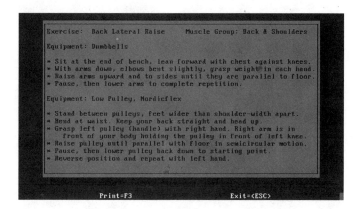

Home Trainer

SportsWorks

Manufacturer: Software Marketing Corp.
Platform: DOS
System requirements: DOS 3.3 or later, VGA graphics, hard drive
Price range: $

Sports fans who want to know all the nitty-gritty details about their favorite competitive pastimes will get a kick out of this huge, text-and-graphics sports database. One hundred and fifty sports in twelve categories are covered in SportsWorks' database, including everything from croquet to gymnastics.

Although the program is DOS-based, its interface is slickly designed and attractive, featuring such modern amenities as a menu bar and interactive buttons. The buttons allow access to various categories of information and control such functions as displaying text and pictures. You can even test your sports savvy with on-line quizzes, or use bookmarks to return easily to previously viewed subjects.

If you've a hankering to use SportsWorks database with another program, you can export text and graphics as ASCII and PCX files, respectively. Data can also be sent to your printer. While SportsWorks is not as multimedia-oriented as some modern Windows programs of its type, it's still a fine value for any sports enthusiast.

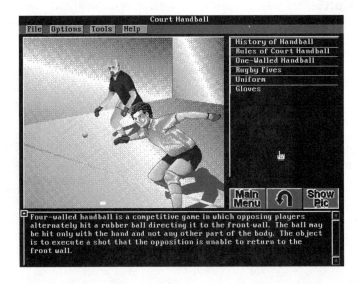

SportsWorks

PharmAssist

Manufacturer: Software Marketing Corp.
Platform: Windows
System requirements: 386 or better, VGA or better graphics
Price range: $$

With all the different drugs your doctor is liable to prescribe, it's easy to get confused about what medications do and how you should take them. PharmAssist can help you sort out these medical quandaries by providing in-depth information about hundreds of drugs including pain killers, antibiotics, allergy pills, tranquilizers, vaccines, and more. Both prescription and non-prescription drugs are covered, making PharmAssist the one-stop resource for drug information.

With PharmAssist, you can find the information you need quickly and easily, just by clicking a couple of buttons. The screen display includes not only text describing each medication, but also color illustrations of what the medications look like. Moreover, the drug information covers everything from how to apply the medication to vaccination requirements for travelers and important first-aid tips.

Additional information, such as which drugs interact with which others and how to get help for drug abuse, may save your life or someone else's. All in all, PharmAssist is the perfect home guide to medicine for anyone wanting to know more about drugs and how they work.

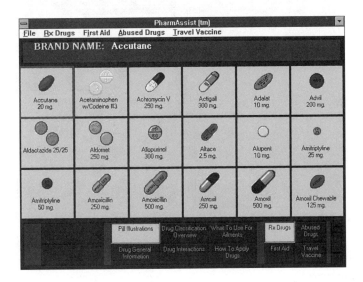

PharmAssist

Home Medical Advisor

Manufacturer: Pixel Perfect, Inc.
Platforms: Windows, DOS
System requirements:
   Windows—4MB RAM, VGA graphics
   DOS—286 or better, VGA graphics, hard disk
Price range: $$

Home Medical Advisor provides extensive knowledge bases covering symptoms, diseases, injuries, medical testing, drugs, poisons, and diet. Each knowledge base is fully indexed so you can find information quickly and easily. In fact, the symptoms section, which is the heart of the program, provides not only a complete index, but also human figures on which you can click with your mouse to jump to symptoms related to specific parts of the body.

For example, if you need information on back pain, you first click the figure's back, and then select the specific topic from the generated list. When you select a topic, Home Medical Advisor quickly finds and loads the appropriate information file, displaying it on-screen in a window, with possible causes for your symptoms listed at the bottom. By clicking a cause, you can skip the diagnostic question-and-answer session and instead receive immediate information on any of the listed possibilities.

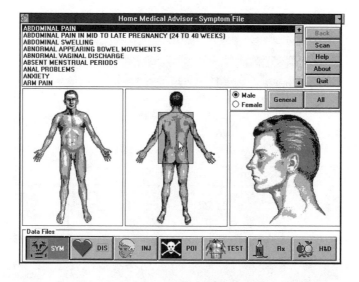

Home Medical Advisor

Clicking the Next button initiates the diagnostic section of the program. At this point, Home Medical Advisor asks a series of yes or no questions; it then uses your answers to diagnose your problem. If you decide to change an answer, you can use the Back button to trace back through the questioning to any point. As you can see, Home Medical Advisor is a valuable addition to any software library. In the case of an emergency, it might even save someone's life.

Holy Bible

Manufacturer: Software Marketing Corporation
Platform: DOS
System requirements: DOS 3.3 or greater, VGA graphics
Price range: $

Although targeted more for the family than for the serious bible scholar, Holy Bible cannot be beat for its sheer beauty. The Windows-like screens and interface are slick and well organized, giving the program a look and feel dramatically different from most DOS programs. Moreover, the photographic-quality images that accompany the text are nothing short of stunning, bringing the stories to life on the screen.

The various books of the Bible are represented by a series of on-screen buttons. When you select a button, you are instantly transported to that part of the book. You can then open a specific chapter or section of the Bible by selecting the appropriate section button. The text is drawn from the King James version of the Bible, with the words of Christ highlighted.

Holy Bible features a fast and sophisticated search function that allows logical expressions including the AND, NOT, and OR operators. Holy Bible also features a slew of options, including bookmarks, a notepad, lessons, and quizzes. In addition, the Maps and Journeys option displays various types of maps, the Timelines option shows biblical events organized linearly, and the Related Topic option lets you explore such subjects as temples, burial rituals, the Hebrew calendar, and more.

Holy Bible

Logos Bible Software 1.6

Manufacturer: Logos Research Systems Inc.
Platform: Windows
System requirements: Minimum
Price range: $$

If you're serious about your Bible studies, this electronic version of the Good Book is considered to be one of the best. Although the product is shipped with the King James version of the Bible, you can purchase add-on modules that offer 13 different Bible versions in English, Greek, and Hebrew. Other types of modules, such as biblical grammar tools, can also be added in to the main program.

Because Logos Bible Software runs under Windows, you can get started quickly and easily with the program. Moreover, Logos' "layered complexity" enables you to choose the expert level at which you'd like to work. Beginners can simply scan through the Bible, while more advanced users can turn on Strong's numbering system, access cross references, create notes, and more. Logos Bible Software boasts especially fast searches, but consumes 20MB of hard disk space—much more than the other Bible program reviewed here.

Logos Bible Software is actually available in three different packages. The regular version 1.6 includes the King James Bible, The Treasury of Scripture Knowledge, a biblical dictionary, and Strong's numbering system. The Dual Version additionally features any one of four other Bible versions. Finally, the Dual Catholic Version includes the New Jerusalem and New American Bibles.

Rock Rap'n Roll

Manufacturer: Paramount Interactive
Platform: Windows, Macintosh
System requirements:
   Windows—386 or better, 4MB RAM, 256-color VGA graphics, sound card
   Mac—LC or better, 4MB RAM, 14" color monitor
Price range: $ ($$ for CD-ROM)

You don't have to be a musician to write wild tunes with Rock Rap'n Roll. This computerized song construction kit lets you piece together hundreds of prerecorded sounds, voices, instruments, and rhythms to create your own masterpiece. Each of the ten studios specializes in a particular type of music, including soul, rock, jazz, reggae, blues, techno pop, big band, and Latin. No matter what your taste in music, there's something here to pull out that latent musical genius you've been hiding.

Rock Rap'n Roll

Each of the studios features ten different rhythm loops that you can combine any way you like to create the driving force behind your song. Just drag the chosen rhythms into the song-a-lizer until you find a combination you like. When your rhythm section is ready to go, turn on the built-in recorder and, using your mouse and keyboard, add voices, guitar solos, symbol crashes, and other sounds to complete your song. You can even plug in a microphone and record your own sounds, including your voice.

Soft Karaoke

Manufacturer: Tune 1000
Platforms: Windows, Macintosh
System requirements:
    Windows—386 or better, sound card
    Mac—LC II or better, System 7, general MIDI-compatible device
Price range: $$

Review copyright 1993 by Compute Publications Int'l, Ltd.
Reprinted by permission.

While PC Karaoke's CD-ROM format offers greater sound quality, Soft Karaoke's MIDI format (no CD player required) offers the greatest flexibility. When you run the program, a tape player-like control panel appears. Using the control panel, you can not only load and run song files, but also manipulate the files in various ways. For example, you can change both the song's tempo and the key. In addition, you can modify the instrumental mix or assign different instruments to different MIDI tracks.

To get this manipulative power, however, you have to give up a certain amount of sound quality. This is because MIDI files are not actual sound recordings, but rather files that control MIDI instruments. To put it simply, all the sounds you hear with Soft Karaoke are generated on a synthesizer, either your computer's sound board or some other external MIDI instrument. The actual quality of the sound depends on the quality of your synthesizer.

Soft Karaoke comes with a microphone and fifteen song files, including favorites like "Dust in the Wind," "Stand by Your Man," and "The Way We Were." Additional disks containing 10 songs each are available from Tune 1000, which offers many disks, including the usual assortments, as well as collections by specific artists like Fleetwood Mac, Michael Jackson, Frank Sinatra, and Elton John.

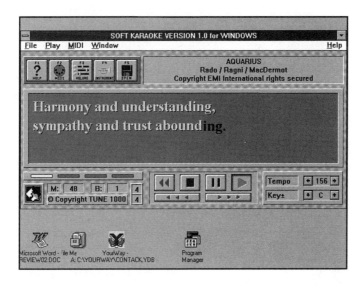

Soft Karaoke

The Card Collector

Manufacturer: AbleSoft
Platforms: Windows, DOS, Macintosh
System requirements:
    Windows—Minimum
    DOS—Hard disk
    Mac—Minimum
Price range: $

Card collecting is a popular hobby of the '90s, and with a program like The Card Collector, you'll be able to keep up easily with the details of your collection. Using The Card Collector, you enter your cards into the database, and the program tracks the total worth of your collection, constructs various types of reports, and provides easy recording of new purchases and sales.

The Card Collector comes packed with complete data for twelve major card sets, including Fleer, Topps, Upper Deck, Bowman, Ultra, and Stadium Club. Data is included for the years 1948 to the present. You can also purchase data disks for football, hockey, and basketball card sets. Moreover, to keep the data you own up to date, AbleSoft provides monthly updates (for a fee, of course) that you can receive on disk or download with your modem.

The Card Collector also allows you to organize your cards in almost unlimited ways. You can search for cards by player names, team names, or flags (such as First Card, Error Card, Special Card, and Rookie card). You can even put together your own custom card sets. If you're running an IBM-compatible computer, both the DOS and Windows versions of The Card Collector come in the same package.

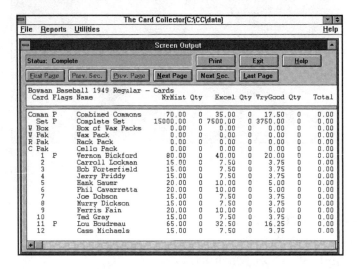

The Card Collector

Part IV

Kid Stuff

O ne of the greatest benefits of having a computer in your home is the leg up it can give to the children in your life in their education. I'm reminded of that "Saturday Night Live" (back when it was funny) parody of Macintosh commercials. The tag line was: "Macintosh, the power to crush the other kids."

In Part IV, you'll find information about working with kids on your computer and knowing how young is too young, plus an overview of major kids' software packages with reviews. And there's much more. Whether you have kids of your own, or are a fabulous aunt, uncle, or friend to kids, if there will be children using your computer, you'll want to read it all.

Here's a free tidbit before you get into the heart of the matter: don't get jealous if the child in your life gets the hang of computing quicker than you do. They've been dealing with computer-like things all of their lives, whereas most adults haven't.

Enjoy the children enjoying your computer. They may be able to teach you something.

Fun, Games, and Learning

Years ago, when microcomputers first began to make their way into homes and schools in significant numbers, many publishers rushed to create "educational" software for kids and adults. Given the limitations of the technology at the time and the narrow definition of education many of these developers brought to the task, a large number of the titles they produced were deadly.

Some of the programs, billing themselves as tutorials, presented page after page of text interspersed with multiple-choice questions. Others took a drill-and-practice approach, asking students to answer questions and then providing feedback in the form of a brief message ("No, try again" or "That's right!"). After the student responded correctly to several problems, the drill programs generally offered a special reward (music, the screen lighting up, an animated effect, and so on).

Software has come a long way since then, but a number of developers and potential purchasers still have a rather old-fashioned view of what is and what is not educational. Many of us fall into the trap of thinking that unless a program feels like "serious" hard work, our children won't learn from it. We sometimes look at programs that focus on factual information and drill kids on a specific body of knowledge and say, "Now, that's educational!"

There are at least two problems with viewing software this way. First, it's easy to lose sight of other aspects of learning when we focus exclusively on right or wrong answers and facts to be memorized. Although there is a definite place for such factual information in any child's education, an even more important role of education is to help our children learn to think and to create—neither of which can be taught through straight drill. In fact, some of the most educationally valuable programs on the market are tools with no obvious instructional content. For example, a good publishing program that offers word processing and clip art capabilities is likely to motivate your child to create stories, letters, and cards for friends, relatives, and teachers—and to refine those writing, spelling, and visual skills necessary to create satisfying results.

A second problem with old-fashioned drills and tutorials is that they usually aren't much fun. In the past, children may have put up with deadly dull programs because the computer was new and exciting to them. Today, the novelty has worn off, and young people have come to expect much more. Not all software has to be "fun" in the sense that a good game or an entertaining movie is fun; tools that allow kids to produce outstanding results or reference software that makes their schoolwork much easier have their appeal as well. But if your child sees a program as "boring," he will never stick with it.

Games and More

A number of the programs that hold children's interest for hours at the computer are educationally oriented games. Some of these are simulation games that place kids in a historically, geographically, or scientifically accurate environment and challenge them to explore, make choices, and overcome obstacles. Many others are today's much-improved versions of drill-and-practice; the drill is now set in an entertaining context that involves game-playing elements (arcade action, mazes, and so on) plus appealing graphics and sound.

In trying to determine what your child is learning from a particular game, you should first consider whether the enjoyment is intrinsic (internal, closely related to the content being covered) or extrinsic (external, unrelated to the content). To explain, let's start with a noncomputer analogy. Suppose that you want your child to practice spelling and vocabulary skills. Many popular activities, such as crossword puzzles, games (Scrabble and Boggle, for instance), and television quiz shows ("Wheel of Fortune"), focus on those skills. All of these activities rely primarily on intrinsic motivation. In each case, the content (letters and words) is central to the game. Although there are some external rewards in the form of points or money earned, the players experience enjoyment derived mostly from successfully manipulating letters to form words or sentences.

An alternative approach, one that focuses more on external motivation, is often taken in schools. Imagine that, instead of suggesting one of the games listed above, you encourage your child to take part in a board game or baseball game involving a set of words he needs to memorize. Each time he correctly spells and defines one of his words, he can progress to another spot on the board or take another base in the ball game. In this case, the game-playing elements (moving around the board or baseball field) are far removed from the content being studied.

Which approach is more educational? In part, that depends on your exact goal. If the point is to master a specific list of words for a test the teacher will give at the end of the week, the extrinsic approach is more efficient. After all, with games such as Scrabble or Boggle, it's impossible to predict which letters players will get and which words they will practice as a result. On the other hand, if your goal is to develop in your child a fascination with letters and words, the first set of games is much more helpful. If your child enjoys playing any one of them, he is likely to walk away with a more positive feeling about word play and language. When walking away from the baseball game, however, she's much more likely to think, "Baseball is fun. I'm glad I got those words right so I could run the bases."

In the software world, we have the same sorts of choices to make. Like the noncomputerized games that encourage word play, some software programs manage to create environments in which the fun, the challenges, and the game-playing aspects are all closely related to the learning that is taking place. Some of the best examples are geography and history games, such as the Carmen Sandiego series, which send players on imaginary trips around the world, using maps to help them navigate and geographic or historical clues to steer them in the right direction. It's hard to separate the game from the content in this case, which increases the likelihood that kids will acquire a renewed interest in maps and in learning about the world.

Many more of the popular educational computer games are on the other end of the spectrum, relying heavily on extrinsic rewards: answer this math problem correctly and you can progress through a maze, spell this word right and you'll shoot down a missile, and so on. In these examples, there are two sets of activities taking place (the maze navigation or arcade action on the one hand and the math or spelling on the other), and there's little logical connection between the two. While we are clearly more enthusiastic about the intrinsic approach, we are not ruling out extrinsic motivation. In fact, many of the games we recommended rely more heavily on extrinsic than intrinsic rewards. (It's definitely a spectrum, by the way, and most programs do a little bit of both.) In part, that's because there are so *few* intrinsically rewarding programs to choose from. But it's also because there are many occasions when the extrinsic reward does work.

An approach such as the baseball example can be more efficient at conveying a set body of knowledge. Furthermore, some topics lend themselves better to exploration than others do. For example, if the subject is mathematical estimation, it's easy to imagine a game in which children navigate through a magical math land, estimating how far they need to go at each turn. However, if the goal is to memorize multiplication facts, it's much harder to think of a game with intrinsic rewards.

A final, and very important, reason for considering games with extrinsic rewards is that some kids respond best to them. The active child who needs to move and run might reject even the most entertaining word game but be willing to play the baseball game and learn a bit of spelling and vocabulary on the side. In the same way, kids who find games like Where in the World Is Carmen Sandiego? too slow-paced, might stick with a geography arcade game, learning to identify countries on a blank map of the world in order to have the opportunity to steer a speeding race car along a track. The social studies content that they are learning may not be as rich, but if the game succeeds in exposing them to a topic they previously ignored, then it certainly has educational value for that child.

Looking at What Else They Are Learning

Whenever you do consider a program that relies heavily on extrinsic rewards, it's helpful to look at those external game-playing elements to see how valuable you think they are for your child. In a sense, there are two types of learning going on: the primary learning that's related to the content area this educational game says it's teaching, and the secondary learning related to the game elements that provide the rewards.

In the case of an arcade-style game, the secondary learning generally involves developing fast reflexes, good aim, and so on. You may decide that these skills are valuable for your child—perhaps he has some difficulty with fine motor coordination but enjoys arcade action and improves his fine motor skills as a result, or perhaps you feel that by "letting off some steam" in this way, your very active kid will be able to concentrate better on other tasks. Or you may choose to steer your child away from the arcade-type games if you feel that they are too violent, if you're convinced that they simply reinforce skills that he already practices for hours each day, or if he is on the other end of the spectrum and hates arcade action.

Other types of secondary learning are common in educational games. When you take into account how much time is often taken by these external tasks, you may feel that some of these games are not worth the time and energy your child spends on them. On the other hand, the secondary skills introduced may be ones that can really help your child. Perhaps a game your child loves involves strategy, problem solving, and deduction-thinking skills that will help him in many aspects of his life. Or perhaps it includes a maze or jigsaw puzzle that encourages him to focus on spatial relations without the time pressure associated with an arcade game. Even if these secondary skills are not closely related to the program's primary goals, they can often be valuable in their own right.

In fact, it's worth considering some games that focus entirely on secondary skills. So far, the games we've discussed in this chapter are the ones that bill themselves as "educational," offering practice in content or skills that fit neatly into specific areas of the school curriculum. But there are a number of other valuable programs that make no such claims even though the skills that they reinforce—problem solving, logical reasoning, spatial relations, and so on—do indirectly relate to a child's performance at school and in life. If your child spends lots of time playing with such "entertainment" software, he just might be learning more than you realize.

In the end, there are many types of learning and many approaches that are educationally valid. If your kid is having a good time using a particular program, if that program focuses on content and skills you feel are important, and if it does so in a way that encourages thinking and creativity, you can feel confident that valuable learning is taking place.

Working Together at the Computer

Many people think of working and playing at the computer as a solitary activity. After all, the computer has one screen and one keyboard, so it's easy to assume that only one person can use it at a time. We imagine a lone computer "nerd" sitting hunched over the keyboard, staring intently at the screen. The glow of the screen is the only light in the darkened room as this solitary soul shuts out the rest of the world and computes.

This image alone is enough to convince some parents not to buy computers for their children. But, even though a number of tasks require solo time at the computer, many computer activities promote group involvement. In fact, educators frequently report that children in their classes work particularly well together when engaged in group activities at the computer. Working together toward a common goal, the children get to know one another better and discover the usefulness of teamwork.

How can you cultivate cooperative learning of this sort in your home? The first step in turning your child's computer time into a social activity is to look for programs that lend themselves well to group use.

Software to Use Cooperatively

Many computer games allow more than one user to play at one time. In most cases, the players take turns trying to win the most points. The computer signals each player when it is time to take his turn. A few of the programs allow two players at the keyboard or two joysticks to be used at once. The players may oppose each other or, in rare cases, cooperate and compete against the computer.

Competitive games are frequently very appealing to kids. While not the ideal way to encourage cooperative attitudes, such games do allow two or more children in your family (or your child and some friends) to socialize at the computer. By making the rules harder for the player who indicates that he is older or more advanced, some programs, such as Broderbund's Treehouse, even allow children at different skill levels (an older and a younger sibling, for example) to compete equitably.

If you're concerned about the effects of too much competition on your children, you can try helping them "turn around" the goals of a competitive game. Rather than competing to get the highest individual score, everyone can work together as a single team to see how high a score the entire group can get. Or, if you have at least four people interested in playing, you can combine both competition and cooperation by encouraging your kids to form competing teams of two or more players.

In addition to the software created specifically for multiple players, many programs designed for individual users can also be used cooperatively. Almost any software that provides a story line or multiple choices lends itself to a group effort. Likewise, adventure games, simulations, interactive storybooks, and programs that allow users to explore freely an imaginary environment are all great ways of getting a group to work together, stopping to discuss possible next moves at each decision point, and proceeding once a consensus has been reached.

You can even use tools such as word processors and paint programs cooperatively. A cooperative effort with this sort of software focuses on the end result and not the process. For example, several members of your family might try writing a group letter to somebody you all care about. The "team" might first create a basic outline of points to cover in the letter. Then each point could be filled in to form a paragraph. Each person might be responsible for a different paragraph, or everybody might contribute to each one. Since all participants can see what is being written and corrections can be made easily, the letter evolves as the group works together.

Team effort can go a long way toward making a challenging program easier and more fun to use. As long as one team member is familiar with the software, the others can learn the ropes relatively painlessly. With a task to focus on and a little bit of coaching, each member of the team is in an ideal position to learn to use the program independently.

Rules and Roles

When children work together at the computer, you will often find them taking turns voluntarily or dividing up the roles based on individual skills and interests. In other words, they may not need your help learning to cooperate if they're motivated by the software and glad to be working together. There are times, however, when adult guidance is needed to help children (especially siblings) learn how to cooperate at the computer.

One approach that works particularly well with children who are at similar skill levels is to agree on a specific role for each participant and then rotate roles periodically so that everyone has the chance to "play" them all. If only two players are involved in a game, for example, one might be the pilot in charge of typing at the keyboard or using the mouse or joystick; the other could be the navigator, providing verbal instructions, reading aloud whatever appears on the screen, and having the final say whenever the two disagree on a move. With additional players, roles such as tactician (the person in charge of finding hints, rules, and shortcuts in the documentation), historian (the note taker who keeps track of what actions the group has taken), and site manager (who is responsible for reminding people of their roles and determining when jobs rotate) can be added.

Of course, you'll want to be flexible about these roles because the kids will probably want to modify them or create new ones. If players are at very different skill levels, you might need to establish nonrotating roles that take advantage of each kid's abilities. For example, a nonreader might never have to take a turn reading at the monitor but could always be in charge of deciding where the group should go next. This can be a great way of allowing younger children to participate in games that might otherwise be too hard for them. However, as the adult, you may find it necessary to monitor play to make sure nobody is ignored or made to feel bad.

If your children respond well to formal rules, you might want to work with them to come up with a list of guidelines to be posted near the computer. In addition to basic computer rules such as "No food near the computer," the list would include rules related to cooperative play. For example, you might use these rules: 1) No one touches the keyboard/mouse/joystick except the pilot; 2) No making fun of other players; 3) Rotate jobs every 20 minutes; and so on.

Working with Your Child at the Computer

So far in this chapter, the role we've described for you is that of a monitor or supervisor, helping your children and their friends learn how to cooperate at the computer. But you may want to be even more actively involved. In fact, if your child does not have a sibling or friend with whom he plays well and is suitably matched, his social time at the computer might be well spent with you. This can be an excellent time for you and your child to relax together.

A larger group of children might welcome your participation as well. For example, kids who are easily frustrated by typing at the keyboard might prefer to have you serve as pilot much of the time while they give the orders. Or you might take the role of special advisor, loading the program and explaining the rules. In either case, your biggest challenge will be to step back and let the kids take the lead. If you're the typist, be sure to type exactly what you are told, even if you know the instructions won't work. If you're an advisor, try to speak up only when your advice is requested. In general, if you spend too much time telling your kids how to use the computer, they will resent the intrusion and come to view computing as just another area in which parents get to tell kids what to do.

If you're lucky (or plan it right), your kids will know more about the program than you do—which gives them the unique opportunity to explain something to you that you don't understand. If you admit that you do not know much about a program but are interested in learning more, your child is likely to delight in teaching you all he knows.

Sometimes the most helpful role you can play is as an interested observer. Acknowledge your child's discoveries and ask him broad questions about the program, the characters, his favorite and least favorite parts, and so on. Simply watching what he chooses to do and letting him know that you are interested can be an excellent way of strengthening your relationship and his self-confidence.

Ownership

If you want your children to view the computer as a tool to be shared, it's important to think carefully about who has access to it and when. Who really owns the computer in your family? If family members view the computer as jointly owned, if they all have some say in the decision to purchase it or in what type of computer to buy, they are more apt to feel free to use it. If the computer was purchased in part for a parent to work on at home, it's important to set aside time when the kids know the computer is theirs—and then step back and let them use it.

If you want your children to work effectively together at the computer, it's also important to find software that appeals to everyone. This may require research and a consensus on which program to purchase. Some families find it helpful for everyone to make a financial contribution. The parents might pay 50 percent of the cost of a program, big sister might pay 35 percent, little brother 15 percent, and so on. If everybody agrees on the purchase and provides his fair share—or at least some share—of the cost, everyone will view the software as an item to be shared.

Location

The location of the computer is also important. With sibling rivalry being as intense as it is, placing the computer in one child's room is not likely to encourage sharing, much less group participation. Ideally, the family computer should be located in a room where everyone can use it and in a position suited to group viewing.

Some families find it useful to place the computer near the television, since most TV rooms are set up to accommodate a large group of viewers. However, this can cause conflicts between those who want to use the computer and those who want to watch TV. It's virtually impossible to accomplish anything at the computer with a television set blaring a few feet away. If you do decide to put both pieces of equipment in the same room, it's important to designate certain times for using the computer and others for watching TV.

A preferable solution is to find a relatively quiet common room (for example, a study, a den with no television, or even the corner of a dining room) where individuals can work alone without being disturbed and where it's also easy to pull up several chairs for a cooperative activity. For those times when a large group will be working together, it's helpful to find a way of placing the screen at a slightly higher level than usual so that everybody can see. A deep computer table helps here as well. By moving the keyboard back away from the screen, more people can view the image on the screen. Keep in mind that even with the best vision, most people cannot read small type on the screen from more than three feet away.

In addition, make sure the screen does not have a glare caused by large windows or bright lights. To do so, look at the screen with the computer turned off. If you can see bright reflections, it may be difficult for several people to view the screen from a slight distance. Close the curtains or leave the light off when using the system.

Watching the Clock

All of us want our children to be able to work and think independently. Equally important is the fact that we want them to develop social skills and learn to work cooperatively with other people. The computer can help with both.

Some parents fear that their children will become "addicted" to computers. For them, the concern is not simply that the child will work alone, but that he will become obsessed, unable to think about anything but computing. The truth is that certain children during certain periods of their lives will indeed become "hooked" on particular computer activities, working on them at every free moment of the day. But, then, kids quite commonly get hooked on all sorts of activities—from reading mystery books to playing baseball.

There's no such thing as "the right amount of time" at the computer, but as with almost any activity your kid loves, you may find it necessary to encourage (or even require) moderation. (See the article "Computing Health and Safety" in Part V for information about the eye strain, muscle aches, and other health problems that can be caused by excessive computer use.) Just as the serious "bookworm" should be encouraged to put down his book occasionally and go outside to play, the serious computer "hacker" should be encouraged to turn off the computer frequently, as well as to welcome others into the experience. Whether your child is a fanatic or a reluctant computer user, you can also help by being supportive, making suggestions that will help him broaden his tastes and outlook, and remembering that whatever game or activity he's obsessed with today will undoubtedly give way to something else in a few months, a few weeks, or even days.

Computers and Your Child's Health

For the most part, a computer is as safe as any other household appliance. But just as with other household appliances, there are some potential health hazards associated with computer use. (Many of them, by the way, are just as applicable to video games as they are to computers.)

Concern about the health effects of computers focuses on several general categories of risk. These include:

◆ Problems related to electromagnetic emissions

◆ Visual problems

◆ Muscle and joint problems

In every case, these risks appear to be directly related to the amount of time spent working on or being near the computer.

Let's begin with the most controversial topic: the possible harmful effects of the electromagnetic field produced by your computer monitor.

Electromagnetic Emissions

Every device that transmits or runs on electricity gives off electromagnetic radiation. This radiation surrounds the object and creates an electromagnetic field (EMF). Some devices, like your toaster or refrigerator, emit very low levels of electromagnetic radiation. Other devices, like high-voltage wires, a kitchen microwave oven, a television, or a computer monitor, give off significantly higher levels. You can't see, hear, smell, taste, or touch electromagnetic radiation, but in today's world, it is everywhere.

No one is certain how normal levels of electromagnetic radiation affect the health of children or adults, but many people are concerned. Occasionally, the fears are based on a misunderstanding of the term radiation. Used to refer to a full range of electromagnetic emissions, "radiation" to many of us connotes X-rays (also known as ionizing radiation), a high-frequency form of radiation that has been proven to increase the likelihood of cancer in animals and human beings. Actually, everybody who has studied the technology behind computer monitors (also referred to as video display terminals or VDTs) agrees that X-ray radiation is not the issue; the tiny amount of ionizing radiation emitted by the cathode ray tube (CRT) within the monitor is effectively screened out by the surrounding glass.

What scientists and consumer advocates do not agree on, however, is how lower frequency electromagnetic radiation—the VLF (very low frequency) and ELF (extra low frequency) radiation given off by computers and a variety of other appliances—affects humans. A number of studies on the subject in recent years have raised concerns and many unanswered questions.

Most of the studies that have been conducted into the health effects of electromagnetic fields fall into one of three categories: 1) studies on the miscarriage rate for pregnant women working many hours a day at computer terminals; 2) experiments with animal embryos to examine the relationship between prolonged exposure to EMFs and birth defects or miscarriages; 3) statistical analyses of cancer rates in children and adults to determine whether proximity to high-power lines (or other wiring configurations causing high levels of electromagnetic radiation) increases cancer risks. The results of the research thus far have been confusing and inconclusive. In each of the three categories, there have been several studies indicating a relationship between EMFs and health problems, and at least as many refuting such a connection.

Even the studies that do find connections frequently raise more questions than they answer. For example, a 1988 study (conducted by Kaiser Permanente Hospital in Oakland, California) that helped draw attention to the potential risks of computer usage by pregnant women, found that only one group of women studied (those with clerical jobs) experienced a higher miscarriage rate the more time they spent at the computer, while other groups (including women in sales or management positions) did not. These findings suggest that other factors, such as stress, may have been responsible for the increases that were found.

Research in the other two areas has been equally confusing. For example, some of the studies of embryos exposed to EMFs showed an increase in miscarriage but not in birth defects; others showed an increase in birth defects but not miscarriage; and still others had results that were not reproducible from one trial to the next. And one of the most recent studies on the effects of power lines (conducted by the University of Southern California) pointed to a link between wiring configurations (related to number, capacity, and proximity of power lines) and leukemia risk but found little evidence that the locations considered riskiest actually had a higher measured level of electromagnetic radiation. Perhaps location with regard to power lines has more to do with other factors, such as traffic patterns, use of defoliant sprays, or socioeconomic status, which in turn might be connected to increased leukemia risk.

Playing It Safe

What, then, can you conclude about the risk that computing poses to your child's health and yours? There is no conclusive evidence that the electromagnetic field created by your computer's monitor can be harmful, but clearly there are enough unresolved questions to suggest that you take a cautious approach. (If scientists do some day conclude that EMFs present a health risk, we'll clearly have to think about protecting our children from much more than computers and TVs; electric lights, hair dryers, and other appliances will be implicated as well.)

In the meantime, here are some suggestions, gathered from a variety of sources, for playing it safe when it comes to computers and EMFs:

- ◆ Because electromagnetic radiation is emitted from all parts of the monitor (in fact, many measurements indicate higher emissions from the sides and back than from the front), it's safest to place a computer in a corner of a room or somewhere else where nonusers are least likely to find themselves near the sides or back of the machine.

- ◆ Don't leave the computer or monitor turned on for long periods of time. If the computer is not in use, turn it off. This can be a nuisance (and might have a slight effect on the life expectancy of your computer), but it is a small price to pay if EMFs do prove to be hazardous.

- ◆ Encourage your children to sit as far as they comfortably can from the computer (or television) screen. Most experts recommend placing the monitor at arm's length (that's an adult arm, with fingers extended) when working at the computer.

◆ In general, it's probably wise to limit the time that children and pregnant women spend at the computer to no more than a few hours a day.

◆ If you are especially concerned, you may want to purchase a special monitor that complies with the recent "MPRII" standards from Sweden, which set maximum acceptable ELF and VLF emission levels. Most hardware companies, including IBM, Apple, Compaq, Dell, NEC, Radius, and many others, offer at least one monitor that meets the MPRII standards.

Visual Problems

While there's much controversy over the danger of electromagnetic fields, there's little disagreement about the fact that prolonged computer use can lead to eyestrain. Whenever children or adults spend a great deal of time on a visual task, they suffer eye fatigue. You are probably familiar with this problem from driving long distances or from reading for extended periods of time. The muscles that control your eyes and focus them simply become fatigued from overuse. The potential for eye fatigue exists for all visual tasks, but it is greatest for those involving close work. Many feel that it's also more of a problem when the close work involves a high-glare device, such as a computer monitor.

Children are especially prone to eye fatigue because their eyes and the muscles that control them have not matured. Extensive reading, close-up television watching, and computing all put great demands on young eyes. The most common result of eye fatigue is that children will become tired and cranky. As every parent can attest, these responses are not unique to computing. When children overdo any activity, they frequently become irritable and irritating. If your child is acting more temperamental than usual, and there is no other obvious cause, long periods of time spent in front of the computer may be the culprit.

Excessive computing may also aggravate existing visual problems. Many children suffer from minor visual impairments that fall into the "nuisance" category. Eventually, these problems require correction, but the remedy may not be necessary until adolescence or adulthood. When children are so taken with computing that they spend much of their free time at the keyboard, however, the "nuisance" visual problem may develop into something that requires correction at an early age.

While there is no evidence that computers can actually cause visual problems, some ophthalmologists worry that overuse at a young age might have a harmful effect on the muscles that control the eyes, making it more difficult for a child to focus his eyes, especially for close-up tasks such as reading. If this occurs, it might be necessary to correct the problem with glasses.

Fortunately, most of these computer-related visual problems can be prevented quite easily. Here are a few suggestions:

- ◆ The most obvious solution is to limit the amount of time your kids spend computing without a break. For children, a brief break every 15 to 30 minutes is recommended. Although it may be difficult to enforce such a rigid time limit on an enthusiastic child, at the very least you should follow the guidelines set for many working adults these days and require a break once every hour. A nonvisual, physical activity—taking a walk, throwing a ball outside, or even accompanying an adult on a trip to the store—is the ideal "spacer" to separate computing sessions.

- ◆ Some professionals suggest the use of eye exercises to help children avoid the problems that might result from computer use. These exercises can be as simple as tracking objects that are moving across the field of vision or focusing on distant objects. One of the ancillary benefits of alternating computer use with other activities is that the alternative activity will often involve visual movements that actually exercise the eyes.

- ◆ It is also a good idea to vary the activities that children undertake on the computer. For example, time at a word processor might be alternated with an action-packed adventure full of moving objects. Alternating activities in this way will make varied demands on young eyes and prevent the fatigue caused by focusing on the same target for too long.

- ◆ Choosing a good monitor is another way of decreasing the risk of eyestrain. Higher resolution monitors are easier on the eyes than low resolution monitors are. If you and your child will be spending considerable time at the computer, it's absolutely essential to have a clear, crisp display.

◆ Finally, it may be important to take steps to decrease the glare from the monitor. Bright and uneven lighting in a room can cause disturbing reflections on the screen. Possible solutions to this problem involve turning off overhead lights, pulling the shades on windows that let in extremely bright light, and turning the monitor so it is neither directly in front of nor exactly opposite the brightest light source. Antiglare screens that can be placed over your monitor are available from a number of manufacturers and are definitely worth considering if your child appears to be bothered by reflections or the general glare of the monitor itself.

If, in spite of these precautions, your child complains about headaches and sore or itchy eyes or suddenly begins having problems with reading or other schoolwork, you should make an appointment with an optometrist or ophthalmologist. Be sure to mention that you have a computer at home and describe the amount of time your child uses it. The doctor may prescribe specific eye exercises, or might fit your child for glasses that are especially suited to the medium-range work involved in computing.

Muscle and Joint Problems

Among people who use computers to earn their living, the greatest number of health complaints is due to muscle and joint problems. For the most part, these problems are of the nuisance variety: a stiff neck, sore shoulders, lower back pain, or tingling in the legs.

There are a few more serious complaints, however. The most common is carpal tunnel syndrome, in which the nerves in the hand are damaged by long and repeated stints at the computer. In its most severe form, carpal tunnel syndrome is a painful condition that can permanently disable an individual.

Children rarely experience muscle and joint problems as a result of computing; they simply don't spend enough time at the computer for such problems to develop. However, it's wise to discourage your children from sitting for long periods of time in an uncomfortable position in front of the computer. One thing you can do is make sure that the chair your child uses is neither too high nor too low. (Special office chairs that can be raised or lowered easily might be helpful if several family members, all of different sizes, will be using the computer at different times.) In addition, encourage your child to sit with correct posture when he is computing. If you can get your child into the habit of sitting up straight and facing the computer directly, it is likely that muscle and joint problems will not develop in the future.

We don't want to exaggerate the risks of extended time spent at the computer, nor do we want to minimize them. By following the guidelines suggested in this chapter, and by encouraging your children to be moderate rather than excessive in their use of computers, we believe you will succeed in creating a safe and happy computing environment for your family.

How Young Is Too Young? Preschoolers Using the Computer

T he topic of computers and young children is a controversial one. Many early childhood educators are reluctant to bring computers into the preschool classroom, and those in the position of advising parents are sometimes adamantly opposed to the idea of computers in the hands of preschoolers. Why?

Most early childhood experts today believe in the importance of a "developmental" approach to educating young children. Such an approach, based in large part on the research of Swiss psychologist Jean Piaget, assumes that children learn by "constructing their own knowledge" when placed in an environment rich with opportunities to explore, to manipulate objects, and to solve problems. In the developmental approach, teachers view counting, reading, and writing in much the same way they view walking and talking; they are confident that children will acquire the new concepts and skills when they are ready to do so—as long as they are given the chance to practice and experiment in a supportive, nonpressured environment.

Some early childhood experts look at software packages designed to drill young children on letters, numbers, and shapes, and worry that computers in preschools will be used to push children faster than they are ready to go, which will encourage them to learn skills in isolation. These educators fear that children who spend lots of time at the computer will become passive or antisocial users. In addition, they are concerned that computers are too abstract for the very young child. They suggest that experience with real paints, blocks, dress-up clothes, and musical instruments is far more beneficial than computerized versions of such experiences. As Ellen Galinsky and Judy David put it in their book, *The Preschool Years* (New York: Ballantine Books, 1991), "In our opinion, the computer offers no learning experience nor fosters any skill for preschool children that cannot be experienced more meaningfully and less expensively in play at home and in good early childhood programs. The value of computers for learning comes later on, when children are older."

But there are a number of other early childhood experts—also strongly committed to a developmental approach—who disagree. While they acknowledge that the market is flooded with software that is not developmentally appropriate for preschoolers, they believe that the right kind of software, used as just one of many learning tools, can make a tremendous difference to young children.

In the Preschool Classroom

In her book *Children and Computers Together in the Early Childhood Classroom* (Albany, N.Y.: Delmar Publishers, 1989), Jane Davidson summarizes much of the research in the field and reports on her own observations of children using computers in preschools. She concludes that computers tend to encourage rather than discourage social interaction and observes that "the children who use computers at the University of Delaware Preschool do not seem passive. Children are jumping up to observe each other's work . . . moving their bodies with the actions of the characters on the screen, and in some cases even dancing to the music on the program."

Charles Hohmann, coordinator of curriculum for the High/Scope Educational Research Foundation (an organization that focuses on the education of young children), agrees. In his book *Young Children & Computers* (Ypsilanti, Mich.: High/Scope Press, 1990), he explains that, for preschoolers in the High/Scope demonstration classroom, "the addition of computers and appropriate software to their environment has [had] positive social consequences," including an increase in cooperative activity (for example, children playing together and helping one another at the computer). And, although he agrees that "the computer provides a symbolic rather than a direct learning experience," he points out that "young children interact meaningfully with symbolic material they encounter in books read or shown to them by parents and other adults." Certainly, a good interactive computer program is no more symbolic or abstract than a book—especially when you consider the new generation of software that allows a child to "turn pages," move objects on the screen, "click" on any word and hear it read aloud, watch and listen as selected characters "come alive," and make choices that determine the outcome of the story.

Finally, when comparing the value of computers to that of concrete objects that children can manipulate, many early childhood educators believe that the ideal is to expose children to all of these options. Computerized graphics programs, for example, should never replace painting, collage, or other "messy" materials in the preschool classroom, but that does not negate the value of the graphics package as a tool in its own right. As Davidson points out, computer art programs "allow the children to create with straight lines and segments of line, something not within their skill level when using crayons, paint, or markers." Her conclusions on this topic: "One would not ban crayons from the room because paint is available . . . . The computer is merely another possible medium with . . . its own limitations and possibilities."

In addition to refuting many of the common fears about computers and young children, the researchers point to a number of other benefits of developmentally appropriate software in the early childhood classroom. For example, educators involved in a Head Start/IBM Partnership project that studied the effects of computers placed at selected Head Start classrooms around the country concluded that developmentally appropriate computer activities increased young children's ability to attend to task, take turns, and follow directions; had a strong positive impact on self-esteem and self-confidence; and enhanced student creativity. (These results were summarized in an article by Tsantis, Wright, and Thouvenelle in the Jan./Feb. 1989 issue of *Children Today* and in a booklet entitled "Computers in Head Start Classrooms," published by MOBIUS Corporation of Alexandria, Virginia.)

In the Home

So far the studies of computers and young children have focused on the school setting. But what does this mean for you as a parent considering a computer for your three- or four-year-old to use at home? Many of the issues are the same; a few are different.

A number of critics of computers for preschoolers have focused on the question of expense. Cost is an issue in a preschool setting because one has to weigh the benefits of a single computer (and accompanying software) against the value of art supplies, puzzles, rubber balls, and so on—all of which can be purchased for less money and used by more children at once. In your home, the issue takes on a slightly different twist. Instead of worrying about how many children you can schedule for this expensive piece of equipment in a single day, you need to worry about how much use your home computer will actually get.

If your only goal in purchasing a computer is to provide your preschooler with access, we suggest that you reconsider. Many preschool researchers find that young children typically spend no more than 15 minutes at the computer before moving on to other activities. If you take the advice of early childhood educators and present the computer as an optional activity in your household, you may find that your youngster spends nearly an hour at the machine one day, 10 minutes the next, and then loses interest totally for a week. Unless there are adults or older children in the family interested in using the computer as well, you may find that you've spent a lot of money on equipment that gets used too rarely to warrant the investment.

On the other hand, if you already own a computer or are considering purchasing one for other purposes as well, we strongly encourage you to invest in a few developmentally appropriate programs for your preschooler to use. He will not be deprived if you don't expose him to the computer, but you may be pleasantly surprised at how quickly and positively he responds to the opportunity to play with this giant electronic toy.

In addition to the benefits found in the preschool studies mentioned in this chapter, there's another reason to consider using a computer with your little one: it's a tremendous opportunity for you to work closely together, to improve your child's communication skills, and to gain some insight into his thoughts and interests. Children as young as two years old can become involved in programs such as Tom Snyder's Reading Magic series, which encourages a parent to boot up the computer, place a child on his lap, and read aloud the story that appears, pausing at decision points within the program to ask the child to choose what should happen next. Other programs that are not necessarily designed as "lapware" can serve that purpose as well. For example, the McGee series from Lawrence Productions (which is especially designed so a nonreader can make choices independently) can also be used with a child too young to use a mouse or other input device effectively. The child can point to a menu choice on the screen and say "go there" or "see chickens" and you can enter the selection he asks for.

Hardware Issues

While we do not suggest buying an entire computer system especially for your young child, there are a few types of add-ons you might want to consider. In particular, owners of MS-DOS computers might consider buying a sound card. An increasing number of programs these days incorporate realistic-sounding speech and sound effects. While they might promise to "play through your PC speaker," they generally sound much better with the help of a special card. (On the Macintosh, such a card is not necessary because the hardware needed to play back high-quality sound is already built into the computer.)

Why should you care about sound quality for your young child? Because programs that "talk" to your preschooler can be extremely beneficial. With improvements in sound technology, software designers are finding themselves able to give directions to nonreaders by speaking those directions aloud. (While there are benefits to time spent with your child at the computer, it's also helpful to find programs that your child is comfortable using independently.) Speech can also provide vital feedback to your child. For example, a talking word processor that names each letter a child presses at the keyboard and reads back entire words (entered by the child or dictated to an adult typist) can be a tremendous tool for the child motivated to learn his letters or begin reading words. Other computerized sounds—conversations between on-screen characters, special effects, background music, and so on—can also add tremendously to the appeal of a program.

The other hardware issue that's worth thinking about is the question of input devices. Many people wonder whether young children can handle the complex task of using a mouse or can locate letters and other symbols easily on the computer keyboard. There is no simple answer to those questions, although the teachers at High/Scope have found that most three- and four-year-olds can learn to use a mouse quite effectively with a few hours of practice. Surprisingly, the children observed in this setting do not seem to have problems with the concept of moving the mouse on one plane (the desk) while the cursor moves on another (the screen); they generally plunge ahead, learning by trial and error. However, most observers agree that using a mouse can be very difficult for those young children who have problems with fine motor skills—especially if the program being used offers very small menu choices or features other tasks requiring precise control.

The keyboard is physically quite easy for the average preschooler to use, although locating letters, function keys, and so on all over the keyboard can be painfully slow for many children. Here again, the issue has a lot to do with software design; developers of effective preschool programs make sure that the keys required for a child to operate the program are minimal and relatively easy to locate.

In general, you are likely to find that the standard input devices (keyboard and mouse) accompanied by well-designed software will be perfectly appropriate for the preschooler over the age of three or three and a half. However, if your child has special needs or generally has difficulty with fine motor coordination, you might consider a touch-sensitive screen, such as the Touch Window from Edmark, which allows him to make choices by pressing directly on the screen.

What Is Developmentally Appropriate Software?

Based on the books mentioned in this chapter and on interviews we conducted with a number of early childhood experts, we have arrived at a list of criteria for you to use when determining whether a software package is appropriate for your preschooler.

Developmentally appropriate software is:

◆ Open-ended and exploratory. It doesn't focus on right and wrong answers but allows children to investigate and discover for themselves.

◆ Easy for a young child to use independently. It does not require reading, has easy-to-understand directions, and only expects children to find a limited number of keys on the keyboard. Furthermore, it is flexible about input devices, allowing a child to use a mouse, the keyboard, or an alternate device—whichever is easiest for that child.

◆ Focused on a broad range of skills and concepts. It works on more than just the numbers, letters, colors, and shapes so often identified as preschool skills. In addition (or instead), it encourages children to classify, to experiment using trial and error, to create and, in general, to think.

◆ Technically sophisticated. It appeals to a child's multisensory learning style, offering attractive graphics, appealing animations, and outstanding sound. It loads quickly and does not have long delays between screens (during which time a young child can become bored).

◆ Age-appropriate. It doesn't push the child to master skills for which he's not yet ready. The images and examples it uses are from real life or are at least understandable to the young child (within his realm of experience).

◆ Playful and fun. It encourages children to imagine, might involve fantasy play, and is definitely enjoyable. Furthermore, the fun is derived from the activity itself, not from some extrinsic reward given if the child succeeds at a given task.

◆ Encouraging. If children experience success when using this software, it helps build their self-esteem.

◆ Expandable. It can be used over and over again without losing its appeal. It offers children plenty of room to grow.

Special Solutions for Children with Special Needs

The terms "special needs" and "disabilities" are very broad. Used to refer to a variety of conditions, they include learning disabilities, behavior disorders, developmental disabilities, communication disabilities such as deafness and blindness, and orthopedic handicaps such as cerebral palsy and trauma-induced paralysis. While it is very hard to give any general advice about such a diverse group, it is safe to say that computers and related technologies have the potential to make a tremendous difference in the lives of children with special needs.

Computers enable "nondisabled" children and adults to accomplish tasks more efficiently. For those with special needs, the computer can play an even more important role: in many cases, it enables them to do things that were impossible (or at least much harder) to do before. This is particularly true of young people with physical or communication disabilities for whom special adaptive devices attached to the computer make it easier to communicate with the outside world. Adaptive devices run the gamut from text readers for blind children to special keyboards and head-operated switches for children with orthopedic disabilities.

Children with learning disabilities can sometimes benefit from special hardware as well. For example, the use of a touch-sensitive screen (built into some monitors or available as a separate unit to place over an existing monitor) can help a child who might otherwise have trouble making the connection between choices on the screen and the mouse or keyboard movements necessary to select them.

While it is beyond the scope of this chapter to list and describe all the adaptive devices that are available to you, the resource directory at the end of this chapter should help you locate an appropriate device for your child if he needs one. In addition, it's helpful to know that certain computers have built-in adaptive features. For example, the Macintosh enables users to modify their systems in order to magnify the screen, make it possible to enter all keyboard entries (Control key combinations, capital letters, etc.) with only one hand, and so on.

What About Special Software?

Children with special needs often have difficulty accomplishing tasks that nondisabled children handle easily. A hearing-impaired child, for example, may have a hard time learning new vocabulary words. A child with a learning disability such as dyslexia may have trouble comprehending printed words.

For some children, especially those with developmental disabilities or other severe learning problems, special software that breaks tasks down into many simple steps is helpful. Such software, available from several of the companies in the directory at the end of this chapter, can be very satisfying to a child who rarely has the opportunity to learn at a comfortable pace and experience real success.

However, it's important not to assume that the average child with disabilities requires special remedial software designed to drill him on the areas he finds difficult. That is a trap that too many school-based remedial programs fall into. Unfortunately, although children with special needs are frequently of average or above average intelligence, they often spend their time at school being drilled on lower-level skills such as vocabulary or "sounding out" words.

One of the problems with this approach is that it emphasizes a child's weaknesses, forcing the child to focus on what he cannot do instead of allowing him to learn compensatory skills and to experience success in other domains. As Richard Wanderman, an educational technology consultant who has years of experience working with students with learning disabilities, explains: "The biggest problem faced by children and adults with literacy problems is that they feel stupid. They need help separating their ability from their intelligence, realizing they can be very intelligent and learning disabled at the same time. As long as a child feels 'dumb,' as long as he's convinced that he'll fail at a task as difficult as reading or writing, why should he even try?"

A learning-disabled student experiences a sense of failure when he is repeatedly drilled in areas in which he is weak. This sense of failure is compounded by the fact that many of the "supplemental" or "enrichment" activities reserved for children who have mastered these basic skills are much more fun than drill. Furthermore, by emphasizing lower-level skills over higher-order thinking and problem solving, we deprive learning-disabled children of practice in the basic life skills that they need to be happy contributing members of society.

In general, our advice to parents who are selecting software for a child with special needs—or, for that matter, for a child who is simply having trouble in certain subject areas—is to look for programs that are fun, that will help your child experience success, and that will encourage thinking, problem solving, and communication skills. Because these are some of the key criteria we used in selecting our favorite software for all children, you are likely to find a number of programs in this book that will be helpful to your special child.

This is not to say that every package that works with nondisabled students will work equally well with children who have special needs. In addition to the general guidelines that we just mentioned, there are other factors to consider when evaluating software for use with a child with disabilities. In particular, it's important for the software to be flexible and easy to customize. For example, if your child will be using a special input device, you'll need to make sure that the software works well with that device. (Fortunately, many adaptive devices today are designed in such a way that they will work with a whole range of standard programs—not just those that were designed specifically for use with that hardware. However, some screen designs or approaches to menuing might make it hard to control certain programs with certain devices.)

For a child with learning disabilities, it's often important to be able to control the speed at which action occurs on the screen, to turn sound effects on or off, and to be able to set difficulty levels. In addition, you'll want to pay attention to a program's overall design to make sure that the screen is not too busy or confusing, the graphics are clear and understandable, the feedback is supportive and encouraging, and the choices are open-ended enough to allow divergent answers and true exploration. A multisensory approach that takes advantage of the sound and graphics capabilities of the computer and somehow encourages tactile exploration as well is particularly helpful to children with special needs.

Self-Confidence and Problem Solving

Making the computer available and accessible is important for all children, but it is even more critical for those with special needs. If at all possible, the computer should be set up in your home so that your child can work independently and comfortably. This practice will promote self-reliance and will encourage your child to use the computer as a general problem-solving tool.

Likewise, you should teach your child how to start the computer, activate software, and use such devices as the mouse and the printer. Even though this might require considerable time and effort on your part and on the part of your child, the investment will be well worth it. In addition to fostering independence, you will be teaching your child skills that will be useful in school and in the world at large.

Although the ability to function independently is important, it's also helpful for you to spend relaxed, playful time with your child at the computer. This shows your child that you are interested in what he is doing, allows him to interact with you in a personal and meaningful way, and gives him an opportunity to do something that children with special needs rarely have the chance to do: "show off." By sitting down with your child at the computer, you give him an opportunity to say, "See what I can do!" Very few activities can contribute more to building your child's self-esteem and solidifying your relationship.

Educational games, such as The Playroom and the McGee series for younger children, or the Super Solvers and Carmen Sandiego programs for older, more advanced kids, can be excellent tools to promote problem solving and build confidence. From the moment your child sits down to learn how the program operates, he is practicing important problem-solving skills. As he progresses through the game, being called upon to solve practical problems through logic or trial and error, he is engaging in the type of thinking required in the real world. If these programs are difficult for your child, you can help eliminate frustration by making play a group experience—with the child taking on the roles at which he is best. Discussing the game with you (or a sibling) as he goes along helps him verbalize what is happening, often solidifying the learning that is taking place.

Communicating and Creating

The greatest challenge faced by most children with special needs is communication. The challenge may be obvious, as in the case of a hearing-impaired or blind child, or subtle, as with a child who has an orthopedic handicap that prevents him from speaking fluently or intelligibly. Problems with receptive communication (listening and reading) or expressive communication (speaking and writing) often frustrate children with special needs and create the impression that they are much less intelligent than they truly are.

Learning to use a computerized writing tool is perhaps the single most important factor in improving a young person's communication skills. For older students, the appropriate tool might be a full-fledged word processor complete with such writing aids as a spelling checker, grammar checker, and on-line thesaurus, and such customizable options as macros (automatic commands that can be created to simplify complex functions to a few keystrokes). For younger children, a simple printing tool like The Print Shop or a large-text word processor to which graphics can be added might be best.

Such writing tools allow children with special needs to think and write far more fluently than might otherwise be possible. The child who lacks the fine motor skills necessary to form letters, who reverses letters and words, or who gets frustrated trying to set a complete sentence on paper, now has the opportunity to produce legible letters with single keystrokes—and to revise as many times as necessary without ruining the appearance of his finished product. Paint programs and other easy-to-use graphics tools also provide special-needs students with the chance to explore, create, and take pride in the attractive art that results.

In addition to providing your child with the tools that make it easier for him to write or paint, it's also important to help him find reasons to want to communicate. One way to promote communication is by subscribing to an on-line service such as Prodigy or CompuServe. (See the article entitled "On-Line Services" in Part V for more information about these and other on-line services.) Such a service can provide your child with access to games, reference materials, and—most valuable—forums where they can interact with electronic pen pals. Parents, too, may find an on-line service useful. Both CompuServe and Prodigy offer forums and other resources that deal with parenting, education, disabilities, and related topics.

A less expensive approach involves using your computer and printer to create a variety of printouts, each with a real purpose. Perhaps there's a person in your child's life with whom he'd like to correspond. If not, you might be able to put him in touch with a pen pal or a mentor to whom he'd enjoy writing. Encouraging children to do other writing with a purpose (for example, shopping lists or Christmas wish lists that will actually be used, fliers for family events such as parties or garage sales, and so on) can do a lot to build self-confidence and to motivate them to improve their communication skills.

Learning More

A variety of resources is available for parents of children with special needs. The organizations and information services listed in the following section don't all deal specifically with computers, but most of them will help you locate support services and other valuable materials (including hardware and software) for use with your child.

Another place to seek help is through your local school district. Your special-needs child should already be receiving services from trained special-education teachers appointed by the district. While there is no guarantee that your child's teachers will have had a lot of experience with his particular disabilities, they should have access to a variety of resources that will help them —and you—learn more. For example, most states have a number of regional centers set up to provide technology demonstrations and other assistance to special-education teachers and administrators. If you're interested in paying a visit to such a center or tapping into other resources that are available to special-education professionals, let your child's teacher know. There's a good chance that he or she will welcome your interest and support and that you can work together as a team to locate the best materials for your child.

Some Valuable Resources for Children with Special Needs

Organizations with a Focus on Technology for People with Disabilities

ABLEDATA, Newington Children's Hospital, 181 E. Cedar St., Newington, CT 06111; (800) 344-5405 (used for both voice and TDD) or (203) 667-5404

This organization maintains a database of thousands of products for people with disabilities. If you are trying to locate computer hardware, software, or any other equipment (seating systems, furniture, and so on), ABLEDATA will take information about your child's disability and the type of device you might be looking for, and then mail you a printout with relevant product descriptions and ordering information.

Alliance for Technology Access, 1307 Solano Ave., Albany, CA 94706; (415) 528-0747

Originally founded by Apple Computer, ATA is now an independent organization with many corporate partners (including both Apple and IBM) and 45 resource centers in 34 states around the country. Each center has its own board of directors and areas of expertise, but all agree on a common goal: to provide people of all ages, with all sorts of disabilities, and at all income levels, with access to technology. Most of the centers offer demonstrations of hardware, lending libraries, workshops, clubs, and more. Call ATA's main number to find out if there is a center near you.

CAST, Inc. (Center for Applied Special Technology), 39 Cross St., Peabody, MA 01960; (508) 531-8555

This center offers training for teachers and evaluation of children with special needs both locally and nationally. In addition to making presentations at numerous conferences, representatives of CAST fly to various sites to help with evaluations and training, or help connect you with local professionals who can assist you in similar ways.

Closing the Gap, P.O. Box 68, Henderson, MN 56044; (612) 248-3294

One of the better-known organizations for teachers, parents, and others interested in the use of technology with special-needs students, Closing the Gap sponsors a national conference each year and publishes a bimonthly newspaper with ongoing hardware and software reviews. One issue a year contains a resource guide to software and hardware. (This guide can also be purchased separately.)

IBM National Support Center for Persons with Disabilities, P.O. Box 2150-H06RI, Atlanta, GA 30301; (800) 426-2133; TDD (800) 284-9482

The National Support Center is a clearinghouse of information about computer-related devices offered by IBM and other vendors. It provides resource guides with listings of equipment for people with mobility, hearing, speech and language, learning, and vision impairments and offers IBM computers and adaptive equipment to qualified buyers at a discount.

RESNA: Association for the Advancement of Rehabilitation Technology, 1101 Connecticut Ave. NW, Suite 700, Washington, D.C. 20036; (202) 857-1199

An organization for rehabilitation professionals, RESNA is devoted to furthering the uses of technology to help people with disabilities. The organization publishes a comprehensive guide, "The Assistive Technology Source Book," which is useful for both parents and professionals in the field.

TAM (Technology and Media), Council for Exceptional Children, 1920 Association Dr., Weston, VA 22091-1598; (703) 620-3660

The Technology and Media division of the Council for Exceptional children is a valuable resource for information about hardware, software, and other technology for children with special needs. TAM publishes a bimonthly newsletter and a quarterly journal, both with a focus on technology in special education.

Trace Research and Development Center, S-151 Waisman Center, 1500 Highland Ave., Madison, WI 53705; (608) 262-6966

Trace is a research center and clearinghouse for information about adaptive devices. If you're having trouble locating the right hardware (and accompanying software) for your child with special needs, Trace is the place to turn; the organization maintains a comprehensive database of adaptive devices on the market today and publishes the Trace ResourceBook with descriptions, ordering information, and help to find the right product for your child.

Worldwide Disability Solutions Group, Apple Computer, Mail Stop 36SE, 20525 Mariani Ave., Cupertino, CA 95014; (408) 974-7910, TDD (408) 974-7911

Through its Disability Solutions Group, Apple offers information to end users about adaptive hardware and software from Apple and third-party developers. Two brochures are available from this group: "Connections," an overview of how computers are being used in special education and rehabilitation and "Toward Independence," a look at access technology.

Other Organizations That Can Help

American Speech-Language-Hearing Association, 10801 Rockville Pike, Rockville, MD 20852; (301) 897-5700, TDD (301) 897-0157

The largest association of speech and hearing professionals, ASHA makes a variety of materials available to parents of children who have hearing and speech disabilities. The association publishes booklets on augmentative communication and may be able to recommend a local professional who can help you with software selection.

Association for Retarded Citizens, 500 E. Border St., Suite 300, Arlington, TX 76010; (817) 261-6003

ARC, with more than 1,200 local chapters, is a strong advocate for developmentally disabled children and adults. Local chapters can provide information regarding services for developmentally disabled citizens and their rights. The Bioengineering program, located in the national office, can make software recommendations.

Council for Exceptional Children, 1920 Association Dr., Weston, VA 22091-1598; (703) 620-3660

In addition to its TAM division described earlier, CEC offers other resources for professionals interested in helping both disabled and gifted children. Two interesting organizations, located in the same building and loosely affiliated with CEC, are the Center for Special Education Technology, a federally funded national exchange, and the Information Center, an extensive library and ERIC clearinghouse with information on a variety of topics, including technology. These resource centers and CEC's two publications ("Exceptional Children" and "Teaching Exceptional Children") are all geared towards professional educators rather than parents, but you can tap into CEC information with help from your child's teacher.

Easter Seal Society, 70 East Lake St., Chicago, IL 60601; (312) 726-6200, TDD (312) 726-4258

You can find local chapters of the Easter Seal Society throughout the country. They provide a variety of services to children and adults with head and spinal cord injuries or speech and language disabilities. These services include technological assistance, as well as therapy, vocational evaluation and placement, and prosthetic recommendations. The Easter Seal Society also offers low-interest loans to help individuals with disabilities purchase computers and related assistive devices. For more information, contact the Technology Related Loan Fund (attn. Sully J.F. Alvarado) at the national office in Chicago.

Exceptional Parent, P.O. Box 3000, Denville, NJ 07834; (800) 247-8080

Exceptional Parent magazine is published eight times a year. It contains a wealth of information for parents of children with disabilities, and periodically includes articles and special issues devoted to technology.

Learning Disabilities Association, 4156 Library Rd., Pittsburgh, PA 15234; (412) 341-1515

Founded by parents, people with learning disabilities, and practitioners, this national organization offers free brochures, sells a variety of other publications, and will help callers find a chapter near them. Local chapters offer support groups and personal resources (medical and legal advice, advocacy with a school system, and so on).

March of Dimes, 1275 Mamaroneck Ave., White Plains, NY 10605; (914) 428-7100

Through its local chapters, the March of Dimes provides information, referral, and support services to parents of children with birth defects. Although they have no special program for information about computer hardware or software, local chapters can be helpful in steering parents in the right direction.

National Association of the Deaf, 814 Thayer Ave., Silver Spring, MD 20910-4500; (301) 587-1788, TDD (301) 587-1789

NAD is an advocacy organization that serves as an information and referral center for parents of hearing-impaired and deaf children. They have no special technology program, but they can generally refer parents to sources of information about computers, software, and telecommunication devices.

National Center for Learning Disabilities, 99 Park Ave., New York, NY 10016; (212) 687-7211

This advocacy group promotes awareness of learning disabilities and lobbies for the rights of learning-disabled children and adults. A general information packet is available from the foundation, as is an annual publication, "Their World." The 1990 edition of this magazine was devoted to technology and its applications to special education.

National Federation for the Blind, 1800 Johnson St., Baltimore, MD 21230; (301) 659-9314

Through its state chapters, the National Federation offers information and referral services to parents of visually impaired children. The NFB has a publication, "Future Reflections," and an extensive collection of reference materials. The National Braille and Technology Center for the Blind is located at NFB's national headquarters and can provide relevant information on computers and software.

National Information Center for Children and Youth with Disabilities (NICHCY), P.O. Box 1492, Washington, D.C. 20013; (800) 999-5599; TDD (703) 893-8614

Although it offers no direct services, NICHCY is a clearinghouse for information dealing with all disabilities. If you are unsure of what information you need or where to get it, this is an excellent resource to consult first. In addition to providing information over the phone, NICHCY publishes several news digests each year. One of the recent issues focused on assistive technology.

Orton Dyslexia Society, Chester Bldg., Suite 382, 8600 LaSalle Rd., Baltimore, MD 21204-6020; (800) 222-3123

A national organization with regional branches, Orton was originally formed as a research organization for professionals studying dyslexia. While many of its members today are medical researchers, a number of teachers and parents are also involved. The society offers a national conference that includes a number of sessions on technology.

United Cerebral Palsy, 7 Penn Plaza, Suite 804, New York, NY 10001; (800) 872-1827

Like many other national organizations, UCP provides a continuum of services through its local chapters. These services range from diagnosis through medical treatment and adaptive housing. UCP offers technological support and is currently engaged in a national demonstration program in which computers are used by young children with cerebral palsy to improve their communication skills.

Some Hardware and Software Vendors

DLM Teaching Resources, P.O. Box 4000, Allen, TX 75002; (800) 527-4747 or (800) 442-4711 (in Texas)

DLM publishes several titles to help children with learning disabilities improve their math and reading fluency, plus a number of more general drill/ tutorial programs that can easily be customized to meet the needs of special-education students. The company also publishes two valuable special-needs resource books compiled by Apple Computer: "Apple Computer Resources in Special Education and Rehabilitation" (a comprehensive guide to Macintosh and Apple II products and resources related to special education) and "Independence Day" (a guide that focuses on adaptive technology and ways in which it can help people with physical or communication disabilities live independently).

Edmark, P.O. Box 3218, Redmond, WA 98073-3218; (800) 426-0856; TDD (206) 861-7679

Edmark is best known for its Touch Window screen, which can be placed over an Apple II, MS-DOS, or Macintosh monitor to turn it into a touch-sensitive screen. The company also produces special education and early childhood software and distributes products from a number of other publishers in the field.

IBM (see IBM National Support Center for Persons with Disabilities above for ordering information)

IBM produces a number of products for disabled users, including a touch-sensitive monitor; SpeechViewer software for use by speech therapists; Phone Communicator to help the hearing- and speech-impaired talk on the telephone; and Screen Reader, a product that reads the computer screen for blind and visually impaired users.

Don Johnston, 1000 N. Rand Rd., Bldg 115, Wauconda, IL 60084; (800) 999-4660 or (708) 526-2682

This company manufacturers the Adaptive Firmware card (for the Apple II) and Ke:nx card (for the Macintosh), which enable users to plug a variety of alternate keyboards, switches, and other input devices into the computer. Don Johnston also distributes software and hardware from a number of other special-education companies.

Laureate Learning, 110 East Spring St., Winooski, VT 05404; (800) 562-6801 or (802) 655-4755

Laureate offers talking software (and a limited amount of hardware) for children and adults with developmental disabilities, language and hearing impairments, emotional disturbances, and acquired cognitive and language disabilities.

Prentke Romich, 1022 Heyl Rd., Wooster, OH 44691; (216) 262-1984

Prentke Romich sells a number of devices, including printers for the blind and other hardware and software that help with communication.

Girls, Boys, and Individual Differences

During the mid-1980s a number of research studies focused on the differences between the way boys and girls viewed and responded to computers. In general, the researchers found that boys were much better represented in computer electives, computer camps, and after-school activities involving computer technology (the boy-to-girl ratio in such voluntary activities was frequently as great as 3 to 1) and that they expressed much more positive attitudes about computers than did their female classmates. Girls generally expressed doubts about their own capabilities with regard to the technology, indicated that they saw computers as more appropriate tools for boys, and deferred to the males in their classes when there were disagreements about who should use the computer for recreational purposes.

Such differences were also reflected in the home, where parents were more likely to purchase computers for their sons than for their daughters and to spend more money on hardware and software purchases when a boy was involved. When girls did have access to computers at home, they generally spent less time on them than did boys with similar access.

The gap between male and female attitudes and behavior was most pronounced in studies that dealt with junior high and high school students. In fact, several of the studies of children under nine or ten years of age found no difference at all between the amount of time boys and girls spent at the computer or how much they enjoyed computer-based activities.

The tendency for girls to lose interest and become less confident about their abilities as they approach adolescence closely parallels what happens to girls' attitudes towards math and science at the same stage in their lives—and raises many of the same questions. Why do our daughters suddenly become less interested and capable in the areas of math, science, and technology? There is little agreement about whether there are any physiological differences that somehow give boys the edge over girls when they reach adolescence, but it does seem clear that the strongest factor at work is social and peer pressure.

A number of studies have shown that girls do as well (or nearly as well) as boys in settings that require both to take the same math and science courses, but that girls in secondary schools generally don't gravitate to such courses when they are optional. (This, of course, increases the gender gap as time goes on, decreasing the likelihood that girls will have the prerequisites to major in math or science in college, even if their interest does increase.) One study of 1,200 ninth graders (reported in "Mismeasuring Women: A Critique of Research on Computer Ability and Avoidance" in the journal *Signs*) showed that boys did better than girls only in those schools where males and females had different self-perceptions about their ability to learn math and science; at sites where the girls believed they could do as well as the boys, there were few differences between the two groups.

Possible Changes

There are a number of research questions still to be answered about boys, girls, and computers. The majority of gender studies reported today were conducted in the mid-1980s, at a time when computers were just entering schools in significant numbers and were being used primarily for computer programming. It's hard to know from these studies whether positive early experiences with computers over several years can make a difference in how girls feel about the technology when they finally reach adolescence. It's also worth asking whether girls continue to see computers as "male" even when they are used not for programming but for writing, art, and other activities less associated with math and science. (This is definitely the direction the technology has moved in recent years.)

Two of the most recent studies, reported in 1989 in the journal *Computers in the Schools*, do show possible evidence of changes in attitudes. In one of the studies, which focused on third and sixth graders who had been working with computers for several years, girls and boys were equally confident about their ability to learn from the computer, and girls were even more enthusiastic about computers than the boys in their class. Because many of the previous studies had shown attitudinal differences starting as early as fifth or sixth grade, the researcher concluded that the positive attitudes in the group she studied might have been the result of early exposure to computers.

The second study (in the same journal) also found that upper-elementary school girls enjoyed computers as much as boys and learned approximately as much from computer software that emphasized map reading and early geography skills. In this case, however, the conclusions focused on the type of software used. Many writers have pointed out in recent years that much of the kids' software on the market takes a traditionally "male" approach, featuring arcade action, explosions, battles, and other images that, for whatever reason, generally appeal to boys more than girls. The program used for this study included none of these elements; instead it focused on a fantasy world (A. A. Milne's Hundred Acre Wood). Perhaps this was the reason for the girls' positive response.

Most of the other evidence we have so far is anecdotal. A number of teachers report that when computers are used for word processing and other activities that appeal to girls as well as boys, there are few differences between the two groups in terms of their enthusiasm level or involvement. While it is still a serious concern that girls continue to be less interested in math and science than do boys, the connection between computers and math and science seems to be decreasing in many young people's minds.

What Parents Can Do

One question you might be asking yourself is, "Does it matter if my girl doesn't love computers?" Parents and teachers actually may be overly concerned with the importance of raising "computer literate" adults. It is certainly not crucial for your child to be fascinated with computers and computer programming in order to do well in college or in the work world. What is crucial, however, is for each of our children to have a sense of confidence and personal self-worth that will allow him or her to deal with all sorts of challenges—on and off the computer—as they arise. Unfortunately, many girls seem to lose some of this confidence as they reach adolescence (at least in the areas of math, science, and related technologies).

What can we do about this problem? Following are some steps you might take to help your daughter keep an open mind about her capabilities and to encourage everyone in your family to examine some of the issues related to males, females, and computers.

We realize that there is a real danger in focusing too much on trends and differences. If your 12-year-old daughter loves computing, you certainly don't want her to get the sense that you're watching and waiting for the day that she'll change her mind. If your 13-year-old son has no interest in video games or "shoot-'em-up" action, the last thing you want is for him to feel that there's something wrong with him.

On the other end of the spectrum, it's important to recognize our children's choices and preferences even when they do conform to stereotypes. You can't force your daughter to be interested in math or science or your son to be interested in writing or human development. You can, however, encourage your kids to question their assumptions, to acknowledge (maybe even laugh at) peer pressures, and in general to be themselves.

What follows is a list of suggestions for ways in which you can encourage your kids to have open minds about technology. Many of the guidelines are adapted from the publications *Does Your Daughter Say "No, Thanks" to the Computer?* (Women's Action Alliance) and *Notes for Parents* (AAAS Directorate for Education and Human Resources Programs, Spring 1990). (For more information about these organizations, see the directory "Some Valuable Resources," later in the chapter.)

◆ Display positive expectations. Don't assume that your daughter will find math, science, or computer programming difficult or that your son will have trouble working peacefully and cooperatively.

◆ If the computer is in your son's room, move it to a more neutral spot. Make sure that your daughter has equal time at the computer—even if she seems willing to defer to a more enthusiastic brother.

◆ Take an interest in what your daughter is doing with computers at school and at home. Let her know that you think her computer interests and skills are important.

◆ Encourage your daughter to enroll in math, science, and computer electives at school and to take part in technology-related after-school programs and summer camps.

◆ If your daughter is reluctant to join programs that appear to be dominated by boys, look for a local Girls Club or Girl Scout troop that offers science-oriented projects. (See the list of valuable resources at the end of the chapter for more information about projects that these two organizations are involved in.)

◆ Give your children nontraditional tasks. For example, next time you take a trip, have your daughter serve as navigator and map reader.

◆ Plan trips to science museums, planetariums, and computer museums with your daughter. Ask her to invite her friends.

◆ Hold family discussions about equity issues, stereotypes, and career options.

◆ Critique computer ads with your children. Compare how often males and females are portrayed and in what roles. Identify the stereotypes and sexist assumptions you encounter.

◆ Be good role models. Girls should see their mothers using the computer, not just their fathers. If you're a mother, take some time to sit down with your kids at the computer—even if it's a new experience for you. Perhaps your daughter can teach you how to use her favorite software.

◆ Visit places where computers are being used in interesting ways. Encourage your daughter to talk with women who have rewarding jobs involving math, science, and technology.

◆ If your daughter says she hates computers, pursue the topic further. Perhaps she simply hates the software she has been exposed to. Help her identify the types of computer activities she does enjoy and locate software that matches her interests.

◆ If your daughter or your son hates arcade action or other imagery used by a particular computer program, look around for alternatives. There are many titles to choose from and not all of them are targeted at the child who loves video games and fast action.

◆ Ask your children about the peer pressure and social attitudes they encounter at school. Does your daughter feel as if her friends expect her to hate math, science, or computers? Does she feel intimidated by the boys in her class and their attitudes towards computers? Does your son expect girls at school to do as well as his male friends?

◆ Talk with your children's teachers. Make them aware of your concerns and the resources you've found useful.

Some Valuable Resources

AAAS Directorate for Education and Human Resources Programs, 1333 H St. NW, Washington, D.C. 20005-4792; (202) 326-6670

The American Association for the Advancement of Science (AAAS) has a division devoted to improving science, mathematics, and technology education in America. This division, the Directorate for Education and Human Resources Programs, publishes and distributes materials for parents, professionals, and policy makers, including suggestions for encouraging girls in math and science. The AAAS also provides materials to help Girl Scout councils train their leaders to conduct science and math activities.

EQUALS, Lawrence Hall of Science, University of California, Berkeley, CA 94720; (510) 642-1823; to find out about a Family Math program near you, call (510) 528-0560

Located at the Lawrence Hall of Science at the University of California, Berkeley, EQUALS publishes a variety of materials related to math, computers, and equity issues. One of their publications, "Family Math," outlines entertaining ways for families to work together to improve children's attitudes about mathematics and the role it can play in their lives. A number of community organizations now offer Family Math workshops based on the ideas outlined in this book.

Girls Inc., 30 East 33rd St., New York, NY 10016; (212) 689-3700

Girls Incorporated offers a program known as Operation SMART, which focuses on science, mathematics, and related technology. Activities include building kites and model airplanes and taking apart computers to see how they work. Check with your local Girls Incorporated affiliate to see if they offer Operation SMART. Or, contact the national office for the Operation SMART activity book.

Women's Action Alliance, 370 Lexington Ave., New York, NY 10017; (212) 532-8330

Women's Action Alliance offers a free booklet entitled *Does Your Daughter Say "No, Thanks" to the Computer?* for parents and one entitled *Do Your Female Students Say "No, Thanks" to the Computer?* for teachers. The Alliance also sells some longer books on the subject, as well as a 1993 video about the Computer Equity Project, which focused on increasing girls' participation in math, science, and technology.

Some Helpful Research Summaries

The results reported in this chapter are summarized in more detail in the following publications:

"The Computer Gender Gap in Elementary School" by Mary DeRemer and "Girls and Microcomputers" by Alfred Forsyth and David Lancy. Published in the journal *Computers in the Schools* (Vol. 6, Nos. 3 and 4, 1989).

"Mismeasuring Women: A Critique of Research on Computer Ability and Avoidance" by Pamela Kramer and Sheila Lehman. Published in *Signs: Journal of Women in Culture and Society* (Vol. 16, No. 1, 1990).

Does Your Daughter Say "No, Thanks" to the Computer?, a booklet published by the Women's Action Alliance, New York.

The Home/School Connection

Although your child's school may be a valuable resource for locating information about good software that will run on your family computer, it's important to realize that many of the programs that work well in schools have little place in a home. For example, there are a number of educational software titles (social studies simulations, graphing tools, and so on) that are designed to be used by a single teacher working with a group of students. Other programs have too narrow a focus to be of lasting value at home, although they fit well in the classroom, where they are used to reinforce an important concept or skill (for example, how to estimate distances or place events in a proper order) and then are set aside for reuse with a new group of students.

In general, parents have to be more conscious than teachers about the entertainment value of software. An educational program might compare favorably in your child's mind to a workbook or lecture—possible alternatives in a school setting. However, the same program might lose its appeal at home when it has to compete with Nintendo, baseball, or phone conversations with friends.

On the other side, there are some excellent home-oriented titles that do not perform well in a school setting. For example, an entertaining program with general educational value for the home market might not make it in the schools if it devotes more time to game playing (navigating through mazes, shooting at targets, and so on) than to the content being covered. In addition, such features as the ability to turn off sound in a program and to save information about how well a number of different players performed are generally far more important to teachers than to parents.

Titles for Both Home and School

In spite of the differences between the two markets, many titles do work well both at home and at school. The publishers of these programs frequently build extra control features into their titles so that they can be altered by teachers to suit a school environment. And they often produce two different versions of the package, containing the same software but different documentation.

The school version of a title generally costs more, and includes a backup disk (to avoid any delays if the main program disk fails and needs replacement) and a teacher's guide with suggestions for classroom activities related to the software. The packaging is also different (frequently the school version ships in a loose-leaf binder rather than a box), which explains why, when visiting your child's school, you may find familiar titles in unfamiliar packages.

In trying to decide whether a program that your kid likes at school is appropriate for home use, it often helps to take a lead from the publishers themselves. While some publishers, including Broderbund and The Learning Company, produce virtually all of their titles for the home market, then create school versions of those they think will sell in education, school-oriented companies, such as Edmark and MECC, offer home versions of only some of their titles. Of course, even if there is a home and a school version of a program your child enjoys, it's important to consider whether it's the sort of program that can maintain your child's interest at home after he has spent hours with it in class.

There are definitely some occasions when a school product not marketed aggressively to families is nevertheless worth considering for your home. If you're involved in home schooling your kids, working with your child over the summer to help him catch up in certain areas, leading any sort of computer-related club for kids, or making technology-related recommendations to your child's school district, you may want to get some school-oriented software catalogs to see what's available.

It's also very helpful to pay attention to what your child is using at school if you're thinking of buying him a word processor or other computerized tool. If you select the same tool he is using at school, he will have to spend less time getting up to speed on the software, and it will be easier for him to complete assignments at home that can then be loaded into the application at school.

The same is true for authoring programs (from programming languages to hypermedia tools such as HyperCard). It's the rare parent or child who has the time and energy to learn to program for pleasure at home. But if your child is already excited about such activities at school, you might want to build on this interest by purchasing a version of the authoring tool for use at home.

Give and Take

In this country, the technical expertise of teachers and school administrators varies tremendously. If the public school system in your state and district (or the private school if your child attends one) has invested resources in buying computers and related technology and in educating teachers about using these tools effectively to enhance the curriculum, your child may be participating in an exciting computer program that will inspire you to learn more as well. Or your child may be lucky enough to be working with dynamic teachers who have taken it upon themselves to make computers and exciting software a part of the classroom. On the other hand, there are many school districts (as well as individual schools within a district) where teachers and administrators are afraid of the technology, where software is outdated or practically nonexistent, or where the computer experts on the staff have lost their jobs due to budget cuts.

If your child's school is staffed with experienced computer-using teachers or a knowledgeable computer resource teacher, chances are these educators will be happy to talk with you about products and ideas that will help your child's computer use at home complement what is happening at school. If, on the other hand, you turn out to be more computer-savvy than the school personnel, you may have the opportunity to help shape the ways in which technology is used in your child's school or district.

Many teachers and administrators will welcome help in this area if it really feels like help and not criticism. For example, if you play an active role in fund-raising for new technology purchases, you will be doing a lot to earn the right to help decide how the funds are spent. You might also volunteer to spend some time in your child's classroom, demonstrating those computer uses your family finds most exciting. If you want to lobby for new technology expenditures in the district, you will also need to identify and seek out the key administrators—those who understand the potential of computers and exciting software to improve education.

When you are spending time in your child's school (either as an observer or as an adviser), it's helpful to be aware of some differences in the home and school technology markets that go beyond the issues of software design described earlier. If you're thinking only of computers and computer software when talking to your kid's teachers about technology, your focus is too narrow. Schools often have access to additional forms of technology that are not found in the typical home. For example, laser videodiscs (an alternative to videotapes that never really took off in the home market because one cannot tape onto a videodisc) are playing an important role in schools today. The videodisc is appealing to educators because it enables them to jump to any segment of the footage, branch to relevant portions of the video, and step through freeze-frame images with the help of a remote-control device, a bar code reader, or a computer hooked up to the videodisc player.

Local area networks that link computers to share data and peripherals are also becoming widespread in schools, opening up an entirely new world of software possibilities. In addition to the many existing software packages that can run on a network (eliminating the need for floppy disk storage and management), there are some new titles that go a step further, taking true advantage of the network's features. These programs involve children working together on different computers in cooperative learning experiences, such as large-group simulations or collaborative writing projects.

Finally, there are some technologies familiar to many home users that take on new uses in the classroom. For example, schools interested in telecommunications have access to a variety of school-oriented services that connect students in different cities, states, and countries so that they can share everything from information about their families to data on acid rain and pollution. Educational television is used in many schools to supplement other teaching materials, and in a number of districts, the medium is becoming increasingly interactive as schools participate in "video teleconferences" with other sites or enroll in "distance learning" courses in which an instructor at a remote site teaches classes via TV.

If you're interested in staying informed about these and other computer-related technologies in the schools, you may want to subscribe to one of the magazines listed in the next section. At the very least, these magazines will provide you with insights about what is possible in education today with the help of powerful electronic tools.

Some School-Oriented Technology Publications Worth Knowing About

The Computing Teacher, 1787 Agate St., Eugene, OR 97403-1923; (800) 336-5191

This journal, which focuses on the instructional uses of computers, is published eight times a year by the International Society for Technology in Education (ISTE). An annual subscription to *The Computing Teacher* costs $55 and includes ISTE membership fees.

Electronic Learning, Scholastic, Inc., P.O. Box 53797, Boulder, CO 80322; (800) 631-1586

Electronic Learning, published eight times a year, September through June, is a magazine for school administrators and computer-using teachers. An annual subscription is $19.95.

Only the Best, ASCO, 1250 North Pitt St., Alexandria, VA 22314-1453; (703) 549-9110

This annual publication is a reference guide to the highest-rated educational software. Reviews are based on evaluations from departments of education, educational magazines, and a number of other school-oriented evaluation groups. The print edition of *Only the Best* costs $25. A floppy disk version (Mac or DOS) is available for $99.

Technology & Learning, Peter Li, Inc., 330 Progress Rd., Dayton, OH 45449; (800) 543-4383

This magazine for administrators and teachers involved in using technology to improve education is published eight times a year. An annual subscription costs $12.

Kids Software

Educational software is probably the number one rationalization for the purchase of a home computer. Luckily, there are thousands of wonderful software titles for kids, most of which are at least mildly educational. Kids software can teach even the very young (as young as age three) to recognize shapes, letters, and words. And older kids can create interactive art, write short stories, or just explore wild and wonderful computer worlds.

Whether you want your kids to get a jump-start on their mathematics or you just want to keep them creatively occupied for a few hours, the programs in this section are sure to bring a grin to any kid's face.

Kid Works 2

Manufacturer: Davidson & Associates, Inc.
Platforms: Windows, DOS, Macintosh
System requirements:
   Windows—4MB RAM, VGA or better graphics
   DOS—286 or better, DOS 3.3 or later, VGA or better graphics,
   hard disk, mouse
   Mac—Minimum (except will not run on a Mac Plus)
Price range: $$

Mom and Dad have Microsoft Works or ClarisWorks, so why shouldn't the kiddies get the "works" too? Kid Works 2 does just that, supplying kids with a story writer, a story illustrator, a story player, and other fun stuff, all in one package. Just about any child will be able to quickly put together his or her own illustrated stories, or just spend hours discovering all the cool things the program can do.

Kids of various ages can put together the rebus-like stories with a combination of words and mini-pictures. The amazing part is that the program can read the story back to the child, using synthesized speech to pronounce just about anything the child types. In addition, the story illustrator provides a full set of graphics tools that are souped up with neat sound effects to keep kids grinning. After the child finishes constructing the story, the story player not only reads the story back, but also displays the child's artwork.

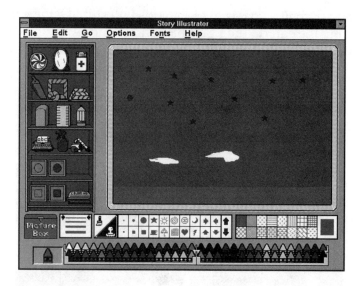

Kid Works 2 for Windows

Reader Rabbit 2

Manufacturer: The Learning Company
Platforms: Windows, DOS, Macintosh
System requirements:
    Windows—386 or better, 4MB RAM, VGA graphics, sound card
    DOS—DOS 3.3 or later, 286 or better, EGA or better graphics
    Mac—Minimum
Price range: $$

Reader Rabbit has been teaching kids about words for a good number of years. In this version of the program for folks aged five to eight, four word games—Word Mine, Match Patch, Vowel Pond, and Alphabet Dance—teach word building, vowel sounds, word concepts, and early dictionary skills.

For example, in Word Mine, kids gather crystals in their mining cart by building words from letter combinations. In Vowel Pond, kids try to catch fish by matching vowel sounds with words that contain those sounds. Match

Patch teaches kids about rhymes, homonyms, and antonyms; kids must match word carrots until the carrot patch is empty. Finally, in Alphabet Dance, kids must alphabetize a list of name cards in order to receive an egg token and watch a funny dance.

Although Reader Rabbit's goal is to teach, kids will still like the games, especially considering the entertaining graphics and sound. And Reader Rabbit offers several different difficulty levels so that you can tailor the program to your child.

Reader Rabbit 2

Creative Writer

Manufacturer: Microsoft Corporation
Platforms: Windows, Macintosh
System requirements:
   Windows—386 or greater, VGA graphics, sound card recommended
   Mac—Minimum
Price range: $$

Kids from the ages of 8 to 14 will flip over Creative Writer, which is one of the most magical word processors ever made. Using Creative Writer, kids can produce their own letters, stories, reports, greeting cards, newsletters, and banners. And the whole process is so much fun, you'll have a hard time stopping them from writing.

Creative Writer features four departments, each of which helps with the writing process. In the library, for example, kids can easily open or delete documents by dragging thumb-nail images to and from the wall. In the Projects department, kids can choose to start a newspaper, greeting card, banner, or other type of document. If your child needs a little creative nudge, she can go to the Idea Workshop, where she can create wacky sentences with the Splot Machine or use the Picture Window to view idea-inspiring drawings. In the Writing Studio, of course, kids compose their actual project.

The program's interface is a delight, featuring colorful icons, with attached sound effects, that allow kids not only to write using a variety of fonts and colors, but also to add clip art, special text effects, borders, backgrounds, and even sounds to their documents. Just exploring the many options included in this wonderful program will keep kids busy for hours.

Creative Writer

The Children's Writing & Publishing Center

Manufacturer: The Learning Company
Platform: DOS
System requirements: Printer
Price range: $$

The Children's Writing & Publishing Center is an introductory word processor with a number of desktop publishing features. Using a set of steps that are easy for even young folks to learn, kids can create and illustrate documents such as reports, stories, letters, newsletters, and fliers. They can even choose between a single-column report format and a two-column newsletter and decide whether or not to include a heading.

Writing & Publishing Center features a simple interface with pull-down menus, on-screen prompts, and help menus. Its tools include basic word processing capabilities (typing, editing, and cutting and pasting, a choice of type styles and sizes, and so on), a 150-picture graphics library, and the capability to import graphics from other libraries. Kids will especially enjoy pasting pictures into their stories and reports, which makes homework time more a treat than drudgery.

While kids love this program and the results they can create with it, many parents who are new to computers also can benefit from the program's simplicity. It's possible to get up and running in a few minutes and to complete a two- or three-page document, including graphics from the library, in less than a hour. After outgrowing Writing & Publishing Center, older kids will want to use The Student Writing Center, also produced by The Learning Company.

The Children's Writing & Publishing Center

Fine Artist

Manufacturer: Microsoft Corporation
Platforms: Windows, Macintosh
System requirements:
    Windows—386 or greater, 4MB RAM, VGA graphics, sound card
    recommended
    Mac—Minimum
Price range: $$

Fine Artist is the companion program to Microsoft's Creative Writer. Kids will adore using this dazzling paint program, which enables them to create not only their own full color paintings, but also posters, comic strips, and even animated picture shows with sound.

In the Painting Studio section of the program, kids can paint their own art masterpieces from scratch or work with one of the included backgrounds, filling in shapes with color much as they would with a coloring book. To keep young artists happily busy, the Painting Studio provides tons of fun tools, including various paintbrushes, a color palette, several rolls of stickers (clip art), a sound generator, and much more. Kids can paint with various shapes, copy parts of a picture from one place to another, resize clip art, add text special effects, erase mistakes, create 3D effects, and even print their pictures.

Fine Artist

Other departments include the Gallery, where kids can open and delete paintings; the Drawing Tricks department, where animated characters show kids how to draw figures and how to create 3D objects; and the Project Workshop, where kids can create comic strips, stickers, and picture shows. The program's easy-to-use interface is much like that used in Creative Writer, making it easy for children to use the program without adult supervision.

Just Grandma and Me

Manufacturer: Broderbund Software
Platforms: Windows, Macintosh
System requirements:
>   Windows—386 or later, 4MB, super VGA, CD-ROM, sound card
>   Mac—4MB RAM, 256-color graphics, CD-ROM

Price range: $

Review copyright 1993 by Compute Publications Int'l, Ltd.
Reprinted by permission.

Based on a book by Mercer Mayer, Just Grandma and Me is a delightful multimedia romp through a storybook come to life. From the first page to the last, readers will be enthralled with a new style of story-telling that is just a hop from a fully interactive cartoon. If a child likes, she can sit back and have the story read to her, complete with animated sequences that build on the original story. Or, if the child likes the hands-on approach, she can use her mouse to click on the many objects on each page, triggering funny mini-cartoons with full sound effects.

Some examples of the silliness to be found in Just Grandma and Me include beach umbrellas that snap shut and rocket into the sky; clams that sing in perfect three-part harmony; a dog that scratches furiously as fleas leap from his fur and escape into the ocean; a starfish that dons a top hat and cane and performs the old soft-shoe; and a raccoon that steps off her beach blanket and jumps around, yelping, on the hot sand. On the educational side, each page's text is also interactive. When a child clicks on a word, the word is highlighted and pronounced, a perfect way for children not only to learn to read new words, but also to discover the way in which sentences are constructed from the words.

Although Just Grandma and Me is targeted at children, it would be a cold adult indeed who wasn't affected by the program's story and sharp sense of wit. The cartoon sequences range from charming to hilarious. In fact, adults and children alike will find it difficult to quit before the entire story has run its course. So, although the program requires little or no adult assistance, it's likely that the "big people" will linger once the program gets started, looking over their offsprings' shoulders. Other titles in the series include Arthur's Teacher Trouble, The Tortoise and the Hare, and The New Kid on the Block.

Just Grandma and Me

Eagle Eye Mysteries

Manufacturer: Electronic Arts
Platforms: DOS, Macintosh
System requirements:
  DOS—386 or better, 256-color VGA, hard disk, mouse and sound card recommended
  Mac—4MB RAM, 256-color graphics
Price range: $

Review copyright 1993 by Compute Publications Int'l, Ltd.
Reprinted by permission.

When it comes to sneaking education in with fun, Eagle Eye Mysteries is sneaky indeed. Children learn about everything from bats and caves to U.S. Presidents while they solve a series of clever mysteries. The educational element is integrated so smoothly into game play as to be almost invisible. Add 256-color graphics and digitized sound, and you've got an educational game few children can resist.

Included in this exciting collection are such intriguing adventures as The Case of the Mysterious Monster, The Case of the Midnight Masquerade, The Case of the Crazy Compass, and The Case of the Reckless Robber. All told, there are almost 75 mysteries organized into three case books—plenty to keep even the cleverest of junior sleuths busy for a long time.

The player's task is to travel around the town, questioning people and gathering clues. To solve the case, the child must pick the five clues that best identify the culprit. Of course, while evaluating the clues, the child also reviews the educational facts she gathered during her investigation! Educational value notwithstanding, the detailed 256-color graphics, original musical score, and digitized sounds and voices make Eagle Eye Mysteries a guaranteed winner.

Eagle Eye Mysteries

Kid Pix

Manufacturer: Broderbund Software
Platforms: DOS, Macintosh
System requirements:
   DOS—EGA graphics, mouse
   Mac—Minimum
Price range: $

Put even the youngest child in front of Kid Pix, and he'll draw, listen and laugh, and then draw some more. While this graphics package is designed for even the youngest user, it offers the normal array of "painting" tools—including lines, rectangles, ovals, erasers, pens, and text—plus many surprising and delightful extras.

The rubber-stamp icon, for example, allows children to choose from a menu of dozens of small pictures and then stamp them on the screen again and again. With the "wacky paintbrush," kids can paint in 32 different patterns. The electric mixer, on the other hand, changes the drawing in a variety of fun and silly ways. Even the erasers are fun: watch your picture disappear into a black hole or explode like a firecracker! If you choose the "?" eraser, you can erase your picture and discover another picture hiding beneath.

Your family will also love listening to the sounds that accompany each action. If you make a mistake, you can undo it while a little voice says "uh oh!" or "oops!" You hear a "kerchunk" each time you use the rubber stamp, the "glug glug" of pouring paint when you fill a shape with color, and the racing engine and screeching tires of a moving van each time you move a piece of the picture. There's so much to do with Kid Pix, that it's more of an experience than a paint program.

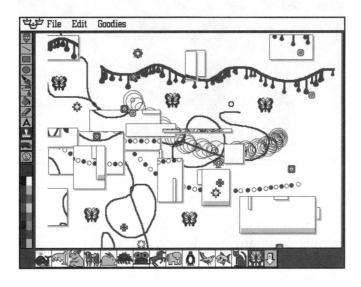

Kid Pix

Treasure Cove

Manufacturer: The Learning Company
Platform: DOS
System requirements: EGA or better graphics, hard disk, mouse and sound card recommended
Price range: $$

Review copyright 1993 by Compute Publications Int'l, Ltd.
Reprinted by permission.

With Treasure Cove, children between the ages of 5 and 9 slip into their swim fins, don a mask and snorkel, and join a fascinating adventure beneath the waves as they solve puzzles, learn about sea creatures, and find treasures. Under the water, the child is armed with only a flashlight and a bubble pump. By capturing sea animals with her bubble pump and exploring the ocean floor with her flashlight, the child advances through the levels of the game, eventually gathering enough gems to win.

Treasure Cove

By replacing the traditional weapons used in video games with the bubble pump, The Learning Company has cleverly avoided violence in Treasure Cove. Animals trapped in bubbles are not destroyed; they are just removed from the screen, after which the child is rewarded. For example, when the child captures an orange sea star, she is given a "puzzler" to solve. These multiple choice questions concentrate on ocean life and usually involve solving simple math problems, finding rhyming words, or completing

384

sentences. If the child answers the question correctly, she is given a clue that she can use to locate gems and the all-important puffer fish, which is required to move on to the next level.

Throughout this underwater adventure, the child will be captivated by Treasure Cove's almost cartoon-quality graphics and humorous animation—especially when the program is run in 256-color VGA. Moreover, Treasure Cove's sound takes full advantage of a Sound Blaster-compatible card to produce snazzy sound effects and a catchy soundtrack.

Where in Space Is Carmen Sandiego?

Manufacturer: Broderbund
Platforms: DOS, Macintosh
System requirements:
 DOS—VGA graphics, hard disk, mouse and sound card recommended
 Mac—4MB RAM, 256-color graphics
Price range: $

Review copyright 1993 by Compute Publications Int'l, Ltd.
Reprinted by permission.

The world's favorite villain, Carmen Sandiego, began her illustrious career in Where in the World Is Carmen Sandiego. Now her crime spree leads into the great expanse of the universe. In this educational game, you must search among 32 different locations for one of 15 suspects. Locations you'll visit include not only the nine planets, but also the sun, the asteroids, Halley's comet, and many moons.

At each location (which is depicted by a digitized NASA photo), you gather clues by questioning witnesses, tapping into V.I.L.E. radio frequencies, or performing a star search for incoming messages from your colleagues. Witnesses and V.I.L.E. radio transmissions immediately give you clues to your next destination. When performing a star search, however, you must first use the star map to lock onto the constellation from which the transmission was sent. Eventually, you catch up with the criminal and make your arrest—assuming, of course, that you arrive in time, don't run out of fuel, and have the proper warrant.

During the course of your investigation, you read about such otherworldly topics as astronauts, astronomers, space explorations, and astronomical terms.

The on-line database stocks all the information you need, including plenty of high-quality photographs and even some fascinating mini-movies. Where in Space Is Carmen Sandiego is yet another top-notch entry into a long and successful line of educational computer games—a fascinating romp through the solar system featuring awesome digitized photos from NASA's own files and a clever gang of cosmic characters.

Where in Space Is Carmen Sandiego?

Busy Town

Manufacturer: Paramount Interactive
Platforms: DOS, Macintosh
System requirements:
  DOS—DOS 3.3 or later, 286 or better, VGA graphics, CD-ROM, sound card, mouse
  Mac—LC or better, 4MB RAM, color graphics, CD-ROM
Price range: $

Busy Town is a place that young kids (ages 3 to 7) will want to visit often, thanks to its many playgrounds filled with exciting and educational things to do. In fact, there's so much to do in Busy Town that it'll be a long time before your kids have exhausted its potential. The program includes over a dozen playgrounds, each of which provides a specific type of activity.

For example, at Bruno's Deli, kids learn about shape and color recognition by helping Huckle Cat serve food and drinks. On the Delivery Truck, kids deliver goods to stores in Busy Town, and along the way they learn about classification, problem solving, and maze tracing. And at Dr. Diane's Hospital, kids learn about body parts by helping the doctor bandage Norbert the Elephant.

Other locations kids can visit include the Fire Station, the Gas Station, Mr. Fixit's Workshop, Captain Salty's Ship, and Storytime. Each playground is easily accessible from the main screen, whose colorful map depicts all of Busy Town. To choose a playground, the child simply positions the mouse cursor and clicks. The program uses digitized voices to help kids find the playground they want.

Busy Town

Math Ace

Manufacturer: Magic Quest
Platform: DOS
System requirements: 286 or better, VGA graphics, hard drive, mouse, and
    Sound Blaster sound card
Price range: $

Review copyright 1994 by Compute Publications Int'l, Ltd.
Reprinted by permission.

Math Ace accomplishes a difficult feat: It makes math fun by merging it with an addicting yet educational game. In Math Ace, you're charged with destroying a virus that's running rampant in a grid of microchips. The longer it takes you to solve a series of math problems, the more microchips the virus munches into silicon dust. Should the virus eat its way to the edge of the grid, you lose. Over the course of your virus stomping, you'll get a chance to play four different games, each loaded with digital sound effects.

Bubble Gum Machine, for example, does a terrific job of teaching probabilities as kids try to guess how many gum balls will drop from the machine. Hide and Seek helps kids place values in a graph, while Function Shoot gives skillful junior mathematicians a chance to show off their understanding of function graphing. All the games do an excellent job of presenting difficult math concepts in an interesting and understandable way.

If a child wants to review his math without the pressure of a ticking clock, he can enter Math Ace's Smart Lab. In the Smart Lab, kids can choose any type of problem from any level in the game. The available topics include Basic Concepts, Arithmetic, Real World, Charts/Graphs, Probability, Geometry, and Algebra. The Smart Lab also features an on-line reference book. With Math Ace, your kids can learn what an exponential function is instead of learning about who's divorcing whom on TV.

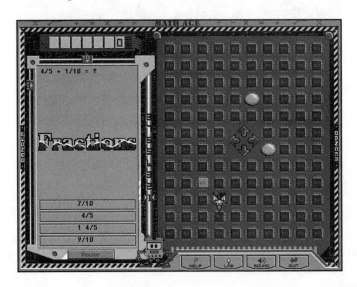

Math Ace

Math Blaster: In Search of Spot

Manufacturer: Davidson & Associates, Inc.
Platforms: Windows, DOS
System requirements:
   Windows—386 or better, 4MB RAM, VGA or better graphics
   DOS—DOS 3.3 or later, VGA or better graphics, hard disk
Price range: $$

Math Blaster is a favorite math drill program that has metamorphosed over the years from Math Blaster to Math Blaster Plus, and finally to Math Blaster: In Search of Spot. Although the new version has much more stringent hardware requirements than previous versions, it features tons of sound effects, digitized speech, and music. The graphics, too, are significantly enhanced, providing high-resolution VGA screens.

Math Blaster features four games for kids aged six to twelve that cover basic arithmetic, fractions, decimals, percentages, estimation, and number patterns. In Trash Zapper, for example, kids solve problems in order to earn tractor beams with which they can retrieve space garbage. In Number Recycler, kids must construct correct equations (i.e. $10 / 2 = 5$), after which the equations are converted into fuel for the rocket. Other games include Cave Runner and the title game, Math Blaster.

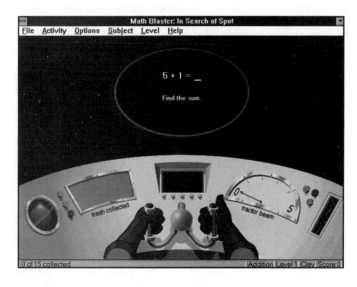

Math Blaster: In Search of Spot

The Treehouse

Manufacturer: Broderbund Software
Platforms: DOS, Macintosh
System requirements:
  DOS—DOS 3.0 or later, EGA graphics, hard drive, sound card
  recommended
  Mac—4MB for color systems
Price range: $

This sequel to Broderbund's excellent program The Playroom will provide
your child with countless hours of enjoyment. Everywhere kids look in the
opening scene there are things to discover and explore. They can write or
draw on the chalkboard in six different colors; look through the telescope and
see a different view each time; or click on the cloud outside the window and
watch it take on different shapes. Cans of worms, spider webs, and a variety
of "inanimate" objects all come to life when your child selects them.

There are also six separate games that can be reached by clicking on objects in
the treehouse. In the puppet theater, kids create animated sentences by piecing together phrases offered by the program. A road-rally game helps kids
practice their math skills while moving around a game board trading chips or
coins. Two of the other games focus on animals. One has children exploring
the world outside of the treehouse while using clues about animal traits to
guess the mystery animal. The second game involves creating animal scenes
while classifying, sorting, and matching.

The Treehouse

Finally, for music lovers, there are several entertaining musical activities. In Musical Keys, for example, kids can play an assortment of famous songs. The child can even write his own music and store it in a songbook. The last activity is a musical maze game to test musical recognition. The child navigates through the maze by matching note sequences played aloud with their written representation. All in all, The Treehouse is filled with surprises that will delight even the very young.

3-D Dinosaur Adventure, Undersea Adventure, Bug Adventure, Kid's Zoo

Manufacturer: Knowledge Adventure, Inc.
Platforms: DOS, Macintosh
System requirements:
   DOS—386 or better, DOS 3.1 or later, VGA graphics, hard disk, sound card
   Mac—Minimum
Price range: $

Thanks to Steven Spielberg, dinosaurs have never been more popular. If your family is interested in these wonderful beasts from the past, 3-D Dinosaur Adventure will keep you enthralled for hours. Featuring realistic-looking film clips, 3-D screens and movies (3-D glasses included), a child's storybook, dinosaur games, and a multimedia reference, there's something for every member of the family. Also featured are actual-voice readings and narrations, as well as a stereo music score.

Bug Adventure is a similar program that features 3-D photos of bugs. Although a 3-D movie is not included, there are many regular bug movies you can watch, including such fascinating subjects as beetles eating a flower or a butterfly leaving its cocoon. Like Dinosaur Adventure, Bug Adventure offers a multimedia reference with real-voice readings and music, as well as a group of bug-oriented games.

If you'd like to go on a tour of the world's oceans, you might like Undersea Adventure, which features not only the usual multimedia reference, but also a marine lab where you can see the insides of squids, sharks, and other marine animals. While Undersea Adventure doesn't include real 3-D movies and images, it does include a pseudo 3-D museum through which you can walk, viewing various displays of sea life.

Finally, although Children's Zoo follows the same format as the other programs reviewed here, it is more appropriate for younger children. Kids can play several guessing games, where they try to identify animals from the sounds the animals make or from an extreme close-up of a body part. Kids can also watch animal movies, identify footprints, and even read a 20-page multimedia story book.

3-D Dinosaur Adventure

Treasure Mathstorm

Manufacturer: The Learning Company
Platforms: Windows, DOS, Macintosh
System requirements:
   Windows—386 or better, 4MB RAM, 256-color VGA graphics, sound card
   DOS—DOS 3.3 or later, 286 or better, EGA or better graphics
   Mac—256-color graphics
Price range: $$

Learning math skills can be a boring process—that is, unless you have Treasure Mathstorm to help you along. In this clever game for kids between the ages of five and nine, the player's task is to restore scattered treasure to

Treasure Mountain's chest. Of course, this job would be a lot easier if the Master of Mischief hadn't buried Treasure Mountain in a dangerous covering of snow and ice.

The player's only chance of completing her mission is to correctly answer math problems to earn the tools she needs to climb the mountain, capture elves, and discover piles of treasure. The problems included in the game help children master such skills as telling time, counting money, and mastering addition, subtraction, multiplication, and division.

The game features lots of charming animations and a catchy background song (which can be turned off, if you like). In addition, the well-designed screen display keeps the player up to date on the game's status, while at the same time providing an attractive view into the game's world. Although your children will probably need a little help getting started with Treasure Mathstorm, once they get going, they'll want to stay.

ZooKeeper

Manufacturer: Davidson & Associates
Platforms: DOS, Macintosh
System requirements:
   DOS—DOS 3.3 or later, 286 or better, VGA or better graphics, hard disk, sound card, mouse
   Mac—System 7.0, 256-color graphics
Price range: $$

Kids under ten years of age with a fondness for animals will enjoy playing ZooKeeper. In this ecological game, the player's task is to bust eco-monsters and clean up the mess they leave in the zoo. Restoring an animal's environment—throwing unneeded items into a recycler and then adding missing objects, such as fruit and plants—may not be an easy job, but it has to be done if the zoo is to have happy animals.

Although ZooKeeper runs off your hard disk and requires no CD-ROM player, the game is loaded with animation sequences and music. Kids will especially like the game's host, an animated monkey with more personality than a roomful of movie stars. In addition, the game's colorful graphics will keep kids enthralled as they discover important information about their favorite creatures.

If a child wants to know more about a particular topic, ZooKeeper's robot can help, by telling the child where on the planet the current animal lives and what kind of climate it's used to. Finally, once the child has properly cleaned up an area, the animals return to take up residence, and the program awards the child with a certificate that can be printed for posterity.

Richard Scarry's Best Neighborhood Ever

Manufacturer: Activision
Platforms: DOS, (Macintosh forthcoming)
System requirements: 386 or better, DOS 5.0 or later, 1MB RAM, VGA or
   better graphics, CD-ROM drive, hard disk, sound card
Price range: $

Young children will adore Richard Scarry's Best Neighborhood Ever, in which they can explore an active town and find fun things to do, watch, and learn. The program is chock full of sound effects, animations, music, and voices, and the best part is that the simple interface allows even the youngest kids to use the program on their own, without the help of an adult.

When the program begins, the child sees a town street, over which she can move a star-shaped cursor with her mouse. Because the star cursor blinks whenever it's over something that can be selected, the child can easily find things to do. Clicking on a selectable item has many different effects. Clicking on the statue in the center of town, for example, triggers a funny animation sequence, whereas clicking on the grocery store lets the child see inside. While inside a building, the same rules apply. Clicking items may trigger short games, funny animations, voices, or sound effects.

As the child moves through the town, she can get help by clicking on any telephone. Because the help system uses real voices as well as graphics to describe the program, even non-readers won't need to go yelling for Mom or Dad. Kids will get a special surprise when they discover their house in Busytown. When they turn on the TV, the show that's on reports on their journey through the town, showing all the places they've visited. A companion program, called Richard Scarry's Busiest Neighborhood Ever, is also available.

Richard Scarry's Best Neighborhood Ever

What's All This
I Hear About . . . ?

I n a salute to the late, great Gilda Radner's Emily Litella character (*"What's all this fuss about our natural racehorses?"*), Part V of *The Home Computer Companion* is dedicated to explaining and possibly illuminating some of the more overworked and underexplained buzzwords in computing.

Buzzwords, as you may know, are words that you run into all over the place: everybody is *buzzing* about them. Unfortunately, you rarely get the details you need to decide whether you're interested or not. You just hear a low roar of "multimedia, multimedia, multimedia" or "PDAs, PDAs, PDAs."

The current list of buzzable words include: multimedia and CD-ROM; portable computers of all stripes, including Personal Digital Assistants (PDAs); PowerPCs; and gobs more. It feels like no one wants to tell you why these things are (or more importantly aren't) hot stuff. They just want to get you buzzing.

So, hold tight while we de-buzz the buzz words. By the way, that's natural *resources*, not *racehorses*. (*"Oh, that's very different. Never mind."*)

Multimedia

M ultimedia is a big ol' juggernaut of a buzzword. You'll see it applied to computers, software, CD-ROM discs and drives, speakers, microphones—you name it. So, what does it mean when a computer thingy is also a multimedia thingy? And is that different from other multimedia thingies you may have heard of before?

Multimedia Is:

In the simplest possible terms (and I can be pretty simple), *multimedia* is applied to a thing (not just computer-related, but anything) that combines two or more different media.

An *object d'art* could be called multimedia if it includes, say, oil paints and pastels (two drawing media). Ted Turner could be called multimedia, because he owns both television and movie companies (two entertainment media).

For a computer-related thing to be called multimedia, it needs to be a piece of software (often based on a CD-ROM disc, which is like a music CD but stores a wider variety of information) that incorporates a combination of text (words), graphics (pictures), sound (music or sound effects), and other dynamic information (things that change over time, like live video clips or animation). For a piece of hardware to claim the name multimedia, it must facilitate the use of multimedia software (such as speakers to help you hear music, a CD-ROM drive to read the discs of software, and so on).

On a computer, multimedia looks something like this:

Text ——

Photograph ——

Control buttons ——

—— Video clip

A scene from Software Toolwork's Oceans Below CD-ROM.

In addition to the labeled media elements, you're missing lovely music and informative narration that doesn't come across well on paper. Sorry.

Multimedia software and hardware are excellent for entertainment (great games), education (learning games, multimedia encyclopedias), reference (more encyclopedic elements, like phone books, catalogs of art, libraries of classic literature), and more. But in order to use and enjoy multimedia software, you must have the computer hardware to handle it.

Choosing the Right Multimedia Hardware

The right multimedia hardware begins with your own computer. Before you unsheathe your credit cards to go on a whirlwind shopping spree for a CD-ROM drive and discs, you should be sure that your computer is up to handling all those media inherent in multimedia.

I Know What You Need

What you really need, if you're serious about getting into multimedia computing, is Alpha Books' *The Complete Idiot's Guide to CD-ROM*, by John Pivovarnick. It covers everything you need to know in delirious and delicious detail.

Multimedia Begins at Home

To get the most (or even anything) from multimedia hardware and software, you need a fairly spunky computer.

For PC owners (and owners-to-be), that means at least a 286 machine with a 10MHz clock speed, 2MB of RAM (4 if you're running Windows, too). However, a more powerful machine (386, 486, or even a Pentium) with a faster (higher) clock speed and more RAM will be even better. You'll have to have at least a 386 machine if you want to run software that wears the MPC label, which is discussed in detail later in this article. And you'll need a VGA monitor and video card capable of displaying 256 colors. (If all of this is Greek to you, you're skipping too far ahead—go back and read Chapter 2.)

For Mac owners (and owners-to-be), that means a Mac with at least a 68030 processor (which is more than half of the current Macintosh and Performa lines) with 4MB of RAM (ample for System 6.0.X users, just enough for System 7). You'll also need a 13-inch or larger monitor that's capable of displaying 256 colors. Again, a better/faster processor (like a 68040-based Quadra, or a RISC-based PowerPC) can only improve things, as can more RAM and a bigger monitor capable of displaying millions of colors. But those things aren't absolutely necessary. And yet again, if this is gibberish, you should go back and check out Chapter 2 (and/or the article entitled "The PowerPC" in Part V if you've got or you want a PowerPC).

If your PC or Mac doesn't seem up to the chore (multimedia software can really put a computer through its paces), you might want to add certain system enhancements (like more RAM or a better monitor) or upgrade your current system to a later model, before you shell out for multimedia hardware. If you don't have a sturdy enough computer, the expensive multimedia hardware may work poorly, if at all, with your existing system.

Adding Multimedia Parts

Once you're satisfied that your computer is up to snuff, you can then deck it out in a style befitting your budget and your needs.

PC owners, to get the full multimedia experience, will need to add a CD-ROM drive, some manner of controller card appropriate for the drive (they often come with the drive—ask before you buy a separate one), a sound card, and speakers and/or headphones to give you full enjoyment of CD sound (whether from CD-ROM discs or music CDs, which most CD-ROM drives can play).

Mac owners get off a little easier. You'll need a CD-ROM drive, and (perhaps) speakers and/or headphones. Macs have the controller card and sound support built-in, so you won't need any additional expansion cards.

Choosing a CD-ROM Drive

There are three main factors that separate good CD-ROM drives from great ones, and they all relate to speed. When it comes to computer hardware, faster is always better and always more expensive.

The first consideration is how many speeds a drive has. A single speed drive is pretty much obsolete (therefore very inexpensive). A drive with two speeds (often called a 2X drive) is better, and drives that have three or more speeds (3X, 4X, and so on) are better—and even more expensive.

At the moment, 3X drives are big, though some 4X drives are starting to make inroads in the marketplace. I wouldn't buy a drive that didn't have at least two speeds; if you can afford 3X or 4X, go for it.

The second speed consideration is access time, which is how long it takes the drive to find the next chunk of data on a disc. Access time is usually measured in milliseconds or ms (for millionths of a second). Average access times range from 650ms (very slow) to 195ms (very fast). I wouldn't buy a drive with an access time slower (that is, a larger number) than 300ms, since that seems to be the speed required of many of the new gee-whiz CD-ROM discs.

The third and final speed consideration when selecting a CD-ROM drive is its throughput or transfer rate. That's how much information it can move from a CD-ROM disc to your computer. The transfer rate is measured in kilobytes per second, or K/S. A drive that transfers data at 150 K/S is slow. A drive that moves 450 K/S is pretty fast. Faster is better. I wouldn't recommend you spring for a drive with a transfer rate of less than 300 K/S.

Anything slower than the recommendations I've made here, and you'll spend a lot of time waiting for things to happen when you play with CD-ROM discs. Video and animation will be choppy. Music and voices may seem to jump and stutter. A faster drive (overall) will keep data flowing smoothly from your CD-ROM disc to your computer. Naturally, balance these speed considerations to stay within your budget—I'm not trying to break your bank, here.

Look for the MPC Label...

IBM-compatible owners will run into the MPC label and/or designation on many multimedia products. MPC stands for Multimedia Personal Computer. Products that wear the MPC label have met a set of standards established by the Multimedia Marketing Council. For a computer to be considered MPC compatible, it must have at least the following hardware and software:

◆ A 386-based PC or better, running with a clock speed of 16MHz.

◆ 2MB of main memory, configured as extended memory.

◆ A VGA card and monitor capable of a 600 x 480 pixel resolution at 256 colors, or 800 x 600 resolution at 16 colors.

◆ An MPC compatible sound card, which includes jacks for speakers, a microphone, stereo-out, and a MIDI port. (Most also include a controller for the CD-ROM drive itself.)

◆ An MPC compatible CD-ROM drive, which has an access time of under one second and a transfer rate of 150 K/S.

◆ You should be running the latest version of Microsoft Windows (3.1) with the built-in multimedia extension.

In my opinion, you should exceed the requirements for the CD-ROM drive and RAM, as suggested in the main text, but this is the published MPC standard. This is the latest version (MPC 2); the requirements for the original standard (MPC 1, or just MPC) are even more lax. And there will probably be an MPC 3 standard (with tougher requirements) issued anytime.

Selecting Multimedia Software

CD-ROM software is an ever-expanding category. Not long ago, it was purely the realm of whiz-bang games and stock photograph libraries. However, as more software companies have come to appreciate the sheer volume of data they can cram onto a CD-ROM disc, those two basic categories have been expanded widely. Today you can find even cooler games, more libraries of clip art and photographs, and enthralling discs of educational, reference, and just plain goofy software.

My own personal favorites include Broderbund's Living Books titles (*Just Grandma and Me*, *The Tortoise and the Hare*, and so on.), which entertain young and old alike with music and animation, while helping kids learn to read. I drool over CD-based collections of classic literature, like Bureau Development's Great Literature CD-ROM, which includes the full text of over 1,800 literary classics, plus some illustrations, plus music, and plus *plus* narration by some famous voices. And I'm a sucker for photo-realistic games like Myst and The Journeyman Project.

I enjoy the games (even if I am reduced to cheating with the hint books), but even more I am in awe of the seamless integration of art, animation, and live-action video. Younger folks (under 20, say) may not be as impressed as I am, because they've grown up with fairly intricate electronic games. I was wowed by Pong, if you're old enough to remember that technically pathetic (but still fun) game.

I won't presume to tell you what to like or to buy. The only advice I'll give is that you should take a list of your system's "qualifications" (like the central processor, the amount of RAM, the monitor specifications, the CD-ROM drive specification) with you when you go shopping. Compare your list (the things you have) with the "System Requirements" information on the software box, whether it's for floppy disks or CD-ROM discs, and make sure you meet or beat the requirements specified on the box.

If you don't have the hardware, don't buy the software. It may not run at all, and if it does, it may run badly. Nothing is more annoying than expecting to have fun with a multimedia game (or whatever), only to wind up sitting there staring at your blank monitor, waiting for something to happen. You could grind your teeth to dust waiting.

The Top 5 Things That Go Wrong with Multimedia Systems (and How to Fix Them)

5. My computer doesn't acknowledge the presence of my CD-ROM drive!

   Check the basics: is the drive plugged in and turned on? (It's hard to tell with some.) Are the cable connections correct and tight? Did you put in a

continues

continued

CD-ROM disc? Did you put it in the right way? What's the most obvious thing you could have done wrong? Check that one again.

4. My computer still doesn't acknowledge the presence of my CD-ROM drive!

Make sure you installed all of the appropriate driver software (the stuff that tells your computer how to deal with the CD-ROM drive, controller, and/or sound cards). Check your drive's manual(s) for installation instructions appropriate to your computer and software.

3. Well, this is great advice—not! My computer *still* doesn't acknowledge the presence of my CD-ROM drive!

Did you turn on the CD-ROM drive *before* you turned on your computer? If your CD-ROM isn't on at startup, your computer doesn't know it's there. Turn on the drive and restart your computer. (PC owners: use the **Control+Alt+Del** key combination. Mac owners: use the **Restart** command under the **Special** menu.)

2. Oh, great! The computer can find the drive, but the CD-ROM software keeps crashing!

You probably don't have enough memory to run the application. Even though the box said "Requires 4MB of RAM" and you have 4MB of RAM installed, part of that memory could be eaten up with system software or extensions.

To see how much memory you have available, PC users can type **MEM** at the DOS prompt. Mac users can use the **About This Macintosh** command from the menu. You may have to remove some non-critical software by editing your AUTOEXEC.BAT file (DOS) or removing some Extensions and Control Panels from the System folder (Mac). Or you can add more RAM to your computer, but that costs money.

1. Now that I've got it up and running, I can't stop playing with *(insert CD-ROM name here)*!

Sounds like a discipline problem to me. Don't start playing until your work is finished. Set time limits for playing with your new multimedia toys—and stick to them. Set an alarm clock to go off after an hour. Ask a spouse, partner, or roommate to rescue you if you don't come out of the office in an hour. Tell him or her to threaten to spank you if you don't behave yourself (of course, that could be the beginning of a whole new batch of discipline problems, so consider the consequences before using this last suggestion).

Laptops and Other Portable Computers

I remember when I was a kid and the big techno-toy was calculators. One day, there was no such thing as a calculator—the next day you could walk into a department store and buy one. They were so small (compared to adding machines) and so very expensive (hundreds of dollars) that our little minds were boggled by them.

Over time, the calculators kept getting smaller and smaller, cheaper and cheaper, and we got rather immune to the wonder inherent in the process. Now we can get a calculator for $5.99, or it can be built into a watch, and we don't bat an eye. We've been jaded by the wonders of technology: things are supposed to get smaller and less expensive over time.

The same thing is happening to computers that once happened to calculators: they just keep getting smaller and (sort of) less expensive. (Unfortunately, with computers at least, every time things get smaller, they get more expensive first.) There's a bewildering array of names applied to small computing devices (not all of which are true computers): portable, laptop, notebook, palmtop, personal digital assistant. What do they all mean?

Size Counts

On the whole, each of these names is supposed to give you a clue to the size of the computer it's applied to. Start with the image of a full-blown desktop computer in your mind, and things should fall nicely into place.

Picture a big, full-sized keyboard, 14-inch monitor, and a CPU that's probably a two-foot square and a couple of inches tall. Not exactly something you'd like to carry with you on a business trip.

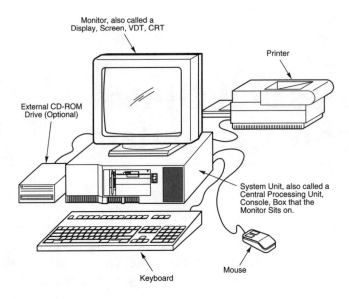

A full-size desktop computer is not particularly portable

Generally, you're pretty safe referring to any small computer as a portable, because they are portable. A *portable* then, is just something that's smaller and easier to carry around with you than a desktop model. The earliest portables were still pretty big and weighed in at over 20 pounds. They often had separate monitors, keyboards, and CPUs that locked together into something like a suitcase or thyroidal briefcase. You really had to want to lug one around with you, and you still needed to set it up on a desk or table to use it.

When the next generation of computers arrived, they were much smaller and had the keyboards and monitors integrated into a one-piece CPU that opened like a book. They weighed in at 15 pounds or less. Instead of having to work at a desk, you could balance one on your knees to work, hence the name *laptop*. (Kneetop just doesn't roll trippingly off the tongue.) You could carry it around in an overnight bag, instead of a suitcase.

Later models got even smaller. They're the size of an average 8 1/5 x 11 inch notebook, and most weigh in at under 10 pounds. Oddly enough, the marketing geniuses decided to call them *notebook computers*, the idea being that carrying one is just like carrying around a pad of paper for taking notes on the run. (At least, that's the impression the manufacturers want you to have.)

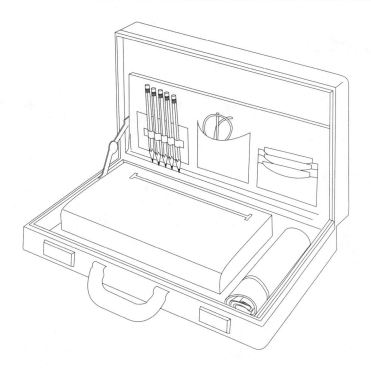

Notebook computers fit neatly into a briefcase

Any of the above small computers work essentially like their desktop siblings. They come in flavors of IBM-compatible or Mac, generally have disk drives and built-in monitors (some even in color), and come with the same assortment of central processor chips (286, 386, and so on for DOS, 68030 and 68040 for Mac). If you care to, you can add a mouse or a keypad. You can hook your portable up to a printer to print. You can add a modem. Almost anything you can add to or do with a desktop machine, you can add to or do with a portable.

All portables can be plugged into power outlets when there's one handy, or can be run off of batteries if there isn't. Because batteries run down quickly, in addition to the usual assortment of utilities for desktop models, portables come with their own utilities to conserve/extend battery life. Otherwise, they're pretty much comparable to desktop machines. In fact, you could own one of these portable machines and never even touch a desktop computer. It's when computers get really small that things start to get weird.

Best of Both Worlds

There are portable computers (Apple's PowerBook Duos, for example) that are designed to be both desktop and portable machines. Out of your home, office, or home office, you can carry a very lightweight portable computer with a built-in monitor and most of the other features you think of when you think "portable computer."

When you get home and want to work at your desk, you close the portable and insert it into a docking station (much as you insert a video cassette into a VCR). The docking station can increase the power of the portable by adding a full-sized monitor and keyboard, and often additional features like more RAM, a math chip, another disk or hard drive, and even an internal CD-ROM drive.

They provide the best of both worlds.

Computing's Twilight Zone: Palmtops and PDAs

When is a computer not a computer? When it fits in the palm of your hand.

Meet the *palmtop*: a computer that fits in the palm of your hand. These babies are so small (How small are they?) that they can't even accommodate a 3.5-inch floppy disk. (Boy, that's small!)

Instead of using disks or hard drives for storage, programs and data are stored in the palmtop's internal memory (RAM and ROM). To get new data into or out of a palmtop, it has to be connected to a desktop or portable computer with a cable, through which information is sent back and forth. You enter your data with a teeny-tiny keyboard (pressing keys with a pencil point, or your teeny-tiny fingers).

This palmtop packs power into a 6-by-3-inch package

Palmtops still perform many of the functions of a desktop or portable computer: you can compose with a word processor, fiddle figures with a spreadsheet, or doodle with a draw program. However, the programs are often stripped-down versions when compared to their full-featured cousins on larger computers.

While they maintain many of the conventions of computers (the keyboard, the monitor, files, and so on) palmtops aren't meant to act as a primary, or even secondary computer. Instead, they supplement your desktop and/or portable computer. You really need to have a regular computer to make use of a palmtop.

Most palmtops aren't manufactured by "computer" companies. Instead, they're made by what are referred to as consumer electronics companies, the kind that make and sell watches and VCRs. Casio and Sharp, among others, make palmtops.

So, when is a palmtop not a palmtop? When it's a personal digital assistant (PDA). They're called *personal digital assistants* because their main functions are the sort of things an executive might hire a flesh-and-blood person to do: track appointments, take notes, remind you of things to do.

PDAs take some mental gear-shifting. They aren't palmtops, but they fit in the palm of your hand. They aren't computers, as we think of computers, but they do computer-like jobs. The reason they aren't palmtops is that palmtops maintain many of the conventions associated with computers: keyboards, monitors, distinct file structures (this is a spreadsheet file, nothing else). PDAs don't.

Rather than being keyboard-based, PDAs are pen-based; you can see the "pen" (actually a rubber-tipped, inkless stylus) in the figure below. Instead of typing on a keyboard, you write it directly on a touch-sensitive screen. The PDA then converts your handwriting to text or your doodle to a picture, and stores it.

Apple's Newton Message Pad PDA (Courtesy of Apple Computer, Inc. Photograph by John Greenleigh)

When a PDA stores information, rather than filing a document as MEMO2.TXT, the PDA just chucks everything into a general pool of digital information, sometimes called "the soup." When you need to find something, you tell the PDA to look for a particular word or phrase (a search string), it skims through the soup looking for every occurrence of the word or phrase. It gives you greater flexibility, because your information isn't locked into any particular format. You can move a phone number from your phone list to an appointment page without going through the same gyrations you might have to use to swap information between two applications on your computer.

When you find that bit of information you need, you can print it (if you're hooked up to a printer), fax it (with a fax/modem), e-mail it to someone on an electronic service or network (also with a modem), or even beam it to another similarly equipped PDA (with the infrared beam built into Apple's Newton Message Pads).

You can use a PDA to keep track of appointments, important dates, lists of things to do, basic math calculations, and note-taking. You can also supplement its built-in functions with additional software.

PDAs are very useful on their own, but most can be hooked up to a desktop computer (usually with a connection kit you purchase separately) to share data back and forth. Why re-enter all the important dates in your life, when you've already got them stored in the calendar program on your computer?

Is a PDA a substitute for a personal computer? No. It's not even a fair comparison, since PDAs aren't really computers. A PDA would be an excellent substitute for all those other things you have choking your briefcase or backpack: an appointment book, notebook, address book, electronic/paper phone book, pocket calculator, pads of expense/mileage reports, and all the ratty crumpled business cards you've collected over the years. Some PDAs, with additional hardware, will even replace your pocket pager—the one that always goes off at the critical moment of a movie, play, or argument.

PDAs make great stand-alone devices, but (with the appropriate connection kit for your computer) get a big + in the "plays well with others" box.

What's Next?

Oh, goodness. Who can tell? Here are some best guesses, but I won't swear to them in a court of law:

◆ As we move further into the Information Age, expect portable computers to get smaller and less expensive, without losing any of the functions you expect from a full-fledged computer.

◆ Look for PDAs to get a little smaller and more powerful, and have more add-in potential.

◆ Look for portables (and perhaps even PDAs) to come with new, smaller CD-ROM drives. The actual CDs will probably be under 3-inches in diameter.

411

◆ Computers (of all sizes) and PDAs will come with (or have as accessories) even more built-in communication options (like wireless cable, cellular telephony) to access the growing information superhighway (see "The Information Superhighway" in Part V).

◆ More "information appliances" (like computers and PDAs) will appear in regular department stores (as opposed to computer stores) as the technology moves out of the domain of so-called computer geeks, and into the realm of (also so-called) regular people.

Beyond that, I don't care to guess. Breakthroughs in technology happen on a regular basis, with little or no warning. With all the money and effort going into defining the Information Age, anything could happen.

It's going to be an interesting Age.

The PowerPC

S peaking of ballyhoo (okay, just *pretend* I was speaking of ballyhoo), a lot of noise is being made about Apple Computer's next generation of Macintosh computers: the PowerPC. It's the computer that made Intel (the manufacturer of the new Pentium processor for DOS machines) run screaming back to the drawing board to play catch-up.

If you haven't been paying close attention to the hype, your impression of the PowerPC may be skewed just short of, or just past, the truth. You may think the PowerPC is some sort of panacea for everything that ails computing. That may (or may not) be completely true.

Some Truth

The truth is that the PowerPC is wicked fast—as much as two to three times as fast as its fastest predecessors. It achieves these amazing speeds by a change of heart, so to speak. Where all previous Macs were based on some variation of the Motorola 680X0 processor chip, the PowerPCs are based on an altogether new beastie: IBM's PowerPC 601 chip. That's right, *IBM's* chip. The old 680X0 chips are known (to byte heads) as CISC chips, for Complex Instruction Set Computer. The new 601 chips are RISC chips, or Reduced Instruction Set Computer.

The gains in speed are, in the main, achieved by reducing the number of instructions the chip needs to perform a particular operation (in addition to changes in the rest of the hardware).

Is It a Mac, IBM, or Both?

If I saw that question on a multiple choice test, I'd have to think twice before circling D: none of the above. The PowerPC is a whole new kind of computer, but its roots are firmly entrenched in the Macintosh.

It's so entrenched that when the lucky folks who get a PowerPC take it out of the box and fire it up, they will see that (to all appearances) the PowerPC works exactly like any other Mac they've seen, only faster. The differences are under the surface, and some are waiting down the road a piece. The software is a clue to the main difference: look in a Macintosh mail order catalog, and you'll see software for Macs and for PowerPCs. PowerPCs can run both kinds.

Macintosh software written for 680X0-based Macs can be run on a PowerPC, but the PowerPC will be running in an *emulation mode*. A special interpreter built into the PowerPC will translate the complex instructions meant for a 680X0 chip, and turn them into the reduced instructions for the PowerPC's RISC chip. In short, the PowerPC will pretend it's an older Mac model.

The software for 680X0-based Macs will at least run a little faster on a PowerPC than on older Macs, but not at the full, blazing speed that's possible on a PowerPC. To take full advantage of the soul of this new machine, you need to run software designed to take advantage of the new chip.

Needless to say, all of the big software companies are hurrying to market PowerPC versions of their best-selling software. That includes Insignia Solutions, the makers of SoftPC and SoftWindows software that emulate a DOS environment, letting you run DOS- and Windows-based applications on your Mac.

Maybe, instead of answering "none of the above" to the question "Is it a Mac, IBM, or both?," I should have answered "all of the above" instead.

What Are the Advantages of Going PowerPC?

The PowerPC is the first fruit of the "unholy alliance" (as I called it at the time) between Apple and former rival IBM. Apple is staking its future on this new breed of Macs, going so far as to say that many 680X0-based Macs will be discontinued as demand for them drops off in favor of PowerPC models. Apple is convinced that the PowerPC is the future of Macintosh computing.

The advantage, therefore, in jumping in and springing for a PowerPC is that you'll remain current in technology. Almost every new Macintosh software product (at least 2 out of every 3 for the first few months, more later) will be aimed at PowerPC owners.

You'll also remain (fairly) current in terms of hardware. While Apple may release newer and zippier PowerPCs, with a PowerPC on your desk, you're pretty much guaranteed an upgrade path (you'll be able to turn your old PowerPC into the new model). Owners of anything other than or older than a few 68040-based Quadra or Centris Macs, will be left out in the cold, since the '040s are the only machines that can be upgraded to a PowerPC.

What Are the Disadvantages of Going PowerPC?

For folks who already own a Mac, the disadvantage is having to wait for all of their favorite ("I use it everyday!") applications to come out in PowerPC versions, so they can make use of the speed that's just itching to get out of the PowerPC's central processor chip.

Those who remember the long (and often expensive) round of software and hardware upgrades that followed the release of System 7 will possibly flinch at the prospect of going through it all again. For folks who don't have a Mac, or any computer, the disadvantage is similar. If you want to work on your new PowerPC, you may have to settle for an old-style Mac software package running in emulation mode until the PowerPC version becomes available. However, you can probably afford to settle for "good enough" or "cheap enough" until the name brand software you desire is ready for your PowerPC.

There's also the question of software compatibility to consider: whenever a new kind of computer becomes available, there's always some program that balks at the new architecture and crashes. It happened both when the '040-based Macs were introduced and (less frequently) when the AV Macs appeared on the scene.

How Can I Be Sure It's Compatible with the Software I Want to Use?

The easiest thing to do is look before you buy. Just as music CDs and cassettes often have stickers that say "Includes the Hit Single!", software will be boasting big stickers saying "PowerPC compatible!" and "PowerPC Ready to Run!" before you can say PowerPC.

Before you run to the computer section of your favorite technology store, cruise the software aisles with a list of your must-have software. If you can't find it in a PowerPC version or a Macintosh version that says it won't crash on you, you might want to wait a little while before you buy a PowerPC.

Take heart, though. All of the tests and reports I've read say that older software and hardware very rarely crash on the new PowerPCs. Granted, everyone loads up their computers differently, and it's impossible to predict what all the various combinations of hardware and software will do, but the odds are sounding pretty good that most of the older Mac software will run on a PowerPC in emulation mode.

Who'd Benefit Most from a PowerPC

I think the people best suited to snap up a PowerPC are those who haven't already made a huge investment in computer hardware and software, but who want to get into computing with a speedy, spiffy, top-of-the-line machine. If they start off with one or two essential applications (such as an integrated Works package, like those discussed in Chapter 20) to get them going, by the time they've mastered them, a broader range of PowerPC software will be available.

Second in line, I think, are folks with old Macs. I'm talking really old: a Mac Plus, SE, or the like. Because technology has advanced so far since those machines were first released, their owners are facing a fairly large number of software upgrades, regardless of the Mac model they choose. Why not upgrade in a big way?

Last in line, I think, are folks who need to stay on the cutting edge. This includes those folks who make their living keeping abreast of new technology (like consultants, who can't consult on a computer platform they've never seen) and those who, by some quirk in their psychological make-up, aren't happy unless they're the first kid on their block with a new toy.

For those of you who aren't sure what you want to do, you can never go wrong just waiting a little while after a new computer is introduced. Invariably, you'll run into someone who owns (or knows someone who owns) the technology in question, and you can ask them what they think.

It's also a great truth that prices tend to drop shortly after a new machine's introduction—if not on the new machine itself, certainly on the machines it's replacing. You may be able to pick up a nice Quadra for a smaller wad of bills, and still be able to upgrade to a PowerPC somewhere down the road.

The Long and Short of It

Unfortunately, the long and short of it is painfully short (at the moment, at least). Should you run right out and buy a PowerPC or PowerPC upgrade? Maybe. If you're willing to proceed in increments, improving your software and hardware slowly, as PowerPC-specific stuff becomes available, sure, jump right in.

Should you sit tight and wait and see what happens with the PowerPC over the next 4–8 months? Maybe that too. It might be prudent to wait until everything you absolutely need is available in a PowerPC version. (However, I only advise prudence to other people. I never touch the stuff myself.)

The absolute least you should do is run right out to the store and test drive one. Wear some dark glasses so you're not blinded by the glitz and hype (you know they'll have only PowerPC software installed to show off its speed). And for safety's sake, leave your credit cards at home or in the hands of a trustworthy friend. The combination of a spiffy new machine and a fast talking salesman is a heady one. Otherwise, you may wind up the proud (if shocked) owner of a new PowerPC.

Avast There, Maties! Software Piracy!

Pardon me while I adjust my eye patch and earring, and tie this darned parrot to my shoulder. (Just kidding about the parrot. We pirates use duct tape.) Batten down the hatches, we're about to wade into some rough and murky waters here, a Sargasso Sea of legal-speak that makes the oceans of computer vocabulary look like a kiddy pool.

What Is Piracy?

Let's stick with the pirate metaphor (*arrrgh, ya' scurvey knave*) for a second here. Aside from buckling swashes and their keen fashion sense, pirates are pretty much known for commandeering stuff that isn't their own: treasure, maidens, ships. Apparently, they made a pretty good living at it, at least until they got caught and hanged (or were made to walk the plank). *Software piracy* amounts to much the same, without the glamour of that roguish lifestyle. It means taking and using something—in this case, software—that isn't yours.

To me (and I know some folks might disagree with this), there are two distinct kinds of software piracy. One is patently wrong, illegal, and relatively easy to spot. The other is less clear-cut, and requires a lot of what philosophy-types call "situation ethics."

The Obviously Piratical

The easy-to-spot sort of software piracy is simple to define. An enterprising person, with a certain amount of computer skills and office equipment, buys an expensive software product. He takes it home, unwraps it, and fires up his computer and photocopier. Instead of installing it, he makes copy after copy after copy of the software disks and manual. He then bundles up his duplicate copies, and sells them to other computer users for less than the cost of the original package.

That's obviously a bad thing to do, and it is illegal. You're taking a product that a company worked very hard to produce (and probably invested a small fortune in developing) and selling it as if you owned the rights to it. That's an infringement of the rights of the publisher. It can get you fined and land you in jail.

However, say you're just a nice guy, who happens to have a bit of software that a friend or colleague could put to good use. So you copy the disks and manuals for him, but no money changes hands. Legally, you and your friend are in the same class as the scum bucket above: you for duplicating copy-righted material, and your friend for using software without purchasing it.

Oblique Piracy

Here's a different situation:

You're a normal, law-abiding citizen who owns a computer. When you bought your personal system you got a copy of, say, Microsoft Works bundled with it. In the course of using it at home, you discovered that you like the word processor and spreadsheet modules in Works a lot more than the complicated ones you use at work.

You copy your Microsoft Works disks, take the copies to work with you, and use them to install Works on the computer there. Did you just break the law? Maybe. The answer to that depends on a couple of things.

◆ Were the disk copies you made the *only* copies you made? If you answer "Yes," you haven't broken the law—yet. If you answer "No," you're busted: come out with your hands up.

◆ While you're using your second copy of Microsoft Works at the office, is somebody else using your copy at home? If you answer "No," you haven't broken the law. Go on your merry, computerized way. If you answer "Yes," you're busted again: the place is surrounded, throw down your mouse and no one will get hurt.

But those are only the answers for Microsoft Works (and most Microsoft products). If you were using a different product, from a different manufacturer (let's say, Apple's Macintosh PC Exchange), you could have been busted as soon as you copied the disk. If you didn't (and I quote) "reproduce on such copy the Apple copyright notice and any other proprietary legends that were on the original copy of the Apple software," you violated the terms of the software license you purchased.

You would get into deeper trouble if you installed the software on a second computer, without purchasing an additional license. The license agreement restricts the software to use on one Apple computer.

Why It's All So-o-o-o Confusing

Here are the some of the problems inherent in deciding what constitutes legal and illegal use of computer software.

The big thing that most people don't realize is that, when you buy a software product, you are not buying the program itself: you are buying the right to *use* the software. The company that produced the program still owns it, they're just letting you use it for a while—and only within some very strict guidelines. Those guidelines, normally called a *software license*, contribute to the confusion in a couple of ways (see the "License To Chill" sidebar for the translation of a typical agreement).

First, nobody reads them (or, if they do read them, they don't understand them because they are written in legal-speak). The agreement is usually printed on the sealed envelope that contains the disks that hold the software you're itching to use. Most folks just tear open the envelope to get at the disks without reading the fine print. The fly in the ointment is that, by opening that envelope, you agree to be bound by the terms of that agreement, the one you never read. You are now officially and completely clueless about the legal uses of the software you just bought.

The second problem is that software companies don't agree on what you can and can't do with their products. In the example above, what would have been a perfectly legal use of Microsoft Works, would have been a perfectly illegal use of Apple's Macintosh PC Exchange. Instead of just one generic license agreement that would apply to all software, you have to read agreements for each and every program you buy. And then you have to remember what constitutes legal usage for each of those programs.

Getting Real

I appreciate the fact that software companies are trying to keep people from buying one copy of a program and giving it to everyone they know. That's fair and fine. A company with a number of employees *should* buy individual copies (or a site license) for all the software its employees are supposed to use. Likewise, your neighbors *shouldn't* come knocking on the door asking to please borrow your Aldus PageMaker disks. They should buy their own, or use your copy on your computer (even that could be illegal under the terms of some of the more elaborate software licenses).

It all comes down to not only what is legal under the terms of the software license, but also what's fair. I think some companies make unreasonable demands of individual software buyers. For example, that whole rigmarole about reproducing all the copyright notices on duplicate copies of Apple's disks is ridiculous. Who's got the time to do that? Moreover, how do you *enforce* something like that?

> "Your honor, the defendant is charged with not putting a little "c" in a circle to denote Apple Computer's copyright on his backup copy of the Macintosh PC Exchange."

They'd get laughed out of court—except maybe on "LA Law."

I think the best idea would be for software companies to lighten up. If they'll come up with one software license for individual users that's reasonable, fair, and written in clear language that says "this is okay and this is not," I'll follow it. (And they can have as many clauses as they want tacked on at the end for government and businesses.) Until then, I'll continue to *try* to do the right thing and follow the spirit, if not the letter, of all these different software license agreements.

License To Chill

The following is an excerpt from the software license that Apple Computer includes with all of its software products. I chose it because it's fairly typical, if a little stricter than most (though some are worse). My translations appear in parentheses. In short, I swear I'm not making this up.

Apple Computer, Inc. Software License

continues

continued

Please read this license carefully before using the software. By using the software, you are agreeing to be bound by the terms of this license. if you do not agree to the terms of this license, promptly return the unused software to the place where you obtained it, and your money will be refunded.

(Listen up! If you so much as insert these disks in your computer, you have to do what we tell you. If you don't like it, don't use our stuff.)

1. License. The application, demonstration, system and other software accompanying this License, whether on disk, in read-only memory, or on any other media (the "Apple Software"), the related documentation and Fonts are licensed to you by Apple. You own the disk on which the Apple Software and Fonts are recorded but Apple and/or Apple's Licensor(s) retain title to the Apple Software, related documentation and Fonts. This License allows you to use the Apple Software and Fonts on a single Apple computer and make one copy of the Apple Software and Fonts in machine-readable form for backup purposes only. You must reproduce on such copy the Apple copyright notice and any other proprietary legends that were on the original copy of the Apple Software and Fonts. You may also transfer all your license rights in the Apple Software and Fonts, the backup copy of the Apple Software and Fonts, the related documentation and a copy of this License to another party, provided the other party reads and agrees to accept the terms and conditions of this License.

(Whatever this junk is you just paid a lot of money for, you only actually own the disk. We, and our playmates (if any), still own everything else. You can make one copy of the disks for emergency backup use, but we own the rights on that too, so you better put all of our copyright notices and fine print on that copy. If you decide to sell your copy to somebody else, you'd better give her every last copy you have, the manuals, and this very long license too. If she doesn't like the license, she can lump it too.)

2. Restrictions. The Apple Software contains copyrighted material, trade secrets, and other proprietary material and, in order to protect them, you may not decompile, reverse engineer, disassemble, or otherwise reduce the Apple Software to a human-perceivable (!) form. You may not modify, network, rent, lease, loan, distribute, or create derivative works based upon the Apple Software in whole or in part. You may not electronically transmit the Apple Software from one computer to another or over a network.

(Did we mention that this stuff is ours? Well, it is, so no peeking. We have no desire for mere mortals to witness our splendor—we would rather work in mysterious ways. You must not tinker with us, either. Only we may make money

off of our stuff, so not only can't you tinker, you may not e-mail or otherwise transmit our stuff.)

3. Termination. This License is effective until terminated. You may terminate this License at any time by destroying the Apple Software, related documentation and Fonts, and all copies thereof. This License will terminate immediately without notice from Apple if you fail to comply with any provision of this License. Upon termination you must destroy the Apple Software, related documentation and Fonts, and all copies thereof.

(This license works until it doesn't. You may end this agreement any time—just destroy everything you have that we own. If you don't do everything we tell you, this agreement will end automatically. We won't tell you that the party's over, but we still expect you to destroy everything you have that we own.)

Although the software license goes on (and on . . .and on), I'll stop here. There's a section devoted to export law and Government End Users that's worse than regular legal-speak. In other words, it's complete gibberish. The rest is legalese for warranty and disclaimer which, naturally, protects the manufacturer (in this case, Apple, but they all do it) more than it does the consumer.

I swear I'm not bitter.

Shareware and Freeware

It may sound like a '90s version of "Simple Simon," but there are a lot of -wares involved in computing, the most basic of which is software. Any one who's even vaguely familiar with the basic concepts of computing understands that software tells a computer what to do with its computing power: Word processing software tells your computer how to process your words; Page layout software tells it how to lay out the various elements of a publishing project on a page; Database software tells your computer how to organize, sort, and extract your data in meaningful and useful ways. And there are a lot more flavors of software available (check out Part III of this book, if you don't believe me).

Many new computer users, however, wind up scratching their heads when they run into the words "shareware" and "freeware." This pair looks like it should be associated with software, but it could be hardware related, too.

Who, What, and -Ware

Shareware and *freeware* are both software varieties. However, rather than being named for what they get your computer to do (as are those mentioned above), they are named according to how you acquire and pay for them.

Usually, when you think of software, you think of computer stores full of rack after rack of commercial products in fancy packages (too much packaging, if you ask me). In a software store you browse the shelves, read boxes, and (if you're *lucky*) get to try out a demonstration copy of the software you're interested in on the store's computer. You select the commercial software package you want, pay for it, get it home, and open it—to find only a disk (or set of disks), a manual, and usually a registration card or some other miscellaneous paperwork.

The price you paid for the package also paid for the manual, the disks, the package design, the research and development time, the programmer's time, the company's advertising budget, and the CEO's quarterly bonus. (And you wonder why you often flinch at the price of software?) On top of that, if you read the article "Software Piracy" in Part V, you know that what you paid for was the right to use the software—you don't even actually own it.

Shareware and freeware work by another whole system entirely.

Share and Share Alike

Shareware is distributed differently. Yes, you will sometimes find it in software and computer stores, but most often, you'll find it on electronic bulletin board services (discussed in "On-Line Services" in Part V) or in catalogs from your favorite user group (see "Computer Pubs" in Part V).

After reading a brief description of the program (or whatever it is) like the one shown below, you acquire it either by downloading it from the bulletin board or by ordering it from a catalog. Or, a friend might just give you a copy. Regardless of how you got it—bang you're ready to run it.

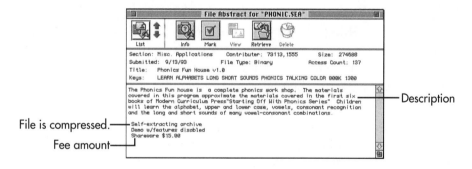

A description of a Shareware file from one of CompuServe's many software libraries

You try the software out. If you don't like it, it may just sink, unremembered, into the oceans of information you have stored on disks or on your hard drive. No loss. If you like it and find yourself using it often, a reminder might pop up on your computer's screen from time to time (like when you start or quit the program), reminding you that you haven't paid for the software yet. Naturally, since you like and use the program, you dig out your checkbook and send the requested shareware fee directly to the program's author.

(They're always good about letting you know how much money to send and where to send it.)

That's the principle behind shareware. You acquire it somehow, and you try it. If you use the program, after a period of time specified in the program's documentation file (from a week to as much as 90 days), you send the author a fee that generally ranges from as little as $5 to as much as $50.

If you think about it, $5–$50 (more in some cases) isn't much to pay for a program you know you like and know you will use—especially if you've ever shelled out hundreds of dollars for a program that turned out to be useless for you. You also have the satisfaction of knowing that your money is going straight to the programmer, and is not lining the pockets of everyone along the distribution chain.

In return for your payment, the author will send you the latest version of the program, information on other shareware he or she has written, and sometimes a printed manual and registration code. The printed manual will let you know how to use the program to its fullest. The registration code will often short circuit the bit of program that keeps reminding you to send in your shareware fee.

Notice in the lower left corner of the figure above that the program is a "Demo w/features disabled." Sometimes the registration code, if there is one, will unlock certain features of the program (as in this figure) that would not operate before you paid the fee. Or, you may just get a new disk with a complete version of the program. The methods and results of registering shareware vary as widely as the software itself.

It's called shareware because you are free to share copies of it with your friends. Unlike commercial programs, you're actually encouraged to give copies away—as long as you include all the information about where to send the shareware fee. With shareware, you are part of the distribution channel. You should *not*, however, give the registration number you paid for to your friends. That isn't kosher.

Shareware operates on the honor system. If you keep and use a piece of shareware, you are honor bound to send the author his or her fee. Every time you keep a shareware program without paying the fee, you build up bad karma points for your next life. You'll come back as a brilliant person who writes fabulous shareware but never gets paid for it. That person will die in abject poverty, unloved and alone. Or maybe you'll just always feel horribly guilty in this life.

Free at Last

Freeware is a horse of a different color: it is a bit of software that is absolutely free. Aside from whatever it costs you in terms of connect charges for an on-line service, a disk, and so on, there are no additional fees.

It's the "finder's keepers" of software. If you find it and like it, you can keep it. Freeware, like shareware, is often discovered through descriptions in on-line services (like the one shown below) or in a catalog. When browsing for software, it's nice to know that there are no additional fees waiting for you down the road.

free!

A description of a Freeware file from one of CompuServe's many software libraries

Often, freeware files are original creations written by programmers trying to solve a pesky little problem that they (or their friends and/or co-workers) have encountered. Or the program might do a silly, fun, or pretty thing to your computer's display that's somehow entertaining, but which doesn't really affect your computer's performance.

Some other freeware files actually used to be commercial programs that, once-upon-a-time, were sold in a store. For whatever reason, the author or publisher let the copyright lapse, moving the program into the *public domain*. Public domain is legal-speak meaning that no one owns the rights to the program anymore, and people are free to do pretty much whatever they want with the program.

Do the "Rights" Thing

Just so you understand a little more about the rights associated with shareware, freeware, and public domain software, here's a little informative primer.

Unlike the elaborate and Byzantine software user agreements that draw the line between legitimate and pirated software (as discussed in the article "Software Piracy" in Part V), freeware and shareware are generally only protected by copyright laws. Even though the authors have chosen to distribute their software through fairly uncontrollable channels, they still retain the rights to their product.

If you get your hands on a piece of freeware or shareware, you do have the right to use it (if you paid the fee on your shareware titles). You also have the right to pass copies on to your friends. You do not, however, have the right to sell copies to your friends (or anyone for that matter) for a profit. You may charge a reasonable fee for the cost of the diskette and duplication or for the use of an electronic service, but you may not charge for the program itself. It isn't yours to sell.

When you see freeware and shareware collections for sale (in a store or mail order catalog, or as part of a book/disk set in a bookstore) the people responsible have gotten the written permission of all the software authors involved. The author's permission gives the vendor the right to sell the software at a profit, sometimes with a percentage of those profits going to the author.

Remember: freeware, though free, is still "owned" by the original author. Shareware may be shared (that is, given away freely), but not sold. Public domain software, on the other hand, is legally owned by no one; you can do with it what you will.

Isn't talking about the law just so much fun?

Other-Wares

From time to time, while cruising through the software libraries of an on-line service like CompuServe or America OnLine, you may run into some quirky little programs that don't fall into either shareware or freeware category. You don't have to send the author money, so in one sense it's freeware. On the other hand, the author does request that you do a little something if you like the program. I call programs with these quirky little requests "otherware" (mostly because "none-of-the-above-ware" just doesn't sound good).

Some of the otherware I've seen (but I'm sure there are other varieties, too) include:

◆ **Postcardware**   If you like and use the program, you're supposed to mail the author a postcard of something in the city where you live, or just an odd postcard.

◆ **Beerware**   If you like and use the program, you're supposed to hoist a tall cool one in the author's name.

◆ **Stampware**   If you like and use the program, you're supposed to send the author a letter using an unusual stamp. (You'll mainly find this one on on-line services with an international membership.) It's a stamp collector's dream.

Keep in Touch

While all of the shareware and otherware programs request a fee or something if you like a program, you should also feel free to contact an author if there's something you don't like about his or her product. Compliments are nice (and we don't hand out enough of them), but constructive criticism helps the authors to improve their work.

If you have something constructive to say ("your program stinks" isn't constructive), make sure you include all the information that will help the author track down the problem. For example, include the make and model of your computer, what operating system you are using, any other applications you had running, and what you were trying to do when the problem occurred. Give the author the same detailed information you would provide a company's technical support person (as described in Chapter 13). Essentially, that's what the author will be doing: providing technical support. Often, an author will have to try to duplicate the problem before he can fix it, and every little bit of information will help.

Also be sure to let the author know how to contact you in case he has some questions to ask. It would also be nice, since you're going out of your way to tell him about a problem or something you don't like, if you could tell him something specific that you do like, too. It will spare his ego and keep things balanced (you know how creative types can be).

Making Your Computer Pay for Itself

I have a friend who owns a house near a major metropolitan hospital. While she was in college, she used to rent out her extra rooms to medical students and interns working at the hospital. She said, "I may not have a job, but my house is up every morning at the crack of dawn, earning its keep."

You may not be able to (or want to) support yourself completely with your computer, but you can certainly make it pay for itself and even make some money toward future expansions and upgrades. TVs and VCRs should be so productive.

A Friendly Warning

Before you quit your job to devote all of your time to turning your computer into a money maker, you should check your local laws about running a business from your home. Taxes and zoning regulations may have an affect on what you can and cannot do from your home. There are also licenses and other red tape to consider. Older folks, who might consider supplementing their retirement income (or folks of any age collecting Social Security or other disability benefits), should check and see how much they can earn before the added income has a negative effect on their monthly benefits.

If you're just going to pick up an odd freelance job or two, these may not be of concern to you. But you won't know unless you check. Read the article "Setting Up a Home Office" for more information on the subject.

There are complete books devoted to all the information you need about using your computer to supplement your income and/or pay for itself (including the laws governing home businesses). If you're seriously (or even frivolously) considering it, you might want to visit your local library or bookstore to pick up a book on the subject(s) that interest you.

Things to Do

Since space won't allow much more here, this is basically a no-frills list of things you could do with your computer to make money. If a project or service requires special equipment, I'll mention that too.

Résumés   A lot of people are looking for work. Around graduation time, colleges are a good source of clients. You should have a laser printer.

Word processing   You could type term papers, correspondence, even contracts for small businesses. You need a high-powered word processor (that does footnotes, indexes, etc.) and a laser printer.

Editorial services   In addition to doing word processing, you could offer to correct grammar, punctuation, and spelling, and even offer to help shape the manuscripts of students and writers in your area. Graduate students working on their theses and dissertations are great clients. You could (conceivably) ghost-write the next kiss-and-tell mega-star autobiography.

Page layout/publishing   You could design flyers, menus, and ads for local restaurants and small businesses. Do the programs for your local church or theater groups or newsletters for your neighborhood clubs. You could even do custom invitations and placecards for swank dinner parties. This requires page layout software and probably a laser printer. A good selection of fonts and clip art couldn't hurt either.

Graphics   Design logos and custom clip art for small and large businesses in your area. Design letterheads, stationery, and other business forms. This requires page layout software, a graphics (paint or draw) program, and probably a laser printer. A good selection of fonts would help, too.

Electronic research services   Use your computer and modem to do on-line information searches for anyone who needs information: writers, editors, students, professionals. There are information services geared toward all manner of professionals, not to mention news services. You need, of course, a modem and membership in a variety of on-line services.

Freelance work   Look in the want ads of your local paper. A lot of companies advertise for people in all categories to do piece work on their computers in their homes. I see a lot of ads for graphics firms and small local newspapers looking for people to do occasional work to help them through seasonal busy periods and special one-time jobs.

Training   If you think you've got what it takes, offer computer tutoring for people who are too afraid to approach a computer alone. Students, parents, grandparents: technophobes come in all shapes and sizes. You'll need to have—and know well enough to teach—the standard assortment of business software, such as Windows (if you have an IBM compatible), Microsoft Word, Aldus PageMaker, and Adobe Illustrator, among others.

Records services   Design, update, and maintain mailing lists and other database-type information for small business in your area. You can extract information for clients on an as-needed basis (like printing mailing lists, etc.). You'll need a good, full-featured database and a printer that can handle labels and (possibly) long print runs.

File conversions   If you have access to both Macintosh and IBM-compatible equipment (or only one computer, but with conversion and/ or emulation software), there are always people looking for ways to convert information from one format to another.

Fax services   With a fax modem, you can fax out information (newsletters, flyers, etc.) that you already word processed or laid out for your clients. With appropriate fax software, you can fax things out in the dead of night, to lots of people, without having to supervise the machine. How's that for good? You'd be making money in your sleep. You might want a dedicated (fax/modem only) phone line.

Job search services   Using your modem and the electronic job search information in the article "Résumés," you could make money searching local, national, and international job listing databases, uploading résumés, and passing on leads to your clients.

Accounting   With a small business accounting package (and, of course, it helps if you're an accountant) you could keep track of small business accounts (payroll, accounts payable/receivable, etc.).

Tax preparation   With computerized tax software, you could do taxes for the masses. You'll need state and federal versions of the software annually, and it will also help your credibility if you have some sort of tax training and know the laws (take a course).

Letters from... You could do a nice seasonal business coming up with personalized and attractive letters from Santa, the Easter Bunny, and other seasonal characters. (Not everyone celebrates Christmas and Easter, so check out other ethnic and religious opportunities, too.)

If you stop and think about it, just about anything you would want to do with your computer could probably be offered as a service to someone who doesn't have access to one. Word processing and records management fall into this category.

As the saying goes, do what you love and the money will follow.

Five Cheap and Easy Ways to Promote Your Services

◆ Post flyers and handbills on telephone poles or bulletin boards at colleges and supermarkets.

◆ Create business cards you can hand out to anyone who seems vaguely interested in your services. (You can even create them yourself with your computer and perforated sheets of card stock, available in computer and office supply stores.)

◆ Take out a small classified ad in your local free paper (ads can cost too much in the bigger commercial papers).

◆ Tell your friends what you're doing. Word of mouth is the best form of advertising because it's free and because people trust their friends' opinions.

◆ Volunteer or heavily discount your services—especially if it's desktop publishing—for a local non-profit group, in exchange for a mention in a program or newsletter. You'll get a warm feeling for doing something good, get some free advertising in a program, and some great word of mouth publicity.

As your business grows, you can venture into more expensive and more professional-looking modes of self-promotion, but everybody's got to start somewhere.

SOHO, SOHO,
It's Off to Work We Go

S OHO is a *big* buzzword right now. Now, while the Soho section of New York City is always buzzing (at least when I go buzzing through it), this SOHO stands for Small Office/Home Office. It's a big buzz because it seems that many of the thousands of white-collar workers who found themselves "reorganized" out of corporate jobs, decided to become businesses themselves, working out of their homes.

The economic hard times and the advent of the Information Age have combined to create a situation not unlike the beginning of the Industrial Age, where many folks set up "cottage industries" to earn a living in their homes. However, rather than turning out assembled goods, the new cottage industries are cranking out information and/or computer-related goods and services.

Whether you're interested in setting up a home office so you can become an information mini-mogul, or you just want to be able to work in a quiet room without interruption, the environment you create for yourself will affect how much and how well you work.

The Heart of the Office

Considering that this is a book about using computers in your home, you can guess what I consider the heart of your home office: your personal computer. Your computer can help your office run more smoothly and efficiently, whether you're taking work home from your regular job or running a small business.

When paired with the appropriate software (just about all the major software types are reviewed back in Part III), a computer can help keep you organized, keep your finances in order (including billing and expenses), maintain your client and supplier lists, and keep track of appointments and projects—in addition to helping you produce the actual product(s) or service(s) that are your stock in trade.

Speaking of your stock in trade, if you just started thinking about starting a home business to supplement or replace your present income, you can get some ideas from the article called "Making Your Computer Pay for Itself." There are plenty of money-making opportunities to choose from, many of which should suit your personality and personal style.

Generally, though, whatever the big, multi-billion dollar companies use *their* computers for, you can use yours for the same (if smaller) purposes. I won't belabor the point any further.

Location Considerations for Your Home Office Workspace

In the best of all possible worlds, your office should be a separate room with a door that closes firmly for two reasons.

The first reason is psychological: you need the sense of being apart from the day-to-day happenings in your home. A door that closes (and locks, if possible) acts as a sound barrier and visual blinder to keep you from being distracted from the business at hand (your business, in fact) so you can get things done. When that door is closed, everyone in your home knows that you're trying to work.

Secondly, there's a financial consideration: if your home office is truly a place of business, and you will be filing (oh, ack!) tax returns on the profits from your business, a separate work-only office will make it easier for you to claim a portion of your rent/mortgage and utilities as a deductible business expense.

If you don't have the physical space for a separate office, you should try to set it up so there is some sense of being in another place. You could use a dividing screen, a curtain/divider, a wall of house plants—anything to give you that feeling of being in a work-place.

'Cause I'm the Tax Man

The reviews are mixed on whether claiming a deduction for the Business Use of Your Home (IRS form 8829) is like a lightning rod for an audit by the tax man. Some say it is, some say it isn't.

The latest advice I've gotten (from a C.P.A.) is that you're safer claiming the deduction if your office is a separate room used only for business-related work. (Are you ever completely safe from an audit?) You're also safer if your business income matches or exceeds any W-2 income from a regular employer.

Calculating the actual deduction involves measuring the square footage of your entire home and that of just your office space, and then figuring out the percentage of space your office takes up. Multiply that percentage by your rent or mortgage to get the figure for your deduction. They don't make it easy.

If you want to claim the deduction, consult an accountant or tax specialist. He'll be able to help you with all the business-related tax mess, so you get all the deductions you are legally qualified to take. And, hey, the cost of the consultation is also deductible!

It will help if the work area is not part of the busiest section of your home, and if it isn't a multipurpose area (like the dining room table) that will require you to set up and remove your computer equipment every time you want to work. A bedroom might be just the place, if your work time doesn't collide with someone else's sleep time.

When you're figuring how much space to commandeer in a room, guesstimate the area you'll need to get set up, and then increase it by half, or even double it if you can. You'll want room to grow and expand as your business takes off and you need (in the immortal words of George Carlin) "More stuff."

As for being interrupted by others in your household, you might try some sort of "do not disturb" signal. I'm thinking of something like the old "tie on the doorknob" signal that dorm-dwellers use to let their roommates know the room is (euphemistically speaking) "in use." Since you'll be wearing your "business hat" at the time, you might want to consider a real hat, like a baseball cap. When you're wearing your work hat, all non-business questions and interruptions must wait until the hat comes off. Just a thought.

Wherever and however you mark your territory, be sure it's near adequate power for your computer and other electricity-sucking equipment you'll need to plug in. Be sure there's good ventilation, too. Then you'll want to pretty it up, so you have something nice to look at while you stew over just the right word or phrase for your memo or advertising flyer.

Office Accoutrements

Once you have your workspace staked out, there's all the necessary accessories to consider: a sturdy desk, good light, comfy chair, and so on. Will you need a photocopier, fax machine, business telephone line? Can you fit all these things in the space you've chosen and still fit in it yourself?

The desk must be big enough for you to sit at comfortably, and sturdy enough to hold your computer, printer, supplies, and whatever else you'll stash on your desk. Hopefully, there will still be some room on which you can actually work. Any other equipment (photocopier, fax, and so on) is optional: you know if you need it. But if you don't need it right away, be sure to leave room to add one or more pieces down the road. Eventually, you'll probably add at least one thing that takes up space. Until then, it's elbow room.

Speaking of Deductions

As you set up, outfit, and operate your home business, make sure you keep records of what you earn and spend. It can be as simple as a spreadsheet or notations on some lined paper, or as complex as using a small business accounting software package to record everything—but keep records. For my money, the best way to keep those records is on the computer.

At the very least, you should have some kind of system for saving and categorizing your expenses. Mine's fairly straightforward: I save every receipt I get and throw them into a big manila envelope. Every now and then I go through and sort them, and enter them into a spreadsheet, with the date of the receipt, a brief description of the item(s), and then the dollar amount(s) listed under the various deductible categories (office supplies, postage, phone, dues and subscriptions, and research, to name a few).

The receipts that have been entered in the spreadsheet are moved into another envelope so they won't be entered twice. It makes everybody happy (especially the poor shlub who gets to do my taxes), and I get all of my legitimate business deductions.

Ignorance Is NOT Bliss

Before you hang out your shingle, pick up your phone. Depending on what type of business you're setting up, you may need to get one or more of these things: a business license; federal, state, and/or local business tax accounts; an employer identification number (if you'll be hiring help). You may also need to check your neighborhood's zoning (especially if clients will be coming into your home) to be sure you can legally run your business from your home.

True Confessions

Hi. My name's John, and I'm a reformed criminal. I didn't do hard time or anything, but I could have.

I'm a writer. I didn't think I was conducting any sort of licensable commerce, pounding away at my keyboard day after day. I thought that as long as I paid my taxes I was safe. I mean, I don't employ anybody but myself (and there are some who will argue that I barely do that).

I was wrong.

Boy, was I wrong. My tax preparer pointed it out to me. She said, "What's your city tax account number?" I said, "My what?"

"Your tax account number. Don't you have a business license?"

"No."

"Uh-oh."

Having an accountant say "Uh-oh" over your tax return is nearly as chilling as having a surgeon say "Uh-oh" over your X-rays.

Fortunately, the matter was easily resolved (though I did have to spend a couple of hours shlepping around City Hall). Going back over my old records showed that I wasn't in line for a major fine or anything. I could have been fined and made to pay back business taxes (with interest and penalties), and I might have had to hire a lawyer, too.

I'm here to say, don't wait. Don't guess. Find out.

You should find out what you need to do to legally run your business *before* you start. You can probably postpone things like getting an employer ID number until you actually have employees, but you should know in advance that you'll need it so there are no nasty surprises later.

Don't ass-u-me (remember that one?) that what you're doing is beneath the notice of the law. It isn't. Sooner or later, someone will notice what you're up to. To avoid problems later, make a few phone calls first. You can get all of the information you need from one or more of the following entities:

◆ A tax professional or accountant

◆ Your local Chamber of Commerce or small business association

◆ A professional group related to your business (like the Author's Guild, for writers, or a business union)

◆ Your local zoning board

◆ Your lawyer, if you have one (or know one you can leech info out of for free)

◆ The revenue and licensing departments at city hall

I put city hall last because most people feel that if they call the actual authorities who could bust them, that they'll somehow "give themselves away." That may be true if you've been operating illegally for a long while, but not if you're just thinking about starting a business. If it makes you feel better, start with the other resources first. You could also try the business section of your local library or bookstore.

Tax, business, and zoning laws vary widely from city to city, so there are no real guidelines to offer, save for one: If you're making money, there's probably a government agency that wants a piece of your action.

It's a good idea to know up front what's expected of you so you can plan and prepare for the day you go legal. There's nothing worse than having to recreate office records from scratch trying to prove you didn't break the law.

The Bionic Résumé

Looking for a new job can be a drag—a real drag. If you're out of work, you've got to deal with that feeling of desperation, that "If I don't find work soon, I'll just _____!" feeling. (Fill in the blank with something appropriate to how depressed you are right now.)

If you're what the media so lovingly calls "underemployed," or if you're looking to make a career change, you have to deal with all of that cloak-and-dagger "Can't let the boss know I'm looking" stuff. Just that problem makes it hard to try to track down another job, but it's even worse if the job you already have is a 9-to-5er. You're working during prime job search hours.

Whichever set of difficulties you are facing, your computer can help. At the very least, it (and your word processing program) can give you shiny, eye-catching résumés that you can subtly alter to favor whatever job you are applying for today. With some additional hardware (specifically a modem) and membership in an on-line service (like America OnLine), it can even help you do the looking.

Résumé *Redux*

The biggest advantages to doing your résumé on your own computer are that you control what it says and looks like, and you can finagle it to suit the interview *du jour*. By "finagle," I am *not* suggesting you lie on your résumé. I may warp the truth a little, but I always manage to get caught when I tell an outright lie.

What I do mean is that you can slant it towards the position for which you're interviewing. The actual finagle might mean doing as little as changing the objective statement (if you use one) to more closely resemble the job you're interviewing for, or it might mean having two completely different résumé styles. In some instances, you might want to have one that emphasizes the previous jobs you've held. In other instances, a résumé that emphasizes the skills you've learned, rather than the jobs themselves, might be more appropriate (especially if you're trying to get out of a particular line of work).

Disclaimer:

I am not, by any stretch of the imagination, a job search professional. I'm a computer geek. Nothing I say here will turn a bad résumé into a good one: it might look better, or read better, but that's about it. Résumés are an art form, really, and I am no artist.

I have had a lot of experience preparing résumés for myself and my friends, and I saw quite a few cross my desk when I was in a position to hire new employees, but all of this is personal—not professional—opinion. I haven't the slightest idea what the current "trend" in résumés might be—and there are trends to them, just like the trends in fashion.

If you have concerns about the content (rather than the appearance) of your résumé, you may want to get a good book on résumé preparation. There are gobs of them in your local library and bookstore. Or, you may want to have your résumé done by a professional. There are gobs of them, too.

Once you have a good, solid résumé in hand, you can redo it on your own computer and tinker with it as suggested here (if you care to).

For example, say you're an elementary school teacher. You want out of classroom teaching, but you still want to work with children in some kind of learning environment. Your objective statement might usually say something like: *Objective: A position that utilizes my childhood-development training and teaching skills in a non-classroom setting.* When you hear of an opening at a children's museum for someone to do informative workshops and presentations on museum-related subjects, you might want to alter the objective statement to something like: *Objective: A position that utilizes my childhood-development training and teaching skills to encourage children and families to learn outside of the classroom.*

The difference is subtle. Both statements say essentially the same thing: you want to teach, but not in a school. The second slants the statement ever-so-slightly closer to the job that's been advertised, without coming right out and saying "I want the job in your museum," which isn't subtle at all.

Some Résumé Tips and Tricks

Résumés are a crapshoot, especially if you send them out in response to ads or rumors of job openings. In nearly 10 years of retail management, I never once hired anyone on the basis of a résumé I received in the mail. Sorry, but it's the truth.

I do believe that a résumé can be an important tool in getting a job, but I think they work better as a post-interview reminder. I also believe that there aren't really any rules for creating the "perfect" résumé, beyond that it should be clean, legible, and accurate, and should honestly represent your skills. It should be printed on heavy weight paper (24 LB, with 25% fiber content—it will say on the box) probably with a laser or other high-quality printer.

The important thing, I think (and again, what do I know), is that the résumé should be representative of you and your style. Here are some simple things you can do to help put yourself in your résumé:

◆ As much as possible, try to "talk on paper" to let your personality through. Rather than falling completely into that stilted résumé grammar, try to have at least one section that reads like you normally speak.

◆ Select a typeface that (while remaining businesslike) shows some of your personal style. Résumés are a formal business document, but within that guideline, there's room to choose one or two fonts (typefaces) that uphold that formality (and aid in its legibility and readability) while showing some personality. Check out the upcoming section "Three Faces of Type."

◆ Bullets (like an asterisk * or dash – in front of a paragraph) can draw attention to important "don't you dare miss this" information. Bullets can be found in a computer font's extended character set or as part of a symbol font (often called *dingbats*). Check your Mac, Windows, or word processor manual for information on using them.

- Remember: less is more. You don't have to list every single job you've had (or skill you learned). Restrict it to the best of the best, the jobs and skills that are most important to the job you want. Back those up with specific accomplishments to show you know how to apply your knowledge.

- Instead of saying "Managed phone and mail order business for store" say, "In managing phone and mail order operations, I increased sales 15% in six months." It not only explains the task you did, but demonstrates how well you did it.

- One or two sentences about your interests and activities outside of work (community service, hobbies, and so on) give whoever is reading your résumé a stronger sense of you as a person (instead of seeing you as just another longhorn in a cattle call).

Three Faces of Type

The proper and improper use of computerized typefaces (fonts) is a book unto itself. Needless to say, we'll barely scratch the surface here.

The thing to remember, appropriate to résumés, is that the choice of typeface can have a subtle, almost subliminal effect on the way a reader perceives the person whose career is summarized on the page. Of course, the perception is also affected by the reader's personal prejudices; a font you think is fun and stylish, may strike the reader as pretentious or precious. It's a fine line to walk, so you have to be careful.

To help you walk that line, here's the same résumé information presented in several different fonts, along with my opinions about each one. How much you agree (or disagree) with what I think will also serve to demonstrate how perceptions vary.

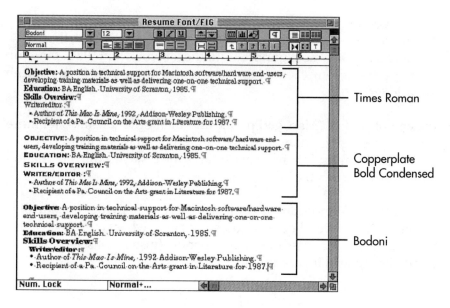

Résumé variations done with Microsoft Word.

Example 1 is done in boring Times Roman (regular, bold, and italic). There's nothing wrong with this classic font, except that it's a classic and is used a lot. There's nothing about it that makes it visually stand out from a crowd.

Example 2 uses two fonts, Copperplate Bold Condensed (for headings) and Bembo (please, no bimbo jokes) regular and italic for the body text. Both fonts are fairly formal. The visual interest comes from their contrast. Copperplate is solid looking, almost heavy, but it's visual "weight" is offset by the lighter "feel" of the Bembo. The combination visually implies a generally serious personality, but with a sense of fun.

Example 3 uses variations of the font Bodoni (Poster, regular, and italic). The Bodoni Poster, used for headings, is heavy but has frills (like in the tail of the J) that keep it from being too serious. The Bodoni Regular, in the body text, has the same overall feeling, but avoids that heaviness. The visual implication is of someone who can be serious if the situation requires it, but who generally isn't.

If you care, I finally opted for Example 2, even though number 3 is closer to the real me. (Just goes to show how little truth there has to be in self-advertising.)

Résumé Mechanics

As you are typing up a résumé in your favorite word processing program, you should keep certain guidelines handy. Unfortunately, how you handle the settings mentioned here varies from program to program. I'll tell you what they are and what you might want to use them for, but you'll have to look them up in your word processor's manual to see how they're controlled in your particular program.

In addition to the basic word processing skills of centering and justifying your text, and applying bold and italics, you should be able to do some or all of the following:

> **Set margins**   The *margin* is the amount of blank space left at the edges of the page. Typically, one-inch margins all around are standard; however, you may want to tweak the exact measurement if you have just a little more information to fit on one page.

> **Set first line indent**   This controls how far from the left margin the first line of a new paragraph will be indented. You'll have to change the indentation to do a *hanging indent*, like those used in the illustration in the section "Three Faces of Type".

> **Set tabs/tab stops**   The *tab stops* are the places to which the cursor jumps when you press the Tab key. Instead of trying to create columns with the Spacebar (yuck!), you should set tabs. It's much easier, looks better in the finished product, and speeds up the typing process (you only have to press the Tab key once where you would hit the Spacebar ten or fifteen times).

Getting the right effect, with the right word processing tool, will give you a much more professional-looking résumé. The sample résumés shown here utilize many of the ideas suggested in this article. Look them over if you need some ideas.

Susan Fields

611 Lois Lane
Metropolis, SM 10874-2061
(515) 555-0666

Qualifications:
- Excellent writing and language skills.
- Strong general office skills, including: data entry and processing, record-keeping, cash reconciliation, and phone work.
- Excellent speller.
- Able to meet deadlines and work well under pressure

Accomplishments:

1993-present	President, Board of Directors, Metropolis Recycling.
1992-1993	Member, Board of Directors, Metropolis Recycling.
1976-1991	Founding member, Coordinator, and President, Ecology Recycling Project.
1985-1989	Member, Smallvillians for Recycling, Steering Committee member, 1986-1988.
1988	Participated in City Council hearings regarding a trash-to-steam plant, and for mandatory recycling for the city of Metropolis.
1975-1977	Member, Board of Directors, Ecology Food Cooperatives.

Employment Experience:

May 1992-Nov. 1993	*Associate*, Law Mart-Smallville, SM
	Telephone receptionist , assisting customers, cashier, member of original set-up crew.
Nov. 1992-May 1993	*Temporary Circulation Asst.*, Metropolis Public Library, Metropolis, SM
	Replacement of circulated materials.
Dec. 1991-Jan. 1992	*Counselor Aide*, Four Ways Addiction Recovery Center, Metropolis, SM
	Responsibilities included introduction and supervision of incoming clients, completion of appropriate forms and records, assisting with client activities and case-management.
Jan. 1984-May 1991	*Administrative Assistant (part time)*, Prisoner Visitation and Support, 1501 Lonely St., Metropolis, SM 10002
	Responsibilities included data entry and record keeping, maintenance of visitation schedules, participation in conference planning and organization, fund-raising, answering telephones and providing information to callers, answering mail inquiries, organizing mass mailings.
1985-1986	*Community Consultant*, Solid Waste Management—Metropolis Resources Council, Metropolis, SM 10803
	Provided technical assistance to communities implementing recycling programs.
1984-1985	*Administrative Assistant/Secretary*-Mark Stetson, Commercial Fund-Raiser, Metropolis, SM
	Responsibilities included typing, file maintenance and phone work, designing forms, receiving and answering correspondence.
1983-1984	*Receptionist*-Jacob Jacobs, D.D.S., 1900 Parker House Square, Metropolis, SM 18203
	Responsibilities included patient scheduling, phones, record maintenance and filing, and billing.
1973-1980	*Coordinator (part-time)*-Ecology Cooperatives, Inc., 2001 S. 36th St., Metropolis, SM
	Responsibilities included daily cash reconciliation, cash register duty, stocking shelves, and inventory maintenance.

Education:

Sept. 1957-June 1959	Business Administration, Metropolis University, University Park, SM

References available upon request.

Kevin L. Stanley

736 East Pleasant Avenue.
Scranton, PA 18519
(717) 555-0003

Educational Background:

Received **Doctor of Divinity** degree at **G & S Theological Seminary**, 6/93.

Recognition and Activities:

Recipient of **Pinafore Preaching Scholarship**, 6/92

Moderator G & S Penzance Church and Piratical Reformation League, 9/90 to 6/93

Secretary of G & S Seminary Association of Black Seminarians, 9/91 to 6/93

Received **A.B.** from **Harvard University** with a concentration in Psychology and Social Relations. 9/78 to 6/82

Recognition and Activities:

Recipient of **Gold Medal Award from the Society of the Performing Arts**, 6/82
Student Body Representative, 6/82
President of Multicultural Arts Society, 9/80 to 6/82

Experience:

Frederick Lane Episcopal Church, Scranton, PA, Student Associate. 9/92 to 6/93
Magnolia Foundation, AIDS Support Group Facilitator and Counselor. 9/90 to 6/93
Community Medical Center, Hemlock Hill, PA, Hospital Chaplain (C.P.E. Basic Unit). 6/92 to 9/92
Mt. Olives Episcopal Church, Scranton, PA, Student Associate. 6/91 to 8/92
Imprudent Insurance Company, Fort McHenry, PA. Assistant Community Relations Consultant, Personnel Administrator, Management Intern, 10/82 to 8/90

References available upon request.

JOHN PIVOVARNICK
2408 PINE ST. APT. A
YEADON, PA 19109
610-555-1212

STATISTICS
Height: 6'3" • Weight: 245 • Eyes: Brown • Hair: Brown • Voice: Baritone

ACTING EXPERIENCE

ROLE	PLAY	THEATER	DIRECTOR
Fagin	*Oliver!*	SPCC	Eileen Kennedy
Nurse Flucker, etc.	*CBLSL PSAs*	Public Access Cable	Michael McGonicle
Henry Irving	*Actor's Nightmare*	Eagen Theater	Holly Salcito
Capt. Brackett	*South Pacific*	Encore Theatre	Agnes Cummings
Algernon	*Importance of Being Earnest*	Univ. of Scranton	Gregory Mercurio
Preacher/Judge	*Rimers of Eldritch*	Univ. of Scranton	J. W. Roberts
1st Voice/Capt Cat	*Under Milk Wood*	Univ. of Scranton	Glenda Jackson
Elwood Dowd	*Harvey*	Encore Theatre	Louis Bisignani
Annas	*Jesus Christ Superstar*	Univ. of Scranton	Agnes Cummings
Amolphe	*School for Wives*	Univ. of Scranton	C. Townsend Alcott
Charlemagne	*Pippin*	Univ. of Scranton	Gregory Mercurio
Marion Cheever	*Next!*	Actor's Circle	Rory Giovanucci
Prospero	*The Tempest*	Univ. of Scranton	Gregory Mercurio
Mr. Katz	*Hot L Baltimore*	Univ. of Scranton	William P. Zahler
Comm. Roseabove	*Oh Dad, Poor Dad...*	Univ. of Scranton	Gregory Mercurio
Rudy/Sgt. Mellors	*A Murder is Announced*	SPT	Louis Bisignani
Woodenshoes	*The Front Page*	SPT	Tony Santinello
Lewis	*Alice in Wonderland*	Univ. of Scranton	John Pivovarnick
Pablo	*Streetcar Named Desire*	SPT	Tony Santinello
Host	*Best of Broadway (radio show)*	PA Blind Association	John Pivovarnick

TRAINING
BA English, Theater minor, 1985, University of Scranton
Dance: Jazz, Ballet, Modern, 3 years
Voice, 2 years

SPECIAL SKILLS
Fencing, Quarterstaff, combat mime, American Sign Language
Character makeup and effects

ACCENTS
Irish, Russian/Slavic, Yiddish/Jewish, High English, Cockney, Southern, assorted others.

TECHNICAL SKILLS
Experienced Stage Manager, lighting technician and operator, carpenter, scenic painter.
(Technical résumé available upon request)

Pounding the Digital Pavement: Electronic Job Hunting

O nce you have a perfect résumé, you'll need somewhere to send it, right? Well, tracking down job leads is one of the most time-consuming parts of the job search. Reading want ads, checking job posting boards, or even asking people who work at companies you're interested in can take lots of time. With a computer and a modem, you can do a lot to speed up the process.

You won't want to neglect other sources for job leads, but many on-line services offer the digital equivalent of a newspaper's classified want ads. As a matter of fact, America OnLine calls theirs "Classifieds Online," and CompuServe calls theirs "Classified Ads" (as shown below). Both offer employment opportunities.

CompuServe

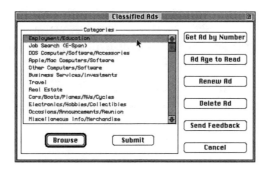

CompuServe's Classified Ads area.

To get to CompuServe's ad area shown above (naturally, you must be a subscriber to the service; see "On-Line Services" for information on joining), use the command **GO: CLASSIFIEDS**. That will bring you to the area shown above. (You may want to skip the general ads and go straight to the job search area; that command is **GO: ESPAN**.) To read the ads, select a category and click on the **Browse** button (or press **Enter**).

Since we're talking about jobs, select **Job Search (E-Span)**. CompuServe presents you with several sets of options to narrow your search. First you'll specify the area of the country through which you want to search (Northeast, Eastern, Midwest, and so on), or you may do a search of the entire country's employment listings.

Next, you'll make a selection for a specific kind of work (Executive positions, Engineer/Architect, Sales/Marketing, and so on). Then you'll be presented with a listing of ads that meet your specifications (particular types of jobs, in a particular part of the nation) like the one shown here.

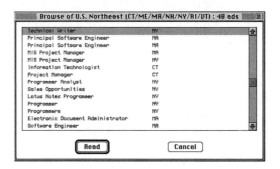

The fruits of our job search labors.

Double-click on the job titles that interest you. You can then read, save to disk, or print out hard copies of each ad that catches your fancy. Each job listing generally includes a job description, qualifications, and contact information should you care to apply for the job.

In addition to the job listings themselves, the E-Span area on CompuServe also offers tips on résumés, interviewing, and finding the "hidden" job market by networking with your peers.

America OnLine

Things work a little differently on America OnLine (AOL); however, you still need to be a subscriber to the service, so you might need to check out the article "On-Line Services" later in Part V.

Just about everything you'd find in your newspaper's classified section can be found in America OnLine's digital version. To get to the classified ads area on AOL (shown below), use the **Keyword: Classifieds**.

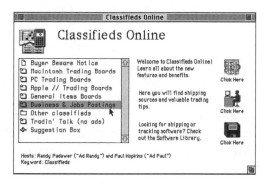

America OnLine's Classifieds Online area.

By selecting the Business & Jobs Postings selection shown in the illustration, you can access two job listing databases: E-Span (the same service we saw on CompuServe) and Help Wanted USA. Both job listing services work the same way on AOL, so we'll just look at Help Wanted USA.

Unlike CompuServe's job search (where you make a series of selections to narrow your search down to the job type and region of the country), on AOL you enter your search parameters as a string of words that are then matched against all of the job listings in the database. The search strings are *Boolean* (as in Boolean Geometry) and may include qualifying words like "and" and "or." Do yourself a favor and read the tips on searching the database (provided on-line). Boolean searches can provide excellent results, but only if you know how to phrase the search string.

In the figure below, I entered "Philadelphia and Macintosh" as my search parameters because I wanted to see how many Mac-related jobs would turn up in a city as large as Philly. Only three did.

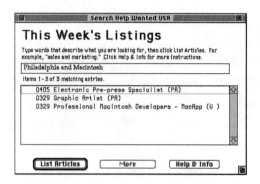

Search results on AOL's Help Wanted USA job database.

Once you've entered your search string (like "Philadelphia and Macintosh" or "Philadelphia" or just "Macintosh"), you can read the ads that match your parameters by double-clicking each entry's name. The ads include job descriptions, qualifications, and various methods of contacting the company should you decide to apply. As on CompuServe, you may save the listings to disk, print them, or ignore them altogether.

While you're at it, you may also want to enter several more search strings (variations on your theme) to see if anything different and exciting turns up under alternate phrasings. It couldn't hurt.

Local Opportunities

As long as you're pressing your computer and modem into service for your job search, you may want to take a few moments and see if you can turn up a local bulletin board (also discussed in the article "On-Line Services") devoted to job openings right in your own area.

In the Delaware Valley (that's Southeastern Pennsylvania, New Jersey, and Delaware) there's the Online Opportunities bulletin board pictured below. It's part of a nationwide collection of bulletin boards that share data with Help Wanted USA (the service we looked at on America OnLine).

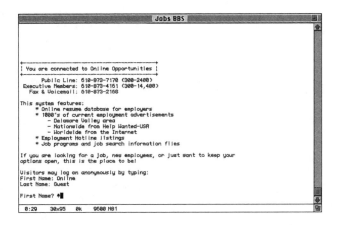

```
════════════════════════ Jobs BBS ════════════════════════

+------------------------------------------+
| You are connected to Online Opportunities |
+------------------------------------------+
       Public Line: 610-873-7170 (300-2400)
    Executive Members: 610-873-4161 (300-14,400)
        Fax & Voicemail: 610-873-2156

This system features:
    * Online resume database for employers
    * 1000's of current employment advertisements
        - Delaware Valley area
        - Nationwide from Help Wanted-USA
        - Worldwide from the Internet
    * Employment Hotline listings
    * Job programs and job search information files

If you are looking for a job, new employees, or just want to keep your
options open, this is the place to be!

Visitors may log on anonymously by typing:
First Name: Online
Last Name: Guest

First Name? ▮

 0:29    30x95    0k    9600 N81
```

Delaware Valley Online Opportunities BBS.

I found the information for this bulletin board tacked onto the end of a job posting on America OnLine. You can probably find one for your local area there too (if not your exact city, at least one nearby). If you don't find one on America OnLine or CompuServe, you may be able to find a phone number for one posted at your local employment office, in the want ads of your local paper, possibly even your local phone book. You won't know until you look.

Unlike a national service like CompuServe, there are no fees associated with a local bulletin board like this one; the only cost to you is your phone bill. (The bulletin board makes its money from selling other services and charging employers a fee. This is as it should be, I think. Why squeeze money out of someone looking for work?)

Through the local bulletin board, you may upload a résumé that prospective employers can look at, download job listings for your area (and possibly nation- and even worldwide). You may even commission a professionally done résumé for yourself.

Considering the amount of time and energy it takes to track down potential employment, any one of these three services is a boon to job hunters. Each gives you the resources to carry on your search for job leads on a national or international basis from the comfort of your own home. In addition, you can access these services in the wee-small hours of the morning, saving the rest of your day for your present job, or interviews and person-to-person networking.

Telecommuting

T his is like one of those riddles kids are so fond of telling: *When is a door not a door? When it's ajar.*

So try this one: *When is a commuter not a commuter? When he's a telecommuter.*

To many, the word "commuting" brings to mind images of rush-hour traffic, jam-packed public transportation, someone reading the newspaper over your shoulder, and women in smart business outfits wearing battered sneakers and white anklets to spare their feet the ignominy of high-heels until they get to work. For a lucky few, commuting brings to mind a different set of images: leisurely drinking a cup of coffee while watching "The Today Show," seeing the spouse/partner off to work, getting the kids off to school, watching the dog chase cars and poop in the petunias. Around, say, nine-ish, it means going upstairs/downstairs/down the hall and opening the office door. You fire up the computer, dial up another computer, and, with the high-pitched whine of computer modems chatting to each other, you're at work.

Tele-*what*-ing?

The word "telecommute" is a hybrid built out of the prefix tele- and the word commute. Tele- means "reaching over a distance, carried out between two remote points, performed or operating through electronic transmissions." You know it and love it from words like *tele*phone, *tele*graph, and the ever popular *tele*kinesis. Commute means "to travel regularly over some distance, as from a suburb into a city and back." (Suddenly, I'm channeling my fourth grade English teacher.)

In short, it means to go to and from your office, your normal commute, by way of electronic transmission. It is not going to work like they do in "Star Trek"; there is no matter-transference beam involved. You don't travel physically by way of electronic transmission (it would be *way* cool if you could), but your work sure does.

Using your home computer, a modem, and a telephone line, you link up with the computer at your job. You can access data, applications, e-mail—anything you would normally do via computer at the work site, you can do just as easily via your computer at home.

Likely Candidates for Telecommuting

Naturally, you can't just tell your boss, "I'm going to be working from home from now on." You need to negotiate that first (and there's more about that later). There are, however, some jobs that lend themselves well to telecommuting.

◆ Computer-dependent work (writers, programmers, some data entry jobs, graphic designers).

◆ Jobs where there is already a computer network in place at the work site. Managers aren't likely to invest a fortune in new equipment for your grand experiment. But if the hardware is already there, the opportunity might also be there.

◆ Jobs in companies that already have an "in-the-field" staff that connects and communicates with the corporate computer from remote locations. Convincing these companies to allow you to telecommute would be easier than trying to convince companies that have no experience of telecommuters.

◆ Jobs with little or no supervision: generally, the boss hands you a job to do and says "Have it back to me by 3:00 p.m. Friday."

◆ Jobs with little or no committee work, where a group is expected to get together face-to-face for meetings, brain-storming sessions, and work groups. If you must put in daily appearances in the office, there isn't much point in trying to telecommute on a regular basis.

Of course, the attitude of your company will also be a deciding factor. A straight-laced, by the book, no-funny-business business will probably not be open to something that (on the surface) sounds as radical and rebellious as telecommuting. It never hurts to ask, though.

Tools of the Trade-off

The basic hardware and software requirements of telecommuting are fairly simple. Both parties (you and your company) must have a computer, modem, telephone line(s), and appropriate communications software.

Especially at home, having more than one telephone line is essential because using a modem on your only phone line will monopolize it while you're working (major trauma if there's a teenager in the house). You may also want a separate voice line for your business, or the phone company's Identa-ring service (which gives you a second phone number with a different ring pattern) on your existing family line. Either way, you'll be able to tell when incoming calls are business- or family-related, and you can answer appropriately.

The company's computer should most likely be a *server*, a computer that is used only to store data and applications in a central location and that is accessed by all the other computers at the site. Otherwise, when you dial in to work, a stand-alone computer will be tied up, and no one else will be able to use it. (Although if that doesn't matter to the company, it shouldn't matter to you either.)

The software you need will vary, depending on the level of interaction you need to have with the company computer. If all you will be doing is working on your computer at home and then transferring a finished file to the company's computer, you may be able to get away with only basic communications software (like those discussed in the Reviews in this book). If you'll need to do more than that (access data and applications from your company's computer, or actually control a computer at the office, for example), you'll need specific client and server software on both machines. The person in charge of the company's network (the network administrator) will be able to tell you what you need to work with the company's particular system.

Also depending on the kind of work you do, you may need to have a fax machine, photocopier, and/or other hardware, software, and business paraphernalia in your home to make telecommuting practical. The article "Setting

Up a Home Office" will give you tips and ideas about setting up your home office in style. A general rule of thumb is that you should have about the same computer equipment at home as you have in your office. If you work regularly with a scanner (or laser printer, or CD-ROM drive, or whatever) in the office, you'll probably need one at home, too.

Crack That Whip!

Once your telecommute has been arranged, get ready for some major adjustments in your life. Working at home requires more discipline and self-control (for me at least) than just about any other work situation. It's very easy to delay "going to work" because the pressures and distractions of home life are in your face all the time. It's very easy to say, "Well, I'll just work a little longer tomorrow. Let me just do these one or two *leetle* things."

If telecommuting is going to be a successful venture for you and your employer, you have to get the work done. Set up a work schedule. It may be a 9 to 5 kind of thing, or (if your company can deal with it) something a little more broken up (like early morning and later evening hours).

The point is to have definite "at work" time and very definite "not at work" time. The "at work" times need to be enough for you to comfortably finish your work. The "not at work" times have to be enough to let you take care of your household, your family, and significant other(s)—not to mention yourself. You need time to unwind and recoup your energies. Otherwise, if you work too much (*guilty as charged, your honor*), your family and friends will feel abandoned and slighted. If you work too little, you may be out of a job or dragged kicking and screaming back into your old commuting routine.

Worst of all, if there aren't set, equitable times for both halves of your existence, you may feel like you work 24/7 (i.e. 24 hours a day, 7 days a week). That's definitely a recipe for burnout. Trust me on this one. (If not me, trust my therapist.)

Working at home (whether telecommuting, or running your own home-based business) can be a most rewarding experience, as long as you can balance between your home- and work-at-home lives.

Uncle John's Top 10 Favorite Things About Working at Home

10. Working in my underwear.

9. Not having to avoid Mexican food on a work day.

8. No office politics and intrigue. (Although I do miss the gossip—*quick*, someone call me with dirt!)

7. The only ego in the office is my own—there isn't room for another one.

6. No Muzak! No Top 40 radio stations! Only music that I like! (Insert evil, maniacal laugh here.)

5. Now that I spend more time away from people, I catch fewer colds.

4. I don't have to go stand outside in the cold and the rain to smoke a cigarette.

3. No more vending machine coffee.

2. No more lunches at my desk.

And my number 1 favorite thing about working from home:

1. No more @#$!*& corporate-zombie-drones breathing down my neck.

Computing Goes Platinum: Senior Services

I
t's a much-touted fact that the "Baby Boomers" are getting old. Around the turn of this century (which isn't too far away), older Americans could move from minority to majority status. U.S. census data shows that the number of Americans over the age of 65 jumped from 26.8 million in 1985 to 29.6 million in 1990.

Freed, somewhat, from the constant obligations of career and family, many folks look upon their later years as a chance to explore and learn (as opposed to settling down into a sedentary routine). Instead of looking after the needs of others, they want to look after themselves—to enjoy and enrich their lives in new and exciting ways. Who can blame them?

Computing offers much in the way of personal enrichment: new challenges to conquer, new skills to learn and master, and a chance to meet like-minded adults both in person and on-line with electronic services like America Online and CompuServe.

Special Needs of Older Computer Users

In addition to the obvious need of computer access, many older computer-geek wannabes may have additional special needs. Emotionally speaking, anyone who was around before computers became commonplace appliances in the home may have to deal with some level of trepidation the first time he or she approaches one. A computer can be a scary thing to the uninitiated (my mother is always afraid she's going to break mine or somehow cause it to explode). Having someone with computer experience introduce a new older user to the computer is probably the least scary approach. In addition, showing is always better than telling, especially when it is necessary to stress the computer's ease of use or to overcome the fear of its fragility.

Any mature person (of any age) dislikes being treated like a child (I know I do). If you are introducing an adult to computers, be sure to show him the ropes as a peer (if you are a peer) or with the respect his age has earned. You aren't somehow better than the person you're teaching; you simply have a skill that he hasn't acquired yet. Provide adult-oriented training materials that approach computing in a light-hearted, easy-to-read manner. Materials that teach in an engaging and non-intimidating manner (like *The Complete Idiot's Guide to the Mac* or *The Complete Idiot's Guide to PCs*) help relieve some of the nervousness associated with learning a new skill.

Older users may also have to cope with physical limitations: a mouse may be difficult to grip and maneuver with arthritis; a monitor may be hard to read because of visual impairment; even a desk or particular type of chair may be difficult to deal with. There are all types of software, hardware, and furniture available to make the computing experience physically easier for folks with special needs. See the article "Special-Needs Computing" for more information on how to deal with those needs.

While many seniors tackle the world of computers on their own or with the help of a friend or family member, many others have found it useful (and more fun) to make computing a team sport by way of SeniorNet, a non-profit organization for adults age 55 and over who are interested in learning about, and with, computers.

Networking with SeniorNet

SeniorNet started out as a research project begun in 1986 by Mary Furlong, Ed.D., Professor of Education at the University of San Francisco, to see if computers and telecommunications could enhance the lives of older adults. Since then, SeniorNet has grown into an organization with over 5,000 members nationwide. (Some members I spoke to on America Online put the figure at more than twice that, over 12,000.) It publishes a wide range of instructional materials and has learning centers in more than 50 U.S. cities (see the section entitled "SeniorNet Learning Centers" at the end of this article).

Learning Centers and Other Benefits of Membership

Learning centers offer classes in word processing, spreadsheets, communications, and other subject areas. Besides functioning as a classroom, learning centers provide a chance for members to meet and compare notes between classes. Members who don't live near a learning center can socialize and learn with other members at national conferences. SeniorNet conferences include presentations, workshops, and exhibits that are aimed at computer users at all levels, novice through advanced.

SeniorNet members also receive a quarterly newsletter, the *SeniorNet Newsline*, which contains informative articles, hardware and software reviews, and step-by-step projects designed for and by seniors. Additionally, members can get discounts on software and computer publications, and can even get special member's rates on America Online, where SeniorNet operates the SeniorNet Online area (shown below).

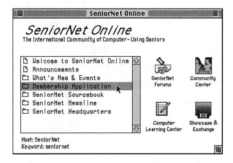

The SeniorNet Online area on America Online.

SeniorNet Online

If the SeniorNet's regional learning centers are like schoolhouses, the SeniorNet Online area of America Online is the playground. Don't get me wrong. The area is just chock-full of serious and helpful information for its members. There are libraries of software, utilities, and text files members can download, and a forum where members can post questions, get answers, and share their views on life, computing, and everything.

The Minimum Requirements, and More. . .

Using an on-line service like America Online requires that your computer be equipped with a modem, telephone line, and communications software. For more information on the hardware and software required, you might want to refer to Chapters 2 (in particular the section on add-on accessories) and Communications Programs in the Review section (the whole chapter is devoted to communications software). For more information about America Online, other on-line services, and the quirks of computer communications, you might want to check out the articles "The Information Superhighway," "On-Line Services," "On-Line Shopping," and "Electronic Pen Pals" later in this part. These articles will tell you everything you need to know to get started.

Visiting the SeniorNet forum (the message area), I followed a spirited exchange in the topic area called "Atheists" and skimmed through some insightful book reviews in an area called (oddly enough) "Book Reviews." Computing is not the only thing on these folks' minds.

But the for-real-and-true playground is the SeniorNet Community Center. The Community Center is an on-line "room" where members can gather to talk in "real-time" (as opposed to the time required to post a message in the forum and wait for someone else to read it and reply).

When I popped in for a visit (see the figure below), it was about 5:30 PM eastern time on a Wednesday. I really wasn't expecting to find anyone about, but I was in a nosy mood so I charged in anyhow. I was pleased to see a gathering of six or eight members chatting, with others coming and going all the while I was there. At one point, there were over a dozen "Netters" (as they sometimes call themselves) in the room, with at least half a dozen different conversations going. There was even some sort of inside joke about "Heather" going on that I just did not get.

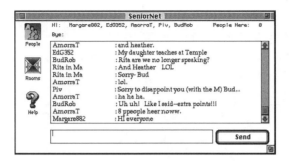

Chatting with the "Netters" on America Online.

One member, operating under the handle "Capn Easy," said his son got him interested in computers when the Capn was 80 years old. He's had his own PC for a little over a year and is "having a ball" with it. Capn Easy told me that his favorite part of SeniorNet is "the interchange of ideas, jokes, etc." Another visitor to the forum, "Daddy Cool," seconded the motion and claimed that "Several of us old codgers have been saved by SeniorNet." When I asked him what he meant by "saved," he asked my age, laughed at my answer, and suggested, "When you're 70–80, you'll understand."

A Sense of Community

The strongest impression one gets when sitting in on a SeniorNet chat, or even just reading through the various postings on-line, is that the SeniorNet members have formed a cozy little electronic community that enjoys the similarities between members (older folks with an interest in computers), but revels in their differences. However, don't get the idea that this is an exclusive club—despite the age requirement for membership. Judging by the warm welcome I received, just about anyone with a civil tongue and sense of fun is welcome to pop in at any time.

Now, if only I could figure out some way to get my technophobic parents to join up. . . .

SeniorNet Learning Centers

Anyone interested in joining SeniorNet (or giving a membership as a gift), should contact the nearest SeniorNet Learning Center for information. You can also join through the SeniorNet Online area on America Online. A single membership is $25 per year ($35 for a couple).

The following table is a listing of the Learning Centers by state. It was taken from the SeniorNet Online informational library.

State/City	Coordinator	Phone #
Alabama		
Huntsville	Anne Parris	205-536-4481
Arkansas		
Hot Springs	Joe Petrek	501-622-1802
California		
Bakersfield	Cheryl Leask	805-327-8511
Culver City	Gordon Jelley	310-202-5855
El Segundo	Robert Fleischman	310-640-8134
Fullerton	Anne Pearson	714-526-2775
Huntington Beach	LeNita Hague	714-960-7671
Oakland	Barbara Chang	510-531-9721
Orinda	Bill Powell	510-524-5939
Sacramento	Maria Lavecas	912-264-5462
Sacramento NE	Edith Buth	916-485-9572
San Francisco	Annette Rose	415-771-7950
San Francisco	Desmond Reeves Sr., Helen Hammack	415-922-7249
San Jose	Phil Carnahan	408-448-6400
San Mateo	Al Ellison	415-377-4735
Santa Cruz	Laura Scribner	408-429-3506

State/City	Coordinator	Phone #
Colorado		
Colorado Springs	Joe Adams	719-685-5721
Florida		
Cocoa	Jim Proesel	407-632-1111, Ext. 4545
Ocala	Diane Leaf	904-629-8351
Tampa	Don Meng	813-974-5263
Winter Park	Geraldine Dixon	407-647-6366
Georgia		
Atlanta/Smyrna	Linda Garcia	404-801-5320
Savannah	Dr. Ruth Garrett	912-651-7559/ 912-351-4520
Hawaii		
Honolulu, Oahu	Virginia Young	808-845-9296
Honolulu- Kokua Outpost	Mabel McConnell	808-528-4839
Kahului, Maui	Art Chenoweth	808-242-1216
Illinois		
Peoria	Sharon Wilkinson	309-682-2472
Indiana		
Indianapolis	Robert Gilmore	317-849-1099
Kansas		
Overland Park	Cathie Peterson, Harold Duvall	913-469-8500, Ext. 3844

continues

State/City	Coordinator	Phone #
Kentucky		
Lexington	Bobbie Newman	606-255-2527
Louisiana		
Baton Rouge	Danna Spayde	504-923-8025
Michigan		
Rochester	Christy Weisenbach	313-656-1403
Missouri		
St. Louis Gateway	Carl VanDyke	314-530-2933
Nebraska		
Omaha	Nikki Ingram	402-552-2359
Nevada		
Las Vegas	Dixie Frisk	702-386-2626
New Jersey		
Ewing	Milt Koosman	609-883-1009
New York		
Valhalla	Shelley Garnet	914-785-6793
New York City	Mary Ann Lewis	212-636-6782
Forest Hills (Queens)	Robert Goodman	718-592-5757
Hudson Guild (Chelsea)	Chris Filner, Bob Himmel	212-924-6710
Upper East Side	Ann Danisi	212-360-7620
Bronx	Patricia Burlace	718-884-0700
Staten Island	Sam Finkelstein	718-981-1500

State/City	Coordinator	Phone #
Oklahoma		
Oklahoma City	Charlene Francis	405-728-1230
Oregon		
Eugene	Teal Korn	503-345-9441
Pennsylvania		
Philadelphia	Dolores Anderson	215-276-6148
Tennessee		
Nashville	Anna Lee Morton	615-327-4551
Texas		
Houston	Dr. Peter Norris	713-963-4151
Nacogdoches	Louise Bingham	409-564-2411
Waco	Rex Hughes	817-666-6154
Vermont		
Essex	Jack Grace	802-878-9530
Washington		
Bellevue (Seattle area)	Gene Rauscher	206-637-1416
Washington, D.C.		
D.C. Area	Joe Schneider, Howard Greer	202-362-9292
Wisconsin		
Appleton	Judy Williams	414-735-4864

But Mom, It's Only a Game...

If you have kids in your house, have kids who visit, or have friends trapped in the monotony of neotony (an indefinite period of immaturity—like my own sad case), sooner or later someone is going to want to use your home computer to play a game. In a household of adults only, choosing what games can and can't be played on your computer isn't much of an issue, unless you don't want anyone else using your computer in the first place. Otherwise, as adults, you should be able to negotiate (with a suitable degree of give and take and compromise on the part of the parties involved) what's an appropriate game for everybody's use.

Throw a couple of younger folks into the mix, though, and you could have problems. With another adult, you can negotiate; you can even just say "No," without provoking a fit of crying. With kids, you should be so lucky. Here are some strategies for dealing with kids, your computer, and games of dubious social value, or that you just don't want them to play.

Choosing Games

Choosing software games for preschool aged children, even up to age 7 or 8, is a breeze because they usually can't/won't fight you on your choice of game. You can pretty much select the games to which you want to expose your children by reading the software package for content and age recommendations. Most kids' software has an age panel on it that says "Suitable for children ages 3 and up," or something like that. This is no guarantee that the game will be good, or that your child will like it, but you can feel fairly confident that the game will be appropriate.

About the time kids break through to the (so called) age of reason—around age 7 or 8—they seem to get the most unreasonable. They know what they want and they want it *now*. They want it because it's cool, or because it's bloody and gross, or because another kid has it. Their desire usually has little to do with the game itself.

This is the stage when dealing with kids and games can be tricky. In a perfect world, there would be a big chart with all the available games on it, listing their appropriateness for various types and ages of kids. Who said the world is perfect? People are different. Kids learn, grow, and mature at different rates.

I won't presume to tell you what's appropriate for your child. If you don't want your kids playing games that involve weapons or violence, that's fine with me. It's also fine if you don't want them playing games with certain themes or with scantily clad people in sexual situations. These are some tips to help you select the games that you feel are appropriate and/or allowable in your home, on your computer.

Not My Kid, Not My Problem

If I, as a so-called expert, don't feel it's right for me to tell parents what to let their kids play, I don't expect you to do it either. When other people's children have access to your computer and collection of grown-up games, you should defer to the parent or guardian's opinion when it comes to letting their kids play your games. Make it plain to the child that it isn't your decision, and accept no "I won't tell if you let me" arguments. No weaseling.

The same rule applies when buying software games for someone else's children. Ask first. It's only polite and right.

Inform Yourself

If you have some concerns about the games your kids are playing on the family computer, you've got no choice: you have to get involved in the game buying process. Before you go shopping with your child, you need to be informed about the game's contents as far as violence, sexual images, or generally gross stuff. Part of the job is already done for you, because the child in question will probably not be shy about saying, "I want such-and-such."

You should ask the child where he saw the game. If he saw it at a friend's house, you could call and ask an adult there what the game is like (or even ask if you could play it yourself before you purchase it for your child). If he heard of the game at school, ask a teacher about it (though, odds are, there won't be anything too objectionable in a game used at school—unless another child brought it).

Sometimes kids just see something in stores or on television and decide they have to have it. Then you need to do some research. Computer magazines (like those discussed in the article "Computer Pubs") will often review kids' games for content and appropriateness. You might want to dig through back issues to see if you can find a review of the game in question.

Game magazines (if you or your child buys them) will also give you some indication of a game's content. However, these magazines (aimed at kids) don't always give the full story on content. They talk more about what's going to make the kids want the game than they do about educational content you might approve of, or other content you may not appreciate.

Other parents or friends may also know something about the game. Pick up the phone. If nothing else, they might be able to point you in a more informative direction.

If all else fails, go shopping by yourself and see if you can check out the package and/or play a demonstration copy of the game in the store.

Go Shopping Together

Not only do kids say the darnedest things, they also buy the darnedest things. If you don't want your kids playing a particular kind of game, you should go shopping with them to steer them away from forbidden games. It will help if you make it clear to the children what is and isn't allowed before you go shopping. Then, if he desires an inappropriate game, you can remind him of the rules.

When confronted with an inappropriate selection, ignore Nancy Reagan: don't "just say 'no.'" Being as specific as you can, explain why the game is inappropriate or unacceptable to you. If you don't know anything about the game, that's an acceptable reason, too. "I don't want you to buy this now because I'd like to know more about it first. We may be able to get it later, or we may not."

Kids are smart. If you explain things to them clearly, with valid reasons, they usually catch on. They may not like it, but they'll understand.

Big Brother Isn't Watching

No matter what your intentions are, you simply cannot watch a child 24 hours a day, 7 days a week. Sooner or later he or she will play a game with content you object to—at a friend's house, in an arcade, at the candy store—somewhere. Different people believe that different things are appropriate for children—that's why the kids next door get to play *Decapitation II: The Final Bloody Conflict* and your kids don't. It doesn't make the kids (or parents) next door somehow better or worse (or bad or good), just different.

Some people will also argue that it's silly to try to shield your children from sex and violence in games because it's on television shows, in commercials, and on billboards in the city where you live. That's why another part of the job of supervising kids (and it is a job) is making sure that they understand the difference between what's pretend (games, movies, television shows) and what's real. Behavior that's appropriate for a character in a game (or TV show, or movie) isn't necessarily appropriate for a real person.

Rating the Games

Folks with concerns over the content of games may have some help coming in the form of a rating system that's being devised by the Interactive Entertainment Industry Rating System Committee (IEIRSC). At the time of this writing, the committee is still being shaped; however, some form of rating system is supposed to be in place for the 1994 holiday shopping season.

The proposal is to establish a ratings panel on the order of the MPAA, the folks who rate the movies G, PG, PG-13, and so on. The ratings will appear on packages (probably as stickers) and will be a simple way for parents to judge games without having to do voluminous research beforehand. The ratings will be applied to cartridge (like Sega and Nintendo) games as well as to disk-based computer software. It will *not* be applied to arcade-type games.

The ratings will act as a supplement for parental discretion, not a replacement. And, like the ratings for movies, not everyone will agree with the committee's decisions. People will still need to do some homework to see if their idea of a "G" rated game jibes with the rating board's idea of a "G" rated game.

What About *My* Games?

While you may have strong feelings about what's an appropriate game for kids, that doesn't mean you can't have and play adult-oriented games yourself. You are a grown-up, after all. The problem is that many of the games need to be installed on a hard drive, which makes it difficult to keep games that aren't appropriate for children away from children. You might want to skip back and check out Chapter 12 for tips on keeping sensitive materials (not just games) out of reach of curious children, nosy house mates, or snooping co-workers.

Rating labels aren't a cure-all. Games will still be produced with content that some people find objectionable, and some companies may not submit their games to the rating board (just like some movies come out without a rating). Also, human nature being what it is, the game that's equivalent to an R or NC-17 movie rating that's unacceptable in your home will attract just as many people as it turns away.

Regardless of the rating system, how it's supervised, and how it's administered, adults will always need to explain to kids what is real and what is made up—what is acceptable behavior to emulate and what isn't. Kids, for their part, will always take that information with a grain of salt and a dollop of peer pressure, and then make up their own minds. In the end, you just do what you can and hope for the best.

Computing Health & Safety

E arlier on—back in Chapter 7 as a matter of fact—we talked about what you can do to keep your computer healthy and safe. Now it's time to turn the tables and give you some ideas on what you can do to keep *yourself* healthy and safe while using your computer.

Please, Don't Hurt Me!

So you're asking yourself, "Geez, how can my computer hurt me?" The obvious ways are easy to spot—that's why they're obvious. While moving it, you could drop it on your foot. A persistent hardware or software problem could cause hair loss (from you pulling it out!), loss of sleep, or even mild loss of sanity. When you finally surrender to that madness and take a baseball bat to your PC, you could be injured by a flying piece of plastic or glass. These are obvious dangers when dealing with any techno-toy.

No, *Really...*

The real dangers to watch out for are more subtle—things you may not even think about until a problem develops. The "problem" may be as simple as a minor headache, or as extreme as severe muscle pain in your neck, back, or wrists.

The exact cause of some of these extreme computer-related problems are hotly debated in the computing and medical communities. Prolonged computer use is suspected of being the cause of some problems, but they may actually be caused by other factors. No one knows for sure. So don't panic, okay? I just want to inform you, not alarm you.

The Eyes Have Had It

That headache you get after you've been working at your computer for a couple of hours may be the result of *eyestrain*, which might also manifest itself as dry/irritated eyes. The bottom line is: your eyes are stressed out and uncomfortable. There are several things you can do to cut down on the potential for eyestrain. Let's talk about each one a bit.

Reducing Glare

The first thing you should do to reduce glare is to position your computer so there isn't any direct light coming from behind you as you sit at the computer (if that's possible). Light from either side is okay, as long as the light doesn't reflect off of your monitor. If repositioning your computer isn't possible, install blinds, shades, curtains, a lot of foliage plants—anything to cut down the amount of light coming through the window while you work. The figure on the facing page shows an el-cheapo shade you can make with cardboard and tape if you're desperate.

Another trick for reducing glare is to change your shirt. If you wear a white shirt and can see it in the monitor, try changing to a darker shirt, which reflects less light. You can also try adjusting the monitor's brightness controls (if it has them) to a level that's comfortable for your eyes.

You may want to purchase an antiglare filter for your monitor. They are sheets of treated plastic or glass that cover your monitor, acting like reverse sunglasses. They reduce the amount of light that bounces off of your monitor and back into your eyes. Shop carefully for filters, though. Some will reduce the contrast on your monitor, making it hard to read; you'll swap one source of eyestrain with another.

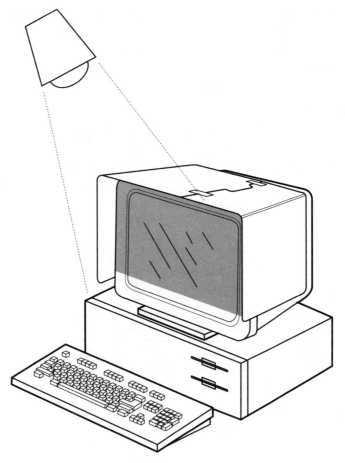

Low-budget glare protection is better than none at all.

Special Glasses

Folks who have reading glasses and wear them to work on their computers
may want to consider getting a new pair explicitly for computer use. After all,
you don't read what's on your monitor the same way you read a book or a
piece of paper. The monitor is at a different angle and is further from or closer
to your face.

An optometrist or ophthalmologist can tell you how to measure the distance at which you work from your screen, as well as the angle at which you hold your head while working. She can then adjust your prescription to one appropriate for your computer work.

Proper Lighting

Proper lighting means about half the light used in a normal office setting. Too much light can wash out the image on your monitor and make it difficult to read. The lighting, like sunlight, should not reflect off of your monitor either. Notice in the next figure that the lights are all pointing away from the computer; this prevents that old glare monster from returning.

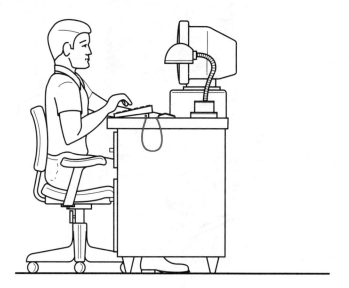

Lights should point away from your monitor.

Distance from Monitor

Maintaining an adequate distance from your monitor will also help reduce eyestrain (and reduce exposure to monitor radiation—a topic that's yet to come). It's generally agreed that you should try to work 24 to 28 inches away from your monitor.

The overall size of most desks and computers often don't give you room to distance yourself enough from your monitor. If you can't work comfortably and allow yourself the space to work, you might want to consider a keyboard tray (that attaches to the underside of your desk and slides out) or a monitor arm (that lets you reposition the monitor, rather than yourself). Both of these items are available in most computer and office supply stores.

What a Pain in the Neck!

Often related to eyestrain is neck pain, the primary victims of which are folks who do data entry from printed material. When you type from copy that's lying flat on a desk, you must constantly reposition your neck and refocus your eyes as you shift between looking at the monitor and looking at the pages on the desk. A copy stand/holder, that positions the pages from which you are typing beside your monitor will reduce neck pain and eyestrain. You'll only need to shift your eyes slightly from the monitor to the pages beside it. Copy stands are also available in most office supply and computer stores.

If you get neck pain associated with cradling a telephone with your shoulder while you work at a keyboard (like Judy, the Time-Life Operator) you may want to invest in a speaker phone (if practical) or a hands-free telephone headset. Maybe then you won't look like Quasimodo at the end of a session on your computer (*"The bells, the bells!"*).

Wheezin', Sneezin', and Rashes

Have you ever noticed how much dust and other fine particulate crud builds up on the front of your television set? A lot. That's because televisions and their kissing cousin, the computer monitor, generate a field of static electricity while they're working. The static pulls in airborne crud, which accumulates on the screen. (You should see mine after a work session with a cat in my lap. My monitor needs a *shave*, it's so hairy.)

While particulate crud is accumulating on the monitor, it's also hovering in a cloud in front of the monitor, right where you stick your face. This smut smog can irritate the eyes, aggravate allergies, and (in the very sensitive) even bring on a rash.

This is another good reason to maintain the 24- to 28-inch distance between yourself and your monitor. You may also want to occasionally clean your monitor with a specially formulated antistatic cleaner made for computer monitors. It will clean off the crud that's already accumulated, and slow down the accumulation process by temporarily reducing your monitor's static field.

Je Suis Fatigué

Just the act of sitting at a desk and staring at a computer monitor can tire you out. And after a long day of pounding those keys, you may find yourself with a sore back to boot.

The answer is just what your mother always told you: sit up straight, young (man/lady)! Don't slouch in your seat. Hunching your shoulders and leaning into the monitor, you're just asking for trouble. Seriously, you should sit with your back straight and your feet flat on the floor. When you type, your wrists should be elevated and loose—sort of like they would be if you were playing the piano. Likewise, you should hold your mouse—not strangle it. (I really should thank the woman who taught me all of this typing-posture stuff in my high school typing class, but I can't remember her name. Sorry. I took personal typing because it was immediately beneficial, and I just wanted an easy "A." It's funny how that laziness worked to my advantage.)

A padded and fully adjustable desk chair with armrests and back support will also help. Or, you may want to consider one of those science fiction-looking kneeling chairs, which are supposed to be wonderful—even if they are odd looking.

If you don't work with relaxed yet proper posture, all of those stresses on your body build up and wear you down. In addition to that end-of-the-day fatigue, you could be setting yourself up for a repetitive stress injury in the near future.

Repetitive Stress Injuries

Repetitive stress injuries (RSIs) represent a whole class of computer-related hazards unto themselves (though they are not strictly computer-related: factory/assembly workers often run into the same problems). Typing and working a computer's mouse are repetitive actions that require a very narrow range of motion. As such, the muscles that control those motions can get boogered up (that's a medical term I just learned) if you use them too much. Tendonitis (pain and inflammation) and Carpal Tunnel Syndrome (*lots* of pain and physical damage to tendons and tissue) can result over prolonged periods. Pain stinks. Carpal Tunnel Syndrome, in extreme cases, can require corrective surgery. (It isn't pretty; my sister's had the surgery twice. Ouch.)

Symptoms of pending difficulty include: numbness and tingling (that "pins and needles" feeling), aching/tiredness in the affected muscles (wrist, arms, shoulders, neck), and outright muscle pain. Any of these symptoms can temporarily affect computer users. They become a concern when they become chronic and/or persistent. When they do, call a doctor—quickly.

The best way to avoid repetitive stress injuries is to listen to your body. If you've been working for, say, forty-five minutes, and your wrists are starting to get tired, stop. Take a break. Do some gentle finger and wrist stretches and exercises. Shake your hands gently at your sides to get the blood flowing again. Do some office aerobics to stretch and limber the affected muscles or gently massage them. Just go do something else for ten minutes. (Personally, I find doing laundry is a great way to break up my computing day. Put in a load; go to work. In 40 minutes, the wash is done: take it out, put it in the dryer, put another load in the wash. It pretty much enforces a schedule of doing something else, with different muscles, for ten or fifteen minutes every hour. But I only do laundry one day a week. . . .)

Additionally, some find the use of keyboard and mouse (or trackball) wrist rests of some benefit. I use both. They give you a padded place to rest your wrists when you're not typing or mousing around. Both keyboard and mouse wrist-rests, like most of the items mentioned, are available in computer and office supply stores, and they come in a terrifying array of fashion colors and patterns.

What About Radiation?

Some will answer, "What about it?" Others will stage protest marches and petition-signings. Computer-related radiation is one of the most highly contentious debates going on today.

The radiation comes from the cathode-ray tube—the picture tube, in television parlance—which works by bombarding the inside of the monitor's screen with a stream of electrons. (It's because of the cathode-ray tube that some folks still refer to monitors as CRTs.) The cathode-ray tube, by its nature, generates electromagnetic fields of varying degrees. The ones you'll hear the most about are usually referred to as VLF or ELF. You pronounce each letter, V-L-F and E-L-F. (If you told someone you were worried that a computer elf was harming you, they'd call an ambulance for you—or send you to the funny farm.)

477

VLF refers to Very Low Frequency electromagnetic fields and radiation. ELF refers to Extremely Low Frequency fields. These fields are generated by electrical appliances—even your refrigerator and toaster—not just your computer. They even surround power lines, which just relay electricity. The electromagnetic fields that surround computer monitors are strongest in the back and at the sides, and they diminish rapidly in strength as you get further away from them. The electromagnetic radiation from these fields is *non-ionizing*, which means it doesn't break apart atoms like ionizing radiation (such as X-rays) can.

These low-level emissions of magnetic radiation have been associated (without a proven cause-and-effect relationship) with increased rates of cancer, miscarriage, cataracts, and birth defects, all very scary problems. Studies have shown, for example, that women who work around computer monitors for more than 20 hours a week have a higher rate of miscarriages. But no one has been able to successfully prove that the emissions cause the health problems. There are too many other variables involved, not only with the monitors and users, but in the surroundings. Offices are full of dangerous and unhealthy factors (including plain old work-related stress) that may be primary or secondary causes of the observed health problems.

So the controversy rages on. In this country there are no accepted standards for what is and isn't safe for electromagnetic radiation exposure. Common sense dictates that, if you're concerned about these emissions, you should at least sit further away from your monitor (or anyone else's), since the radiation level decreases rapidly with distance.

You can also take further steps. Some antiglare filters also shield users from part of the electromagnetic radiation. You can also purchase monitor cowls, which reduce VLF and ELF emissions. A company called NoRAD manufactures a full line of antiradiation devices. If you'd like more information, you can give them a call at 1-800-262-3260.

If you're purchasing a new monitor, look for one that says it conforms to Sweden's limits on ELF and VLF emissions. Or, you could purchase an LCD (liquid crystal display) or LED (light emitting diode) monitor like those built in to many laptop computers. They don't use a cathode-ray tube and, therefore, don't emit electromagnetic radiation.

To my way of thinking, even though the dangers aren't proven, there are simple things I can do to reduce the risk of exposure. Why not play it safe and just do them? I always play safe, or I don't play at all.

Speaking Of Safety

There are two other things you might want to think about (while I have you in this heightened state of safety-consciousness): home and computer security.

If you're the kind of person for whom personal safety and the security of your home are big concerns, you might want to put your computer to yet another use. You can, in fact, equip your computer to act as a home monitor. With entry sensors (that tell you when a door or window has been opened) and motion sensors (that, well, detect motion), you can turn your home computer into Security Central. You can also add smoke detectors and emergency pagers of the "I've fallen and can't get up" variety. And there are simpler versions that control lights and appliances, turning them on and off on timers to make it look like you're at home when you aren't.

If you're interested in these possibilities, you can find advertising in the back of most popular computer publications. The main drawback of these systems is that you have to leave your computer turned on while you're away or when you want to use the alarm options while you're at home.

While you're thinking about how your computer can help you feel more secure, you might want to return the favor by making your computer feel secure. There are a few companies that offer computer insurance to protect your hardware and software investment. Your home computer may not be covered by a typical homeowner's or renter's insurance policy. Ask your insurance agent, to be sure.

No coverage? No problem, you can call Safeware at 1-800-800-1492. Their policies start at as little as $49 per year, and cover your computer against theft, fire, and water damage. Earthquake protection (and protection against other acts of God) will cost extra.

Special Needs Computing

ere's a great big secret: almost everything in this world is geared toward the lowest common denominator. Whatever most people appear to do or think or have or feel is considered "normal," and the world at large is structured around that concept of normalcy.

And here's another great secret: Everybody's got at least one thing that knocks them right out of the "normal" range. Since abnormal is the norm, here's how we cope: We coast through the stuff we're "normal" in, and adapt in the areas we aren't.

This chapter is about adapting computer technology to whatever may be "abnormal" about you or me or someone we know. Computers are too wonderful a tool for folks to avoid them simply because they're designed for statistically average folks with two hands, ten fingers, two average eyes, ears, and all that other "normal" junk. They can be adapted to almost any special need.

There is, in fact, so much information and technology out there to help folks adapt computer technology to their needs, that there's too much to cover in this chapter. So here's the deal: I'll talk about specific things like accessories that are available to adapt your computer, and broad categories like adapting to vision and motor skill deficiencies. Then I'll give you some resources to help you track down the things I didn't have space for that deal with very specific issues.

Hidden Treasures

Maybe when you bought your Macintosh or IBM compatible computer, you and your family members didn't have any difficulty using it. But something happened—simple aging, disease, an accident, anything—and now you need to adapt your computer to a new set of needs.

Macintosh Goodies

When Apple Computer started their "One person, one computer" philosophy, they realized that not all people use a computer the same way. From the start, they included software to help users tailor their Macs to their needs. In every set of System software disks, there is a set of control panels that make Macs easier to use for folks with impaired vision and/or motor skills.

The Views control panel (shown here), introduced with System 7.0, lets the user specify the font (typeface) and font size for file and folder names and the other text displayed in windows on the desktop. In addition, it lets the user choose what information is displayed and the size of the small icons that appear when listing files and folders by name. Changing the settings in the Views control panel can ease eyestrain for folks without visual impairment and make life much easier for folks with mild to moderate impairment.

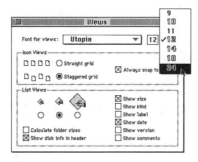

The Macintosh Views control panel.

The CloseView control panel is on the Tidbits disk, from your original set of System disks. This control panel enables you to enlarge a part of the screen display for easy reading or to provide a bigger target to click on with a mouse or other input device. You can set magnification as low as 2x (double) or as high as 16x.

For folks unable to execute multiple-key combination (like ⌘-S for Save), Apple provides the Easy Access control panel, which is also found on your Tidbits System disk. Easy Access gives you three sets of customizing options: Mouse Keys, Slow Keys, and Sticky Keys.

With the Mouse Keys options, you can substitute keys on your Mac's numeric keypad (on an extended keyboard) for mouse movement. Slow Keys lengthen the amount of time between when a key is pressed and when a character appears on the screen, which helps to avoid unwanted keystrokes. The Sticky Keys option lets you press a key combination (like ⌘-S for Save) one key at a time, instead of having to press both keys simultaneously.

The Mac's Easy Access control panel.

All of the control panels mentioned here are discussed fully (including installation and instructions for use) in your *Macintosh User's Guide.*

Speaking of/to Computers

Folks with visual and/or manual impairments may also benefit from the new line of computers that you can actually speak commands to. These computers let you tell them what you want them to do. Any command that is in a menu can be spoken aloud, and the computer will execute it. You can also have your computer read a text file to you (don't confuse this with a screen reading utility, which I'll discuss later).

Currently, Apple's AV (for audio-visual) Macs, and Compaq's Presaria computer come with this option as part of the package. I'm sure that, eventually, you'll be able to buy the voice recognition software for other comparable machines.

The technology isn't perfect yet. You still need to do some manual work with the keyboard and/or mouse (it won't type a document for you). And if you don't speak clearly, the computer can grossly misinterpret some of your spoken words. But it's a start, and it will improve as the bugs are worked out.

To obtain information about the many Mac-related disability solutions available, check the Resources appendix under Macintosh Disability Resources.

MS-DOS

Users of DOS-compatible computers can get a suite of utilities, called AccessDOS, similar to those for the Mac. Developed by the Trace R & D Center at the University of Wisconsin-Madison, AccessDOS makes using MS-DOS easier for people who are movement and/or hearing impaired. It includes utilities for:

◆ Single-fingered typing of key combinations.

◆ Ignoring accidental keystrokes (like Slow Keys for Mac).

◆ Adjusting the key repeat rate.

◆ Controlling the mouse pointer with the keyboard.

◆ Controlling keyboard and mouse with an alternative device.

◆ Providing a visual cue when the computer makes a sound.

You can turn the utilities on and off as needed, and there's extensive on-line help. AccessDOS is available free from Microsoft's Customer Sales and Service (see the Resources appendix.)

If you have a modem and membership in either CompuServe or GEnie (see "On-Line Services" in Part V) you can download any or all of the AccessDOS components from either service or from Microsoft's Download Service (look in the Resources appendix for more information).

For Windows Users

There is also a suite of utilities similar to AccessDOS that's available for users of Microsoft Windows. It's called the Windows Access Pack. It too is available free from Microsoft's Customer Sales and Service and by modem from the bulletin board services mentioned above.

Other Visual Accessories

Now we get into the areas where there are *so* many options available, that it would be impossible to review or recommend any particular product.

For folks with severe visual impairment I can't think of a better thing to have than a screen reading utility. A screen reader makes computers (especially those with a picture-based interface, like Macs and Windows machines) completely accessible to blind and visually impaired users.

Screen readers replace visual elements of the screen (icons, menus, etc.) with spoken words. Generally, they also replace mouse movement with keyboard commands (a Braille keyboard may help, too). When an item is selected on-screen, the computer speaks the icon or file name, reads the list of menu commands, and allows the user to respond to audio rather than visual cues.

There are a variety of screen readers available for most computer platforms (Mac, DOS, Windows). There will be help on where to find them, coming up.

Help with Motor Skills

People with limited motor abilities have a vast array of computer accessories available to them.

There are simplified and adjustable keyboards to make typing and keystroke commands easier, and macro programs that can reduce a complex set of actions to a single keystroke. Users with only one hand can install special keyboard "maps" in their computers (Mac or IBM-compatible), which reconfigure a two-handed keyboard to left or right hand keyboards. People who cannot use their hands, but have good head and mouth control, can replace their mouse- or trackball-like pointing device with a headpiece that lets you turn and puff (instead of pointing and clicking).

None of these options require expensive, high-end computer systems, but they can be expensive in and of themselves. A headpiece pointing device for Macintosh (the Prentke Romich HeadMaster) ranges in price from just under $1000 (for a basic model), to almost $1800 (for a wireless model).

Hearing Impaired Users Can Save Money!

While there aren't many computer accessories specifically for the hearing impaired, you can put your computer and modem to good use, and save some money, too.

Many commercial telecommunications software packages (like those reviewed in this book) are capable of emulating (pretending to be) a TDD (Telecommunications Device for the Deaf). A *TDD* is a device that attaches to your telephone and allows you to type a conversation back and forth with another TDD user. Instead of having to buy a stand-alone TDD (sometimes called TTYs, or text telephones), you can use your computer and modem, and save yourself the extra expense. If you've already got a TDD, you can use your computer and modem as a spare.

Resources

If you'd like help tracking down an accessory mentioned here, or need solutions for a specific set of computer-related hassles, check Appendix B.

You can also find a wide variety of information (with a modem and membership) on any of the national computer services (such as America Online and CompuServe). I think all of them have a forum devoted to disabilities.

In the meantime, have fun and happy computing!

Attention Employers!

Since the Americans With Disabilities Act (ADA) took effect, if you are concerned or confused about how to make your office computers accessible to disabled employees, you have a resource of your very own. The Technology Assistance Act set up ten regional centers to help employers with information and referrals. You can call 1-800-949-4232, and you'll be connected to the center in your region.

Virtual Reality

Virtual reality is a tough concept to nail down. In fact, it's virtually impossible. (I just *had* to say that.) But let's take a whack at it. The problem of explaining what it is stems from the fact that what most people think of virtual reality comes from what they've gleaned from network television ("Wild Palms" and "Mad About You") and the movies (*Lawnmower Man*), two industries not well known for their accurate information integrity.

Virtually Virtual Reality

If you look at the phrase "virtual reality," you'll notice that it's made up of two words: "virtual," meaning (and I'm paraphrasing here) so close that it might as well be the real thing; and "reality," meaning whatever reality means (I'm not touching that one). But if a "virtual impossibility" is something so difficult that it may as well be impossible, then a "virtual reality" is something so nearly real that it may as well be real.

When virtual reality gets bandied about in books and magazines and on television shows, it is generally referring to computer software and hardware that creates a three-dimensional representation of a thing or place that "looks" and "feels" so much like the real thing, it could fool you into thinking it is that real thing. Usually (in movies at least) this is accomplished by a sort of sensory immersion: your body gets covered in things that simulate the normal sensory input you get from the world, making the virtual world "feel" and "look" real.

In the computer world, you see the virtual world through goggles that don't let you look at anything else. You touch the world through gloves that at once send your hand gestures to the computer to issue commands (pick up that vase) and return tactile information that fakes your hand (in that glove) into thinking you're holding a vase. You can then put it down, pour the water out of it, or throw it against a virtual wall, just like you could with a real vase.

Some forward-thinking people (and fans of *Star Trek: The Next Generation* and *Deep Space Nine*) even envision a virtual reality scenario that gives you the same sensory experience, but without the ton of hardware strapped to your body.

If you're looking for the "total body contact" type of virtual reality, you'll have to get in line and wait with the rest of us. While it is being worked on in research labs all over the place, that kind of virtual reality is still (by conservative estimates) five or more years down the road. Unfortunately, movies, television, and fiction tend to focus on the finished product, regardless of its current state of undress.

What's in Your Future?

When full contact virtual reality arrives, what sorts of things will you be able to do with it? Practically anything. If it can be imagined and programmed into a computer, you'll probably be able to do it with virtual reality hardware and software. Here are just a few ideas:

- ◆ Virtual sports: take your position as tight end on your favorite football team and prepare to tackle and be tackled by officially licensed representations of famous sports figures.

- ◆ Virtual dating: strap on your cybersuit and log into a Virtual Hernando's Hideaway, where you can meet your virtual date (made up by a computer) or a virtual representation of a real person who's also suited up and on-line. If you take a liking to each other and promise to respect each other in the morning, virtual dating could lead to virtual mating.

- ◆ Virtual learning: instead of packing a lunch and trundling your kids off to the school bus every morning, you might just have to pack them into their VR suits. Students could then log-on and meet in a virtual classroom. (But will they be able to pass virtual notes? And if they get caught, will they get virtual detention?)

- ◆ Virtual testing: imagine having to successfully perform a VR simulation of a new surgery technique in order to first learn the technique and again later to maintain your board certification. Would you believe there could be virtual driving and piloting tests? It could happen.

VR also promises a lot for folks with physical impairments that prevent them from experiencing some physical activities. Imagine being able to put on a VR suit and play baseball (or anything) when before VR your arms or legs (or lack of same) prevented you from it. Very cool.

Will I be Able to Use My Current Computer?

Let's put it this way: probably. When VR products are finally sold to the consumer market, what are then the high-end computers will most likely be able to use the VR goodies. VR won't succeed commercially if people have to buy expensive new computers to use the other expensive new VR stuff. I mean, it won't be much of a consumer market if people aren't consuming.

Whether that will be the computer you have on your desk right now, or the one you'll be buying two or three years from now is beyond my knowledge. It depends on how fast they can get VR products to the consumer market and what technological advances happen in the meantime. While a million years is a mere snip of time in geological time frames, two years is practically an epoch in terms of technology.

In the Meantime . . .

It's easy enough to say, "You'll just have to wait," but it's a lot harder to do. If you want or need a VR fix right now, you have a couple of options available to you.

In the World at Large

While you're waiting for your virtual date to call you up and give you his or her virtual address and v-mail node, there are a number of things currently available that are getting kind of close to that sort of virtual reality. And they're probably all happening in a mall near you.

◆ Virtual games: there are limited VR implementations on the market where you buy a ticket and put on a glove and goggles, and you can blast other players with virtual ray guns. There are also simulations of dangerous adventures: flying helicopters, jets, and even the space shuttle.

◆ Virtual rides: buy a ticket, and you can ride a virtual roller coaster or a rocket to Mars. They're enclosed capsule-like things with a movie screen in the front. You watch the movie simulation while the capsule shakes, rattles, and rolls you as appropriate to the "ride." These used to be pretty lame, but they're getting better.

If you don't have a mall nearby, or the mall isn't VR-friendly, you can always take a trip to Las Vegas, Nevada. Since every state in the nation, it seems, is legalizing some form of gambling (lotteries, if not casino-type gambling), Vegas has remade itself into an entertainment Mecca—in addition to a gambling one. Many casino-hotels offer high-tech rides and entertainment based on virtual reality principles. If nothing else, it will give your children something to do (since kids aren't allowed on the gambling floor), and it will give you a chance to do something other than plug quarters into a slot machine.

In Your Own Little Corner of Your Own Little Room

There are a number of games and computer applications that will let you get a feel for what virtual reality will be like in the future. Playing many CD-ROM games is like stepping into another world. Games like The Journeyman Project by Presto Studios, and Myst (shown below) from Broderbund Software, create detailed photo-realistic worlds that incorporate live-action video and animation. It's easy to get lost in these virtual worlds (I've lost uncounted hours to Myst, and I'm afraid to continue the Journeyman Project because the time-loss potential looks just as high).

A view of the Channelwood Age in Myst. It really is a whole 'nother world.

For More Info...

You can learn more about CDs, CD-ROM, and multimedia-type games in the Reviews section of this book.

However, if games aren't your style, you can concoct your own virtual world with programs like Virtus WalkThrough. Virtus WalkThrough, for example, lets you create a cyberspace of your own, either patterned after the real world (like the house shown in the figure below) or completely of your own imagining. You can also launch yourself into cyberspace, without the physical sensations of virtual reality, by firing up your modem and meeting and greeting the folks you meet on an on-line service, such as those discussed in Part V of the book in the articles on the information superhighway and on-line services.

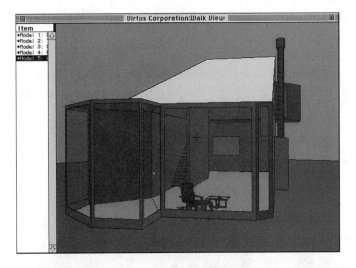

A virtual house, constructed with Virtus WalkThrough. It's called WalkThrough (oddly enough) because you can walk through your creation as if it were a real, three-dimensional space.

While we amuse ourselves with *virtual* virtual reality, I'm going to go on a diet. I don't want to look too chubby in a VR suit when the real thing comes along.

The Information Superhighway

G o ahead, get them out of your system now. You know, the obligatory information "highway" puns: digital speed bumps, road kill, rest stops, passing lane, fast lane, cruise control, and so on. I'll wait.

Unless you've been spending time on another planet, you've probably heard and seen piles of hype about the information superhighway: from Vice President Gore on C-Span or in commercials by your phone company, cable company, on-line services, and computer companies. You've even seen commercials by people and wondered who they are or what their stake is in all this.

There's been lots of fluff about the information superhighway, but not much you could call substance. No one wants to answer the questions that are probably foremost in your mind—like what is it exactly? When will it happen? And, what's in it for me?

The trouble is that nobody's quite sure, yet, what the actual thing will be like; they only know what they want it to do. You'll hear phrases like "movies on demand," "shopping at home," "video telephones," and even "home news services" (like those used by newspapers and television news programs), all pouring right into your home via fiber optic cables.

So What Is It? A Phone Thing? A Cable Thing? A Computer Thing?

When you get right down to the nitty gritty, it's a computer thing. It will all be based on computer technology. However, you might not use a "computer" (at least not a desktop computer as you currently know it) to access and travel the information superhighway. You'll probably use some sort of information appliance that's hooked to your television. The monitor will be a television, or at least be like a television. The keyboard and mouse will probably be replaced by some simpler control, on the order of a television's remote control. At the heart of it, however, will be computing power similar to that of a desktop computer. Naturally, you should be able to use your computer with appropriate hardware and software to access many of the same information services.

TV Services You're Likely to See

Name any TV service or program, and I'd say you'll see it, probably a couple of times and under different names. Take every pay-per-whatever service you can think of (pay-per-view, shopping, on-line services—and don't forget your psychic pals and other 900-number services) and multiply them by about 10 or 20.

Think about it. They're promising that something like 500–1000 information "channels" will be available, all offering a variety of services. Right now, many cable systems offer in the vicinity of 80 channels, and there are still long stretches of time when there's nothing worth looking at on the tube. One of the biggest challenges to the info-highway will be finding enough stuff to fill all of those new channels with quality shows and services that people will actually want to use.

Most likely, any goof with the capital necessary to start one will have an information service of some kind. Infomercials (like those for the Flowbee vacuum-cleaner-barber-thingy) could be an entire network instead of just an hour commercial. Ted Turner will launch his "Toons on Demand Network," so you can pay $3 to watch Bugs Bunny in "What's Opera, Doc?" whenever you want ("Kill da WA-bbit, kill da WA-bbit").

There will be as many goofy things to do as serious or practical ones. Some of the ones you may actually want to use (although I will watch "What's Opera, Doc?" as often as I can stand it) might include:

◆ The (insert movie studio name here) Channel, where you can sort through all of the movies in a studio's vaults and watch one whenever you want.

- The Video Conferencing Channel, like the current 3-way calling option available to most phone users, only with pictures and more callers. You'll be able to call people you choose (like family members on holidays), or one of those 900-number talk lines so you can talk to scantily clad strangers. (At least it will force people to be honest; no more Orson Welles look-alikes saying they look like Jean-Claude Van Damme.)

- The (insert department store name here) Channel, where stores like Sears, J.C. Penney's, Bloomingdales, and K-Mart let you sift through their basic stock and order anything you'd normally run out to a mall or store to get. And don't forget supermarkets and companies that already have a strong catalog mail-order business (like Land's End or L.L. Bean).

- The News Channel, where you'll be able to specify a search word or phrase, and any news story that contains that word or phrase will be marked for you. You can then read/watch the stories, and (if they're what you're looking for) save them to a disk, a video tape, or print them out. You could also get whole newspapers and magazines the same way—without those annoying subscription and perfume cards.

- Probably, there will also be channels that reproduce the form, substance, and function of most of the on-line services that are currently available. Instead of dialing into America Online with your computer and modem, you could access it just by changing the channel.

Local "Programming"

Just as you find commercials for local stores and restaurants on television now, when the info superhighway rolls up to your door, you'll be able to order goods and services from local retailers, too. Imagine, not just movies, but *pizza* on demand! Sweet and sour pork! Groceries! They will all be available with the push of a few buttons on your "information appliance." (You may ooh and ahh at will.)

Local newspapers, maybe even video news, will be dropped in your digital mailbox, rather than chucked behind your rose bushes or up on your roof. The entire range of services that will be available on a national level will probably be available from merchants in your area.

TV Channels—So You Mean It's a Cable Thing?

Well, that depends on who wins the media slug-fest. Right now the phone companies and the cable companies are going toe-to-toe to see who gets to deliver the superhighway to your door. The phone companies have the advantage of already being in more homes than cable companies, but in order to take charge of the superhighway, they have to reconstruct their systems to make total use of fiber optics (because regular, old-fashioned phone lines and switching systems can't handle the extra burden of digital video and text the way fiber optics can).

The cable companies have the advantage of already having systems in place that are "interactive." In most cable systems, you can pick up your cable remote (or telephone) and order a pay-per-view event, such as a movie or a boxing match. It isn't "on demand" yet, though. You have to watch when the event is scheduled to run, not whenever you feel like it—which is one of the big selling points for the information superhighway. With the systems that are being proposed, you would be able to see any TV show at any time you wanted. (That's just a small part of the big picture. But for those of us who haven't seen Letterman since the '80s because he comes on too late, it's going to be great.)

Whichever industry wins the slug-fest (or even both if it's a draw) will then have to refine and restructure the way they deliver information to accommodate all of the different kinds of services that will be funnelled to your television or home computer. That's going to be a big, long-term, expensive job.

Haven't We Got an Info Highway Already?

The answer is a resounding "Yes and No." Yes, we can already do most of the things the media-types are hyping about the superhighway.

Pay-per-view delivers movies all the time, if not exactly when we want them. QVC and the Home Shopping Club (among other cable shop-at-home channels) offer around the clock shopping, but you have to want what they're showing at that given moment. You can't call up and say "I'm looking for a Navajo Squash Blossom necklace, or something similar—show me what you have." You have to wait until they're doing a western jewelry show and hope they have what you want. Likewise, the commercial computer services, like America Online, CompuServe, and even your small, local bulletin boards also offer shopping, information, and even real-time discussions and e-mail correspondence.

While we can already do many of the things the pundits promise in this brave new world of information, we have to use different tools to do them, and many are only available at certain times. The thing about the superhighway (if you can believe the hype) is that it will be whatever you want, whenever you want it, through one central "information appliance."

Roadblocks on the Information Superhighway

Sorry, I thought I got all of those puns out of my system. I guess I was wrong. Right now, the only things standing between us and the world of unlimited access and information are three big concerns: economic, social, and legal concerns.

Dollars and Sense

The economic concern is easy: who's got the money to put the machinery in place. The government has decided it can't do it alone, so they want to just help shape the network (sometimes called the NII, National Information Infrastructure) but let the private sector pay for and build it.

Whoever wins the job is going to spend, and then make, an awful lot of money. That's why there's so much competition between potential service providers. Whoever controls the actual network (the phone, cable, or other lines) will make money from both subscribers (like you and me) and providers (like movie studios and department stores).

To Have and Have Not

The social issues are a little stickier. Will the advent of the information super-highway create a new class system? We already have class distinctions based on income. Will there be a new set of digital outcasts based on who has access to information and who doesn't? If we want to avoid that, who picks up the tab for folks who can't afford the equipment and fees to participate?

If we don't provide the wherewithal to access the network, how do we get the information to these folks? The already disenfranchised may, for lack of vital information (such as voting information, network-based health and education programs, even job listings), become complete outcasts. How do they change their status if they don't have the access to the information they need in order to change?

Is Big Brother Watching?

Then there are the legal issues: Do we want unlimited national access to what some might consider digital pornography, or is there some way to restrict it without infringing on the First Amendment rights of the producers, service providers, and folks who want to use such services? Do the rights to freedom of speech and a free press apply when there is no actual speech, and no presses, paper, and ink involved?

There's also the privacy issue. The various law enforcement branches of the government (such as the CIA and FBI) want to build easy-access wire-tapping support into the information infrastructure. They want to be able to listen in on the exchanges between criminals and/or terrorists who might use the back alleys of the network to plan and execute crimes. Law enforcement agencies would also like to limit what you can do to protect your data from being accessed by unauthorized users (via a coding system known as encryption) so that the law enforcers can decode anything traveling the superhighway. Essentially, it's no good tapping the private correspondence of people if you can't read it once you have it.

There's also a plan to mandate the inclusion of a computer chip into all tele-communication devices (telephones, modems, fax machines, you name it). The chip, known as Clipper or the Clipper Chip, would allow government agencies to locate and monitor any communications device anywhere that has the built-in chip. They would be able to do all this without the current need to get a warrant or prove probable cause, and without any other protections to privacy guaranteed by the Constitution and the Bill of Rights. While the goal is to prevent and prosecute crimes and criminals, everyone's privacy would be affected by such a measure.

The agencies claim that law abiding people have nothing to fear. So the public-spirited part of me says "fine." Catching crooks and other no-goodniks is a good thing, especially if you can catch them before someone dies or something blows up. Yet, the privacy-minded side of me gets nervous just thinking about who will be making decisions to tap or not to tap. That's the kind of paranoia-inducing junk my grandparents fled the old Soviet Union over. I'd feel much better knowing that there wasn't some government drone in an office somewhere, whose only job is to figure out where I am, what I'm doing, who I'm talking to, and whether or not I pose a threat to national security. Trust me: I'm not dangerous.

If You're Concerned...

I know I'm concerned about the right to privacy for us regular folks who spend a good bit of time on-line. If you are too (or if you just want more information before you decide to panic), there are two organizations you can join or contact to ask for more details. (These are the Internet addresses I'll be giving you; that's the geekiest way for computer geeks to correspond. You'll need to have at least membership in an on-line service with the Internet access to use them. Check out the Internet information later in the book for ways to send electronic mail to the Internet addresses.)

The Electronic Frontier Foundation is a group that any concerned person may ask for information or may join if he wants to enlist in the campaign. Contact them by sending e-mail to: **membership@eff.org**. Or you may want to send e-mail to Computer Professionals for Social Responsibility (CPSR). Their e-mail address is: **cpsr.info@cpsr.org**.

Someday Soon . . .

So when will the information superhighway fall into place? Not for some time yet. First the issues discussed above have to be resolved to everyone's satisfaction. Give that a couple of years.

Then the machinery has to be put in place, which means another year or two before even limited services can be offered. Count on a few more years for the real gee-whiz stuff (video conferencing, everything-on-demand, and so on). My guess would be, then, shortly after the turn of the century. We'll finally get to see whether 2001 the year looks like *2001* the movie—and we'll be able to watch that movie whenever we want. I'll make the popcorn.

On-Line Services

The realm of on-line services and digital computer-to-computer communications is almost like a parallel dimension. It really is another world. Call it cyberspace, Cyberia, the datasphere, hyperspace—call it anything you like—just call it (with a modem, of course).

Some say this parallel dimension is the true foundation of the global village, because a bureaucrat can't sneeze in one nation without a bunch of on-line types saying "*Gesundheit!*" and pondering at length of the implications of that sneeze. In the last few years, e-mail and on-line postings have kept us informed on the status of cities after earthquakes and riots and governments after coup attempts, and have given us information in spite of traditional media blackouts (for instance, some dish on a famous trial or investigation where a judge has issued a gag order).

While some folks sit, sigh, and wonder why the information superhighway hasn't beaten a path to their doors yet, others are cruising an information two-lane highway, just waiting for the road crews to come along to widen it and up the speed limit.

An On-Line Road Map

You'll find more information about, and references to, on-line services and telecommunication accessories salted throughout this book. For example:

◆ Modems are discussed in Chapter 2.

◆ Communications software is reviewed in the "Reviews" section.

◆ Other related topics, including on-line job searches, telecommuting, senior services, special needs computing, the information superhighway, on-line shopping, electronic pen pals, the Internet, and computer clubs, are covered in the sundry articles here in Part V.

The sheer amount of information about the on-line world should give you an idea of its important role in the future of computing. Not to mention the fact that it's a lot of fun. To help you better understand the on-line services that are available, this article is a round-up/review of the major players, some of the smaller players, and players we haven't seen but who are warming up in the wings. We will also give you tips for tracking down small home-brew bulletin boards (BBSs) in your own home town.

The opinions expressed here are purely my own. I say that because I'm highly opinionated on the subject, and I know it. You aren't me, and you don't have my needs and tastes (or lack of taste). Don't let my opinion sway you too much. You've got a brain; make up your own mind.

P Is for Prodigy

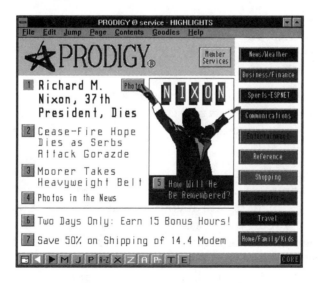

The Prodigy Highlights screen, Windows version.

If you've read *The Complete Idiot's Guide to the Mac*, you know I don't like Prodigy. But I was taken to task over my dismissal of it by some friends who like and use Prodigy, so (in the interests of fairness) I thought I'd try it again and see if it has changed since last I used it.

Prodigy has changed, but not enough for my tastes. It's slow (some folks refer to it as *Plod*-igy), it's difficult to use (too many steps to do simple tasks), and the range of services offered is painfully shallow compared to other on-line services. Plus, it's expensive (see the sidebar entitled "Prodigy Pricing").

Many of the features (like sending unlimited e-mail) that are part of the package price with services like America Online, cost you extra on Prodigy. Likewise, many of the features that are the big draws on other services (such as live real-time chat rooms) are missing from Prodigy. The Prodigy interface is clunky and tedious (and, frankly, unattractive).

The most annoying problem, in my opinion, is the flood of junk mail you get from Prodigy's on-line vendors (which takes time to delete even if you don't read it). The constant barrage of advertising across the bottom of the screen is also crass. The ads are drawn before the parts of the screen that you want to see, which also takes up your time while the meter is ticking. (Maybe I'm just spoiled.)

To be fair(ish), Prodigy *has* drawn an impressive array of special celebrity guests to their service. Sue Grafton, author of one of my favorite series of mystery novels (*A Is for Alibi* through *K Is for Killer*), was the *celeb du jour* the last time I was on-line. I love her.

Other fun areas on Prodigy include gobs of shopping, sports/weather/news coverage, tons of on-line events and contests (many involving celebrity appearances), horoscopes, and lots of special interest boards on which to read and post responses.

If all you're interested in doing is reading and posting messages in the wealth of bulletin board areas, reading news (top stories, weather, sports), and shopping, Prodigy might be worth your time and money. If there are younger folks in the house, Prodigy is especially worthwhile; it's very wholesome. But if you're looking for live chat, you want to send more than 30 e-mail messages (of one hundred or fewer words) a month, and you want to download a wide variety of software and information, Prodigy may not be the way to go.

Prodigy Pricing

Prodigy offers seven different pricing plans. Their basic "Value Plan" costs $14.95/month, for which you get unlimited hours in the free "Core" areas, and two hours in the "Plus" (extra charge) areas. You also get 30 free e-mail messages (not full messages, necessarily, but per page messages—roughly 100 words). After you exhaust your free time, you're charged $0.06/minute in the Plus areas. Additional messages are $0.25 per message page (of about 100 words). (These prices are current as of the time of this writing but, like everything in life, are subject to change without notice.)

You can get a Prodigy startup kit in book and computer stores, but it's expensive. You can get a nearly free one (just a charge for shipping and handling) by calling 1-800-PRODIGY. Prodigy software (and all on-line service software) is regularly included in a promotional package when you buy a modem.

CIS Is for CompuServe Information Service

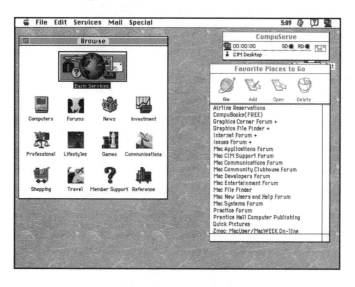

CompuServe Information Manager, Macintosh Version.

I use CompuServe on a pretty regular basis. I guess that makes me a CIS-sy. CompuServe is probably the world's largest centralized base of on-line information (not counting the Internet, because its information is spread out over a lot of different computers). CompuServe has nearly a thousand different subject areas, most of which are primarily aimed at business professionals and/or computer business professionals. There's even an extensive on-line mall, where you can order just about anything from the comfort of your home, office, or home office.

You can find jobs, look up a phone number listed in any Yellow Pages in the U.S., get stock market quotes, and research news stories by selective retrieval (you post a search string—a word or phrase—and the service will return any and all news stories containing that string). There is an incredible amount of information. You can also read and post material to and from discussion boards, download software, and contact thousands of other users via e-mail and live discussions in the forums.

All this business-targeted stuff is available at a business-like price: it's expensive (see the sidebar entitled "CompuServe Pricing" for details) and you don't get any "free" hours each month, as you do on other services. In spite of the cost, if what you're looking for is information (and lots of it) for personal or work-related use, CompuServe is probably a wise investment. However, if you're more interested in the social aspects of the life on-line, you may be happier with another service. The lack of any free hours really kills the urge to chat. (I know I keep saying to myself, "This is nice, but not for $5 an hour. Those 900 numbers are cheaper.")

You can access CompuServe with just about any telecommunications software, but it makes navigation very difficult for beginners. You're better off investing in CompuServe's Information Manager (shown in the figure at the top of the section) or CompuServe Navigator. Either package will give you a friendlier interface and will save you time and money on-line.

The Information Manager is good for folks who like to surf around and explore. The Navigator will automate your sessions so you can log on, snag your e-mail, download files, and get out of there with a minimum of time and fuss. Both are available in book and computer stores and by mail order. The Information Manager costs around $40, and the Navigator runs approximately $70. Both include usage credits to offset the cost of the software, and both are available for most computer platforms.

CompuServe Pricing

If you buy the boxed version of the CompuServe signup kit (about $40), you get a copy of its CompuServe Information Manager software and a $25 usage credit. Hourly charges, under CompuServe's Standard Plan, are $4.80/hour for modem speeds from 300 to 9600 baud; 14400 baud modems are charged $9.60/hour.

Many of CIS's "information bases" incur additional charges by the hour and/or minute. You're always warned before you access a service with additional charges. There are no extra prime time charges for using the service between the hours of 6 AM and 6 PM, Monday through Friday.

As always, prices are current as of the time of this writing but, like everything in life, are subject to change without notice. Alternate pricing plans are available. You can get more information by calling 1-800-848-8199.

AOL Is for America Online

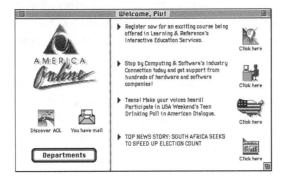

America Online, Macintosh Version.

Personal prejudice rears its ugly head again. America Online is my favorite on-line service. I started using it four computers ago, back in the dark ages when I had an Apple IIe. I'm hooked.

If CompuServe has a business-like feeling, America Online sort of feels like a big ol' fraternity/sorority house. In fact, I'd go so far as to say that, in tone, it's an exact opposite of CompuServe. CIS is business, with fun tucked away in odd little corners. AOL is fun, with business tucked away in stodgy little corners. (You can access Morningstar Financial Services while you read the juicer bits of chat in the "Gossip Gossip Gossip" chat room.) As for myself and others I know, I work on CompuServe, and I play on America Online.

AOL is a graphics-based system with plenty of menus and buttons to help you navigate. It's very easy for beginners to get the hang of. There's also help around all of the time in the form of Guides, Help Rooms, and live Customer Service representatives.

AOL is also teen-friendly. There are lots of areas for kids, ranging from Online Teachers that help with homework questions to entertainment areas and teen chat rooms. There's also a Parental Guidance feature that allows parents to restrict access to adult-oriented chat and information areas. There are live Game Rooms, interactive casino-type games, and live conferences scheduled nightly.

A big attraction on AOL is the variety of non-computer-related discussion areas and chat rooms. You can find the full spectrum of interests: chat rooms and forums devoted to fundamentalist Christians are just a stone's throw away from rooms and forums where gay and lesbian members meet and exchange information. Talk about diversity.

Don't think computer-related topics are given short shrift. The Industry Connection has information, software, and support forums for hundreds of computer hardware and software manufacturers. There are even on-line versions of some of your favorite computer magazines.

I think AOL is a great choice for beginners, because of its ease of use. It's great for families with older children. It's great for folks who don't want to be serious and talk shop all the time. Am I gushing, here? Slap me.

AOL Pricing

America Online costs $9.95/month, which gets you 5 hours of free usage. Additional hours are $3.50/hour. There are no prime time surcharges, nor are there additional charges for high speed access (currently 9600 baud is the highest speed you can use).

Pricing is current . . . *blah-blah-blah* . . . subject to change . . . *blah-blah-blah.* (I'm tired of typing it, you must be tired of reading it).

Because of its graphical interface, you do need special software to access AOL. It's available in Mac, DOS, Windows, and Apple II-family (IIe, IIc, IIGS) formats. You can find Mac and Windows versions in book and computer stores for about $20, which covers the cost of a book (not a manual, an honest-to-goodness book) and includes 10 hours of free on-line time.

You can get just the software (all versions) for free by calling 1-800-827-6364.

Under Construction: eWorld

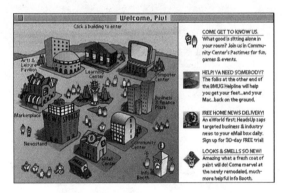

Apple's eWorld

Apple Computer is launching its own on-line service, called eWorld (for electronic World), and it's pretty exciting. eWorld is built on a version of America Online's software, so the interface is graphical, very friendly, and downright *pretty*. The service is still being built at the time of this writing (it should be generally available by the time you read this). Many services and features were not in place or were only partly in place when I went snooping, so I can't really say more than "Looking good!"

eWorld uses a city metaphor (you can see it in the figure above). Want to send someone an e-mail message? Click on the *eMail Center*. Want to meet people? Go to the *Community Center*. An impressive list of folks have signed on to offer services on-line, including heavy-hitters like Claris Corporation and WordPerfect, such user groups as BMUG and the Boston Computer Society, and news services from *USA Today* and Tribune Media Services.

Unfortunately, the service will be Macs-only for a while. A DOS/Windows version will be announced sometime after the Mac version is released to the world at large.

I've never been in on the ground floor of an on-line service before. It will be interesting to watch it grow and change and to see what sort of adult it grows into.

---

eWorld Pricing

Since the service is still under construction, everything about it is subject to change, not just the pricing. Right now, it looks like entrance to eWorld will cost you $8.95/month, with two free hours of non-prime-time usage. Additional hours will cost $4.95.

There will be a prime time surcharge of $2/hour when you log on between 6 AM and 6 PM, Monday through Friday. There will not be a surcharge for high-speed access. Currently the highest speed available is 9600 baud.

Like AOL, eWorld requires special software. You can get a free start-up kit by calling 1-800-775-4556.

GEnie, Delphi, and Others

While the really big services try to have something for everyone, there are some smaller services around that only do a few things and do them well. Two of them are Delphi and GEnie.

Delphi's biggest selling point is that it's the only service (right now) that offers full, reasonably priced access to the enormous resources of the Internet. GEnie's known for its powerful e-mail features and for the enormous variety of its discussion areas. More people seem to have something to say on any given topic—and say it—on GEnie than on just about any other service.

Both are reasonably priced alternatives (see pricing sidebar) for folks who want to dabble in on-line services, but who don't yet know if they need all of the resources of CompuServe or America Online. Neither require special software; you can use whatever telecommunications package you own.

Delphi and GEnie Pricing

Neither service has a sign-up fee.

Delphi offers two pricing plans: 10/4 and 20/20. The 10/4 plan costs $10/month with 4 free hours of usage. Additional hours are billed at $4 per. The 20/20 plan is a bargain for heavy-users: $20/month with 20 hours of usage; additional hours are only $1.80 each. However, there is a $9/hour surcharge for prime-time usage for either plan.

GEnie will set you back $8.95 a month, with 4 free hours. Additional hours are $3/hour, and there's a $9.50/hour prime-time usage service charge. You'll also pay an additional $6/hour for high-speed access. Prices are higher in Canada.

Contact Delphi at 1-800-544-4005 for details. To let GEnie out of its bottle, call 1-800-638-9636.

Bulletin Board Services (BBSs)

While you're poking around with that generic communications software, you might want to see if you can turn up a small free bulletin board in your own hometown. They're generally free and lots of fun, and are a wonderful introduction to using your computer to communicate with the world at large—without the expense of learning the ropes on a pay-as-you-go service.

You can generally find a local bulletin board by asking around at your local computer store or user group meeting, or by calling someone in the computer department at your local high school or institution of higher learning. Once you find one, there's usually a listing on-line of other bulletin boards in your area. When you get comfortable surfing the datasphere in a smaller environment, you can move on to bigger challenges.

Just be warned: many local bulletin boards are run as hobbies by their SYSOPs (System Operators) and are subject to the whims of their owners. And since many SYSOPs are teenagers, you can imagine how whimsical those whims may be. I know of one local board that has to shut down every time the SYSOP has to type a letter or do his homework—he's only got the one computer.

The point is, don't expect the same level of professionalism and privacy from local boards that you'll see on the major commercial services. In some cases you may get it—but don't *expect* it.

See you around the planet.

On-Line Shopping

Some people shop to live; others live to shop. Unfortunately for me (but fortunately for the national economy), I fall into the latter category. Sometimes the only thing that saves me from being the victim of drive-by shopping is the fact that, most times, I'm too busy to be bothered. But sometimes it's just too convenient, and I go nuts. QVC, the cable shopping channel, mail order catalogs, and infomercials shown in the dead of night present multiple shopping opportunities.

Not to be left behind, on-line services are doing their bit to bolster consumer confidence in the world. Most of the major on-line services offer some level of shopping. Whether it's for access to EAAsy Sabre (American Airlines' on-line ticketing service) or a matter of sending flowers to a loved one or joining a service like the "Something [Book, Cake, Coffee, Fruit...] of the Month Club," on-line services offer new and wondrously strange ways of spending your hard-earned money.

Ranking the Services

This is a list, in order of personal preference, of the best of the big services for ease of shopping (including quantity of vendors, quality of vendors, and ease of finding them):

4. eWorld: This is last only because the service is in development right now. They do have some impressive folks lined up, so they may move up if the reality matches the potential. #4 with a bullet (it may be moving up in ranking).

3. America Online: AOL gets high points for ease of use and finding, but their vendor list is small. EAAsy Sabre (a flight booking system) is the best vendor of the bunch there. To be fair, most of the companies in the *Industry Connection* will let you order products via e-mail, but they aren't in the shopping section, so I didn't count them.

continues

continued

2. Prodigy: The service's crass commercialism is relentless, but you can certainly shop-till-you-drop. The hardest part is avoiding the vendors. All vendors use the same order form, so ordering is simple and consistent.

1. CompuServe: CIS strikes the perfect balance. They want you to shop in their Electronic Mall, but they don't bully you into it the way Prodigy does. CIS boasts hundreds of vendors (two of which specialize in my favorite addiction: coffee). And though navigating the Mall can be difficult at first, it doesn't take long to catch on.

Vendors Galore

As you might expect in a computer-based environment, computer hardware, software, and supplies are readily available for sale in on-line shopping centers. America Online (in the Travel and Shopping department), Prodigy (in Shopping), and CompuServe (in their Electronic Mall) feature Computer Express as an on-line vendor. America Online also offers access to Comp-u-Store, a stand-alone on-line shopping service, via a gateway. In addition, CompuServe offers access to some widely known mail-order services, such as MacWarehouse and the Mac and PC Zone catalogs.

All the big services offer a way to search for and book the best airline tickets on-line. America Online and Prodigy give you access to American Airlines' EAAsy Sabre, the system used by many travel agents to book flights. I use it to check out flight availability between Philadelphia and Las Vegas, Nevada. You never know when you're going to need to make a fast getaway.

Both Prodigy and CompuServe offer Hammacher Schlemmer as a vendor of interesting, high quality (and high priced—you get what you pay for) goodies and gifts. There's exercise equipment, fruit and cheese baskets, office supplies, insurance—just the volume of *stuff* you can shop for on-line may be intimidating.

Most shopping quests can be accomplished in a few minutes if you have an inkling of what you want and of what kind of vendor is likely to carry it. On-line services usually offer some sort of search mode, either for each vendor, or for all of them. That can speed things up considerably. After all, you shouldn't have to spend too much money when you're looking to spend money.

Other Shopping Opportunities

You don't necessarily need membership in a big on-line service to be able to shop with your computer and modem. You may not have the huge selection of vendors to go after one at a time, but you can most certainly shop.

Here are a few of the shopping options you'll run into:

◆ Computer hardware and software companies often have their own electronic bulletin boards. In the main, they offer support, software upgrades, and some communication with other product users. Most, however, give you the chance to buy more of the company's products. Check the Customer Service and Support section(s) of your manuals for company BBS numbers.

◆ Local stores, with computer geek employees, may offer their own bulletin board service. Where I live, our local branch of Borders bookstore has a bulletin board where you can (in addition to other things) order any book in stock or special order one of the titles they don't carry. Ask around in your favorite stores or look in the back of local computer or consumer publications for leads.

◆ Other local bulletin boards, in order to meet their expenses without charging their members a fee, sometimes offer on-line shopping for local businesses, or they'll have advertising offering special member discounts when you shop in the store.

As construction of the information superhighway gets underway, look for more specialty and other retail stores to offer on-line shopping in anticipation of the day when everyone is plugged-in, logged-on, and licensed to shop.

Off-line Shopping

One of the more interesting trends in shopping has been the creation of the CD-ROM-based catalog. Naturally, it's only interesting if you have (or have access to) a computer with a CD-ROM drive.

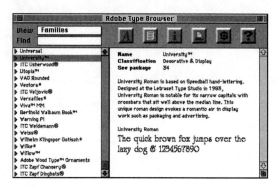

Adobe's Type On Call CD-ROM

The early CD catalogs (like Adobe's Type On Call, shown above) were primarily for computer fonts. Then Macintosh software became available. And while that field is growing (you can find CD software catalogs for just about every computer platform now), the newest application is shopping for other consumer items.

You can get regular merchandise catalogs on CD now: everything from ties and watches to tropical vacations. When you see something you like in the catalog, you generally call a toll-free number (with your credit card in hand) and place your order.

If you're purchasing fonts or software, you'll receive a code to unlock the software from your CD, and then you can copy it to your hard drive or diskettes. General merchandise is shipped right to your door, just as it is with paper catalog shopping.

CD-ROM catalog vendors include Apple Computer Software Dispatch (free CD for Macintosh software, 1-800-937-2828); En Passant ($14.95), for general merchandise from 18 companies (1-800-437-4121); and Magellan Systems The Merchant (free CD for general merchandise, 1-800-561-3114).

Many computer software stores and mail order companies offer their own CD-ROM software catalogs. Prices range from free to relatively cheap ($5–10).

Look for much more CD-ROM-based shopping as vendors catch on to the new idea. Many will, since mailing a few ounces of CD is much less expensive than mailing a few pounds of catalog.

When shopping on-line or off, be warned that the old dodge of "Oops! I left my credit card at home" doesn't work when you're already at home. You'll have to think of another.

Digital Pen Pals

One of the greatest things about using on-line services (the big national and international ones, as well as small bulletin boards in your hometown) is that they give you the opportunity to meet wonderful people you might not ordinarily meet.

Right off the bat, you have something in common: you're both computer users who travel cyberspace. If you happened to meet in a special interest area, odds are you also have that interest in common, too. Shy folks (like yours truly) thrive in on-line chat rooms, once they realize that

♦ You can't be seen.

♦ No one knows who you are.

♦ You're "judged" not on superficial qualities like your looks or your keen fashion sense, but on the quality of your chat: your sense of humor, intelligence, and your opinions.

♦ By creating a new screen name, you can completely remake yourself into who you want to be (like the stereotypical dateless teen who becomes a digital lothario when he logs on).

Corresponding via e-mail and meeting for on-line chats can be a source of great fun, the start of a friendship, even a romance. I don't know of a talk show on the planet that hasn't, at one point or another, done a story about couples who have met and fallen in love on-line. It happens all the time.

Where the Boys and Girls Are

Naturally, to meet people on-line, you need to be a member of a service (like those discussed in "On-Line Services" in Part V), and have a computer and modem hooked up to a phone line.

The easiest place to meet people and chat on America Online is in the People Connection: an ever changing landscape of chat rooms devoted to a wide range of topics and interests. It helps if you think of the People Connection as a sort of Chat-break Hotel. You enter it through a Lobby, and from there you can go to any of the other rooms that are open, create a public chat room of your own, or find a private room for private talk.

Lobbying for Chat

Once you've logged on to America Online, you enter the People Connection by selecting the word **Lobby** from your **Go To** menu (regardless of what computer you're using). You'll land in a Lobby that looks surprisingly blank (like the one shown below); it is actually a hotbed of activity.

The lobby only looks blank because you just arrived. Soon, lines of chat will begin to scroll across your screen. You can help the chat along by typing a general "Hello" to the group in the text box at the bottom of the window shown above; it's only polite to say hello when you enter a room, even if you're only going to hang back and watch for a while. Once you've got a feel for the personalities in the lobby, you can stay and read the chat, join in, or you can find a different room that sounds interesting to you.

People coming in   People going out

Click here to see
a full list of the
people present.

Click here
for a list of
open rooms.

Click to go to
other areas.

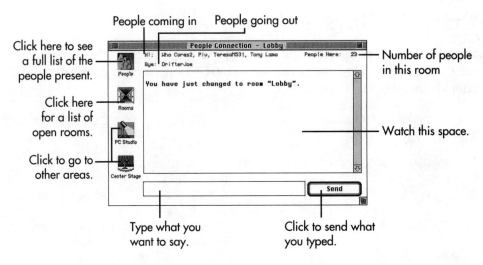

Number of people
in this room

Watch this space.

Type what you
want to say.

Click to send what
you typed.

The People Connection lobby of America Online.

To find another room, click on the **Rooms** button at the left-hand side of the window. It will present you with a list of Active Public Rooms, like the one shown here (of course, the room names are likely to be very different). You can scroll through the list until you've read all the room names available. You'll probably have to click on the **More** button a few times; when the More button appears gray, you've hit the end of the list.

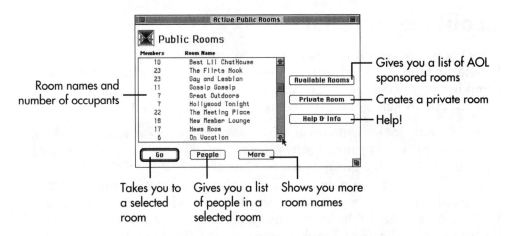

Room names and
number of occupants

Gives you a list of AOL
sponsored rooms

Creates a private room

Help!

Takes you to
a selected
room

Gives you a list
of people in a
selected room

Shows you more
room names

The Public Rooms Listing—there's something for everyone. If not, you can create your own room.

To switch to another room, click on the name of the room you want to enter, and hit your **Enter** key or click on the **Go** button. You'll land in the selected room if it isn't full. Public rooms have a maximum capacity of 23, so you may be asked if you want to go to a similar room. (You can always say "No," and select another room that isn't full.)

I (feeling lonely and unloved) decided to stick my nose into the Romance Connection room (shown below), so I could flirt shamelessly with strangers. As you can see in the picture, the first thing I did was say "Howdy" to the room. (My screen name is PIV, by the way—say hello if you see me.)

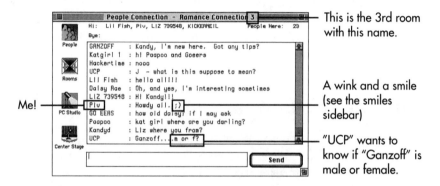

This is the 3rd room with this name.

A wink and a smile (see the smiles sidebar)

"UCP" wants to know if "Ganzoff" is male or female.

Me!

Chatting up the Romance Connection

Once you've found a room you feel both comfortable and interested in, you can partake of the conversation and start making friends. It isn't difficult at all, once you get passed the initial attack of shyness.

A Room of One's Own

If, by some chance, you can't find an existing room that appeals to you, you can always create a room of your own and wait for other interested users to pop in.

To create a room of one's own all you have to do is click on the **Rooms** button to the left of every chat window. It will give you the room listing shown earlier. Click on the **Available Rooms** button, and you'll get a listing of **Member Rooms** and a button you can click to create a room. You'll be asked to type in a room name and press **Enter**. You'll then find yourself in your newly created room.

You'll be in the room alone, but don't panic. Wait a few minutes and see if someone you can chat with pops in. It takes time for people to scroll through the list of room names to see them all. Some folks are shy about entering a room with only one or two people in it. Give it a few minutes before you give up.

If you already have on-line friends you'd like to chat with without strangers barging in, you can create a private room by clicking the **Private Room** button beside the room listing. Since the room name isn't listed anywhere for the general public, only people who know it can get in. It's like having an unlisted phone number: only the people you give your number to can call. Here, only people to whom you give the private room name can enter. Create a private room by using the **Private Room** button beside the room listing. You'll be asked to enter a name for your new room; type it in the box and press **Enter**.

Outside the People Connection

If you can't quite overcome your shyness to chat with up to 23 people at a time, there are other places to meet folks on America Online. One such place is the Lifestyles & Interests area. You can access it by using the Keyword: Lifestyles. (You invoke keywords by pressing **Command+K** on a Mac or **Control+K** on a PC, and then typing the keyword.) You'll see the screen shown below, which allows you to choose from more than 40 different special interest areas.

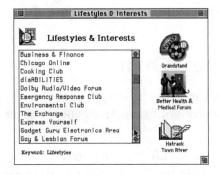

Lifestyles of the interesting.

Eventually, you can develop a chat-like relationship without the pressure (and immediacy) of chatting face to face. You can take the time to think a little before you respond. You may even want to correspond via e-mail with people whose views you agree and/or disagree with. Whether you choose live chat, or time-delay messages, on-line services like America Online offer you the chance to express yourself in new and interesting ways, and to win friends and influence people.

On-Line Etiquette

Just as you should behave a certain way when you're involved in face-to-face interaction, there are certain loose rules of behavior that make life on-line a little more pleasant for everyone involved. In addition to the normal rules of politeness and civility that help in any situation, there are some that are specific to computer communications. Here's a little primer to help you get started. These apply no matter what service you may be using.

Chat Room DOs and DON'Ts

DO:

♦ Say "hello" when you enter a new chat room.

♦ Try to get a feel for conversations already in progress before you start a new topic.

♦ In a crowded room, address comments to specific people by screen name so everybody knows who's being spoken to (especially questions, otherwise everyone or no one will answer).

♦ Give other people a chance to respond to one comment before you send another. Others may not type as quickly as you do, or a lot of people may be trying to talk at once, which can slow down everybody's chat.

♦ Don't be embarrassed to ask for help. Everyone's been a novice at one time. Most folks are happy to help.

DON'T:

- ◆ TYPE IN ALL CAPITAL LETTERS! It's considered shouting, and rude.

- ◆ Don't enter words or sentences one letter at a
  t
  i
  m
  e
  It's called "scrolling," and it is considered rude because it monopolizes a room.

Correspondence DOs and DON'Ts

These apply to e-mail messages, as well as to postings on a message board. In some circumstances, they can even apply in a chat room.

DO:

- ◆ If you're responding to a particular part of a message, refer to it by quoting a portion. You should >>>set your quote off with indicators like these, on a line by themselves<<< before your comments. It will refresh the memory of the person who wrote the original, and save new readers from searching for the original to figure out what you're talking about.

- ◆ Stick to the subject at hand. Long message *threads* start to drift off the subject. The last message in a thread called "Apples and Oranges" shouldn't be about a movie you saw last night (unless it was a film about apples and oranges, of course).

DON'T:

- ◆ Make personal attacks on people whose views you don't like or disagree with. Feel free to point out how or why you disagree with their ideas or comments, but questioning their parentage won't change their minds.

- ◆ Similarly, don't take criticism of your own postings personally. Message areas are called "forums" for a reason: they're there to encourage the open exchange of information and ideas, and to foster discussion. Name calling doesn't quite hit the mark. You're better than that.

Beware the Weirdos

The on-line world is just like the world outside your door: it's full of every type of person you can think of. There are the crooked and the dangerous, as well as the angels and sweethearts.

It's unfortunate, but you can be sexually harassed or be the victim of prejudice and/or ignorance, and you can meet people who want to rob you and hurt you. I've seen it all and been the recipient of some of it. You don't have to put up with it.

If you're harassed on-line, you can report the offending person to the customer service area of the service you're using. Get the offending party's name (or number) and quote, as accurately as possible, the text of the offensive or harassing remarks.

To protect yourself from fraud or crime, use your head. Just because you're in the safety of your own home doesn't mean you're immune to danger. Don't give anyone information in a chat room or via e-mail that you wouldn't hand out to any stranger on the street. Don't give out your address or phone number. Don't give your credit card or long distance card numbers. You don't even have to give your real name if you don't want to.

The only people on-line who need that kind of information are the on-line service's new accounts staff, and you generally only have to provide that information once (when you first subscribe to the service). Use your head. Don't be a victim.

Smiley Faces and Other Shorthands

When we talk in person, we get a lot of information from audio (tone of voice) and visual (smiles, arched eyebrows) cues that just aren't present on-line. It can make it difficult to figure out how to interpret some comments.

Think about how many different ways you could interpret "You're such a goof!" with different audio and visual clues attached. If someone is laughing with you when he says it, he may be impressed with your bizarre sense of humor. With no facial or vocal twists, he could be dismissing you as a jerk. With teeth bared, he could be threatening you with physical harm.

Folks on-line have developed little shorthands (mostly made with punctuation keys) to represent facial expressions used when communicating hard-to-interpret messages. (You have to turn your head to the left to see these faces.) A face is generally made up of a colon (:) for eyes, a minus sign (-) for a nose (noses are optional, not everyone uses them), and a parenthesis mark () for a smile or frown.

:-) is a basic smile.

:) is a noseless smile.

;-) is a wink and a smile.

:-D is a big ol'smile.

:-(is a basic frown.

:-| is non-judgmental.

:-x says my lips are sealed.

=8-O means I'm shocked!

:-* represents a kiss.

There are hundreds of variations. Some folks even have combinations to represent themselves. A guy with a crewcut, glasses, and a mustache might represent himself with **[8-{)**. You'll catch on with practice.

Another set of shorthand that takes getting used to (IMHO) is the use of abbreviations like IMHO (In My Humble Opinion) to substitute for commonly used phrases. They save typing, but can leave you scratching your head trying to figure out what they mean. Some of the more common ones include:

LOL = laughing out loud

ROFL = rolling on floor laughing

IMNSHO = in my not-so-humble opinion.

GMTA = great minds think alike

If you see one you don't understand, just retype it and add a question mark **(IMNSHO?)** and someone will translate. If you translate a shorthand for someone else, you may even get hugged {} in return. If you're very nice to someone on-line, you might get a really big hug. {{{{{}}}}}

I'm Gonna Sit Right Down and Write Myself a Letter

By the way, if you want to contact one of the authors of this book on-line to try out your new skills:

John Pivovarnick can be reached at the screen name **PIV** on America Online, or at **70713,3554** on CompuServe. From Internet, or any service with Internet access, he can be reached at **piv@aol.com**.

Making the World Your Oyster: The Internet

I f you browse through your local bookstore's computer book section, you'll probably notice dozens of titles attempting to demystify the Internet. The number of those books grows almost daily. But all the demystifying in the world won't help you if you don't understand what the Internet is in the first place. It takes some explaining.

The Internet Is NOT an On-line Service!

In spite of the fact that the Internet is like an on-line service in many ways (you log into it with your computer and modem, you can send and receive files and e-mail, and so on), it is not an on-line service like those discussed earlier in this part. An on-line service implies a central location (one big computer you dial into) with one company in charge (like America Online or CompuServe)—a standard assortment of services with a standard set of fees for connecting and using them. Generally, you can only access a big service with its own software package (often referred to as *proprietary software* because they are its proprietors, and you can only use it with their service).

The Internet, on the other hand, is made up of an International Network of computers, without any one computer as its home base. These networked computers are frequently owned by colleges, universities, government offices, and private corporations, none of which are actually in the business of running an on-line service. Since it's a conglomeration of computers, no one entity is in charge of it. Likewise, there's no set kind of computer in the network, except that most of them are big mainframe types, running operating systems other than DOS or the Mac OS. Many of them are UNIX based, an operating system for real propeller heads.

Well Then, What Is It?

In *very* simple terms, the Internet is a collection of computers, linked together via modems and phone lines. It's a network of computer networks that spans the world. In this networked world, there are many types of information for the taking.

Newsgroups

Contained in the net are all types of information and discussion groups that members can read and respond to. The topics range from basic computing to current events and politics, from human sexuality, alien abductions, and Star Trek trivia to The Grateful Dead and… well, you get the idea. If you have an interest in anything, you can probably find information about it on the Internet.

These individual discussions are called *newsgroups*. The various newsgroups are lumped together under the heading of *USENET* (for User's Network). You can find newsgroups devoted to a single topic (like AIDS information) or a group of related topics (like the entertainment media).

E-Mail

E-mail is another of the big features of Internet. You can send electronic mail to anyone anywhere in the world who has an Internet account. You can also send e-mail to just about anyone who has a membership on a large-ish on-line service with Internet access.

In addition to sending individual messages, you can subscribe to an e-mail list, which is like subscribing to a free on-line magazine. You'll then receive batches of mail relating to particular topics that interest you.

FTP, Gophers, and Webs (Oh, My!)

Netters, as some Internet users refer to themselves, are fond of obscure acronyms and abbreviations—partly because they're fun, partly because they're like secret handshakes (you can always tell a netter by the apparent gibberish he spouts), and partly because they save time in typing, like a system of shorthand.

Some of the more common and/or important mystery words you'll run into include:

◆ **FTP (File Transfer Protocol)**   The way text and application files are sent and received through Internet. It's also the name of the application program used to move those files.

◆ **Gopher**   A way of browsing through tons of information on the Internet. Internet member organizations, and even some individual users, have created Gopher "servers" that provide menus of items that you retrieve by double-clicking. Sometimes a double-click will bring you information, sometimes another set of menus. The new menus may be on the server you originally connected with, or they may be on a different server halfway around the world. It's called Gopher for two reasons: it's a way to go-fer information (get it?) and it was developed at the University of Minnesota, home of the Golden Gophers.

◆ **World Wide Web (WWW)**   Not to be confused with *World Wide Pants*, the production company for "Late Night with David Letterman." World Wide Web is a *hypertext* system (like the Mac's HyperCard, or the PC's HyperPad) that allows users to navigate through linked documents. If you select a topic in one document, it will take you to more information (on that same topic) in a different, linked document.

Because of these and other mystery expressions, I recommend that you get a good book on the Internet before you jump in with both feet.

How Do I Get Connected?

The Internet itself is free. However, there is no way for most average people to hook into it without an intermediary service (a.k.a. "service provider"), which is basically someone with a big, powerful computer that's connected to the Internet with a big, powerful cable. Your computer calls the service provider's computer, which in turn connects your computer to the Internet through its cable.

There is not one fixed price that service providers charge. Some are free; some are cheap (charging $5 a month to belong); and others are bloody expensive (hundreds, even thousands, of dollars a year). You'll learn all about the types of services and types of providers shortly.

Good News/Bad News

The Internet has a lot going for it. For one thing, there are more people connected to the Internet than there are to all the on-line services combined. If you need to send e-mail to someone, your chances of being able to reach him through the Internet are excellent. The down side of that is that there is no central directory of users. There are a number of ways to search for people on the Internet, but the only reliable way to send someone e-mail is to get his full Internet address beforehand.

Another positive point (or negative point, depending on the sort of person you are) is that there's very little censorship on the Internet. Most on-line services are monitored closely for the form and content of messages. Each takes their own slant on what is or isn't "acceptable" for posting. (Prodigy has a reputation for severe censorship; America Online is a little more liberal.) If you're trying to discuss a controversial topic on an on-line service, you may get very frustrated at having your messages zapped before anyone else has a chance to reply to them.

On the Internet, discussions in e-mail groups and newsgroups can be of a more frank, uncensored nature. (That's not to say that anything goes. In order to protect freedom of expression, there is a code of conduct.) A wide range of people from around the world contribute to these frank discussions, so there is just more of everything: more files, more programs, more varied information, and more points of view. Variety is the spice of life on the Internet.

But again there is a down side. The bad news is that the diverse, patchwork nature of the Internet can make it very difficult to find the topics you're looking for, and sometimes you don't want to wade through everyone's uncensored opinion on that topic to find the information you need.

Since no one owns the Internet, there is no "big brother" imposing usage rules, as there is with an on-line service. If an on-line service is like a stream running through private property, the Internet is like an ocean—vast, uncontrolled, and unowned. The negative side to this is that since no one is in charge, there is no central place to ask questions or get help. You're pretty much on your own, unless your service provider decides to help you.

Help!!!

If you think you want to go wading in the deep and chilly waters of the Internet, don't be shy. Get help first. Buy a good book related to accessing the Internet that's geared toward your kind of computer. There are a million of 'em.

May I shamelessly suggest *The Complete Idiot's Guide to the Internet*. It's a painless introduction to the highways and byways of the Internet connection. While the book will be helpful to anyone, it even comes with a DOS-disk (sorry Mac users) of useful listings and utilities to make your life a little easier. Just a suggestion.

And then there are viruses. Most on-line services take responsibility for making sure all of the software uploaded to their systems is virus-free. *Viruses*, if you haven't heard about them, are nasty little bits of computer programming that are hidden inside of other applications. When you run the application, the virus "infects" your computer. The infection could be as harmless as a "Gotcha!" message that appears on your screen, or as destructive as a virus that scrambles all of the data on your hard drive.

Most of the scary viruses you hear about are introduced and spread via the Internet. It's not necessarily dangerous to you if you use protection (please pardon the expression). There is a wide variety of virus protection, detection, and elimination software available. You'll find more information about those software programs in the "Reviews" section.

Okay, I'm Ready To Get Connected

Hooking into Internet can be a Byzantine procedure. Depending on the access you want (full access, e-mail-only, USENET only), you may have to look hard and/or pay a lot. It's not always an easy chore. (I've been looking for a reasonably priced way to fully access Internet for a year now. No luck yet.) Some methods of connection are easier and cheaper than others. Here's a rundown of some of them.

Free Local Access?

Before you go scrambling around your hometown looking for a service that offers Internet access, stop and ask about the Internet at your school or place of business. Many corporations, government offices (city, state, and federal), and colleges are already part of the Internet. You may only have to ask for an account.

In many cases, access to the Internet on your job or at your school is free or subject to a $5–$10 startup fee. If you're trying to buy the access from a company or college, the rates are usually a little better than those for commercial services, since these providers aren't out to make a profit, just to meet expenses.

You may also be able to get access through your local library. (Of course, you may not be able to log on from your home; you may have to physically go to your local library and use one of their computers.)

Going Through an On-Line Service

Yes, I know, I told you that on-line services are not the same as the Internet. But many on-line services are now offering limited access to the Internet through their services. It's kind of like the on-line service is acting as your Internet service provider, in addition to providing the other features they offer as a regular on-line service.

Almost all on-line services offer Internet *gateways* through which you can send and receive e-mail from Internet addresses, or even send through Internet to a member of an on-line service of which you aren't a member. (For example, you can send e-mail from your CompuServe account to a friend who only uses America Online.) And all of the big on-line services are racing to add more and more Internet access to their basic services. America Online is the first to add more than just e-mail. AOL's Internet Center (shown below) enables you to access newsgroups and e-mail lists and is in the process of adding *file transfer protocol* (FTP, for uploading and downloading files) and remote login options (where you use AOL as the intermediary service to log directly into the Internet).

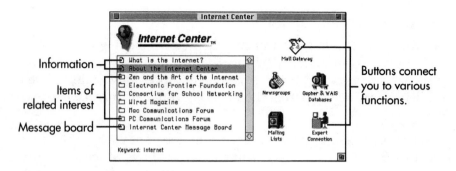

America Online's Internet Center.

Delphi, a smaller on-line service, already offers *full* Internet access, but Delphi isn't as easy to use as those (like CompuServe, America Online, and the new eWorld) that have a graphical (menu- and icon-based) interface. You have to type commands to do everything, which isn't easy for beginners. Even old hands run into trouble at times.

By the end of 1994, you should find things evened out among the major services, and all of them will be offering full (or nearly full) Internet access. Whether it will be less expensive to use them, instead of a local connection point, is yet to be seen, but it will certainly be easier.

Finding a Service Provider

Your final option for gaining Internet access is to find a local Internet service provider. This may be difficult: not all major cities have them. My editor in Indianapolis, for example, has to call Chicago (a long-distance call, of course) to connect to her service provider. If there's one in your town, you'll be able to save a substantial amount of money in long-distance charges.

You really need to beat the bushes to find an Internet access option you can access easily and afford. Check the back of your favorite computer magazines. Ask around at your local user group meetings. Ask at your favorite computer store. Someone, somewhere, may know where and how you can connect to the Internet locally.

Once you've selected a service provider, he will ask you what type of account you want. Don't stare blankly at him when the time comes—be prepared. Read the next section.

Types of Service Available

Service providers offer different levels of Internet access for different prices. The most basic connection is e-mail only; it's a very cheap type of service to get, but all you can do is send and receive e-mail messages.

With a dial-in direct connection, you log into a service provider's computer as if your computer were a terminal of that computer (that is, as if your home computer were part of the service provider's network). The provider's computer is already a part of the Internet, so your computer has immediate access to the Internet files and information. The chain of connection would look something like:

You—Host/Internet

A dial-in direct account will cost you about $100 to set up, and then a monthly fee to maintain. (This can be as little as $15 a month, but most cost more, and there's no "standard" fee scale).

With a dial-in terminal (also called "dial-up") connection, you log onto the service provider's computer and tell that computer what you want it to do. That computer connects to the features of the Internet that you want to access. Any files you retrieve are sent to the service provider's computer and stored there. If you want to download them to your computer, another step is necessary. That chain of connection would look something like this:

You—Service Provider—Host/Internet

A dial-up connection will cost you less to set up (possibly as little as $20, but frequently more) and then monthly or sometimes hourly charges on top of that.

There are a couple of big advantages to dial-in direct over dial-in terminal. One is that it's easier and faster to download files from other computers. The other is that you can buy (or download for free) special software that makes your interface with the Internet much more graphical and fun to use. For example, a program called Mosaic (for Mac and Windows) lets you navigate the Internet with the familiar graphical point-and-click environment. To use this kind of software, you need a dial-in direct account (or a permanent connection, which is discussed next).

The permanent connection is the most expensive kind—over $1000 a month on the average. Your service provider has one of these, and he charges you money to dial into it. If you have a permanent connection, you can be your own service provider! A permanent connection uses a cable that connects directly to the Internet, bypassing your telephone line. It's a much faster, more efficient connection. Lots of businesses use permanent connections, but permanent connections are out of the price range of home users.

What Kind of Software Do I Need?

Unlike a service like America Online, where everyone uses a similar proprietary software package to access their service, many Internet users can use any telecommunications package to get connected. Some service providers may require you to log in with certain software, but there is no universal "Internet software" you can ask for by name.

If you use a dial-in direct or permanent connection, you can take advantage of some of the software available that makes the Internet easier to navigate. A popular program called Chameleon provides a group of utilities that make World-Wide Web, Gopher, and FTP easier; Mosaic enables you to visit many World-Wide Web sites in a graphical fashion.

An Alphabet Soup of Internet Connections

You'll hear hundreds of confusing acronyms on the Internet. Cyberspacers love to speak in abbreviations—it makes them feel like insiders. Here are a few that might be thrown at you.

TCP/IP   Transmission Control Protocol/Internet Protocol. Often used to refer to a direct connection to a computer that is part of the Internet. It's so direct that it doesn't involve modems and phone lines. It's the kind of connection you'll have if your company, school, or government office is already part of the Internet.

SLIP   Serial Line Internet Protocol. A kind of dial-in direct connection that uses a modem and phone lines. You dial into a TCP/IP computer that is part of the Internet.

CSLIP   Compressed SLIP. A SLIP variation (see above).

PPP   Point-to-Point Protocol. Another SLIP variation (see above).

UUCP   Unix-to-Unix Copy Program. An Internet connection that allows only mail and some newsgroup information to be sent to your computer. A low-end dial-up connection.

Fun Things to Do on the Internet

The following list gives you an idea of some of the fun things you can do on the Internet.

◆ Read a book. *Project Guttenberg* (named after the guy who printed the first book) is an electronic library containing many complete books as text files you can download and read. Very cool. It's at **mrcnext.cso.uiuc.edu** in the **letext/directory**.

◆ Go to a museum. Digital versions of photographs and other *objects d'art* from the Smithsonian Institute can be downloaded via FTP and enjoyed at your leisure. They're at **photo1.si.edu** in the **pub/images/directory**.

◆ Speak out. You can e-mail President Clinton and Vice-President Gore at their Internet addresses: **president@whitehouse.gov** and **vice.president@whitehouse.gov** respectively (and respectfully). No, Socks doesn't answer e-mail, so don't waste your time.

◆ Annoy co-author, John Pivovarnick. Send him e-mail at **piv@aol.com**. Okay, don't annoy him. Send him your questions and/or comments about this or any of his books. He loves to get e-mail, and promises to answer.

More Fun Stuff from *Bitnet*

Bitnet (Because It's Time NETwork) is a large network connected to the Internet. Back in the day when Internet access was horribly expensive, Bitnet offered a cheap alternative. It still exists, and still hums with wild and funky LISTSERV lists that act a lot like the Internet's newsgroups.

You can get a current list of Bitnet LISTSERV discussion groups by sending an e-mail message to **listserv@bitnic.educom.edu**. In the body of the message (not the subject or anywhere else), type **list global**. By return e-mail, you'll be sent a copy of the current listing of discussion groups. Try not to get addicted (*yeah, right*).

There are too many other things to list. The potential for fun is practically unlimited. Log on. Poke around. Have a digital adventure.

Rare Birds of a Feather: Computer Clubs

I count myself among the lucky few. Many of the people in my life share my love of computers—in fact, the love of my life was a bigger computer geek than me. Others are less fortunate. Many computer owners have no one with whom to share the joys and pains of computing. Either there isn't anyone to talk to, or the people in their lives just don't care or understand.

It's hard to get someone excited about conquering a computer-related problem, when they never understood the problem in the first place. Moreover, it's hard to get help solving a computer problem, if everyone you know knows less about computers than you do.

That's where *user groups* enter the picture.

User Whats?

A *user group* is a group of computer users who meet regularly to share their computing experiences with their peers. User groups don't necessarily meet in person: they may meet through a monthly newsletter or a user group-run electronic bulletin board, or they may "meet" and interact via a special area on a commercial on-line service like CompuServe or America Online.

The people in these groups come from all walks of life, are of all shapes and sizes, and have all kinds of other interests. The only thing they have in common is an interest in using computers. That's why they're called "user" groups.

Acronyms, such as BMUG (Bee-MUG), BCS, or the occasional WUG variation, abound in user group names. BMUG used to stand for the Berkeley

Macintosh Users Group; now it just stands for BMUG, since they've expanded into some Windows support as well. BCS is the Boston Computer Society. Any group with WUG as part of its acronym will probably be a Windows User Group.

There are teeny-tiny user groups that meet in people's homes, and there are larger groups that meet in church basements and on college campuses. And, there are enormous national and international groups that could probably *never* get all their members together in one spot.

Tracking down a local group requires some footwork, but not much. The next time you're in your favorite computer or software store, ask if anyone knows about a local user group and how to get in touch with a representative. You can do the same thing the next time you're at your local college campus or continuing education center.

If you have a local computer publication, check the classified ads in the back. If you get a national computer publication, check the ads in the back and scan the articles. Ask your friends who use computers. Call the computer department at your local college or high school. Older computer users (age 55 and over) might also want to check out "Senior Services" in Part V for information on SeniorNet.

Apple Computer also refers folks to user groups (both big and small) with their User Group Connection. Although it's primarily for Apple-related user groups, you'll soon be able to get PC group information from them as well. Call them at (408) 461-5700.

If you don't have a local group, you may want to form your own. Apple Computer has put together a fantastic guide to "starting, sustaining, and enjoying an Apple User Group in your community, university, or K-12 school district." The book is called *Just Add Water*, and you can get it from the Apple User Group Connection at (408) 461-5700. While the book is geared toward Apple-related user groups, the broad concepts will help you start any kind of group you care to form.

I'm Not a "Joiner"

Hey, cool. Far be it from me to say you've got to join a group. It's not like I won't ever speak to you again if you don't. For those who would rather avoid a full-fledged commitment to a group, you can get many of the same benefits from user group areas on the big electronic services. You won't get all the benefits, but you get a lot. You'll need a modem and membership in one of the on-line services to go this route. See "On-Line Services" in Part V for information on the hardware and software requirements.

CompuServe

CompuServe Information Service (CIS) is huge. Finding anything on it by just poking around can be time consuming and, therefore, expensive. To track down user group information, I used the **Find** option available under the **Services** menu in the CompuServe Information Manager (CIM). The **Find** option may be in a different location on your computer, so check your manual(s) for information specific to your setup. Using "user group" as a search string, I turned up seven forums (see the next figure). I decided to poke my nose into the WUGNET (Windows User Group Network) Forum.

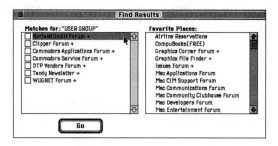

CompuServe Find Results: Desperately seeking user groups.

You have to join a forum to get full access to *its* files and information. If you simply visit, you may not be able to get anything other than information about the forum. Joining is as simple as pressing your **Enter** key. Once you join, you get full access. The WUGNET Forum looks like this:

Up-to-the-minute info
about the forum

Any messages
posted to you

All the messages

The meeting room

Other users
visiting the forum

Software and
information files

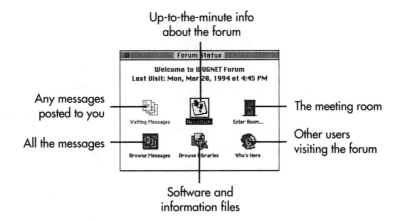

The WUGNET Forum on CompuServe

The WUGNET Forum libraries offer you informational text files, shareware and freeware applications, and demos of commercial programs (so you can try them before you shell out big bucks for the package). You can also read and post messages in the Message area, or pop into the WUGNET room to chat with other forum members in "real time."

This information (and overall setup) applies to almost all of the forums on CompuServe—even the Macmillan Computer Publishing Forum (**GO: MACMILLAN**), where you can exchange messages with me and other authors from the Macmillan publishing family.

America Online

Unlike CompuServe, America Online puts all its user groups in one area—the User Groups Forum, shown next—accessed by using the keyword **UGF**. (You use keywords in America Online by pressing the **Command+K** key combination on a Mac or **Control+K** on a PC, typing in the Keyword, and pressing **Enter**.)

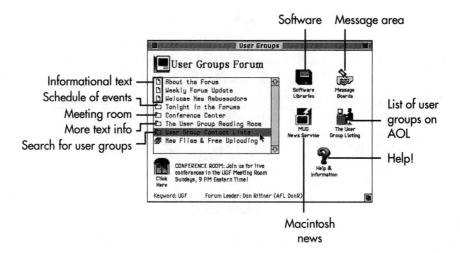

The User Groups Forum on America Online.

America Online (AOL) offers the same features as CompuServe. I like AOL's arrangement better because you can access all the User Group forums (see the next figure) by clicking on the **User Group Listing** button.

AOL's rogues' gallery of user groups.

The combination of access to user group information and all the support from manufacturers and software companies, gives members of an on-line service all the information and help they could ever use. And it's fun, too.

Computer "Pubs"

That's "pubs" as in "publications," not as in "public houses," where you go to drink away your computing woes. You should never drink and compute: you could crash.

If you want to stay current and on the cutting edge in the world of computing, or even if you just want to get better at what you're already doing, you need to read. There are dozens upon dozens of computer magazines, newsletters, and books designed to keep you informed and learning all the time. You actually *can* learn something new every day.

Magazines

There are magazines based on the kind of computer you own (*MacWorld* and *PCWorld,* for example), some devoted to particular applications (like Windows and WordPerfect), and even some devoted to particular computer uses (*Home Office Computing* springs to mind). The right magazine will keep you up to date on hardware and software upgrades, corporate mergers (who bought whom), new products, and good old fashioned industry gossip.

Finding the "right" magazine(s), however, can be quite a challenge. Some are aimed at programmers, others at novices. Some target corporate, big-budget buyers; others target shallow-pocketed home users. A few even try to be all things to all people. Which one is for you?

Hunt a Little, Read a Little

It's difficult to say that a person with certain characteristics would do well with a particular magazine. Everybody approaches computing with his own set of goals and needs. Likewise, people learn at different rates, and some pick up information better when it's presented in one format than in another.

The best thing you can do to determine what's best for you is haul yourself down to the local library, computer store, bookstore, or newsstand. Browse through the assortment of magazines available that cover your computer type (Mac or IBM), your interests (personal computing, business, or games), and your experience level (novice, intermediate, or advanced). In a library, or store that's amenable to serious browsing, read an article or two from each of the magazines you've selected to see whether they appeal to you and if you can follow along without having to run to a computer dictionary.

Speaking of Computer Dictionaries . . .

If perchance you do need to run to a computer dictionary, may I suggest *The Complete Idiot's Guide to Computer Terms* by Joe Kraynak. It's arguably the best computer dictionary on the market for beginners.

When you've narrowed the field down to one or two (or even three) magazines that appeal to you, buy the latest copy of each, take them home, and read them cover to cover. Then buy them again next month and do the same. After two months of reading the same magazine(s), you'll get a feeling for which ones cover the topics that interest you, in a way that interests you. You'll also see which magazines are essentially the same magazine with different covers and by-lines. Subscribe to the one or two that impress you most favorably.

In a family or multi-user situation, you might want to take the other users along for the ride. The younger folks might want a game magazine. A teacher might want a magazine slanted toward education professionals.

Some Obvious Choices

While you may have a hard time telling the difference between the contents of *Macworld* and *MacUser*, or *PCWorld* and *PC Computing*, there are some magazines that stand out as the only magazines focusing on particular needs and readers. This list covers some of the obvious choices (but again, magazines come and go, so look before you accept these as the only choices available).

◆ *PC Novice* (1-800-472-4100) takes their mission statement "Personal computers in plain English" very seriously, delivering easy-to-understand information to beginning and intermediate PC users.

- *Home Office Computing* (1-800-288-7812) is about the only magazine completely devoted to setting up and running an effective home office. It covers both Macintosh and IBM computers, as well as related hardware and software.

- *Mac Home Journal* (1-800-800-6542) is the only Mac magazine aimed specifically at the needs of home/family Mac users. It's written at a level accessible to novice users, with columns devoted to beginners and more advanced users.

- *Wired* (1-800-SO WIRED) is *the* journal of computer culture and counter-culture. It's less about computers and computing and more about the *zeitgeist* of the digital age. Think of it as a cross between *The Saturday Evening Post* and *Elle*, with a healthy dose of lysergic acid thrown into the mix.

Alternatives to Magazines

Traditional paper magazines aren't the only game in town. There are fleets of electronic magazines being distributed on the major on-line services. Since there's no lengthy typesetting/publishing routine to go through (most magazines are a month or two old by the time you get them), the news from an on-line publication is very current. Some are serious substitutes for your favorite magazines, others are vanity-ventures where one person gets to rant and rave on whatever topic appeals to him that day. (These vanity 'zines can be very entertaining, even if they are uninformative.)

The easiest way to find electronic publications is to log onto the service of your choice and use the service's Find command (they all have one). Enter the word "Magazine" as the search string, and you'll turn up piles of magazines and newsletters. *TidBITS*, for Mac users, is one of my personal favorites.

Since they're freely distributed, read 'em and enjoy. If you don't like them, you've only lost a snip of time and the few cents it cost you to download them.

Book Me, Dan-o!

Books, like magazines, target different audiences with different needs, but in more detail than a magazine article could ever dream of using. A good library of basic references is an excellent substitute for cranky and badly written software manuals. It also provides the means of helping you decide what will be the next phase of your growth into the world of computing. It's much better, I think, to spend $15 on a book that discusses CD-ROM drives in detail, than to spend $400 on the drive itself, only to discover you have no need for one.

When shopping for computer books, I suggest the same approach as when shopping for magazines: browse and read until they threaten to throw you out of the store. You really should know that you can relate to an author or publisher's style and method of presentation before you shell out money for those books. Don't waste money on a book you can't relate to.

The Scoop on Macmillan Computer Publishing

It may seem like a shameless plug here, but I wouldn't work for (much less plug) a publisher I didn't respect. The following list describes the various divisions (or *imprints* as they're sometimes called) that fall under the umbrella of Macmillan Computer Publishing, the folks who brought you this book.

If you like this book, you may want to consider others. If you don't (please let us know why, and we'll try to do better), this can serve as an object lesson, illustrating the different kinds of books produced by different publishers.

◆ Alpha Books publishes books for the beginner and for users who want to get the job done without having to get into the advanced details of the programs. They publish the "10 Minute Guides," "One Minute References," and "The Complete Idiot's Guides."

◆ Brady Publishing publishes books written by expert or well-known authors who can teach and demystify the machines and software. They publish the works of leading industry experts, who are high-profile proven authors in personal, business and professional computing. Brady has also begun to publish many books on computer games.

continues

continued

◆ Hayden Books & Adobe Press. Hayden publishes books on Macintosh products including hardware and software, desktop publishing, graphic design, computer graphics in general, and convergences between Macintosh and Windows in the desktop publishing and graphics fields. Adobe Press covers Adobe software, helping the user with the operation and use of the programs.

◆ New Riders Publishing develops and markets high-quality products to train and support CAD (Computer-Aided Design) users and professionals, experienced computer users, and professionals in Windows, networking, and database applications. The user level of their books ranges from beginner to advanced.

◆ Que Publishing addresses the major software titles with beginner, intermediate, and advanced level books. They publish the popular "Using" series of books, which cover many software packages; programming titles, which cover compilers and database programs; and books on a variety of hardware topics.

◆ Sams Publishing focuses on books about programming languages, databases, operating systems, networking, and new technologies (multimedia, graphics, morphing, virtual reality, sound, and so on). These books are written for everyone from beginners to advanced readers, although most of the programming/database/networking books are aimed toward intermediate-to-advanced readers.

Where computer magazines will give you news and reviews you can use, books will give you a solid foundation to expand your computing horizons. We could all use our horizons expanded.

Software Publisher Index

AAPEX Software Corp.
952 Greg Street, Suite 101
Sparks, NV 89431
(800) 728-7650

AbleSoft
4824 George Washington Hwy.
Suite 103
Yorktown, VA 23692
(800) 545-9009

Access Software
4910 W. Amelia Earhart Drive
Salt Lake City, UT 84116
(800) 800-4880

Activision
11601 Wilshire Blvd., Suite 1000
Los Angeles, CA 90025
(310) 473-9200

Arabesque Software Inc.
2340 130th Avenue NE
Bellevue, WA 98005
(800) 457-4243

Aris Multimedia Entertainment, Inc.
310 Washington Blvd., Suite 100
Marina Del Ray, CA 90292
(310) 821-0234

Autodesk
11911 North Creek Parkway South
Bothell, WA 98011
(800) 228-3601

Best!Ware
300 Roundhill Drive
Rockaway, NJ 07866
(800) 322-6962

Books That Work
285 Hamilton, Suite 260
Palo Alto, CA 94301
(800) 242-4546

Borland International Inc.
1800 Green Hills Road
Scotts Valley, CA 95067
(800) 331-0877

Broderbund Software
500 Redwood Blvd.
Novato, CA 94948
(800) 521-6263

Bureau of Electronic Publishing, Inc.
141 New Road
Parsippany, NY 07054
(800) 828-4766

Campbell Services, Inc.
21700 Northwestern Hwy.
Suite 1070
Southfield, MI 48075
(313) 559-5955

Central Point Software
15220 Northwest Greenbrier Parkway
Beaverton, OR 97006
(800) 964-6896

ChipSoft Inc.
6339 Nancy Ridge Drive #103
San Diego, CA 92121
(800) 964-1040

**The Church of Jesus Christ
of Latter-day Saints**
The Family History Department
Ancestral File Operations Unit
50 East North Temple Street
Salt Lake City, UT 84150
(801) 240-2584

Claris Corp.
5201 Patrick Henry Drive
Santa Clara, CA 95052
(408) 727-8227

Cliffs Notes, Inc.
P.O. Box 80728
Lincoln, NE 68501
(402) 423-5050

Compton's NewMedia Inc.
2320 Camino Vida Roble
Carlsbad, CA 92009
(800) 862-2206

**Computer Associates
International Inc.**
One Computer Associates Plaza
Islandia, NY 11788
(800) 225-5224

Corel Corp.
1600 Carling Avenue
Ottawa, Ontario
Canada K1Z 8R7
(800) 836-3729

Datastorm Technologies Inc.
3212 Lemone Blvd.
Columbia, MO 65201
(314) 443-3282

Davidson & Associates
P.O. Box 2961
Torrance, CA 90509
(800) 556-6141

Delrina Corp.
6830 Via Del Oro, Suite 240
San Jose, CA 95119
(800) 268-6082

**Digital Communications
Associates, Inc.**
1000 Alderman Drive
Alpharetta, GA 30202
(800) 348-3221

The Dumbbell Press
One Kennedy Drive
South Burlington, VT 05403
(800) 859-1969

Electronic Arts
1450 Fashion Island Blvd.
San Mateo, CA 94404
(800) 245-4525

Expert Software
800 Douglas Rd.
North Tower, Suite 355
Coral Gables, FL 33134
(305) 567-9990

Fractal Design Corp.
335 Spreckels Drive
Aptos, CA 95003
(800) 647-7443

The Freesoft Company
105 McKinley Road
Beaver Falls, PA 15010
(412) 846-2700

Grolier Electronic Publishing Inc.
Sherman Turnpike
Danbury, CT 06816
(800) 285-4534

HyperGlot Software Co.
P.O. Box 10746
Knoxville, TN 37939
(615) 558-8270

Individual Software Incorporated
5870 Stoneridge Drive, #1
Pleasanton, CA 94588
(800) 331-3313

INFOBUSINESS
887 South Orem Blvd.
Orem, UT 84058
(801) 221-1100

Insignia Solutions, Inc.
1300 Charleston Road
Mountain View, CA 94043
(800) 848-7677

Interplay Productions, Inc.
17922 Fitch Avenue
Irvine, CA 92714
(714) 553-6678

Intuit Inc.
155 Linfield Avenue
Menlo Park, CA 94026
(800) 624-8742

JIAN Tools for Sales, Inc.
127 Second Street
Los Altos, CA 94022
(800) 346-5426

Knowledge Adventure, Inc.
4502 Dyer Street
La Crescenta, CA 91214
(800) 542-4240

The Learning Company
6493 Kaiser Drive
Fremont, CA 94555
(800) 852-2255

Lifestyle Software Group
63 Orange Street
Saint Augustine, FL 32084
(800) 289-1157

Lotus Development Corp.
55 Cambridge Parkway
Cambridge, MA 02142
(800) 831-9679

LucasArts
P.O. Box 10307
San Rafael, CA 94912
(415) 721-3300

Magic Quest
125 University Avenue
Palo Alto, CA 94301
(415) 321-5838

Maxis Software
2 Theater Square
Orinda, CA 94563
(510) 254-9700

McAfee
2710 Walsh Avenue
Santa Clara, CA 95051
(408) 988-3832

MECA Software Inc.
55 Walls Drive
Fairfield, CT 06430
(800) 820-7457

Microsoft Corporation
One Microsoft Way
Redmond, WA 98052
(800) 426-9400

MicroTac Software, Inc.
4375 Jutland Drive, Suite 110
San Diego, CA 92117
(800) 366-4170

Multicom Publishing
1100 Olive Way, Suite 1250
Seattle, WA 98101
(206) 622-5530

Mustang Software Inc.
P.O. Box 2264
Bakersfield, CA 93303
(800) 999-9619

Nolo Press
950 Parker Street
Berkeley, CA 94710
(510) 549-1976

Novalogic
19510 Ventura Blvd., Suite 200
Tarzana, CA 91356
(818) 774-0600

Origin
110 Wild Basin Road, Suite 230
Austin, TX 78746
(512) 328-0282

Paramount Interactive
201 West 103rd Street
Indianapolis, IN 46290
(800) 992-0244

Parsons Technology Inc.
One Parsons Drive
Hiawatha, IA 52233
(800) 223-6925

Pinpoint Publishing
P.O. Box 7329
Santa Rosa, CA 95407
(800) 788-5236

Pixel Perfect, Inc.
10460 S. Tropical Trail
Merritt Island, FL 32952
(407) 777-5353

PKWare, Inc.
9025 North Deerwood Drive
Brown Deer, WI 53223

Polaris Software
15175 Innovation Drive
San Diego, CA 92128
(800) 722-5728

Power Up Software
2929 Campus Drive
San Mateo, CA 94403
(415) 345-5900

PushButton Software Inc.
1700 W. Park Dr.
Westboro, MA 01581
(800) 277-7874

Qualitas, Inc.
7101 Wisconsin Avenue, Suite 1386
Bethesda, MD 20814
(301) 907-6700

Quarterdeck Office Systems, Inc.
150 Pico Blvd.
Santa Monica, CA 90405
(310) 392-9851

Que Software
201 West 103rd Street
Indianapolis, IN 46290
(800) 992-0244

Reality Technologies, Inc.
2200 Renaissance Blvd.
King of Prussia, PA 19406
(610) 277-7600

ScreenMagic
820 Florida Street
San Francisco, CA 94110
(415) 648-8056

Shapeware Corp.
1601 Fifth Avenue, Suite 800
Seattle, WA 98101
(800) 446-3335

Sirius Publishing Inc.
7655 E. Gelding Drive, Suite B-1
Scottsdale, AZ 85260
(800) 247-0307

SoftKey International
201 Broadway
Cambridge, MA 02139
(800) 227-5609

Software Marketing Corporation
9830 South 51st Street
Building A-131
Phoenix, AZ 85044
(602) 893-3377

Software Publishing Corp.
3165 Kifer Road
Santa Clara, CA 95056
(800) 336-8360

Software Solutions
5 Park Plaza, Suite 825
Irvine, CA 92714
(714) 553-6575

The Software Toolworks
60 Leveroni Court
Novato, CA 94949
(415) 883-3000

Sound Source Unlimited
2985 E. Hillcrest Dr., Suite A
Westlake Village, CA 91362
(805) 494-9996

Spinnaker Software Corp.
201 Broadway
Cambridge, MA 02139
(800) 826-0706

Stac Electronics
5993 Avenida Encinas
Carlsbad, CA 92008
(800) 522-7822

Symantec Corp.
10201 Torre Avenue
Cupertino, CA 95014
(800) 441-7234

Synergistic Software
P.O. Box 186
Issaquah, WA 98027-0186
(206) 391-5361

T/Maker
1390 Villa Street
Mountain View, CA 94041
(415) 962-0195

Timeworks International
625 Academy Drive
Northbrook, IL 60062
(800) 323-7744

Tune 1000
295 Forest Ave., Suite 1000A
Portland, ME 04101
(800) 363-8863

Viacom New Media
1515 Broadway
New York, NY
(212) 258-6000

Virgin Games, Inc.
18061 Fitch, Suite C
Irvine, CA 92714
(714) 833-8710

WordPerfect Corp.
1555 N. Technology Way
Orem, UT 84057
(800) 451-5151

WordStar International, Inc.
One Harbor Drive, Suite 111
Sausalito, CA 94965

World Library, Inc.
12914 Haster Street
Garden Grove, CA 92640
(800) 443-0238

Xenon Educational Systems, Inc.
1253 University Drive, Suite 216
Coral Springs, FL 33071
(305) 345-9209

Accessibility Resources

Apple Computers

Apple Computer runs a free service called Macintosh Disability Resources. They maintain an extensive library of information offering Mac-related solutions for disabilities. You can contact them (by voice) at 1-800-795-1000, or (by TDD) 1-800-755-0601.

Trace R&D Center

For help with access to any sort of computer, you can contact the Trace R&D Center at the University of Wisconsin-Madison by calling 608-263-2309 (voice), or 608-263-5408 (TDD). You may also write to them at:

> **Trace R&D Center**
> S-151 Waisman Center
> 1500 Highland Ave.
> Madison, WI 53705-2280

National Information System

Within the United States, you can find resources in your local region by contacting the National Information System (NIS), an information and referral service for people with disabilities. You can call them at 1-800-922-9234 (voice/TDD) or fax them at 803-777-6058. If you live in South Carolina, call them at 1-800-922-1107 (voice/TDD); if you live outside the U.S., call them at 803-777-6222 (voice/TDD). You can also write to them:

National Information System (NIS)
Center for Developmental Disabilities
University of South Carolina, Benson Bldg.
Columbia, SC 29208

Microsoft AccessDOS

You can receive AccessDOS, a set of DOS utilities that makes DOS more accessible for people with disabilities, by calling Microsoft's Customer Sales and Service at 1-800-426-9400 (voice) or 206-635-4948 (TTY). It says in my copy of the MS-DOS 6 manual that AccessDOS costs $5, plus sales tax, shipping and handling. When I called the 800-number above, they said it was completely free—not even shipping and handling. Free is good.

With your modem, you can also download AccessDOS from Microsoft's Download Service (MSDL) by dialing 206-936-MSDL (6735). The service is available at any time except between the hours of 1:00 and 2:30 AM Pacific time.

Bibliography

Basham, Tom. "On Strike: Origin's Strike Commander." *Computer Gaming World*, August 1993, pp. 132.

Carey, Theresa W. "M.Y.O.B. and DacEasy Heat Up Windows Accounting Fray." *PC Magazine*, March 29, 1994, pp. 37–38.

Carlson, Kyla K. "War of the Words." *PC/Computing*, August 1993, pp. 124–150.

Claiborne, David. "PIM Puts Data in its Place." *Windows Magazine*, February 1994, pp. 128–130.

Coleman, Terry. "The Ultimate Gambit." *Computer Gaming World*, January 1994, pp. 42–44.

Dille, Ed. "Comanche CD: Fly Missions Over Digital Terrain." *Electronic Games*, April 1994, pg. 82.

Ellison, Carol. "CorelDRAW, Version 4.0." *PC Magazine*, January 25, 1994, pp. 186–188.

Finnie, Scot. "Hate Doing Windows?" *PC/Computing*, February 1994, pp. 32–34.

Gartner, John. "Database Arrives in Windows." *Windows Magazine*, February 1994, pp. 124–126.

Gilliland, Steve. "CA-Simply Accounting for Windows." *PC Magazine*, January 25, 1994, pp. 202–203.

Gilliland, Steve. "Microsoft Profit." *PC Magazine*, January 25, 1994, pp. 206+.

Gilliland, Steve and Ted Stevenson. "The Works: Not Just for Beginners Anymore." *PC Magazine*, April 26, 1994, pp. 185–209.

Goble, Gordon. "Out of the Pits." *Computer Gaming World*, February 1994, pp. 32–34.

Gomolski, Joseph R. and Barbara Cole-Gomolski. "Keep More of What You Make." *PC/Computing*, March 1994, pp. 32–33.

Greenberg, Allen. "Passing Judgment on a Pop Icon." *Computer Gaming World*, March 1994, pp. 42–43.

James, Jeff. "Trading Spaces." *Computer Gaming World*, December 1993, pp. 132–134.

Karney, James. "Microsoft Publisher 2.0 Lays Out Big Improvements." *PC Magazine*, October 26, 1993, pg. 44.

Keizer, Gregg. "Digital Dollars & Silicon Cents." *PC Magazine*, January 25, 1994, pp. 235–244.

Keizer, Gregg. "ECCO: Your Life as an Outline." *PC Magazine*, September 14, 1993, pg. 50.

Keizer, Gregg. "InfoCentral Can Pull Your Life Together." *PC Magazine*, June 14, 1994, pp. 37–38.

Labriola, Don. "PFS:Publisher." *PC Magazine*, May 17, 1994, pp. 202–204.

Landau, Ted. "MacWrite Pro." *MacUser*, September 1993, pp. 70–71.

Lindstrom, Bob. "Myst." *Electronic Entertainment*, January 1994, pp. 92–93.

Macaraeg, Brendon M. "Publish It! for Windows." *PC Magazine*, May 17, 1994, pp. 204–206.

Malloy, Rich. "Q&A for Windows: DAVE Will Help You Build Queries." *PC Magazine*, December 7, 1993, pg. 56.

Mann, Richard. "Links 386 Pro." *Compute*, January 1993, pp. 118–119.

Mendelson, Edward. "Documents Take the Center Stage." *PC Magazine*, November 9, 1993, pp. 108–112+.

Mendelson, Edward. "WordPerfect 6.0 for Windows Heads Into New Territory." *PC Magazine*, December 7, 1993, pp. 37–38.

Miller, Chuck. "The Arrival of a Long-awaited Guest." *Computer Gaming World*, August 1993, pp. 54–56.

Olafson, Peter. "Dracula Unleashed." *Electronic Entertainment*, February 1994, pg. 102.

Olsen, J.W. "Five Scripture Titles Offer Spiritual Well-Being." *PC Magazine*, October 12, 1993, pp. 496–497.

Olsen, J.W. "Five Ways to Get on Speaking Terms with Mac Disks." *PC Magazine*, January 25, 1994, pg. 50.

Olsen, J.W. "Three Tutorials Break the English Barrier." *PC Magazine*, February 22, 1994, pp. 402–404.

Perenson, Melissa J. "Columbia's Quotations Add Wit to Your Work." *PC Magazine*, March 15, 1993, pg. 50.

Perenson, Melissa J. "SportWorks: A Medal-Quality Guide to Sports Through the Ages." *PC Magazine*, December 21, 1993, pg. 449.

Powell, James E. "The Big Word Processors Go Toe to Toe." *Windows Magazine*, March 1994, pp. 260–268.

Powell, James E. "In Search of the Perfect PIM." *Windows Magazine*, June 1994, pp. 264–282.

Powell, James E. "Visio 2.0: Drag-and-Drop Graphics." *Windows Magazine*, January 1994, pg. 151.

Quain, John R. "300 Clemens Titles on CD-ROM." *PC Magazine*, January 11, 1994, pg. 426.

Rabinovitz, Rubin. "The Ideal CD-ROM Reference Library." *PC Magazine*, August 1993, pp. 554–557.

Robinson, Earle. "QmodemPro Does Windows Well." *PC Magazine*, March 15, 1994, pg. 54.

Rubenking, Janet. "Two Programs for Expectant Parents." *PC Magazine*, January 25, 1994, pp. 412–413.

Stevenson, Ted and Kathy Yakal. "Dancing to a New Tune." *PC Magazine*, March 15, 1994, pp. 235–263.

Stinson, Craig. "Excel 5.0 Extends Both Features and Usability." *PC Magazine*, March 15, 1994, pp. 37–39.

Stinson, Craig. "Quattro Pro 5.0 Excels at Modeling." *PC Magazine*, October 12, 1993, pp. 37–38.

Stinson, Craig. "Spreadsheets: Less Is More." *PC Magazine*, January 11, 1994, pp. 189–243.

Trivette, Donald B. "Planning for Your Dream House." *PC Magazine*, March 29, 1994, pp. 406–407.

Vogt, Christopher E. "Make Tax Season a Bit Less Taxing." *Windows Magazine*, March 1994, pp. 98–102.

Walnum, Clayton. "Eagle Eye Mysteries." *Compute*, December 1993, pp. 106–107.

Walnum, Clayton. "Just Grandma and Me." *Compute*, May 1993, pp. 84–85.

Walnum, Clayton. "Math Ace." *Compute*, April 1994, pp. 80–81.

Walnum, Clayton. "Spotlight: PC Karaoke and Soft Karaoke." *Compute*, November 1993, pg. 100.

Walnum, Clayton. "Treasure Cove." *Compute*, June 1993, pp. 76–77.

Walnum, Clayton. "Where in Space Is Carmen Sandiego?" *Compute*, November 1993, pp. 108–109.

White, Ron. "WordPerfect 6.0 for Windows Does It All." *PC/Computing*, December 1993, pp. 70–72.

Wolf, Scott. "Rebel Assault." *PC Entertainment*, March/April 1994, pg. 89.

Yakal, Kathy. "Peachtree Accounting for Windows." *PC Magazine*, January 25, 1994, pp. 223–227.

Yee, Bernie. "Strike Commander." *PC Games Magazine*, August/September 1993, pp. 20–21.

Books

Hanson, Larry. *Everything You Wanted to Know About the Mac.* 2nd ed. Indianapolis, IN: Hayden Books, 1993.

Kraynak, Joe. *At Home with Your PC.* Carmel, IN: Alpha Books, 1992.

Kraynak, Joe. *The Complete Idiot's Guide to Buying & Upgrading PCs.* Indianapolis, IN: Alpha Books, 1994.

Kraynak, Joe. *The Complete Idiot's Guide to PCs.* Indianapolis, IN: Alpha Books, 1994.

Kraynak, Joe. *The First Book of Personal Computing.* 4th ed. Carmel, IN: Alpha Books, 1990.

Pivovarnick, John. *The Complete Idiot's Guide to CD-ROM.* Indianapolis, IN: Alpha Books, 1994.

Pivovarnick, John. *The Complete Idiot's Guide to the Mac.* Indianapolis, IN: Alpha Books, 1993.

Price, Jonathan. *Virtual Playhouse.* Indianapolis, IN: Hayden Books, 1994.

Salpeter, Judy. *Kids and Computers: A Parent's Handbook.* Carmel, IN: Sams, 1992.

Walnum, Clayton. *Adventures in Artificial Life.* Indianapolis, IN: Que Corporation, 1993.

Glossary

access time   The average time it takes a device (usually a disk drive) to find a random piece of data on a disk. Access time is measured in milliseconds (the lower the number, the faster the drive). Good access times are between 15 ms and 20 ms. (See also *transfer rate*.)

ADB   Short for Apple Desktop Bus, this is the standard way of connecting mice, keyboards, and a few other peripherals to the Macintosh.

antiglare screen   A screen or filter that fits over your monitor to prevent light from bouncing off the screen into your eyes.

application   Also know as a *program*; a set of instructions that enable a computer to perform a specific task, such as word processing or data management.

ASCII file   A file containing characters that can be used by any program on any computer. Sometimes called a *text file* or an *ASCII text file*. (ASCII is pronounced "ask-key.")

AUTOEXEC.BAT   A batch file that DOS reads whenever you boot or reboot your IBM-compatible computer. This file contains a series of commands that DOS automatically reads and executes.

backup copy   An exact duplicate of a file or a disk.

batch file   Any PC file that contains a series of commands. You run a batch file just as you would a program file (by entering its name at the DOS prompt). The most common batch file is AUTOEXEC.BAT.

baud   A unit for measuring the speed of data transmission, which is usually used to describe the speed at which a modem transfers data, such as 2400 baud. A more accurate measure of transmission speed is bps (bits per second).

BIOS (basic input-output system)   The startup instructions for a computer. The BIOS tells the computer how to control traffic between the various elements that make up the computer, including disk drives, the printer, the ports, and the monitor.

bit   The smallest piece of data a computer can store. A bit can be only one of two values, either 0 or 1.

boot   To start a computer with the operating system software (usually DOS, or for Macintoshes, System 7) in place.

bulletin board system (BBS)   A program that enables a computer to automatically answer the phone when other computers call. The BBS allows the calling computer to copy files to it (*upload* files) and copy files from it (*download* files). Although you can purchase a BBS program to set up your own BBS, most users work with BBSs set up by computer companies and professional associations.

buffer   A place in memory in which to store data temporarily, while it's waiting to print, for example.

bus   A superhighway that carries information electronically from one part of the computer to another. There are three such highways:

- A *data bus* carries data back and forth between memory and the microprocessor.

- An *address bus* carries information about the locations (addresses) of specific information.

- A *control bus* carries control signals to make sure traffic flows smoothly, without confusion.

byte   A group of eight bits that usually represents a character or digit.

cache   Pronounced "cash," this is a part of memory that speeds up your computer's *access time* by holding the most recently accessed data from a disk. The next time the computer needs the data, the computer gets it from memory rather than from the disk, which would be much slower. Sometimes called a *RAM cache*.

capacity   A measure of how much data a disk can store. For example, a 5.25-inch high-density floppy disk can be formatted to store 1.2MB; 1.2MB is the disk's *capacity*.

card   See *expansion card*.

CD-ROM (Compact-Disc Read-Only Memory)   A storage technology that uses the same kind of discs you play in an audio CD player for mass storage of computer data. A single disc can store over 600MB of information. Pronounced "see-dee-rahm."

cell   The box formed by the intersection of a row (labelled 1,2,3...) and a column (labelled A, B, C...) in a spreadsheet. Each cell has an *address* (such as B12) that defines its column and row. A cell may contain text, a numeric value, or a formula.

CGA   Short for color graphics adapter. An early, crude color display technology. The term is used to refer to both the monitor and the graphics card that powers the monitor.

click   To move the mouse pointer over an object or icon, and press and release the mouse button once without moving the mouse.

clip art   A collection of graphic images meant to be copied and pasted into other documents.

clipboard   A temporary storage area that holds text and graphics. The Cut and Copy commands put text or graphics on the clipboard, replacing the clipboard's previous contents. The Paste command copies clipboard data to a document.

CMOS (Complementary Metal-Oxide Semiconductor)   Pronounced "see-moss," this is an electronic device (usually battery operated) that stores information about your computer.

cold boot   To turn on the power to your computer with the operating system in place.

COM port   Short for communications port. A receptacle, usually at the back of the computer, into which you can plug a serial device such as a modem, mouse, or serial printer. If your computer has more than one COM port, the ports are numbered COM1, COM2, and so on. The Mac's printer and modem ports are COM ports.

command   An order that tells the computer what to do. In command-driven programs, you press a specific key or type the command to execute it. With menu-driven programs, you select the command from a menu.

communications software   Software that allows a computer (equipped with a modem) to communicate with other computers through the phone lines.

compress   To compact files so that they take up less space.

computer   Any machine that accepts input (from a user), processes the input, and produces output in some form.

conventional memory   The first 640KB of memory in a PC.

CPU (Central Processing Unit)   See *microprocessor*.

crash   Failure of a system or program. Usually, you realize that your system has crashed when the display or keyboard locks up. The term *crash* is also used to refer to a disk crash or a head crash. A disk crash occurs when the read/write head in the disk drive falls on the disk. It's like when you drop a phonograph needle on a record (remember records?). A disk crash can destroy any data stored where the read/write head falls on the disk.

cursor   A horizontal line that appears below characters. A cursor acts like the tip of your pencil: anything you type appears at the cursor. (See also *insertion point*.)

cut and paste   An editing feature that allows you to copy or move information from one location to another on the screen or in a document.

data   The facts and figures that you enter into the computer and then are stored and used by the computer.

database   A type of computer program used for storing, organizing, and retrieving information. Popular database programs include Q&A, Access, and Approach.

density   A measure of the amount of data that can be stored per square inch of storage area on a disk.

desktop publishing (DTP)   A program that enables you to combine text and graphics on the same page and manipulate the text and graphics on-screen. Desktop publishing programs are commonly used to create newsletters, brochures, flyers, résumés, and business cards.

dialog box   In many programs, you can enter a simple command to perform some task like saving a file. However, you may need to enter additional information before the program can perform the task. In such cases, the program may display a dialog box, which allows you to carry on a "conversation" with the program.

directory   Because large hard disks can store thousands of files, you often need to group related files in separate directories on the disk. Think of your disk as a filing cabinet and think of each directory as a drawer in the cabinet. By keeping files in separate directories, it is easier to locate and work with related files.

disk   A round, flat magnetic storage medium. See *floppy disk* and *hard disk*.

disk drive   A device that writes data to a magnetic disk and reads data from the disk. Think of a disk drive as being like a cassette recorder/player. Just as the cassette player can record sounds on a magnetic cassette tape and play back those sounds, a disk drive can record data on a magnetic disk and play back that data.

DOS (disk operating system)   DOS, which rhymes with "boss," is an essential program that provides the necessary instructions for the computer's parts (keyboard, disk drive, central processing unit, display screen, printer, and so on) to function as a unit. MS-DOS is a disk operating system, as is the Mac's System 7.1.

DOS prompt   An on-screen prompt that indicates DOS is ready to accept a command. It looks something like C> or C:\> on an IBM-compatible.

double-click   To press and release a mouse button (usually the left one) twice quickly without moving the mouse.

download   To copy files from another computer to your computer usually through a modem. See also *upload*.

drag   To hold down a mouse button (usually the left one) while moving the mouse; usually used for selecting or moving an object on-screen.

EGA   Short for enhanced graphics adapter, a semi-early color display technology. This term is used to refer to both the monitor and the graphics card that drives the monitor.

e-mail   Short for *electronic mail*, e-mail is a system that enables people to send and receive messages from computer to computer. E-mail is usually available on networks and on-line information services.

EMS (Expanded Memory Specification)   See *expanded memory*.

emulation   The ability to copy or act like. A hardware device, such as a printer, can emulate a more standard printer brand, for example.

environment   An electronic setting in which you perform tasks on your computer. Microsoft Windows, for example, displays a graphical environment that lets you enter commands by selecting pictures instead of by typing commands. This makes it easier to use your computer (assuming you know what the pictures stand for).

executable file   A program file for IBM-compatibles that can run the program. Executable files end in .BAT, .COM, or .EXE.

expanded memory   A special way for IBM computers to use memory beyond 640 kilobytes. With expanded memory, additional memory is added to the computer in the form of memory chips or a memory board. To access this additional memory, an expanded memory manager reserves 64 of the standard 640 kilobytes as a swap area. The 64 kilobytes represent four *pages*, each of which consists of 16 kilobytes. Pages of data are swapped into and out of this 64-kilobyte region from expanded memory at a high speed. Not all programs can use expanded memory. See also *extended memory*.

expansion card   An add-on circuit board for a new device, such as spare memory, a mouse, or a modem, for example. Fits in a spare expansion slot in the back of the computer.

expansion slot   An opening on the motherboard (inside the system unit) that allows you to add devices to the system unit.

export   The capability of an application to save a file, usually with a Save As command, in a format easily used by another application.

extended memory   The same sort of memory that makes up the one megabyte of base memory that most PCs have. Extended memory is directly available to the processor in your computer, unlike expanded memory in which data must be swapped into and out of the base memory. See also *expanded memory*.

extension   In DOS, each file you create has a unique name. The name consists of two parts: a file name and an extension, separated by a dot. The file name (to the left of the dot) can be up to eight characters. The extension (which is optional and to the right of the dot) can have up to three characters.

For a Mac, an extension is a bit of software that loads at startup, expanding the Mac's capabilities.

field   In a database record, a field contains a single piece of information (for example, a telephone number, ZIP code, or a person's last name).

file   A collection of information stored as a single unit on a floppy or hard disk. Files always have file names to identify them.

file allocation table (FAT)   A map on every disk that tells the operating system where the files on the disk are stored. It functions like a classroom seating chart. On a Macintosh, it's part of the desktop file.

fixed disk drive   A disk drive that has a non-removable disk (as opposed to floppy drives, in which you can insert and remove disks).

flat-file database   A database program that allows you to work with one database at a time (as opposed to a relational database).

floppy disk   A wafer encased in plastic that stores magnetic data (the facts and figures you save). Floppy disks are the disks you insert in your computer's floppy disk drive (located on the front of the computer).

font   Any set of characters of the same *typeface* (design) and *type size* (measured in points). For example, Times Roman 12-point is a font: Times Roman is the typeface, and 12-point is the size. (There are 72 points in an inch.)

format (disk)   Formatting creates a map on the disk that tells the operating system how the disk is structured. The operating system uses this map to keep track of where files are stored.

format (document)   To establish the physical layout of a document, including page size, margins, running heads, line spacing, text alignment, graphics placement, and so on.

freeware   Programs that you can use for free. Also called *public-domain software*.

function keys   The 10 or 12 F keys on the left side of the keyboard, or 12 F keys at the top of the keyboard (on some keyboards, there are both). F keys are numbered F1, F2, F3, and so on, and are used to enter specified commands in a program.

graphical user interface (GUI)   Pronounced "gooey"; A type of program interface that uses graphical elements, such as icons, to represent commands, files, and (in some cases) other programs. The Mac's operating system is a GUI, as is Microsoft Windows.

graphics card   An add-on circuit board that enables your computer to display graphics on-screen.

hard disk   A disk drive that comes complete with a non-removable disk. It acts as a giant floppy disk drive and usually is encased in your computer.

Hayes compatible   Used to describe a modem that uses the Hayes command set for communicating with other modems over the phone lines. Hayes-compatible modems are usually preferred over other modems because most modems and telecommunications software is designed to be Hayes compatible.

Hercules graphics adapter (HGC)   A monochrome (black and white) graphics standard.

hot-key   A key or key combination that you can press while in a program to access another program or to execute a command.

hypertext   Key words that are linked to related subject matter (usually on a help screen).

icon   A graphic image on-screen that represents another object, such as a file on a disk.

import   To bring a file created in one program into another program.

initialize   To reset a computer or program to some starting values. When used to describe floppy or hard disks, the term means the same as to format.

insertion point   A blinking vertical line used in some word processors to indicate the place where any characters you type will be inserted. An insertion point is the equivalent of a *cursor*.

install   To copy program files to a hard disk or to floppy disks so that you can use the program on your computer.

integrated program   A program that combines the features of several programs, such as a word processor, spreadsheet, database, and communications program. The names of integrated programs usually end with the word "works."

interface   A link between two objects, such as a computer and a modem. The link between a computer and a person is called a *user interface*, and refers to the way a person communicates with the computer.

keyboard   The main input device for most computers.

kilobyte (K)   A unit for measuring the amount of data. A kilobyte is equivalent to 1,024 bytes.

launch   To start an application. It can also be called *starting* or *running* an application.

load   To read data or program instructions from disk and place them in the computer's memory, where the computer can use the data or instructions. You usually load a program before you use it or load a file before you edit it.

logical drive   A section of a hard disk of memory that is treated as a separate disk and is assigned its own letter (on a PC) or icon on a Mac.

macro   A recorded set of instructions for a frequently used or complex task. Macros resemble small programs, and can be activated by pressing a specified key combination.

mail merge   A process that allows you to combine a single letter with a list of names and addresses to create a series of form letters, all addressed to different people.

math coprocessor   An add-on chip that takes some of the load off the microprocessor by performing arithmetic functions and graphics processing.

MDA   Early monochrome (black and white) monitor/video card standard.

megabyte   A standard unit used to measure the storage capacity of a disk and the amount of computer memory. A megabyte is 1,048,576 bytes (1,024 kilobytes). This is roughly equivalent to 500 pages of double-spaced text. Megabyte is commonly abbreviated as M, MB, or Mbyte.

memory   An electronic storage area inside the computer that's used to temporarily store data or program instructions when the computer is using them. The computer's memory is erased when the power to the computer is turned off.

memory-resident   Also known as TSR or terminate-and-stay-resident, a program that remains on call after you leave it. You can run the memory-resident program and then load another program on top of it.

menu   A list of commands or instructions displayed on-screen. Menus organize commands and make a program easier to use.

microprocessor   Sometimes called the Central Processing Unit (CPU) or processor, this chip is the computer's brain; it does all the calculations.

modem   An acronym for modulator/demodulator. A modem is a piece of hardware that enables a computer to send and receive data through an ordinary telephone line.

monitor   A television-like screen on which the computer displays information.

mouse   A hand-held device that you move across the desktop to move an indicator, called a mouse pointer, across the screen. Used instead of the keyboard to select and move items (such as text or graphics), execute commands, and perform other tasks.

mouse pointer   An arrow or rectangle that appears on-screen and moves when you roll your mouse. You use the mouse pointer to select text, draw, and enter commands.

MPC (Multimedia PC)   A standard used for multimedia equipment and software to ensure that the equipment and software will work together smoothly.

MS-DOS (Microsoft Disk Operating System)   See *DOS*.

multimedia   The combination of text, sound, video, graphics, and animation for use in presentations. Multimedia presentations are often stored and played back using CD-ROM discs.

multitasking   The capability to run more than one program at the same time. Some programs, such as the DOS shell, enable you to switch between two or more programs (task switching), but do not allow a program to perform operations in the background (multitasking).

NuBus   A high-speed slot that accepts cards that work with a Macintosh's central processor to supplement its functions. The information is fed along a data path called a *bus*, like a Mac's ADB (Apple Desktop Bus), which feeds a Mac information from the mouse and keyboard.

on-line   Connected, turned on, and ready to accept information. Used most often in reference to a printer or modem.

on-line service   Any commercial service accessible via a modem. CompuServe, Prodigy, Delphi, GEnie, and America Online are a few examples.

open file   To read a file from a disk into your computer's memory so that the computer and you can work with it.

OS   Short for operating system. See also *DOS*.

parallel port   A connector used to plug a device, usually a printer, into the computer. Transferring data through a parallel port is much faster than transferring data through a serial port, but parallel cables can reliably carry data only 15 or 20 feet.

parameter   An extra piece of information added to a command. For example, in the command COPY MYFILE.TXT, the COPY command has the parameter MYFILE.TXT, which is the name of the file to copy.

parity bit   In modem communications, the bit used to make sure that the information being transferred is not being corrupted during transmission.

partition   A hard disk can be divided (or *partitioned*) into one or more drives, which DOS refers to as drive C, drive D, drive E, and so on. Mac partitions are given their own icons on the desktop. (Don't be fooled; it's still one disk drive.) The actual hard disk drive is called the *physical* drive; each partition is called a *logical* drive.

path   The route that the computer travels from the root directory to any subdirectories when locating a file.

PDS   Processor Direct Slot. A slot that feeds information directly into the central processor of a Macintosh computer (as opposed to sending it through a bus).

peripheral   The system unit is the central part of the computer. Any devices attached to the system unit are considered *peripheral* (as in "peripheral vision"). Peripheral devices include the monitor, printer, keyboard, mouse, modem, and joystick. Some manufacturers consider the keyboard and monitor as parts of the computer, not as peripherals.

physical disk   The actual disk drive that you can see and touch, as opposed to the *logical disk* drive.

pixel   A dot of light that appears on the computer screen. A collection of pixels forms characters and images on the screen. Think of a pixel as a single peg in a Lite Brite toy.

ports   The receptacles at the back of the computer. They get their name from the ports where ships deliver and pick up cargo. In this case, the ports allow information to enter and leave the system unit.

POST (Power-On Self-Test)   A series of internal checks the computer performs on itself when it is first turned on. If the test reveals that any component is not working properly, the computer displays an error message on-screen giving a general indication of which component is causing problems.

program   A group of instructions that tell the computer what to do. Typical program types include word processors, spreadsheets, databases, and games.

prompt   A computer's way of asking for more information. The computer basically looks at you and says, "Tell me something." In other words, it is *prompting* you or prodding you for information or for a command.

protocol   A group of communications settings that control the transfer of data between two computers via a modem.

pull-down menu   A menu that appears at the top of the screen listing various options. The menu is not visible until you select it from the menu bar. The menu then drops down, covering a small part of the screen.

query   The process of asking a database program to retrieve one or more records that match a given set of criteria.

random-access memory (RAM)   Where your computer stores data and programs temporarily. RAM is measured in kilobytes and megabytes. In general, the more RAM a computer has, the more powerful the programs it can run.

read-only memory (ROM)   A set of permanent instructions that tell a computer how to coordinate its various components and get to work. Also refers to any memory storage that can be looked at (read) but not changed (written to).

record   Used by databases to denote a unit of related information contained in one or more fields, such as an individual's name, address, and phone number.

relational database   A database program that allows you to combine data from more than one database file (as opposed to a flat-file database).

resolution   A measure of image quality that refers to the number of pixels horizontally and vertically on the screen. The resolution of most VGA graphics screens, for example, is 640 × 480. The greater the resolution (the more pixels on the screen), the better the image quality.

ROM BIOS   See *BIOS*.

run To load a program into your computer's memory so that you can use the program.

save file To save the information from your computer's memory to a named file on disk.

scanner A device that converts images, such as photographs or printed text, into an electronic format that a computer can use. Many stores use a special type of scanner to read bar-code labels into the cash register.

scroll To move text (or other data) up and down or right and left on a computer screen.

SCSI (Small Computer Systems Interface) Pronounced "skuzzy," this is another way of connecting peripherals to a computer.

shareware Programs that you can test drive for free. If you like the program and wish to continue using it, you are legally obligated to pay the developer of the program.

shell A program that enables you to enter commands to the operating system by choosing them from a menu. Shell programs make it easier to use the operating system.

software Any instructions that tell your computer (the hardware) what to do. There are two types of software: operating system software and application software. *Operating system software* (such as DOS) gets your computer up and running. *Application software* enables you to do something useful, such as type a letter or chase lemmings.

sound board Sometimes called an *audio board,* a circuit board that plugs into an expansion slot inside your computer and gives the computer a greater capacity for producing sounds.

spreadsheet A program used for keeping schedules and calculating numeric results. Common spreadsheets include Lotus 1-2-3, Microsoft Excel, and Quattro Pro.

stop bit A bit that acts as a space between words in modem communications. It tells the computer where one byte of data stops and the next one begins.

style A collection of specifications for formatting text. A style may include information for the font, font size, font style, margins, and spacing. Applying a style to text automatically formats the text according to the style's specifications.

super VGA   Graphics mode that, right now, is quickly becoming the high-end standard. This term is used to refer to both the graphics card and the monitor.

surge protector   Also known as a *surge suppressor*, a unit that stands between the computer and the electrical outlet to prevent any sudden increases in power from damaging the computer.

switch   A value you can add to a command to control the manner in which the command is carried out. For example, in DOS, you can use the /V switch with the COPY command to have DOS verify that the copied files are exact duplicates of the originals.

SYSOP   Short for System Operator and pronounced "SIS-op," it's the person in charge of a bulletin board system.

trackball   A device often used with laptop computers that works like an upside-down mouse. A trackball requires less desk space than a mouse, because instead of moving it around the desk, you roll it in place to move the pointer. Some arcade video games use devices similar to trackballs. (Remember "Missile Command"?)

transfer rate   A measure of how much information a device (usually a disk drive) can transfer from the disk to your computer's memory in a second. A good transfer rate is in the range of 500 to 600 kilobytes per second. The higher the number, the faster the drive. (See also *access time*.)

uninterruptible power supply (UPS)   A battery-powered device that protects against power spikes and power outages. If the power goes out, the UPS continues supplying power to the computer so you can continue working or can safely turn off your computer without losing data.

upload   To send data to another computer, usually through a modem and a telephone line or through a network connection.

VGA   Acronym for video graphics array. A very common high-resolution monitor/graphics card standard.

virus   A program that attaches itself to other files on a floppy or hard disk, duplicates itself without the user's knowledge, and may cause the computer to do strange and sometimes destructive things. In the worst case, the virus may attack the computer by erasing files from the hard disk or by formatting the disk.

warm boot   Also called reboot, the process of reloading the computer's operating system when the computer is already running. In DOS, you can reboot by holding down the Ctrl key and the Alt key and pressing the Delete key. On a Mac, use the Restart command under the Special menu.

widow/orphan   A *widow* is the last line of a paragraph that appears alone at the top of the next page. If the first line of a paragraph gets stranded at the bottom of the page, it is called an *orphan*. Just remember that an orphan is left behind.

wild card   Any character that takes the place of another character or a group of characters. Think of a wild-card character as the wild card in a game of poker or the blank pieces in Scrabble. If the Joker is wild, you can use it in place of any card in the entire deck of cards. In DOS, you can use two wild characters: a question mark (?) and an asterisk (*). The question mark stands in for a single character; the asterisk stands in for a group of characters.

windows   A way of displaying information in different parts of the screen. Often used as a nickname for Microsoft Windows.

word processor   A program that lets you enter, edit, format, and print text.

write-protect   To prevent a computer from adding to or modifying data stored on a disk.

WYSIWYG (What-You-See-Is-What-You-Get)   A way of displaying your work on-screen so that it resembles the work as it will appear when you print it out. Pronounced "wizzy-wig."

Index

E

e-mail, 559
  etiquette, 520
  Internet, 525
E-Span (job listings), 447
Eagle Eye Mysteries, 381-382
Easter Seal Society, 358
Easy Access control panel
  (Macintosh), 481
Easy installation (Macintosh),
  126
Ecco Professional 2.0 (PIM),
  204-205
Edmark, 361
education, 4
educational software, 115-116,
  290-322, 325-329, 343-344
  communication, 354-355
  developmentally
    appropriate software,
    348-349
  gender differences, 362-368
  hardware requirements,
    347-348
  home computer use, 345-346
  preschool use, 344-345
  problem solving, 353
  resources, 355-361
  school use, 370-372
  special software, 351-352
  vendors, 374-395
EGA (enhanced graphics
  adapter), 559
electricity, *see* power supply
electromagnetic emissions,
  336-338
Electronic Arts, 381-382, 545
Electronic Frontier Foundation, 497
Electronic Learning, 373
electronic magazines, 541
electronic mail, *see* e-mail
emulation, 559
Encarta, 271-272
encryption, 96

enhanced graphics adapter
  (EGA), 559
environment
  lighting, 474
EQUALS, 367
ergonomics, 33-34
  see also user health issues
error messages, 99-100
etiquette (on-line services),
  519-521
eWorld, 505-506, 509
Exceptional Parent, 358
executable files, 560
exiting
  TeachText, 92
  Windows, 85
expanded memory, 560
expansion cards, 560
expansion slots, 27
Expert Landscape, 180-181
Expert Software, 180-181, 545
exporting files, 560
extended memory, 560

F

Family for Windows, 310-311
Family Ties, 308-309
FATs (file allocation tables),
  561
fields (databases), 560
File Manager (Windows),
  80-85
File Transfer Protocol (FTP),
  526
FileMaker Pro, 158-159
files, 561
  ASCII, 555
  AUTOEXEC.BAT, 555
  backing up, 97-98, 555
  batch files, 555
  compressing, 129-130,
    231-232, 235-236, 558
  copying, 64-65
  deleting, 65-66
  downloading, 559

executable files, 560
exporting, 560
file extensions, 560
importing, 562
Macintosh, saving, 93
moving, 66-67
naming, 67
protecting data, 96-98
README (Macintosh), 125
saving, 135, 567
transferring between
  Macintosh and IBM,
  240-241
undeleting, 66-68
Windows
  copying, 81-83
  deleting, 83
  moving, 81-83
  multiple files, 83-84
  naming, 83
Fine Artist, 379-380
fixed disk drives, 561
floppy disks, 561
  caring for, 44
  DOS, 58
  drives, 12
  formatting, 561
  software requirements, 122
fonts, 561
FORMAT command (DOS),
  59
formatting
  disks, 59, 561
  résumés, 443-445
  text, 561
Fractal Design Corp., 545
Fractal Design Painter,
  170-171
The Freesoft Company,
  192-193
freeware, 424-429, 561
freezes, 100
French Assistant, 297
FTP (File Transfer Protocol),
  526
full backups, 98
function keys, 561

G

H

I